# HP ProLiant Servers AIS

# Official Study Guide and Desk Reference

# Hewlett-Packard® Professional Books

## HP-UX

## UNIX, LINUX

## COMPUTER ARCHITECTURE

## NETWORKING/COMMUNICATIONS

## SECURITY

## WEB/INTERNET CONCEPTS AND PROGRAMMING

| | |
|---|---|
| **Amor** | E-business (R)evolution, Second Edition |
| **Apte/Mehta** | UDDI |
| **Chatterjee/Webber** | Developing Enterprise Web Services: An Architect's Guide |
| **Kumar** | J2EE Security for Servlets, EJBs, and Web Services |
| **Little/Maron/Pavlik** | Java Transaction Processing |
| **Mowbrey/Werry** | Online Communities |
| **Tapadiya** | .NET Programming |

## OTHER PROGRAMMING

| | |
|---|---|
| **Blinn** | Portable Shell Programming |
| **Caruso** | Power Programming in HP OpenView |
| **Chaudhri** | Object Databases in Practice |
| **Chew** | The Java/C++ Cross Reference Handbook |
| **Grady** | Practical Software Metrics for Project Management and Process Improvement |
| **Grady** | Software Metrics |
| **Grady** | Successful Software Process Improvement |
| **Lee/Schneider/Schell** | Mobile Applications |
| **Lewis** | The Art and Science of Smalltalk |
| **Lichtenbelt** | Introduction to Volume Rendering |
| **Mellquist** | SNMP++ |
| **Mikkelsen** | Practical Software Configuration Management |
| **Norton** | Thread Time |
| **Tapadiya** | COM+ Programming |
| **Yuan** | Windows 2000 GDI Programming |

## STORAGE

| | |
|---|---|
| **Thornburgh** | Fibre Channel for Mass Storage |
| **Thornburgh/Schoenborn** | Storage Area Networks |
| **Todman** | Designing Data Warehouses |

## IT/IS

| | |
|---|---|
| **Anderson** | mySAP Tool Bag for Performance Tuning and Stress Testing |
| **Missbach/Hoffman** | SAP Hardware Solutions |

## IMAGE PROCESSING

| | |
|---|---|
| **Crane** | A Simplified Approach to Image Processing |
| **Gann** | Desktop Scanners |

# HP ProLiant Servers AIS
## Official Study Guide and Desk Reference

*Bryan Weldon*
*Shawn Rogers*

www.hp.com/hpbooks

Prentice Hall
Professional Technical Reference
Upper Saddle River, New Jersey 07458
www.phptr.com

**Library of Congress Cataloging-in-Publication Data**

A CIP catalog record for this book can be obtained from the Library of Congress.

Editorial/Production Supervision: *Andrew Wahnsiedler/Lori Lyons*
Composition: *Julie Parks*
Cover Design Director: *Jerry Votta*
Cover Design: *Sandra Schroeder*
Cover Photography: *George Lange*
Art Director: *Gail Cocker-Bogusz*
Manufacturing Buyer: *Maura Zaldivar*
Acquisitions Editor: *Jill Harry*
Editorial Assistant: *Brenda Mulligan*
Marketing Manager: *Dan DePasquale*
Publisher, HP Books: *Mark Stouse*
Manager and Associate Publisher, HP Books: *Victoria Brandow*

© 2005 Hewlett-Packard Development Company, L.P.
Published by Pearson Education
Publishing as Prentice Hall Professional Technical Reference
Upper Saddle River, New Jersey 07458

PRENTICE
HALL
PTR

**Prentice Hall PTR offers excellent discounts on this book when ordered in quantity for bulk purchases or special sales. For more information, please contact: U.S. Corporate and Government Sales, 1-800-382-3419, corpsales@pearsontechgroup.com. For sales outside of the U.S., please contact: International Sales, 1-317-581-3793, international@pearsontechgroup.com.**

Company and product names mentioned herein are the trademarks or registered trademarks of their respective owners.

Printed in the United States of America

First Printing October 2004

ISBN 0-13-146717-4

Pearson Education Ltd.
Pearson Education Australia Pty., Limited
Pearson Education Singapore, Pte. Ltd.
Pearson Education North Asia Ltd.
Pearson Education Canada, Ltd.
Pearson Educación de Mexico, S.A. de C.V.
Pearson Education — Japan
Pearson Education Malaysia, Pte. Ltd.

*I dedicate this book to the HP team, a wonderful group of dedicated people working together to not only build HP as a worldwide leader, but more importantly, who strive to make the world a better place.*

*—Bryan Weldon*

*I dedicate this book to my wonderful wife, Kellie, and my beautiful children, Cameron and Carlie.*

*—Shawn Rogers*

# Acknowledgements

This book is the result of years of efforts by dedicated technical and training professionals in the Compaq and Hewlett-Packard Industry-Standard Server training group. We would like to jointly recognize the following individuals who have contributed greatly to the training materials and other technical resources that were used liberally in the creation of this work:

The ISS Training team: led by Brian Duelm, Chris Walsh, Ron Felder, Ken Clark, and Steve Pryor. Contributing members of this team include Ellen Chadick, Gretchen Holloman, Richard Hykel, Brent Keadle, Jason McGee, Bill Patton, Stephanie Pounds, Chris Powell, Bill Shields, and Lance Taylor.

The HP Certified Professional team: Brian Beneda, Chuck Mundt, Karen Petrini, for their work on the competency model and exam development for the ProLiant AIS and ASE programs.

Renata Golden, owner of Golden-Ink, contributed to the writing and editing of much of the content used throughout this study guide.

Contributing subject-matter experts include Georg Fest (Navcom Switzerland) and Radomir Bozic (2ETC, Belgrade).

We would want to express our appreciation to the outstanding team at Pearson Education: Jill Harry for her unwavering support, extreme patience, and excellent project management skills; Andrew Wahnsiedler for his editorial contributions; and Brenda Mulligan for her outstanding administrative assistance.

*—Bryan and Shawn*

I would like to thank my family for their support and patience.

I would like to thank my friends and associates throughout HP. Thanks especially to Ron Felder for his management sponsorship, guidance, and encouragement of the new ProLiant AIS and ASE programs.

Thanks also to my coauthor and friend, Shawn Rogers, who has provided the book-writing expertise to transform this unruly content into a usable study guide. It has been an honor and pleasure working and learning from Shawn over the past seven years.

*—Bryan Weldon*

I would like to thank Kellie, Cameron, and Carlie for their love and support. As with all of my other authoring endeavors over the years, the sacrifice to give Daddy "book time" was real and required an extra measure of patience and endurance.

I would like to thank my friends and associates in the HP Certified Professional Program. Thanks especially to Tony Croes and Susan Underhill for their encouragement and support for my authoring efforts.

Thanks also to my coauthor and friend, Bryan Weldon, who has provided the technical and content leadership for this book. I have worked with Bryan for many years and found him to be the consummate IT professional, an exemplary Compaq/HP customer advocate, a dedicated Scouter, and an all-around nice guy.

*—Shawn Rogers*

# CONTENTS

**CHAPTER 3**

# Processors and Multiprocessing   *27*

**CHAPTER 4**

# Memory and Cache   47

# Bus Architecture   *77*

## CHAPTER 6

# Server Storage *111*

### CHAPTER 7

# Disk Array Technologies    *147*

**CHAPTER 8**

# Introduction to Fibre Channel   *173*

**P A R T  TWO**

# HP Server Technologies *201*

**CHAPTER 9**

# The HP ProLiant Server Line *203*

**CHAPTER 10**

# HP Rack and Power Technologies   *211*

**CHAPTER 13**

# HP Array Technologies 253

**PART** FOUR

# Systems Integration *281*

**CHAPTER 14**

## Evaluating the Customer Environment *283*

**CHAPTER 15**

## Installing, Configuring, and Deploying a Single Server *301*

**PART** FIVE

# Systems Management *341*

**CHAPTER 16**

# Introduction to HP Systems Management *343*

**CHAPTER 17**

# HP Lights-Out Management Technologies *365*

**PART** SIX

# Performance  *383*

**CHAPTER 18**

# Installing Hardware Options and Upgrades  *385*

**CHAPTER 19**

# Availability  *397*

**CHAPTER 22**

# Problem Resolution, Performance Issues, and System Maintenance *433*

## APPENDIX A

# AIS Competencies   *475*

## APPENDIX B

# Answers to Learning Checks   *479*

## APPENDIX C

# Sample AIS Exam   *509*

# Index   *517*

# The Accredited Integration Specialist (AIS) Credential

Welcome to the world of HP ProLiant servers. This book provides a foundation upon which you can build your knowledge and skills for selling, servicing, and supporting the HP ProLiant server products.

If you are pursuing the HP *Accredited Integration Specialist* (AIS) credential, this book is your main resource for beginning your study. In fact, if you attend the training courses that prepare you for the exams in these credentials, your instructor will expect that you have an understanding of the technical concepts presented here.

One of the main reasons for this book is to allow HP technical instructors to use valuable instruction time focusing on HP value-added technologies and hands-on labs, instead of explaining technologies considered to be "industry standard." This book has the support and endorsement of both the HP Certified Professional Program and the HP training departments, and is recommended as a preparatory resource for all ProLiant server-focused credentials.

This book is organized into seven parts, as described in the following sections.

## Part 1     Industry-Standard Server Technologies

Part 1 of this book examines each major subsystem of an industry-standard server, including server chipsets, processors and multiprocessing, memory and cache, server storage, array technologies, and Fibre Channel.

Part 1 is intended as an overview of those technologies that are not proprietary to HP servers. The chapters in Part 1 serve as a foundation for discussing HP technologies in later chapters.

**Part 2**     # HP Server Technologies

Part 2 of this book provides a high-level introduction to important HP server-related technologies. Chapter 9 explains how the HP ProLiant server line is categorized by line and by series. This information is vital for applying the right HP server solution to the customer solution. Chapter 10 provides an overview of HP rack and power technologies.

**Part 3**     # HP Storage Technologies

Part 3 of this book explains the HP storage products and technologies. Chapter 11 explains the implementation of the SCSI standards in HP ProLiant servers. Chapter 12 explains key network storage technologies, such as *direct-attached storage* (DAS), *network-attached storage* (NAS), *storage area networks* (SANs), and the HP *Enterprise Storage Architecture* (ENSA). Chapter 13 explains HP server drive array technologies.

**Part 4**     # Systems Integration

Chapter 14 discusses methods for evaluating the customer environment and determining the best solution. After that solution has been determined, it must be deployed. The skills for installing, configuring, and deploying a single-server solution are explained in Chapter 15.

**Part 5**     # Systems Management

HP ProLiant servers have long been differentiated from competitor's products by their manageability. Several management technologies are explained in Part 5. Chapter 16 introduces you to HP systems management. Chapter 17 focuses on HP Lights-Out management technologies, including iLO and RILOE.

**Part 6**     # Performance

After the server solution has been deployed, the attention then turns to optimizing the server's performance. Chapter 18 discusses techniques for installing a variety of hardware options and hardware upgrades. Chapter 19 discusses server availability, and what measures can be taken to increase the level of availability in HP ProLiant servers. Chapter 20 provides guidelines for optimizing server storage.

| Part 7 | **Problem Resolution** |
| --- | --- |

After the server solution has been deployed and optimized, circumstances might arise where troubleshooting is required to resolve a particular problem. Chapter 21 focuses on backup strategies that should be used to prevent data loss when a problem occurs. Finally, Chapter 22 explains the HP troubleshooting methodology.

# Industry-Standard Server Technologies

Industry-standard servers are composed of several key subsystems, and each subsystem plays a vital role in the overall performance of the server.

Part 1 of this book examines each major subsystem of an industry-standard server. This part discusses each subsystem in detail, and then the remainder of the book explains how these individual components come together in the HP ProLiant server family; this book also emphasizes the HP value-added innovations to these industry technologies.

Here is an overview of the chapters in Part 1.

**Chapter 1** **Introduction to Server Technologies**

Chapter 1 provides a high-level overview of the key components and subsystems that make up an industry-standard server.

**Chapter 2** **Server Chipsets**

The chipset provides a foundation to the overall architecture of a server. To eliminate bottlenecks and increase performance, the chipset must provide an optimized and balanced architecture.

**Chapter 3** **Processors and Multiprocessing**

To select the appropriate server for a particular task, you need to consider several factors related to the server processor, such as how processors work, what innovations make processors work faster, how processor types differ, and how multiprocessor servers differ from single-processor servers.

**Chapter 4** **Memory and Cache**

Chapter 4 explains the differences between memory and cache, and how both work. This chapter also examines some of the technical innovations that have increased memory and cache performance and their fault-tolerant capabilities.

**Chapter 5** **Bus Architecture**

The internal computing components of a server are connected by a collection of pathways, known as buses, that differ in width and speed. This chapter explains the types of buses, how they function, and the different bus technologies commonly found in today's industry-standard servers.

## Chapter 6    Server Storage

Two popular types of hard drive technology are currently offered in the server systems industry: ATA/IDE and SCSI. This chapter explains the differences between these technologies, and how each technology is implemented in an industry standard server.

## Chapter 7    Array Technologies

RAID technology is based on the theory that a group of smaller drives is more efficient than one large drive. The basic premise of fault-tolerant RAID is that an intelligent manager can handle a drive array so that it can withstand the failure of any individual drive in the array without losing data. Chapter 7 explains the various RAID levels and how drive arrays work.

## Chapter 8    Introduction to Fibre Channel

Fibre Channel is an integrated set of standards developed by the *American National Standards Institute* (ANSI). Fibre Channel technology is an industry-standard interconnect serial data transfer architecture that delivers a high level of reliability, throughput, and distance flexibility for the server industry. Chapter 8 explains foundational Fibre Channel concepts and terms.

Each of these chapters provides a foundation for discussing HP server technologies in later chapters of this book.

# Introduction to Server Technologies

This chapter provides an introduction to key server technologies that are explained in much more detail throughout the remainder of the book. After reading this chapter, you will be able to briefly explain the function of the following key server components and subsystems:

- System boards
- Processors
- Memory
- Bus
- Chipsets
- Storage
- Power
- Racks
- System clock

Understanding how server architecture subsystems work together enables you to select and configure a server to meet specific application needs and provide the highest performance.

Building an HP server requires integrating system components into an architecture that meets specific server design requirements and provides the highest level of overall quality. HP designs each ProLiant server with a set of subsystems to create a balanced, high-performance, and cost-effective computer architecture. HP server architecture designs are rigorously tested throughout the design and manufacture process.

This chapter provides an overview of the key components found in HP ProLiant servers, including system boards, processors, chipsets, buses (I/O interconnects), memory, storage components, power, and mechanical components (e.g., server and component chassis).

## 1.1    System Boards

A server system board, shown in Figure 1–1, is an integrated circuit board containing most of the processing components. System boards come in three types: *active*, *passive*, and *modular*.

The active board is the traditional system board (motherboard) that has embedded, active chipsets.

The passive system board does not contain embedded chipsets. Instead, it functions like an interconnect board, linking several integrated circuit component boards together.

**Figure 1–1**

*System board.*

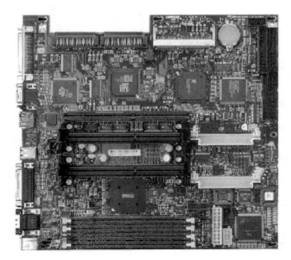

A modular system board is a hybrid between the active and passive types. It contains some embedded chipsets and acts as an interconnect board for upgradeable, integrated circuit component boards.

HP uses both active and modular system boards in the ProLiant family of servers. The active board design offers the most cost-effective solution for entry-level servers and density-optimized servers. The modular board design provides maximum scalability and component upgrades in a server.

## 1.2   Processors

The processor, shown in Figure 1–2, functions as the brain of the server, controlling all activity among the server components. A processor is composed of several components, located on the same integrated circuit and working together.

The most commonly used processors in the server industry are 32-bit processors. ProLiant servers use 32-bit Intel processors. HP engineers work closely with Intel to ensure compatibility between the processor and the other server components.

## 1.3   Memory

Memory stores data needed by other components. It is used in several areas of the server, including the main system, cache, video, and drives.

Memory is sometimes called *RAM* (random access memory). The basic types of RAM include *dynamic ram* (DRAM) and *static RAM* (SRAM).

DRAM, shown in Figure 1–3, is the most common memory type found in server memory subsystems. This memory technology is inexpensive but very slow compared to processor requirements.

SRAM is used most exclusively in cache implementations. This memory technology is extremely fast, but is more expensive than DRAM and generates significant heat.

**Figure 1–2**

*Typical system processor.*

**Figure 1–3** *Typical DRAM memory.*

## 1.4  Bus

A *bus* is a set of electrical circuits used to transport binary data that has been converted to electrical signals, enabling communication among all of the components of a server.

Many types of buses work together in a server to provide high performance with minimal bottlenecks. The basic types of buses found in a server include the following:

- **Processor bus**—Is internal to the processor
- **Backside bus**—Connects the processor or processors to the on-board cache memory
- **Frontside bus**—Connects the processor to the system controller chipset
- **Memory bus**—Connects the main memory to the memory controller
- **Local I/O bus**—Connects high-speed internal and external I/O devices to the I/O controller hub
- **Expansion I/O bus**—Connects I/O ports, expansion I/O controllers, and expansion slots to the I/O controller hub

Each server bus type is made up of two electrical lines, which are also known as buses.

The first type is the *address* or *control* bus. This bus identifies the desired location within a target device where data might reside. It also carries control signals that indicate the purpose of the data transfer, such as whether a device is supposed to read or write the data.

The second type is the *data bus*. Data moves between any two devices over the data bus. The data can be instructions for the microprocessor or information the microprocessor is transmitting. This information can pass to or from the memory or I/O subsystem.

## 1.5  Chipsets

The *chipset* is the central nervous system of the server. It controls communications and data exchange between all server components and determines the overall functionality of the server.

A chipset is a set of *application-specific integrated circuits* (ASICs) that has many basic server-logic functions integrated into one or more chips. Functions integrated into the ASICs include the system controller, the memory controller, the I/O controller, and the program interrupt controller.

Most ProLiant servers use industry-standard chipsets designed by ServerWorks. Servers in the 700 series use a chipset designed internally by HP. Sometimes HP adds additional ASICs designed by HP to perform specific functions, such as system management.

## 1.6  Storage Components

Disk drives are a relatively fast, reliable, and economic way to store and access data, applications, and operating systems. Server storage typically consists of removable storage and permanent storage.

Removable storage includes CD-ROM drives, disk drives, and tape backup drives.

Permanent storage includes IDE disk drives and SCSI disk drives.

### 1.6.1  Drive Arrays

HP is a leader in drive array storage technology. An array, sometimes called a *RAID array*, is a set of disks that acts like a large single disk, thereby providing higher performance and data fault tolerance than a multidisk system.

Because storage needs have expanded beyond the server and the types of storage devices have increased, the need for a high-speed connection between servers and storage devices has become critical. Storage solutions designed to meet these needs include the following:

- **Direct-attached storage (DAS)**—Storage devices directly, internally, or externally connected to the server, such as disk drives, tape drives, and external storage systems.

- **Storage area network (SAN)**—A dedicated, centrally managed, secure information infrastructure network that enables direct physical access to common storage devices or a storage pool.

- **Network attached storage (NAS)**—Dedicated, self-contained, intelligent servers that attach directly to the existing LAN. Data is transferred to and from clients over industry-standard network protocols using industry-standard file-sharing protocols.

- **HP Enterprise Network Storage Architecture (ENSA)**—Brings SAN, NAS, and DAS together in an architecture that meets enterprise storage requirements.

## 1.7 Power

Server components require a tightly controlled and regulated supply of power. The power supply must be adequate to support the electrical load of the server in its standard configuration and support any added or upgraded components.

The server power components are a critical part of server fault prevention and fault tolerance and should be able to (1) predict and avoid failure, (2) allow preventive maintenance before failure, and (3) keep the server running in the event of component failure.

ProLiant servers include power-system designs that provide reliability through fault prevention and fault-tolerant features, including intelligent power supplies and fans, and redundant power supplies and fans. A typical power supply is shown in Figure 1–4.

**Figure 1–4**

*Typical server power supply.*

The power subsystem includes power, thermal, and airflow components.

Power components can be classified by whether they are internal or external to the server.

Internal power components include the power supply, the *voltage regulator module* (VRM) (sometimes called the *processor power module*, or PPM), fans, and system board thermistors.

External power components include *uninterruptible power supply* (UPS) and cables, the power-distribution unit, and the redundant A/C power source.

## 1.8 Racks

A *rack* is a metal frame or cabinet into which computer components can be mounted. Racks typically ship in standard widths of 19 or 23 inches; height is specified by a *unit* (U) of measure that is 1.75 inches from top to bottom. An HP Rack System/E is shown in Figure 1–5.

HP racks ship in a variety of sizes, from 14U to 47U, to offer a range of rackmount capacity. Additional features include ventilated doors and side panels, sliding shelves, and locks. HP also offers a variety of options, including a selection of rack-mountable monitors and keyboards, console switches, and cable-management solutions.

In addition, HP offers online tools to help customers design and configure a rack solution to best fit their space, capacity, and power requirements.

HP racks are designed for optimal adaptability, extendibility, strength, mobility, ease of use, and stability.

**Figure 1–5**

*HP Rack System/E.*

## 1.9    System Clock

A system clock coordinates the activity of the server components. The clock is actually a crystal. When electrical current is applied to the crystal, it vibrates at a constant rate. The number of vibrations is measured in *megahertz* (MHz).

Each vibration is known as a *clock cycle* or *clock tick*. The clock cycles act as a sort of drumbeat that drives the work of all other components. Every action a component makes takes place on a clock tick.

Some components work faster than others, getting their work done in fewer clock cycles. The challenge in server design is to connect all the components in a way that provides a constant data flow through the system but minimizes bottlenecks. The design of the server, combined with the user configuration of the server, determines whether a subsystem works to enhance performance or works as a bottleneck to restrict overall performance.

Data flow in a server can be viewed in a hierarchical, fastest-to-slowest, logical block diagram. Data must move through the system effectively from fast to slow and back. To keep the faster subsystems (processors and memory) working efficiently, the system depends on controllers, memory buffers, parallel buses, and concurrent read and write processes.

## ▲ LEARNING CHECK

1. *Which type of system board is most commonly found in HP ProLiant servers and has active embedded chipsets?*

    A. Active

    B. Passive

    C. Modular

2. *Which type of memory is most commonly found in server memory subsystems?*

3. *What is the function of the address or control bus?*

4. *What is a dedicated, centrally managed, secure information infrastructure that enables direct and physical access to common storage devices or a storage pool known as?*

    A. Drive array

    B. Direct-attached storage

    C. Storage area network

    D. Network attached storage

5. *Which server component coordinates the activity of the server components and regulates server data flow?*

    A. Memory

    B. Processor

    C. System clock

    D. System bus

# Server Chipsets

This chapter provides an overview of server chipset innovations. After studying this chapter, you should be able to do the following:

- Define the term *chipset* and explain how the chipset provides the foundation of a server's architecture.

- Describe the original PC architecture and explain its performance limitations.

- Describe the dual independent bus architecture and explain its performance limitations.

- Explain how bus mastering technology reduced bottlenecks and improved server performance, and describe its performance limitations.

- Describe the memory and I/O controller (MIOC) technology and explain how it reduced memory bottlenecks.

- Describe parallel I/O bus technology and explain how it reduced I/O bottlenecks.

- Describe the highly parallel system architecture, and explain how its dual-memory controller technology reduced system bottlenecks and improved performance.

- Explain how the crossbar switch reduced bottlenecks at the memory and I/O controllers.

- Describe the innovations implemented in the ProFusion chipset and explain the ProFusion architecture.

- Describe the innovations implemented in the F8 chipset architecture, explain its high-bandwidth capabilities, and list its key advantages.

**15**

A chipset is a collection of the microchips on a server motherboard that control the features and the functions of the motherboard. The chipset determines how much memory can be installed, which processors can be used, and which types of interfaces the computer can support.

The chipset provides a foundation to the overall architecture of a server. To eliminate bottlenecks and increase performance, the chipset must provide an optimized and balanced architecture.

This chapter explains how chipsets have evolved. This information provides a foundation for our discussion of other server components in later chapters.

Note that several terms introduced in this chapter are further explained in subsequent chapters of this book. It is the old chicken and egg quandary. For the chapters in Part 1 of this book, it will be helpful to read through them a first time, and then cycle back through them before you take the Accredited Integration Specialist (AIS) exam.

## 2.1 Original Server Architecture

The original PC system architecture started out with one bus with a single speed and the same bus width to all peripherals, as illustrated in Figure 2–1.

Two main performance bottlenecks resulted from this architecture. First, because only one system bus was available for all devices, only one device could use the system bus at a time. When one device was using the bus, all other devices had to wait their turn for attention. Second, all bus transfers, both system and I/O, were restricted to the same bus speed.

In this architecture, approximately 96% of all data transfers were between the processor and memory.

## 2.2 Dual Independent Buses

To alleviate the problems caused by a single system bus, the next step was to split the bus into two independent buses. This was known as *dual independent bus architecture*. This architecture is shown in Figure 2–2.

HP introduced the first dual independent bus design. This design allowed the memory bus between the processor and memory to operate at a higher speed than that of the I/O expansion bus. An I/O bridge was used to synchronize data transfers between the two buses.

**Figure 2–1**

*Original
PC system
architecture.*

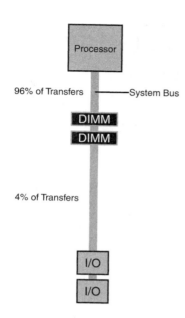

**Figure 2–2**

*Dual
independent
bus
architecture.*

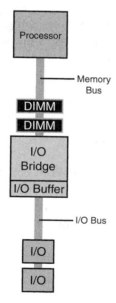

In this architecture, the bottleneck now shifted to the I/O bridge. All
I/O devices were contending with the I/O bridge to communicate with the
host bus. To solve this problem, buffers were added to the bridge. If the
bridge was busy transferring data from one I/O device, it would buffer the

**Figure 2–3**

*Bus mastering.*

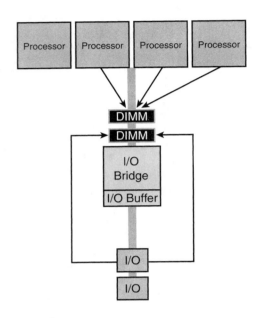

data from other I/O devices. When the bus was free, the bridge sent the buffered data. This enabled the I/O devices to continue working and not wait for a response from the bridge.

## 2.3   Bus Mastering

The next step in server evolution was *bus mastering* technology, as illustrated in Figure 2-3.

With bus mastering, multiple bus master devices contended for access to system memory. Multiple processors could transfer data directly to main memory. I/O adapters could also transfer data directly to main memory.

Although enabling I/O devices to be bus masters freed up processor resources, it caused contention for memory.

## 2.4   MIOC Architecture

The problem of memory contention was solved when HP introduced the first data-flow manager, a tri-bus arbitrator that acted as a *memory and I/O controller* (MIOC). This architecture is illustrated in Figure 2–4.

**Figure 2–4**

*MIOC architecture.*

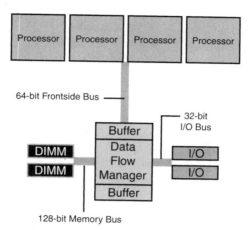

The data-flow manager provided three main functions: (1) bus arbitration; (2) timing; and (3) buffering between the processor, memory, and I/O.

In this architecture, the width of the memory bus was increased to 128 bits to allow multiple concurrent I/O transactions.

## 2.5   Parallel I/O Buses

The bottleneck now shifted to I/O access and I/O bus speed. Multiple I/O devices in a server were located on one bus and were limited to one bus speed.

This limitation was solved by adding *dual-peer* and *triple-peer* I/O buses. This design was possible by adding more I/O controllers called *bridges*, as shown in Figure 2–5.

With this design, peripherals on any bus have independent access to the processors and memory. This design also allows I/O buses to operate at different speeds, separating the slow I/O from faster I/O. Buffers in the bridges allow I/O transfers to queue, reducing latency.

The key benefits of this design included the following:

- Twice the I/O bandwidth of single-bus systems—267MB/s (533MB/s) compared to 133MB/s (267MB/s)
- Support for more PCI devices than single-bus systems
- Balance of I/O workload and performance by placing high-usage peripherals (such as the graphics controller and disk controller) on separate buses

**Figure 2–5**

*Parallel
I/O bus
architecture.*

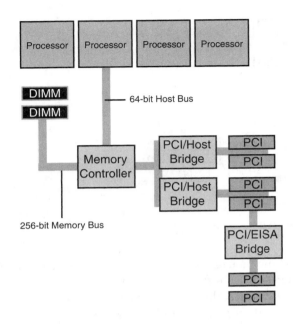

## Highly Parallel System Architecture

Peer I/O buses moved the bottleneck from the I/O subsystem back to the memory controller. Dual memory controllers were the next step in chipset evolution. This system architecture design was called the *Highly Parallel System Architecture* (HPSA), and is shown in Figure 2–6.

This architecture also featured dual peer PCI buses. HP co-developed this powerful technology with ServerWorks and was the first to bring it to market.

HPSA servers employing dual memory controllers processed memory requests in parallel, enabling memory bandwidth to achieve up to 1.6GB/s with 100MHz (2.12GB/s with 133MHz) SDRAM.

HPSA components include the following:

- Assisted Gunning Transceiver Logic plus (AGTL+) bus
- Intel Pentium II and III processors
- Dual Wide-Ultra SCSI controllers
- Dual-peer PCI buses
- Dual memory controllers
- Interleaved memory

**Figure 2-6**

*Highly Parallel System Architecture.*

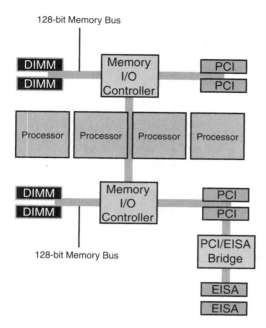

128-bit Memory Bus

DIMM
DIMM
Memory I/O Controller
PCI
PCI

Processor | Processor | Processor | Processor

DIMM
DIMM
Memory I/O Controller
PCI
PCI

PCI/EISA Bridge

EISA
EISA

128-bit Memory Bus

## 2.7  Crossbar Switch

The next step in chipset evolution was to reduce the bottleneck at the memory I/O controllers by replacing the controllers with a crossbar switch, as illustrated in Figure 2–7.

The crossbar switch has five ports: two to the memory subsystem, two to the processor subsystem, and one to the I/O subsystem.

Employing mainframe techniques, the crossbar switch enables each of the five main ports to transfer data at high speed to each of the other ports, allowing concurrent read/writes between processors, memory, and I/O. Although there are two physical system buses, the buses present one system image logically to the operating system.

## 2.8  ProFusion Chipset

The next evolution was the *ProFusion* chipset, shown in Figure 2–8.

Jointly developed by HP and Intel, the ProFusion chipset uses a unique two-port (bus) memory design with 1.6GB/s memory bandwidth (2 × 800MB/s), allowing simultaneous access to memory on both ports.

**Figure 2–7**

*Crossbar switch.*

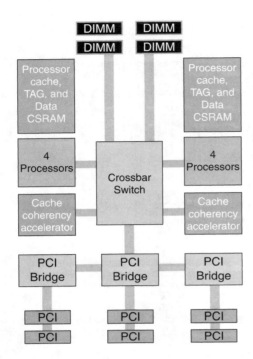

The ProFusion Memory Access Controller (MAC) manages two separate memory controllers on separate memory buses. This technique employs high-speed *synchronous DRAM* (SDRAM) interleaved on a cache line basis. One controller manages all of the odd cache line addresses, and the other manages all of the even cache line addresses. As a result, latency is reduced when accessing two consecutive cache lines in address order. The MAC arbitrates the access by the two processors on the two main system buses to the memory and I/O system.

The ProFusion Data Interface Buffer (DIB) provides the data path control and buffering between the AGTL+ buses and memory. The DIB consists of buffers between the processor, I/O AGTL+ buses, and memory. If the required *dual inline memory module* (DIMM) is busy when the MAC initiates a memory cycle, the DIB temporarily stores the address and forwards it to the memory on the next available cycle.

**2.9** **F8 Chipset**

The next evolution of HP system architecture design is the *F8* chipset architecture, which is based on the ProFusion chipset. HP leveraged experience

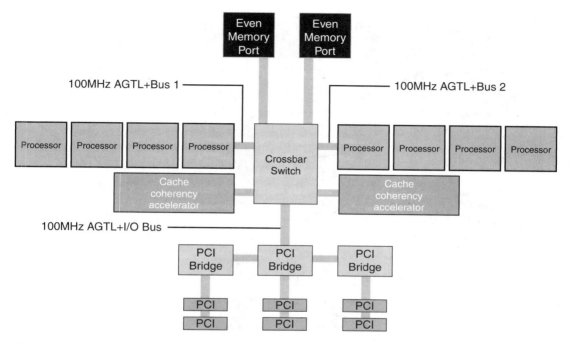

**Figure 2–8** *Intel-based server block diagram.*

gained with the ProFusion eight-way architecture to develop the F8 eight-way multiprocessing architecture. The F8 architecture is shown in Figure 2–9.

HP developed the F8 chipset with a multiport, nonblocking crossbar switch to optimize efficiency and allow simultaneous access to memory, processor, and I/O subsystems.

The F8 chipset supports multiple PCI-X bridges and incorporates the HP embedded PCI Hot Plug controller for high availability in the I/O subsystem.

### 2.9.1 F8 Chipset Architecture

The F8 chipset was designed for even higher performance by optimizing the crossbar switch component and increasing bandwidths to match the processing power of the Intel Xeon MP processor.

The design includes a large buffer capable of holding 128 cache lines, 13 read ports, and 4 write ports

These features increase the number of concurrent transactions in the switch, and include a cache-coherency filter and a patent-pending Guaranteed

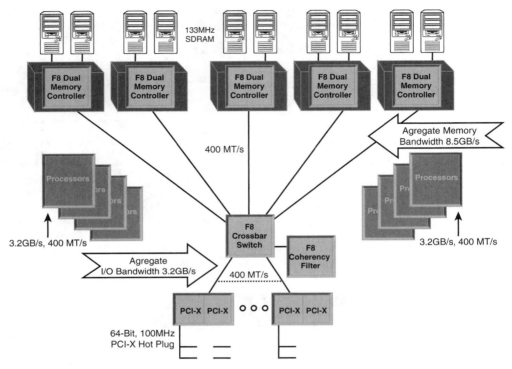

**Figure 2–9** *F8 chipset.*

Snoop Access algorithm to reduce the amount of cross-bus traffic. All of these features increase efficiency and improve the scalability of the F8 architecture.

For example, a bus operating at 100MHz and transferring four data packets on each clock would have 400MT/s (*mega transfers per second*).

The F8 chipset includes several innovations that provide high bandwidth, including scalable memory performance, PCI-X bridges, and Hot Plug RAID Memory.

### 2.9.1.1 SCALABLE MEMORY PERFORMANCE

HP engineers ensure scalable memory performance by increasing the memory bandwidths to an aggregate of 8.5GB/s, which is 33% more than the bandwidth of the processor buses combined. This design provides ample headroom for computing needs because each processor bus has four times the bandwidth of the Pentium III Xeon processor bus.

### 2.9.1.2   PCI-X BRIDGES

The F8 chipset can include up to four industry-standard dual PCI-X bridges in the I/O subsystem, each with embedded PCI Hot Plug controllers. Because each bridge can support two PCI-X bus segments operating at speeds up to 100MHz, the chipset can easily accommodate peripherals using high-speed interconnects, such as Gigabit Ethernet and Ultra320 SCSI.

### 2.9.1.3   HOT PLUG RAID MEMORY

Servers that enable Hot Plug RAID Memory use RAID DIMMs to provide fault tolerance and enable the hot replacement and the hot addition of memory when the server is operating. This eliminates unplanned downtime in the case of a DIMM failure.

When the memory controller in the F8 chipset needs to write data to memory, it splits the cache line of data into four blocks. Then each block is written, or striped, across four memory modules. A RAID engine calculates parity information, which is stored on a fifth cartridge dedicated to parity. With the four data cartridges and the parity cartridge, the data subsystem is redundant so that if the data from any DIMM is incorrect or any cartridge is removed, the data can be rebuilt from the remaining four cartridges.

## 2.9.2   F8 Chipset Advantages

When compared to a *cache-coherent Non-Uniform Memory Access* (cc-NUMA) architecture, the F8 *symmetrical multiprocessor* (SMP) architectures provide (1) a simpler programming model, (2) reduced average latencies overall, and (3) the ability to use standard operating systems and applications.

The F8 chipset from HP delivers these additional advantages:

- Eliminates potential bottlenecks by using very high bandwidths to match the processing power of the Xeon MP processor
- Eliminates potential bottlenecks using optimized crossbar switch capabilities
- Expands online replacement capabilities to include Hot Plug RAID Memory

The F8 chipset includes five memory controllers with HP Hot Plug RAID Memory and a multiported crossbar switch. The F8 chipset supports the following:

- 8.5GB/s of aggregate memory bandwidth
- 3.2GB/s of bandwidth for each processor bus

- 32GB of Hot Plug RAID Memory (40 DIMMs)
- Up to four 100MHz PCI-X bridges with hot-plug support
- Eight Pentium IV Xeon processors

## ▲ Summary

This chapter covered the chipset and I/O evolutions that have occurred over the life span of the industry-standard server, beginning with the original server chipset architecture and ending with the latest chipset technologies in the F8 architecture.

## ▲ LEARNING CHECK

1. *Define the term* chipset.

2. *What are the two main performance bottlenecks in the original PC chipset?*

3. *What was the main benefit of the dual independent bus architecture? Where was the bottleneck with this architecture?*

4. *What server subsystem was the point of contention with bus mastering technology?*

5. *What were the three main functions of the memory and I/O (MIOC) technology?*

6. *Which system architecture first provided peripherals with independent access to processors and memory?*

7. *Which architecture provided dual-peer PCI buses and employed dual memory controllers that processed memory requests in parallel?*

8. *What innovation enabled each of the five main ports to transfer data at high speed to each of the other ports, allowing concurrent read/writes between processors, memory, and I/O?*

9. *What chipset uses a two-port (bus) memory design with 1.6GB/s memory bandwidth (2 × 800MB/s), allowing simultaneous access to memory on both ports?*

10. *What three advantages does the F8 chipset have over the NUMA architecture?*

# Processors and Multiprocessing

One of the core competencies required of an HP *Accredited Integration Specialist* (AIS) is this:

"Explain and recognize processor technologies."

This chapter will assist you in meeting this core competency by providing information on the following key objectives:

- Explain how processors work, including the function of these key components:
  - Execution unit
  - Control unit
  - Registers
  - Decode unit
  - Prefetch unit
  - Data cache
  - Branch target buffer
  - Bus unit
  - Instruction cache
- Explain how key processor innovations have improved processor performance, including the following concepts:
  - Pipelining
  - Superscaler processing
  - Hyper-pipelining

- Dynamic execution
- Explain how logical processors work in conjunction with hyper-threading technology.
- Explain the technical concepts behind multiprocessor servers, including these key concepts:
  - Asymmetric multiprocessing (AMP)
  - Symmetric multiprocessing (SMP)
  - Tightly coupled
  - Loosely coupled
- Explain the key requirements to consider when mixing processor types in an industry-standard server.

To select the appropriate server for a particular task, you need to consider several factors related to the server processor, such as how processors work, what innovations make processors work faster, how processor types differ, and how multiprocessor servers differ from single-processor servers.

It may seem logical to assume that processor speed is the sole factor to consider when choosing a processor for a particular application. For example, it seems perfectly reasonable to assume that a server with a 1GHz processor will always perform better than a server with an 800MHz processor. However, this is not always the case. Many factors besides processor speed affect how well a processor performs in a particular situation.

This chapter explains those factors and examines concepts that you need to know to make sure you make the right processor decisions.

## 3.1 How Processors Work

At the most basic level, a processor is a group of components that execute instructions. An instruction is an order (such as add, subtract, or compare) that a computer program gives to a processor. Instructions are written in binary code, which means they are represented by 1s and 0s. The binary code opens and closes gates between two devices in the processor that need to communicate with each other. This process moves information from one device to the other.

Typically, a programmer creates a new application with a high-level programming language. Commands in the high-level programming language correspond to several instructions. When the programming is complete, a compiler converts the high-level program into instructions. This process is illustrated in Figure 3–1.

### 3.1.1 Processor Components

The key components in a processor are illustrated in Figure 3–2, and are described as follows:

- **Prefetch unit**—A holding place for instructions and operands that a processor will need.
- **Decode unit**—A component that breaks an instruction into its constituent parts.
- **Execution unit**—A component that performs the actual data processing, such as adding and subtracting. The execution unit can be further divided into two other components: (1) the *arithmetic logic unit* (ALU), and (2) the *floating-point unit* (FPU).

**Figure 3–1**

*The process of building instructions for a processor to perform.*

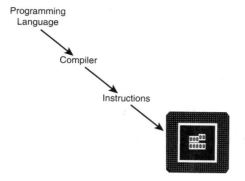

**Figure 3–2**

*The main components of a processor.*

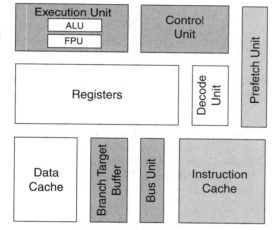

- **Control unit**—A component that acts as a scheduler for the execution units.
- **Registers**—A small number of memory locations used by the control and execution units to store data temporarily.
- **Level 1 (L1) cache**—A small, fast memory area that holds recently used instructions and data.

Some processors are designed around the Harvard architecture. In this architecture, the L1 cache is divided into an *instruction cache* (Icache) and a separate *data cache* (Dcache), as shown in the graphic.

- **Branch target buffer**—A register that stores recently taken branches to aid in branch prediction.
- **Bus interface unit**—A component that controls access to the address and data buses.

### 3.1.2   How Processors Handle Instructions

In general, a processor goes through five stages when it receives input.

#### 3.1.2.1   STAGE 1: FETCHING INSTRUCTION

The prefetch unit searches for an instruction to handle the input. First it looks for an instruction in the L1 cache (or the Icache portion of L1). If it does not find the instruction there, the prefetch unit looks for it in successive layers of the memory hierarchy.

After the correct instruction is found, it is stored in the L1 cache. The prefetch unit fetches the instruction from the cache and sends it to the decode unit.

#### 3.1.2.2   STAGE 2: DECODING INSTRUCTION

The decode unit breaks the instruction into its basic elements, such as an index, data, and the operation code. The decode unit sends the decoded result to the control unit.

#### 3.1.2.3   STAGE 3: EXECUTING INSTRUCTION

The control unit sends the decoded instruction to an execution unit, such as the ALU. The execution unit completes the command, such as adding, subtracting, multiplying, and dividing.

#### 3.1.2.4   STAGE 4: TRANSFERRING DATA

If the instruction is a command, the data it needs to complete the command is transferred to the execution unit from the registers.

#### 3.1.2.5   STAGE 5: WRITING DATA

If required, the execution unit writes the result to a register and data cache.

### 3.1.3 Clock Synchronization

| | Clock Cycle 1 | Clock Cycle 2 | Clock Cycle 3 | Clock Cycle 4 | Clock Cycle 5 | Clock Cycle 6 | Clock Cycle 7 | Clock Cycle 8 | Clock Cycle 9 | Clock Cycle 10 |
|---|---|---|---|---|---|---|---|---|---|---|
| Instruction 1 | Fetch instruction | Decode instruction | Execute instruction | Fetch data | Write data | | | | | |
| Instruction 2 | | | | | | Fetch instruction | Decode instruction | Execute instruction | Fetch data | Write data |

Each stage that the processor goes through is synchronized with the system clock. If each stage takes one clock cycle to complete, one instruction will be processed in five clock cycles. After five cycles, the next instruction can be processed

## 3.2 The Processor Performance Evolution

Engineers have constantly searched for ways to improve processor performance. One way to remove performance bottlenecks is to make the processor do more in one clock cycle. This has been accomplished through pipelined processors, superscalar processors, hyper-pipelined processors, dynamic execution, and the *Explicitly Parallel Instruction Computing* (EPIC) model.

### 3.2.1 Pipelined Processors

In April 1989, Intel introduced the i486 processor, which was the first pipelined processor.

A pipelined processor does not wait for one instruction to be completed before it begins another. Instead, when the prefetch unit completes the first stage and sends an instruction to the decode unit, it immediately starts working on the next instruction. As soon as the decode unit finishes one instruction, it immediately begins working on the next, and so on. This is illustrated in Figure 3–3.

### 3.2.2 Superscalar Processors

The Pentium processor was introduced in 1993. The Pentium added another execution unit to the processor. This innovation also allowed the Pentium to have two pipelines. When both pipelines were operating simultaneously, the

**Figure 3–3**

*How a pipelined processor works.*

| Fetch | Decode | Execute | Transfer | Write |
|-------|--------|---------|----------|-------|
| | | Instruction 1 | | |
| | | Instruction 2 | | |
| | | Instruction 3 | | |
| | | Instruction 4 | | |

**Figure 3–4**

*"Two instructions in flight" with a superscalar processor.*

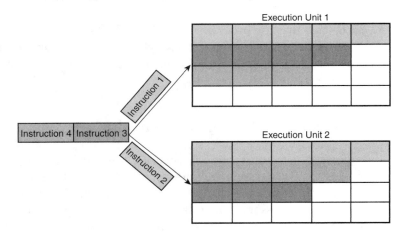

processor could execute two instructions during one clock cycle. This is also known as having "two instructions in flight," and is illustrated in Figure 3–4. A processor that can execute more than one instruction per clock cycle is a superscalar processor. Pentium II and Pentium III processors are superscalar processors, each having five execution units.

### 3.2.3 Hyper-Pipelined Processors

Adding execution units is one method of increasing the number of instructions that a processor deals with in one clock cycle. Expanding the number of steps, or stages, in the pipeline is another method. The Pentium processor has a 5-stage pipeline, the Pentium Pro processor has a 12-stage pipeline, and the Pentium 4 processor, introduced in 1999, has a 20-stage pipeline, as shown in Figure 3–5.

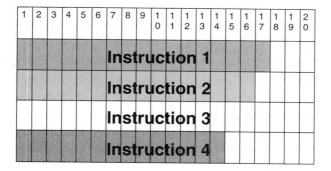

| 1 | 2 | 3 | 4 | 5 | 6 | 7 | 8 | 9 | 1 0 | 1 1 | 1 2 | 1 3 | 1 4 | 1 5 | 1 6 | 1 7 | 1 8 | 1 9 | 2 0 |
|---|---|---|---|---|---|---|---|---|---|---|---|---|---|---|---|---|---|---|---|

Instruction 1

Instruction 2

Instruction 3

Instruction 4

**Figure 3–5**  *20-stage pipeline of the Pentium 4 processor.*

Increasing the number of stages in a pipeline might at first seem illogical. An instruction that previously took only 5 cycles to complete now might take as many as 20 cycles. One benefit, however, is that by breaking the work into smaller steps, the processor has to do less work in each step. The system clock speed can be increased significantly, and more instructions can be completed in the same amount of time.

> **EXAMPLE**
>
> A hyper-pipelined processor can complete 11 instructions in 20 cycles. Without the pipeline, the processor could complete only two instructions in 20 cycles, making a hyper-pipelined processor 5.5 times faster.

### 3.2.4  *Dynamic Execution*

In 1995, Intel introduced the Pentium Pro, the first processor based on the P6 architecture. Part of the P6 architecture is a set of technologies known collectively as *dynamic execution.*

Dynamic execution consists of out-of-order execution, branch prediction, and speculative execution. These technologies are designed to help overcome pipeline hazards—performance problems in hyper-pipelined processors that can be caused by pipelining in some situations.

A pipeline hazard blocks the pipeline until the hazard is removed. This is called a *pipeline stall.* The deeper the pipeline, the more costly (in performance terms) a pipeline stall can be. A 20-stage pipeline might have to wait

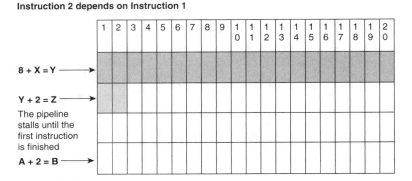

**Figure 3–6** *An example of a pipeline stall.*

as many as 19 cycles to process the correct branch. A 10-stage pipeline would have to wait only 9 cycles in the same type of situation. This concept is illustrated in Figure 3–6.

Two types of common pipeline hazards are dependence problems and branching problems.

Dependence problems are handled by a processor function known as *out-of-order execution*. Branching problems are handled by a processor function known as *branch prediction*. A final processor function that helps resolve pipeline hazards is known as *speculative execution*. Each of these functions is explained in the following subsections.

### 3.2.4.1 OUT-OF-ORDER EXECUTION

Dependence problems occur when one instruction needs data from another instruction to complete its operation. If the first instruction is not complete before the second instruction needs the data, the pipeline must wait until the first instruction is complete.

To handle dependence problems, processors perform out-of-order execution. Instead of holding up the pipeline when it is waiting for the first instruction to finish, the processor can process other instructions that do not depend on the first instruction. The results of these instructions are stored until they are needed later. When the first instruction has finished processing, the dependent instruction is introduced into the pipeline. The result is that fewer cycles are wasted.

**EXAMPLE**

Here is an example of out-of-order execution. Suppose a processor needs to execute the following three instructions:

Instruction 1: 8 + X = Y

Instruction 2: Y + 2 = Z

Instruction 3: A + 2 = B

Notice that Instruction 2 depends on Instruction 1. A processor that can perform out-of-order execution could introduce Instruction 3 (which has no dependencies on previous instructions) into the pipeline before Instruction 2. When Instruction 1 is complete (and Instruction 3 is already far down the pipeline), Instruction 2 is introduced into the pipeline, as illustrated in Figure 3–7.

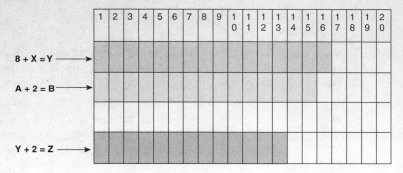

**Figure 3–7**  *An example of out-of-order execution.*

### 3.2.4.2  BRANCH PREDICTION

Branching instructions check a condition, and then execute one branch of instructions if the condition is true, or another branch of instructions if the condition is false.

The branching instruction might take up to 20 cycles to complete, but the prefetch unit keeps filling the pipeline. It could send instructions from the wrong branch into the pipeline before the branching instruction is complete.

When this happens, all the instructions in the pipeline are stopped until the instructions from the wrong branch are flushed from the pipeline, as illustrated in Figure 3–8.

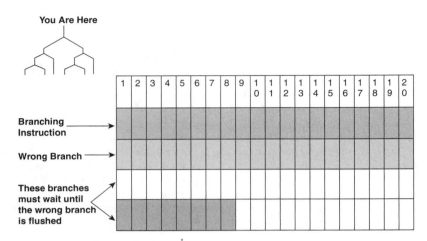

**Figure 3–8** *An example of a branching problem.*

Branch prediction helps mitigate branching problems. During branch prediction, the first time a branch instruction is executed, its address and that of the next instruction executed (the correct branch) are stored in the *branch target buffer* (BTB). The processor uses this information to predict which way the instruction will branch the next time the processor executes it. Branch prediction is correct more than 90% of the time.

When the first instruction is used again, the processor prefetches the branch that was correct the last time, so the wait is minimized and incorrect guesses need to be flushed less frequently. When branch prediction is correct, executing a branch does not cause a pipeline stall.

### 3.2.4.3 SPECULATIVE EXECUTION

Speculative execution is the third component of dynamic execution. It is a blend of branch prediction and out-of-order execution.

A processor that can perform speculative execution will predict the path that a branching instruction will take and begin executing nonconditional instructions in that path. (This is different from branch prediction, which only prefetches the instructions, but does not execute them.)

Instead of writing the instruction results to the general purpose registers as it normally would, the processor stores these speculative results in temporary registers. When the branching instruction is resolved, the precalculated results can be taken from the temporary registers and written to the general registers in the order they were issued.

### 3.2.5 EPIC

In May 2001, Intel introduced the Itanium processor, which is based on the *Explicitly Parallel Instruction Computing* (EPIC) model.

In the EPIC model, a compiler bundles three groups of instructions together. Each bundle includes a few bits, called a *template*, that tell the execution units whether the instructions are dependent or independent. Intel calls this explicitly parallel because the compiler tells the execution units which instructions can be processed in parallel. The Itanium processor does not have to determine the processing order the way a processor with out-of-order capabilities must.

EPIC architecture also handles branching in a new way. Each instruction has a 1-bit predicate. The predicates for the instructions in one branch are set to true; the predicates for the instructions in the other branch are set to false.

A branching instruction is sent to the processor followed quickly by both branches. The processor determines whether the branching instruction is true or false. If it is true, only the instructions with a true predicate are processed. If the statement is false, only instructions with a false predicate are processed. There is no need to flush the pipeline for mispredicted branches.

## 3.3    Logical Processors and Hyper-Threading Technology

Intel Xeon processors include two sets of registers, or architecture states, on a single core. This makes each physical processor act like two logical processors. The execution units and other resources within the core are shared by the two architecture states, enabling the processor to keep the execution units working more often. As a result, a processor with hyper-threading technology can increase performance 30% over the same processor without hyper-threading technology.

With hyper-threading technology, the two logical processors can execute different tasks, or threads, simultaneously using shared hardware resources. From a software or architecture perspective, this means operating systems and user programs can schedule threads to logical processors as they would on multiple physical processors. From a micro-architecture perspective, this means that instructions from both logical processors will persist and execute simultaneously on shared execution resources. The result is that more transactions are processed, so many Internet and e-business applications see faster response times.

**Figure 3–9**
*Operating
systems
schedule
threads to
separate
processors
and to
separate
logical
processors.*

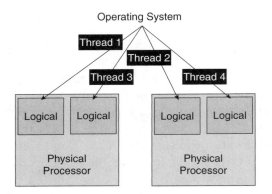

### 3.3.1   Thread Scheduling

Operating systems that recognize logical processors manage them as they do physical processors, scheduling tasks or threads to them. With more than one Xeon processor installed, operating systems can schedule threads to separate processors and separate logical processors on a single physical processor simultaneously, as shown in Figure 3–9.

Because of the way the processors are counted and subsequently identified by the operating system, threads are always scheduled to logical processors on different physical processors before scheduling multiple threads to the same physical processor occurs. This optimization allows software threads to use different physical execution resources when possible.

The operating system disables a second logical processor when it is not needed by issuing a halt instruction. This prevents the second logical processor from repeatedly checking for work, which can consume significant execution resources.

## 3.4   Multiprocessor Servers

A server with more than one processor is known as a *multiprocessor server*. One method of meeting the demand for more computing power is to include more than one processor in a server.

The term *way* is used to indicate the number of processors in a server. For example, a four-way server, such as the HP ProLiant DL580 G2, has four processors. An eight-way server, such as the HP ProLiant DL760, has eight processors.

Several factors can affect the performance of a multiprocessor server. For example, an operating system must be able to handle multiprocessing

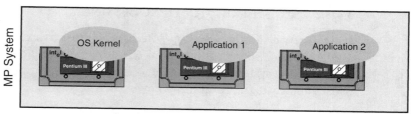

Asymmetric multiprocessing (AMP)

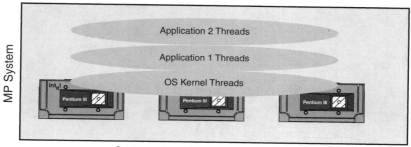

Symmetric multiprocessing (SMP)

**Figure 3–10** *AMP vs. SMP.*

environments. Different operating systems handle multiprocessing differently. In some cases, the operating system sends all I/O interrupts to a single processor; in other cases, however, processors share I/O interrupts.

When designing a multiprocessor system, engineers must decide (1) how the processors will share the workload, and (2) how the processors will share memory and I/O resources.

## 3.4.1    Sharing the Workload

Two methods exist for a multiprocessor server to share the workload among the processors—*asymmetric multiprocessing* (AMP) and *symmetric multiprocessing* (SMP). A comparison of these techniques is shown in Figure 3–10.

### 3.4.1.1    ASYMMETRIC MULTIPROCESSING

In asymmetric multiprocessing, specific tasks are assigned to specific processors. This method can be inefficient because, depending on the type of applications, the workload among processors is unevenly distributed. Adding a new processor in an AMP system does not guarantee increased computing power. In some cases, however, keeping a single process on one processor is desirable.

### 3.4.1.2 SYMMETRIC MULTIPROCESSING

In symmetric multiprocessing systems, each task is executed on the next-available processor, resulting in excellent load-sharing capability. However, the operating system must be able to support SMP. Adding a new processor usually increases the computing power.

Most HP industry-standard servers use SMP for multiprocessing.

### 3.4.2 Sharing Memory and I/O Resources

Two architectures are available for designing a multiprocessor system to share memory and I/O resources—tightly coupled and loosely coupled.

### 3.4.2.1 TIGHTLY COUPLED

In the tightly coupled architecture, all processors share all memory and I/O resources, as shown in Figure 3–11. The operating system manages all the resources. If memory fails, all processors are affected. This requires a system bus that is common among all the processors and shared components.

Most HP industry-standard servers are based on a tightly coupled architecture.

### 3.4.2.2 LOOSELY COUPLED

In the loosely coupled architecture, each processor has memory and I/O resources assigned to it and, in a sense, acts as an independent computer, as illustrated in Figure 3–12. It does not share its resources with the other processors, but it does communicate and cooperate with them. If memory fails, only the processor using that memory is affected.

HP Himalaya servers use a loosely coupled architecture.

### 3.4.3 Other Factors

Several other factors can affect the performance of a multiprocessor server. For example, an operating system must be able to handle multiprocessing environments. Different operating systems handle multiprocessing differently. In some cases, the operating system sends all I/O interrupts to a single

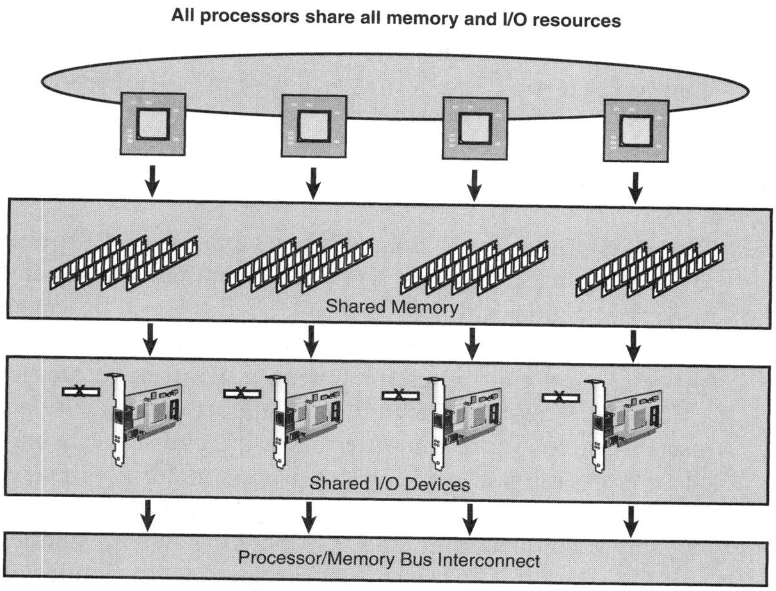

All processors share all memory and I/O resources
Shared Memory
Shared I/O Devices
Processor/Memory Bus Interconnect

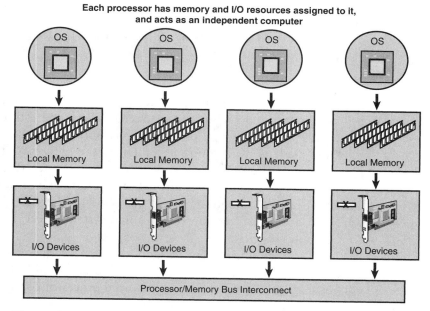

**Figure 3–11** *Tightly coupled architecture.*

Each processor has memory and I/O resources assigned to it, and acts as an independent computer
OS
OS
OS
OS
Local Memory
Local Memory
Local Memory
Local Memory
I/O Devices
I/O Devices
I/O Devices
I/O Devices
Processor/Memory Bus Interconnect

**Figure 3–12** *Loosely coupled architecture.*

processor, but in other cases processors share I/O interrupts. When designing a multiprocessing solution, you must plan carefully to ensure that the solution that you design works well with the customer requirements.

## 3.5   Mixing Processors

The Intel processor line includes several families of processors with varying core frequencies, L2 cache sizes, and steppings. Customer desire for investment protection and their growing need to scale processing power and to redeploy server components make the ability to mix processors in dual-processor and multiprocessor systems a significant customer benefit.

To ensure full protection and support under manufacturer warranties, users must configure computer hardware and software according to manufacturer guidelines. In the case of processors for use in servers, guidelines of multiple vendors must be reconciled: those of the processor manufacturer, the server manufacturer, and the operating system vendor. The question of vendor support for Intel processor mixing is clouded by differences in vendor testing programs and vague wording of vendor support policies.

> **! IMPORTANT**
> Four-way platforms, starting with the Intel Xeon processors, no longer support processor mixing.

With the rapid introduction of new processors and the race to bring new products to market, no vendor has sufficient time and resources to test every possible combination of mixed processors for all potential problems. Intel conducts its own testing program for the processors it markets and publishes identified errata and workarounds on the Intel website.

For compatibility testing through its Windows Hardware Quality Labs and certification through the Microsoft Windows Logo Program for hardware, Microsoft Corporation requires that systems meet defined processor configuration restrictions.

Other operating system vendors might have their own qualification procedures for multiprocessor servers. HP, other manufacturers, and users are free to do additional validation of mixed processor configurations if they choose.

### 3.5.1 Processor Steppings

Processor steppings are versions of the same processor model (for example, the Intel Pentium III Xeon processor) that vary only slightly, usually to improve performance or manufacturing yield. Each stepping requires changes to the system ROM. For each processor stepping that it produces, Intel provides a microcode patch for inclusion in the system ROM.

Each Intel processor stepping has a unique processor ID, and its microcode patch contains the same processor ID. The microcode patches are stored in a table within the system ROM. HP and other server vendors must continually add newly released Intel patches to keep their ROMs current.

After a processor has been installed, stepping identification can be problematic because a heat sink typically covers the top of the processor chip. Utilities provided with operating systems might help. For example, under Windows NT, a system administrator can use the Windows NT Diagnostics utility to identify the stepping level of each installed processor. Alternatively, a system administrator can use the Survey utility to view the steppings of installed processors.

### 3.5.2 Intel Support for Processor Mixing

Based on the information available on the Intel Web site at the time of this writing, Intel supports mixed steppings of processors only if all processors in a system meet the following criteria:

- Have identical family and model numbers as indicated by the CPU ID instruction.

- Operate at the same frequency—that is, at the highest frequency rating commonly supported by all the processors.

- Have the same cache size.

- The processor with the lowest feature set must be the bootstrap processor.

The bootstrap processor is the primary processor in a multiprocessor system. It is the main processor that starts the system and from which it loads the operating system and performs most functions. The remaining processors in a multiprocessor system are application processors.

### 3.5.3   Operating System Support for Processor Mixing

Like Intel, operating system vendors support the mixing of processors only if all processors in a system meet the following criteria:

- Have identical family and model numbers.
- Operate at the same frequency.
- Have the same cache size.
- The processor with the lowest feature set must be the bootstrap processor.

Statements from operating system vendors tend to be vague about support for mixed processor steppings. The most common operating systems typically do not inhibit the operation of servers containing multiple processors with different steppings.

## ▲ Summary

This chapter explained the key concepts relating to processors and multiprocessing that you need to understand in order to properly recommend an HP ProLiant server solution.

## ▲ LEARNING CHECK

1. *What is an instruction?*

2. *Match the processor component with its function.*

| | |
|---|---|
| Prefetch unit | A small, fast memory area that holds recently used instructions and data |
| Decode unit | A component that controls access to the address and data buses |
| Execution unit | A component that breaks an instruction into its constituent parts |
| Control unit | A small number of memory locations used by the control and execution units to store data temporarily |

| Registers | A register that stores recently taken branches to aid in branch prediction |
| L1 cache | A component that performs the actual data processing, such as adding and subtracting |
| Branch target buffer | A holding place for instructions and operands that a processor will need |
| Bus interface unit | A component that acts as a scheduler for the execution units |

3. *Put the following steps in order to describe how a processor handles input:*
   A. Executes instruction
   B. Writes data
   C. Fetches instruction
   D. Transfers data
   E. Decodes instruction

4. *Match the technology with its description:*

| Pipelined | A processor that does not wait for one instruction to be completed before it begins another |
| Superscalar | A processor with an expanded number of steps that it uses to complete an instruction |
| Hyper-pipelined | A processor that can execute more than one instruction per clock cycle |
| Branch prediction | A processor in which the compiler tells the execution units which instructions can be processed in parallel |
| Out-of-order execution | A technology in which the first time a branch instruction is executed, its address and that of the correct branch are stored in the branch target buffer |
| EPIC | A processor technology that can process instructions first that do not depend on another instruction |

5. *Match the technology with its description:*

| | |
|---|---|
| Asymmetric multiprocessing | All processors share all memory. |
| Symmetric multiprocessing | The next task is executed on the next available processor. |
| Loosely coupled | Tasks are assigned to specific processors. |
| Tightly coupled | Each processor has memory assigned to it and, in a sense, acts as an independent computer. |

6. *When mixing processors, to which processor core frequency should the core frequency of each processor be set?*

7. *Which processor should be installed as the bootstrap processor?*

# Memory and Cache

After studying this chapter, you should be able to do the following:

- Describe the characteristics of and differences between dynamic RAM (memory) and static RAM (cache).

- Explain how data is written to, stored in, and read from memory.

- List the technologies that can be used to improve memory performance.

- Describe memory failures and the fault-tolerant technologies used to protect memory, including the following:

  - Parity
  - Error checking and correcting (ECC)
  - Advanced ECC

- Explain the function of cache memory.

- Discuss methods to improve cache performance.

This chapter explains the differences between memory and cache, and how both work. It also covers some of the technical innovations that have increased memory and cache performance and their fault-tolerant capabilities.

**47**

## 4.1     Memory and Cache

Figure 4–1 shows the main components of a basic computer system. Notice how the key components are connected by the address bus, control bus, and the data bus. Together these three components make up the "system bus."

Server performance is substantially increased if the system buses are utilized on every clock cycle. As technical innovations have consistently increased processor speed and capacity, systems designers have been challenged to find ways to keep the system buses fully utilized at every clock cycle.

### 4.1.1   DRAM

It became apparent early in the evolution of computers that magnetic storage technologies such as tapes and hard disk drives would not be able to keep up with the processor demands because of their slow speed. Memory modules were the innovation that met the challenge to keep up with the increasing speed of processors. Figure 4–2 shows a typical memory module.

Memory modules use *dynamic RAM* (DRAM) technology to store and read data for the processor.

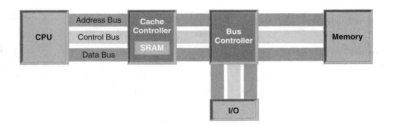

**Figure 4–1**   *Diagram of a basic computer system.*

**Figure 4–2**   *Memory module.*

A DRAM module stores bits of data in capacitors. (A capacitor is an electronic device that can hold an electrical charge.) A capacitor that is holding a charge is equivalent to a binary 1. A capacitor without a charge is equivalent to a binary 0.

DRAM is called dynamic RAM because capacitors cannot hold a charge indefinitely. A significant limitation of a DRAM module is that the charge in a capacitor completely drains in a matter of milliseconds if left alone. To keep the data intact, the capacitors must be recharged thousands of times per second. During the recharge process, the memory chip cannot be used to send data to or receive data from the processor.

The capacitors on a DRAM module are arranged in grids, sometimes called a *memory matrix* or a *memory chip*, as illustrated in Figure 4–3. The rows and columns of the grid are electrically conductive traces etched on the chip. The intersection of a row and column is called a *cell*. Each cell, which is identified by its row and column address, contains a transistor and a capacitor.

## 4.1.2 SRAM

To overcome the limitations of DRAM, engineers developed cache. Cache uses a group of transistors arranged as a flip-flop circuit, or latch, to store data. A latch is an electronic circuit that alternates between two states. When current is applied, the latch changes to its opposite state. Figure 4–4 shows a Pentium Pro Processor with a 512KB cache.

Cache is known as *static RAM* (SRAM) because, unlike capacitors, latches do not have to be refreshed. This makes cache much faster than memory.

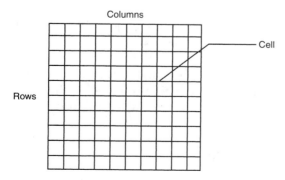

**Figure 4–3**  *The memory matrix.*

**Figure 4–4**

*Pentium Pro Processor with 512KB cache (on left).*

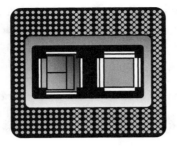

**Figure 4–5**

*FC-PGA processor on a silver heat sink.*

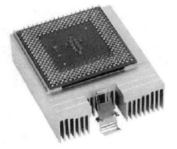

Through the years, engineers have added layers of cache between the processor and memory. Methods have been developed to move cache from the system board to the actual processor. Some Xeon processors, for example, have three levels of cache on the processor.

### 4.1.2.1   LIMITATIONS OF SRAM

Despite its speed, cache does have limitations. First, it is more expensive than DRAM. DRAM stores a bit in a single capacitor, but an SRAM latch requires six to eight transistors to store the same bit. The more transistors, the more expensive the chip is to produce.

And second, the transistors in the latches make cache very hot. Special cooling mechanisms, such as heat sinks, must be developed to channel the heat away from the processor. This also increases the cost of SRAM. Figure 4–5 shows an FC-PGA processor on a silver heat sink.

## 4.2   How Memory Works

Memory chips were originally attached directly to the system board of a computer. As the need for more memory increased and the space on the system board started to become scarce, memory chips were mounted on cards

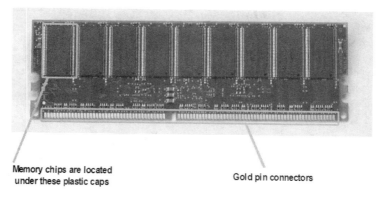

Memory chips are located
under these plastic caps

Gold pin connectors

**Figure 4–6**  *DIMM.*

called *memory modules.* Figure 4–6 shows a typical *dual inline memory module* (DIMM). Notice the parallel rows of memory modules and the gold pin connectors.

The *single inline memory module* (SIMM) was one of the first types of memory modules developed. Memory chips were mounted on one or both sides of a SIMM, but electrical signals from both sides were routed to the same set of gold pins. SIMMs could handle only 32 bits of data at a time.

Today's HP ProLiant servers are built to handle 64 bits of data at a time, so SIMMs were eventually replaced by DIMMs. DIMMs have memory chips on both sides, and each side has separate pins for a total of 144 pins. Some DIMMs have 168 pins. The extra pins handle *error checking and correcting* (ECC) capabilities. (ECC is explained later in this chapter.)

The electrical traces from the memory chips are routed from the memory chips to gold pins located at the bottom of the memory module. The pins snap into slots on the system board or a memory board.

An *application-specific integrated circuit* (ASIC) known as the *memory controller* sits on the system board. The memory controller controls the memory bus, the pathway between the processor and the memory modules. The memory bus has two parts: the address bus and the data bus. Figure 4–7 illustrates how the memory controller utilizes the address bus and data bus.

In addition to the address and data pins, a typical memory module has other pins that it uses to communicate with the memory controller. The *row address strobe* (RAS) and *column address strobe* (CAS) are pins used to communicate the address of the cell the memory wants to set. Typically, they carry a high voltage. The memory controller communicates with the memory chip by changing the voltage of the RAS and CAS.

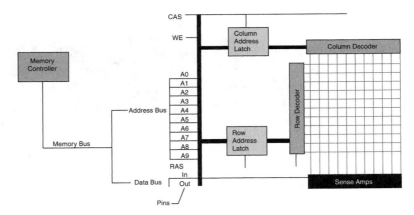

**Figure 4–7**  *The memory controller uses the address bus and data bus to communicate with memory.*

The memory controller uses the *Write Enable* (WE) pin to indicate whether an operation is a read or a write.

To read or write data, the memory controller sends a row address to the RAS and a column address to the CAS through the address pins.

For a write operation, data is sent through the Data In pin to the cell at the intersection of the addresses.

For a read operation, a sense amp measures the charge of the cell at the intersection. If it is charged, the sense amp indicates a 1 on the Data Out pin. If it is not charged, the sense amp indicates a 0 on the Data Out pin.

A memory cell can hold 1 bit of data, but a processor is designed to work with data in bytes. When the processor needs to store data in memory, it sends 8 bytes of data and an address through the system bus to the memory controller. The memory controller breaks each byte of data into 8 bits and uses the address that the processor sent to determine a row and column address. The memory controller sends each of the 8 bits to a different memory chip on the module. All 8 bits will have the same address, just on different chips.

When the processor requests data, the memory controller sends the same request to each chip, receives the bits of data, and reassembles them into the requested byte, as illustrated in Figure 4–8.

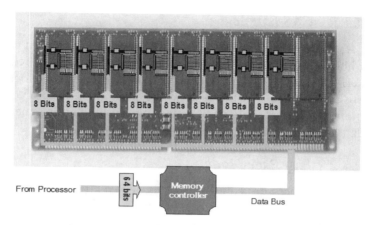

**Figure 4–8** *How the memory controller distributes data to the memory chip.*

## 4.3 Improving Memory Performance

Although processor speeds have increased dramatically, memory speeds continue to lag behind. One way that engineers try to improve memory performance is to shorten memory latency. Memory latency is the length of time it takes for a DRAM module to return data to the memory controller. Two main factors affect memory latency: access time and cycle time.

Access time is the amount of time it takes for data to show up on the data bus after the row is activated by RAS

At the beginning of a read operation, the memory controller lowers the RAS voltage, which sets the row address on the row address latch. The time it takes for the RAS line to fall to a predetermined low level is referred to as *tRAC*. The longer tRAC is, the longer the access time will be.

Later in the read operation, the memory controller lowers the CAS voltage, which sets the column address on the column address latch. The time it takes for the CAS line to fall to a predetermined low level is referred to as *tCAC*. Similar to tRAC, the longer tCAC is, the longer the access time will be.

Cycle time is the amount of time between read operations.

At the end of a read operation, the memory controller increases the voltage on the RAS and CAS lines to indicate the end of the operation. The time it takes to increase the voltage on both lines to a predetermined high level is called the *precharge delay*. The next operation cannot occur until after the voltage on both lines is high enough. The longer the precharge delay, the longer the cycle time.

### 4.3.1    CAS Latency

CAS latency is a number that refers to the ratio—rounded to the next higher whole number—between column access time and the clock cycle time. It is derived from dividing the column access time by the clock frequency and raising the result to the next whole number. The lower the CAS latency number, the less amount of time required for the first memory access in a data burst transfer.

### 4.3.2    Fast Page Mode

When a processor requests data, its next request is usually for data in the same row, or page. Therefore, to speed data to the processor, a technique called *fast page mode* (FPM) was developed. In FPM, when a processor makes a request for data, the memory controller retrieves the requested data plus an additional three columns of data from each memory chip.

The memory controller then assembles the data into four 1-byte chunks. Together these chunks are called a *word*. The memory controller sends, or bursts, the word to the cache, which stores it in a cache line. The cache then sends the requested byte of data to the processor.

If the next processor request is for data from the same page, the request can be filled quickly from the cache line. This is known as a *page hit*. If the requested data is not in the same page, the data is retrieved from memory. This is known as a *page miss*. A page miss can more than double the amount of cycles it takes to retrieve the data.

FPM decreases latency by eliminating the cycle time for RAS for the last 3 bits of data.

### 4.3.3    Extended Data Out DRAM

A drawback of FPM is that the data from one column had to be sent to the Data Out pins before the next column could be activated. Memory designers overcame this limitation in 1996 by introducing *Extended Data Out* (EDO) DRAM.

EDO decreases latency by activating the next column while data is still on the Data Out pins. This change to DRAM timing results in a 20% to 30% decrease in the amount of time it takes to get data from the memory module to the memory controller.

## 4.3.4 Synchronous DRAM

FPM and EDO are both asynchronous technologies because they do not function according to the system clock. They have their own timing mechanisms that coordinate reading and writing data to memory with the system clock.

In 1997, *synchronous DRAM* (SDRAM) was introduced. SDRAM relies on the same clock used by the memory bus. This development eliminated the need for the special timing mechanisms.

SDRAM differs from asynchronous RAM in another significant way. SDRAM DIMMs contain multiple banks of chips. While the memory controller is receiving data from one bank, it can precharge a row in the other bank. This process reduces the amount of time that the controller has to wait for data to be available.

## 4.3.5 Double Data Rate RAM

*Double Data Rate* (DDR) memory effectively doubles the number of data transfers per clock cycle by sending data on both the rising and falling edge of each clock signal. Engineers often call this transfer method a double-pumped bus. This technique is illustrated in Figure 4–9.

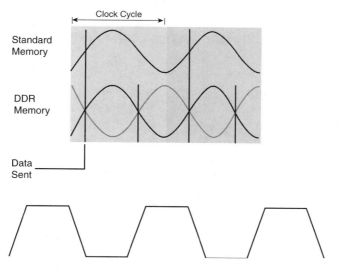

**Figure 4–9** *DDR RAM can transfer data on both the rising and falling edge of each clock cycle.*

The net effect is that DDR RAM can send or receive twice as much data to or from the processor in one clock cycle. Therefore, although a memory bus might run at 100MHz or 133MHz, it can have an effective data transfer rate of a standard 200MHz or 266MHz bus, respectively.

A clock cycle is best represented as a wave, with a rising edge, a falling edge, and a plateau between the edges. SDRAM DIMMs transfer data only on the rising edge of the clock cycle.

DDR RAM was introduced in ProLiant ML530 G2 and DL580 G2 servers in 2002.

### 4.3.6   Comparing DDR Memory and SDRAM Memory Technologies

Performance is enhanced using DDR memory architecture and modules by taking advantage of transferring data on both sides of the clock.

The naming convention for DDR RAM relates to the peak bandwidth, rather than the clock rates like that used by PC100 and PC133 SDRAM.

DDR PC1600 SDRAM has the same data bus width as PC100 and PC133 SDRAM (64 bits plus ECC bits), but because it transfers data twice per clock cycle, PC1600 memory has twice the effective data transfer rate of PC100 DIMMs.

Although both PC133 SDRAM DIMMs and DDR PC2100 SDRAM DIMMs are used on a 133MHz memory bus, PC2100 SDRAM has twice the effective data transfer rate of PC133 DIMMs because of DDR technology on a double-pumped bus.

In addition, CAS latency on PC1600 DIMMs is 2 or 2.5 clocks, a half-clock faster than the CAS latency on PC100 or PC133 DIMMs. CAS latency on PC2100 DIMMs is 2.5 clocks, a half-clock faster than the CAS latency on PC133 DIMMs.

Physically, the DIMM types look different, as shown in Figure 4–10. The DDR DIMMs are smaller—only 1.2 inches high, as compared to the 1.7 inches for the PC133 and PC100. In addition, DDR DIMMs have a single notch in the gold connectors; PC100 and PC133 DIMMs have a double notch.

### 4.3.7   Comparing DDR SDRAM to RDRAM

Most industry-standard servers have not implemented *Rambus DRAM* (RDRAM), which has a wider data bus and a faster clock speed than SDRAM. One reason is that no enterprise-class chipset is available for RDRAM memory systems.

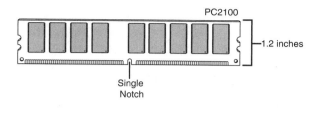

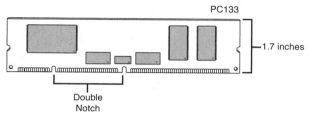

**Figure 4–10** *A comparison between a PC 133 SDRAM DIMM and a PC2100 SDRAM DIMM.*

Other reasons that SDRAM is implemented in servers instead of RDRAM include

- Because of architectural limitations, the maximum memory supported by RDRAM chipsets is much lower that those designed for servers using SDRAM.
- RDRAM DIMMs are much more expensive than comparably sized SDRAM DIMMs.
- Latency in RDRAM is 14 to 18 clocks (compared to 2 or 2.5 clocks for PC1600 SDRAM).
- RDRAM consumes more power and subsequently produces more heat than SDRAM DIMMs.

### 4.3.8 Pumped Buses

DDR memory works on a double-pumped bus. A pumped bus sends data more than once per clock cycle. It does this by using more than one clock. The clocks are out of phase with each other. Data is sent when their strobes intersect.

When four clocks are used, the bus sends data four times per clock cycle, because there are four intersections per cycle. This is known as a *quad-pumped bus*. Figure 4–11 illustrates the differences between buses.

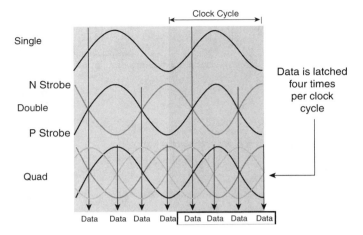

**Figure 4–11** *Data transfer cycles for pumped buses.*

### 4.3.8.1 HOW DOES THAT COMPUTE?

The maximum data transfer rate is calculated using the following formula:

$$\frac{\text{Bus speed (MHz)} \times \text{Bus width (bytes)}}{\text{Cycles/Transfer}}$$

In a 64-bit, 100MHz system, data is sent across the system bus once every clock cycle:

$$\frac{100\text{MHz}}{1} \times \frac{8 \text{ bytes}}{1} = 800\text{MB/s}$$

In a quad-pumped Xeon system, data is sent across the system bus four times every clock cycle:

$$\frac{100\text{MHz}}{1} \times \frac{8 \text{ bytes}}{4} = 3200\text{MB/s} = 3.2\text{GB/s}$$

Therefore, a quad-pumped Xeon system has the same data transfer rate as a 400MHz single-pumped bus:

$$\frac{400\text{MHz}}{1} \times \frac{8 \text{ bytes}}{1} = 3200\text{MB/s} = 3.2\text{GB/s}$$

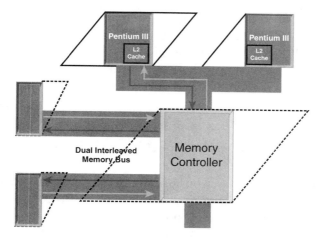

**Figure 4–12** *Interleaved memory technology.*

### 4.3.9 *Interleaved Memory*

Interleaved memory technology increases the amount of data obtained in a single memory access.

When data is written to memory, the memory controller distributes the data across DIMMs in a bank, as shown in Figure 4–12. When the processor sends a read request to the memory controller, the memory controller sends the request to all DIMMs in the bank simultaneously. The data at the requested address is returned along with data from subsequent sequential addresses. The memory controller interleaves the data from all the DIMMs to put it back in its original order.

Because more than one DIMM is used in this transaction, the amount of data that can be written or read is larger than if a single DIMM were used. For example, in dual-interleaved memory, where two DIMMs are used, the processor can read and write twice the amount of data in one memory access. In four-way interleaved memory, the processor can read and write four times the amount of data in one memory access.

The data is sent to the processor cache in anticipation of future data requirements. The processor uses the faster cache, which now contains much more sequential data than in a non-interleaved system, to fulfill subsequent requests until it cannot find the data it needs. At that point, it sends another request to the memory controller.

Using interleaved memory, the processor cache can meet the data requests from the processor more than 98% of the time, which provides two benefits. First, the bus between the processor and the cache runs at the processor speed. The bus between the cache and memory runs at a much slower speed. Interleaved memory fills the cache more quickly, so the processor fills its cache faster. Second, because most requests are filled from cache, fewer requests are sent to the memory controller. As a result, there is less chance that the second processor will have to wait to access the memory controller.

## 4.4    Memory Failures and Fault-Tolerant Memory

Because memory is an electronic storage device, it has the potential to return information different from what was originally stored. The probability of memory failures has increased in recent years, as shown in Figure 4–13.

There is a direct correlation between increased memory capacity and an increased *annualized failure rate* (AFR), the probability of one memory failure in one year. Several factors are driving increased memory capacity:

- DRAM density is growing.
- More DRAM chips are populated on each DIMM.
- DRAM chips are being stacked on top of each other to create higher-capacity DIMMs.
- More DIMM slots are available in servers.

The probability of memory failures increases 3% for every 1GB of installed memory. The probability jumps to 48% when the memory is increased to 16GB. The AFR increase is true whether the memory increase is caused by increased DIMM capacity or additional slots in the system.

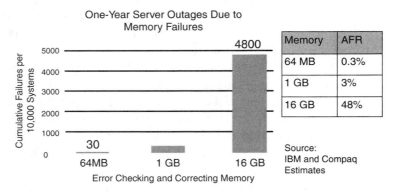

**Figure 4–13** *Probability of server outages due to memory failure.*

Recent moves to reduce power consumption in servers also contribute to memory failures. As memory module voltages decrease, the signal margin also decreases, making the signal more susceptible to noise. As a result, memory error rates increase.

Two kinds of errors can typically occur in a memory system, hard errors and soft errors.

A hard error occurs when there is a physical problem such as a defective DIMM or a broken connection. A hard error recurs unless the problem is repaired. HP tests every DIMM that is placed in its servers to reduce the number of hard errors a customer might encounter.

A soft error occurs randomly when an electrical disturbance near a memory cell alters the charge on the capacitor. A soft error does not indicate a problem with a memory device because after the data is corrected, the same error does not reoccur.

Soft errors are more prevalent than hard errors. Research has shown that the number of soft errors increases with memory capacity. Based on 460 soft errors per year for 10,000 computers with 64MB of memory each, approximately 3 soft errors will occur per computer per year for every 4GB of memory.

HP has used a number of technologies to detect, and in many cases correct, soft errors. These technologies include parity checking, *error checking and correcting* (ECC), and advanced ECC.

## 4.4.1   Parity Checking

The first error-detecting technology used in memory was parity checking. It was originally designed for desktop computers. A system that uses parity checking adds a parity bit to each byte when data is written to memory, as shown in Figure 4–14.

The system counts the number of 1s in the byte. If it is an even number, the parity bit is 0. If it is an odd number, the parity bit is 1.

**EXAMPLE**

1110011 = 1 for parity
1100011 = 0 for parity

When the system reads the byte from memory, the memory controller recalculates the parity bit and compares it to the stored parity bit. If a single bit in the byte has changed, the new parity value will not match the stored

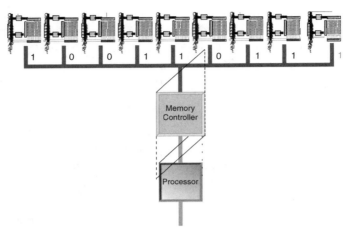

**Figure 4–14** *Parity checking adds an extra parity bit to each byte.*

parity value. The controller knows that a soft error has occurred and shuts down the system to avoid data corruption. No error is logged.

Although parity checking detects many errors, it does have some drawbacks. Parity checking can detect only odd numbers of single-bit errors. If two soft errors occur in the same byte, the parity bit will be correct although the byte is corrupt. In addition, parity checking does not know which bit is bad and cannot correct it.

### 4.4.2 ECC

ECC memory was introduced in Compaq Systempro XL servers in 1992, and is used in all ProLiant servers. ECC memory can detect up to 4-bit errors in a single byte. More importantly, it can correct single-bit errors.

ECC systems are similar to parity systems, with one important difference. Instead of calculating a parity bit for each byte of data written to memory, ECC systems calculate a 72-bit syndrome (checksum) for every 64 bits of data. The checksum contains the 64 bits of data and 8 check bits. Figure 4–15 illustrates this concept.

On a read operation, the memory controller recalculates the checksum and compares it to the original. If the syndromes do not match, the system knows that an error has occurred. It uses the checksums to determine which bit is corrupt and corrects the error before sending it to the requesting device.

Some soft errors are multibit errors, which traditional ECC cannot correct and which will cause an ECC system to fail. The potential for multibit errors increases with memory capacity. For example, servers with 1GB of

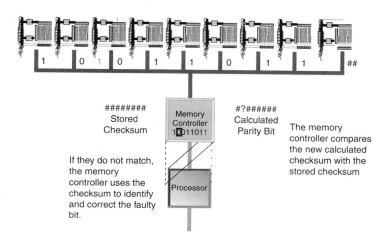

**Figure 4–15**  *ECC memory technology.*

memory using ECC are protected against memory failures only about as well as servers with 64MB of memory using parity checking. With each new generation of servers, memory capacity increases—and so does the potential for system failures.

## 4.4.3   Advanced ECC

To improve memory protection, Compaq introduced *advanced ECC* (AECC) technology in 1996. HP and other server manufacturers continue to use this solution in current server product lines.

Standard ECC devices can detect and correct a single-bit error during a read from a DIMM. This prevents the error from causing the server to shut down. Standard ECC memory also detects multibit errors, but it cannot correct them. AECC can correct a multibit error that occurs within one DRAM chip on a DIMM and thus can correct a complete DRAM chip failure.

AECC performs memory writes, and it reads and corrects memory errors in a system with four DIMMs.

### 4.4.3.1   MEMORY WRITE

During a memory write in an AECC system, a 256-bit cache line is sent from the processor to the memory controller. The data in the cache line is divided into four 64-bit data words, which are sent to four *error detection and correction* (EDC) circuits.

Each EDC circuit generates 8 bits of ECC data that it adds to the 64-bit data word to form a 72-bit syndrome. The memory controller sends the syndrome to 4 DIMMs. Each DIMM has 18 DRAM chips, 9 on each side, for a total of 72 DRAMs. For each syndrome, the memory controller stripes the data across all 72 DRAMs, sending 1 bit to each chip.

### 4.4.3.2   MEMORY READ

When a device requests data from memory, the 72-bit syndrome is retrieved from the DRAMs and sent to the EDC circuits. The circuits run several ECC algorithms on the data to ensure its integrity. Then the EDC circuit strips the extra 8 bits of ECC data from the syndrome and sends the data back to the requesting device.

### 4.4.3.3   MEMORY ERRORS

If an EDC circuit detects a single-bit error within a syndrome, it can correct the error before sending the data to the requesting device.

Advanced ECC can detect and correct up to a 4-bit error, if all the errors originate from the same DRAM.

When a DRAM fails, it sends a single bit of corrupt data to each EDC circuit. Each circuit detects and corrects the error sent to it before sending the data to the requesting device.

AECC can detect and correct up to four single-bit errors, if all the errors originate from different DRAMs and go to separate EDC circuits. Advanced ECC cannot correct multibit errors if errors from different DRAMs are sent to the same EDC circuit.

## 4.5   Advanced Memory Protection

HP ProLiant technologies now provide advanced memory protection methods and options that avoid downtime caused by memory failure. These technologies include the following methods that protect data still contained in memory:

- Online spare memory
- Single-board mirrored memory
- Hot-plug mirrored memory
- Hot-plug RAID memory

These options are implemented at the hardware level, independent of the operating system, and work with ECC technology to provide an additional level of protection against memory failures.

Each of these advanced memory protection options is explained later in this book in Chapter 19, "Availability."

## Cache

Although retrieving data from memory is much faster than retrieving data from hard disk drives and tapes, it still cannot keep the processor pipeline full. Cache is implemented to help keep the pipeline full and the processors processing data efficiently.

Like memory, cache stores data in grids. Instead of using capacitors, however, the grids in cache are made up of latches. Because the latches do not have to be refreshed, cache can read and write data much faster than memory.

Cache works off the principle of data locality. When a processor requests data, there is a high probability that the next request will be for data stored in close proximity to the initial data that was requested. When a processor requests data from memory, memory sends the requested data plus the nearby data. All data is then stored in cache. Therefore, subsequent data requests can usually be filled from the faster cache rather than from the slower memory.

### 4.6.1  Cache Levels and Placement

Cache was originally located on the system board between the processor and memory. It was connected to the processor through the system bus, as shown in Figure 4–16. Eventually, cache was incorporated into the processor. Current processors usually contain more than one cache. The first-level cache is called L1 (Level 1), the second-level cache is called L2, and so on.

L1 cache is the fastest of all the caches, but it holds the least amount of data. Because it is connected directly to the processor, it operates at the same speed as the processor. It can deliver data in as little as 10ns.

L2 cache was also originally located on the system board and connected to the processor through the system bus. That meant it was slower than L1 cache, but still faster than memory. Now all processors used in ProLiant servers include L2 cache as part of the processor. The L2 cache is connected to the processor through a backside bus. The backside bus speed depends on the processor, but normally runs at the speed of the processor.

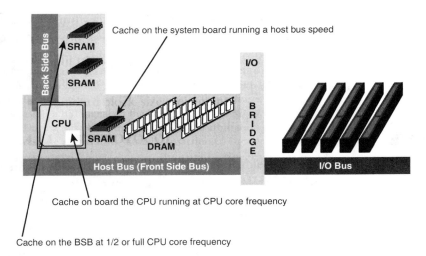

**Figure 4–16** *Cache levels and placement.*

When L2 cache moved to the processor package, cache on the system board became known as *L3 cache.* L3 cache runs at the speed of the system bus, which is still faster than the memory bus. The Itanium processor now has L3 cache located on the processor. This opens the possibility for an L4 cache on the system board.

Each level of cache is bigger than the last. L2 holds a copy of everything in L1, and has room for additional data. L3 holds a copy of everything in L2, plus additional data. L2 and L3 can deliver data in about 20 to 30ns. In contrast, main memory delivers data in about 60ns because it runs at the speed of the memory bus. In comparison, hard drives can take as long as 12ms to return data to the processor.

## 4.6.2  Cache Lines and Tag RAM

Although DRAM is generally designed with only a few rows to make refreshing easier, SRAM does not have that limitation. As a result, cache is usually designed with many rows and only a few columns.

> **EXAMPLE**
>
> A 512KB cache has 16,384 rows (or cache lines) and 32 columns.
> ($16,000 \times 32 = 512,000$)

Each row in the cache is known as a *cache line*. In newer processors, when the processor requests data, main memory returns the single byte of data requested and it also prefetches the next 31 bytes. The 32-byte chunk is stored in a cache line. This is known as a *cache line fill*. If the processor requests data from the additional 31 bytes (which it often does), it can retrieve the data quickly if it is already in a cache line.

A smaller SRAM chip, called the *tag RAM*, stores the memory address for the data in each cache line. When the processor requests a piece of data, the cache controller compares the address in the request with the addresses in the tag RAM. If the cache controller finds the address, it returns the associated data to the processor. This is known as a *cache hit*. If the controller does not find the address, it is known as a *cache miss*.

## 4.7    Improving Cache Performance

Engineers are always looking for ways to increase the efficiency of every clock cycle. Over time, several enhancements have been made to cache and memory design to speed up the time it takes the system to read and write data.

### 4.7.1   Single-Processor Operation

In single-processor systems, the L2 cache size is not as critical as in multi-processor systems. 256KB is usually sufficient for L2 cache in single-processor systems. A memory access from the processor only competes for the system bus with a bus master PCI card. Doubling the cache size from 256KB to 512KB results in a performance gain of 3% to 5%. Larger cache sizes have better hit rates, but the relative incremental gain in single-processor systems is offset by the cost. Figure 4–17 illustrates this concept.

### 4.7.2   Multiprocessor Operation

In multiprocessor systems, up to four processors per processor bus must compete for memory and I/O access rights. The system bus therefore becomes a severe bottleneck, and the increase in traffic results in a decrease in performance. Additional processors will not improve performance proportionally.

With four processors on a single bus, it is very likely that a processor requiring data from main memory will have to wait before getting access to the system bus. If the processor has a large cache, however, it has quick and easy access to much of the data it will need. Performance will therefore increase substantially.

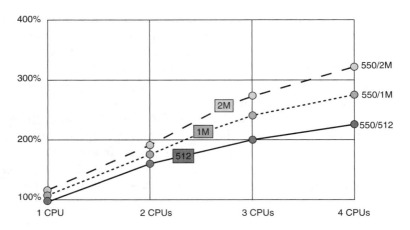

**Figure 4–17** *Performance gains with different levels of cache.*

## 4.7.3  Cache Architectures

The speed at which cache can fill a request from the processor partially depends on where the data from main memory is stored in the cache. The two main cache architectures are look-aside cache and look-through cache.

### 4.7.3.1  LOOK-ASIDE CACHE

Early processors that did not use cache sent memory read and write requests to the system bus. Although the requests were intended only for memory, every device connected to the bus received the request and had to filter out whether the request belonged to it. Because only one device could use the system bus at one time, the memory requests slowed system performance.

When cache was implemented, the processor still sent the request to the system bus where both cache and memory received the request. If a cache hit occurred, the cache controller would terminate the request to the other devices on the system bus. If there was a cache miss, the request continued as normal. This type of architecture is known as *look-aside cache*, as illustrated in Figure 4–18.

The advantage of look-aside cache is that if there is a cache miss, memory has already been notified and can complete the request quickly. If there is a cache hit, however, memory has wasted time precharging the rows and columns, and the other devices on the system bus had to wait to use the bus.

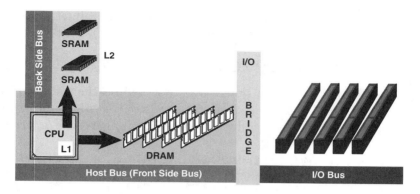

**Figure 4–18** *Look-aside cache architecture.*

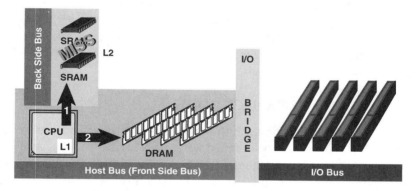

**Figure 4–19** *Look-through cache architecture.*

### 4.7.3.2 LOOK-THROUGH CACHE

Look-through cache reduces the number of requests that the system bus receives. When a processor sends a read request in this type of system, the request goes to cache first. If there is a cache hit, no request is passed on to the system bus, thereby keeping the bus free for other devices to use. If there is a cache miss, the cache controller transfers the request to the system bus. Figure 4–19 illustrates this concept.

The advantage of look-through cache is the overall reduction in the number of memory requests on the system bus. The disadvantage of look-through cache is that main memory does not begin looking for data until after the cache has determined there is a cache miss. This delay is commonly called the *lookup penalty.*

Look-through cache has been used in all Intel processors introduced after the Pentium processor.

## 4.7.4   Writing to Cache

The method that a system uses to write to cache and to memory can affect the speed of the system. The method used to write information to the cache depends on whether the cache is write-through cache or write-back cache.

### 4.7.4.1   WRITE-THROUGH CACHE

When the processor writes a piece of data, it updates the L1 cache, which updates the L2 cache, which updates the L3 cache (if there is one), which updates main memory. This update process can take many clock cycles to complete. If the processor needs the data again soon, it has to wait until the data has been updated in main memory.

This type of cache architecture is known as *write-through cache* because the system must write the data through all the memory levels before it can be used again.

### 4.7.4.2   WRITE-BACK CACHE

To minimize the time the processor has to wait to retrieve data it has just written, engineers designed write-back cache.

In write-back cache, the processor updates the L1 cache, but main memory is not updated immediately. Instead, a special status bit attached to the cache line, sometimes called the *dirty bit*, is flagged to indicate that the data has not been written to memory yet. This keeps the memory bus clear for other requests.

If the processor requests the data again, the cache controller checks the status bit to see whether the data in the cache line is the same as the data in memory. If not, data is written to memory before it is returned to the processor.

If the processor wants to write a piece of data, the cache controller looks at the status bit to see whether the data in the least recently used cache line has been written to memory yet. If not, the cache controller initiates the write to main memory before overwriting the cache line with the write request of the processor.

## 4.7.5   Bus Snooping and Bus Snarfing

A single processor is not the only device in a server that might try to read or write to memory. In multiprocessing systems, other processors might try to

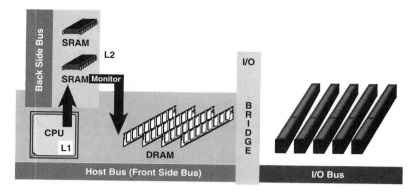

**Figure 4–20** *Bus snooping.*

access memory. Many newer servers contain devices known as *bus masters*. Bus masters can access memory without going through the processor.

In write-back systems, one of these devices could request data from memory, but the memory might be stale. Cache might contain dirty data that has not been written to memory yet. In this case, the device making the memory request could get bad data.

To prevent this from happening, cache controllers are designed to "listen in" to the system bus traffic for any memory requests made by bus masters. This is called *bus snooping*, and is illustrated in Figure 4–20.

When the bus master is trying to read from memory, the cache controller checks to see whether newer data is in cache. If it is, the cache controller puts the request of the bus master on hold until it updates memory with the most current data.

When the bus master is trying to write to memory, the cache controller captures the data being written and writes it to cache. This method of capturing data is known as *bus snarfing*.

## 4.7.6   Reading from Cache

The speed at which cache can fill a request from the processor partially depends on where data from main memory is stored in the cache.

### 4.7.6.1   FULLY ASSOCIATED CACHE

The cache might be designed so that data from main memory can be stored in any cache line. This is known as *fully associated cache.*

In fully associated cache, moving data from memory to cache is quick. The data replaces the cache line with the oldest data. Finding this data later, however, can take a long time. In a 512KB cache, the cache controller might have to look through all 16,384 cache lines before it finds the data that it needs.

### 4.7.6.2 DIRECT MAPPED CACHE

Another cache architecture, known as *direct mapped cache*, assigns a group of addresses to each cache line. This makes it quicker for the cache controller to determine whether a piece of data is in the cache.

The controller has to look at only one address in the tag RAM—the one to which the requested address is assigned. If the requested address matches the one in the tag RAM, it is a cache hit. If not, the cache controller does not have to look at any other tag RAM addresses and it can move on to the next step.

Direct mapped cache can cause cache thrashing. Cache thrashing describes a situation with multiple cache misses, frequent memory accesses, and frequent cache updates.

---

**EXAMPLE**

The processor requests a piece of data from one address (D1). Main memory sends D1 to the processor and to cache. D1 is assigned to cache line 1 (CL1).

The processor immediately requests a different piece of data (D2). D2 also happens to be assigned to CL1. The cache controller looks for D2 in CL1, but gets a cache miss because the chunk containing D1 resides in CL1.

The cache controller sends the request to the next levels of memory until there is a cache hit. At this point, D2 replaces D1 in CL1.

---

The processor is running a loop and asks for D1 again. Again there is a cache miss because D2 is now occupying CL1. This process could continue until the loop is finally finished. During that time, the cache hit rate would be 0%.

### 4.7.6.3 SET-ASSOCIATIVE CACHE

Most cache architecture today is a compromise between direct mapped and fully associative cache. It is called *set-associative cache*.

Set-associative cache assigns a group of memory addresses to a specific group of cache lines known as a *set*. Depending on the cache, each set can have two, four, or eight lines. In two-way set-associative cache, data from a group of memory addresses can fill either of two cache lines. Using the previous example, D1 could fill CL1, and D2 could fill CL2.

Compared to direct mapped cache, it might take the cache controller slightly longer to find the data because it has to check two addresses in the tag RAM. However, the increased number of cache hits makes up for this. In general, the more cache lines in each set, the more likely a cache hit will occur. However, the more cache lines in each set, the more cache lines the cache controller has to check for a match.

## ▲ Summary

This chapter focused on memory and cache, first explaining the differences between memory (dynamic RAM) and cache (static RAM).

The next topic was how memory works. This chapter covered DIMMs and SIMMs and how memory is used to store and retrieve data.

Several innovations have come about that have improved memory performance over the years. These innovations include FPM, EDO, SDRAM, DDR RAM, and interleaved memory.

As memory technologies have evolved, several factors have combined to increase the possibility of memory failures. The next topic focused on the various means by which memory can be made more tolerant to faults, including parity checking, ECC, and AECC. HP and Compaq have pioneered the development of more advanced memory technologies, including online spare memory, single-board mirrored memory, hot-plug mirrored memory, and hot-plug RAID memory. These advanced technologies are explained later in this book.

Finally, this chapter discussed how cache is used to enhance system performance and the various cache architectures and technologies.

## ▲ LEARNING CHECK

Answer the first four questions with DRAM, SRAM, or both.

1. *Which technology uses capacitors to store data?*

2. *Which technology is faster?*

3. *Which technology is used in cache?*

4. *Which technology stores data in a grid?*

5. *What innovation did DDR RAM introduce?*

    A. Transfers data on both the rising and falling edge of each clock cycle

    B. Distributes data across DIMMs in two banks

    C. Adds a parity bit to each byte when it writes it to memory

    D. Corrects single-bit errors

6. *Which memory technology doubles the amount of data obtained in a single memory access from 64 bits to 128 bits?*

    A. DDR RAM

    B. Online spare memory

    C. Hot-plug RAID memory

    D. Interleaved memory

7. *Match the fault-tolerant technology with its description:*

| | |
|---|---|
| Parity | This technology uses a checksum to analyze an error, determine which byte is corrupt, and correct it. |
| ECC | Four memory controllers each write one block of data to one of four DIMMs. A fifth memory controller stores parity information on a fifth DIMM. |
| Advanced ECC | A memory bank with a faulty DIMM automatically fails over to a spare bank of DIMMs. |
| Online spare memory | The memory controller writes the same data to identically configured banks of DIMMs on two memory boards. |
| Hot-plug mirrored memory | The memory controller adds a bit to each byte when it writes the byte to memory based on the number of 1s in the byte. |
| Hot-plug RAID memory | This technology corrects multibit errors that occur on a single DRAM chip. |

8. *What is the benefit of cache in a server?*
   A. Fills data requests from the processor more quickly than memory
   B. Doubles the amount of data that can be stored on the hard drive
   C. Decodes instructions to make the processor work faster
   D. Increases the clock speed of the memory bus

9. *Which cache stores the first data checked by the processor?*

10. *Which bus connects the L2 cache to the processor?*
    A. Frontside bus
    B. Backside bus
    C. System bus
    D. PCI bus

11. *What is the function of the tag RAM?*

12. *Match the cache implementation to its definition:*

| | |
|---|---|
| Look-aside | A cache controller listens in to system bus traffic for any memory requests made by bus masters. |
| Look-through | When a bus master is trying to write to memory, the cache controller captures the data being written and writes it to cache. |
| Fully associated | A bit attached to the cache line is flagged to indicate that the data has not yet been written to memory. |
| Direct mapped | Data from main memory can be stored in any cache line. |
| Set-associative | The system must write the data through all the memory levels before it can be used again. |
| Write-through | Both cache and memory receive memory requests. If there is a cache hit, the cache controller terminates the request to the other devices. |
| Write-back | A group of memory addresses is assigned to each cache line. |
| Bus snooping | If there is a cache hit, no request makes it to the system bus. |
| Bus snarfing | A group of memory addresses is assigned to a specific group of cache lines. |

# Bus Architecture

After studying this chapter, you should be able to do the following:

- Describe the characteristics of and differences between dynamic RAM (memory) and static RAM (cache).

- Explain how data is written to, stored in, and read from memory.

- List the technologies that can be used to improve memory performance.

- Describe memory failures and the fault-tolerant technologies used to protect memory, including the following:

  - Parity
  - Error checking and correcting (ECC)
  - Advanced ECC

- Explain the function of cache memory.

- Discuss methods that can be used to improve cache performance.

The internal computing components of a server are connected by a collection of pathways, known as *buses*, that differ in width and speed. This chapter explains the types of buses, how they function, and the different bus technologies commonly found in today's industry-standard servers.

## 5.1   Bus Architecture Overview

As shown in Figure 5–1, internal system buses provide parallel data transfer paths between these key server components:

- Chipset controllers
- Processor
- Cache
- Main memory
- Peripheral buses

Buses are responsible for moving addresses and data between server components. Control signals indicate what the components are to do with the addresses and data they receive.

**Figure 5–1**

*Typical buses in a server.*

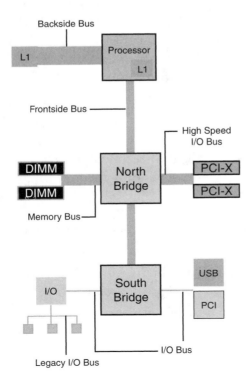

The number of electrical lines in the bus determines the bus width. Just as the width of a highway limits how much traffic can pass through, the width of the bus limits how much data can transfer at a time.

Bus width is measured in bits. A 16-bit bus transfers 16 bits, or 2 bytes, at a time over 16 wires; a 32-bit bus uses 32 wires to transfer 4 bytes simultaneously, and so on. This bus width limits maximum data transfer between components.

The bus does not initiate the data transfer. The processor and chipset controllers initiate the data requests and accomplish the transfer across the bus.

In some cases, addresses and data travel on separate physical buses: an address bus and a data bus. In other cases, they use the same bus.

When a system uses the same lines for both addressing and data, it is called *multiplexing*. Multiplexing gives a set of bus lines and bus connections more than one function. A system controller might first assert the bus with a control signal to transfer addresses across 32 lines of a bus, and then reassert a new control signal to use the same 32 bus lines to transfer data.

## 5.1.1   Address Bus

The address bus has a dual role. First, it is used to transport the source and destination addresses of data to be transmitted on the data bus. To access the data within a device or memory, its address must be placed on the address bus by an initiator, such as the processor, controller, or bus master.

Second, it identifies memory locations generated by the processor, bus masters, or direct memory access (DMA) controller. For a device to move any data, the address bus has to identify the desired target location within a target device where data might reside.

The range of addresses within memory that a single processor can access is known as the *address space*. The number of lines, or bits, available to the address bus determines the address space. The size of the address space is calculated by raising the number 2, which is binary with each line or bit being a 0 or 1, to the exponent $n$: $2n$. The exponent $n$ is the number of lines in the address bus, which is the same as the size in bits of the address bus.

---

**EXAMPLE**

An Intel Pentium processor has 32 address lines, which provides 232 addresses or 4GB of address space.

The widths of the address bus and maximum addressable memory for the Intel processor family are listed in the following table.

| Processor | Address Lines (Bits) | Theoretical Maximum Addressable Memory |
|---|---|---|
| 8086 | 20 | 1MB |
| 80286 | 24 | 16MB |
| 80386 and 80486 | 32 | 4GB |
| Pentium | 32 | 4GB |
| Pentium Pro | 36 | 64GB |
| Pentium II, III, and 4 | 36 | 64GB |
| Pentium II Xeon and III Xeon | 36 | 64GB |
| Xeon | 36 | 64GB |
| Itanium | 64 | $2^{64}$ GB |

**Note**    The ability of the processor to access the maximum address space can be restricted by the chipsets and the operating system.

## 5.1.2  Data Bus

The data bus is the internal pathway that carries data to and from the processor or to and from memory. Data moves between any two devices over the data bus. The data can be instructions for the processor or information the processor is transmitting. This information can pass to or from the memory or I/O subsystem.

The width and speed of the data bus directly affect performance and significantly influence system throughput. The bus width is the number of lines or wires that make up the bus. Each line or wire of a data bus can carry 1 bit of information.

The width of the bus is equal to the number of data pins on the processor or other device. Data buses are designed in multiples of eight lines because each line carries 1 bit of data and 8 bits make up a byte. Therefore, the data bus width indicates how many bytes the bus can carry during each transfer. A 32-bit bus can transmit 4 bytes at one time; a 64-bit bus can transfer 8 bytes per cycle.

The following table shows the width of the data bus for various Intel processors.

| Processor | Data Bus Width |
|---|---|
| 8086 and 80286 | 16 bits |
| 80386 and 80486 | 32 bits |
| Pentium and Pentium Pro | 64 bits |
| Pentium II, III, and 4 | 64 bits |
| Pentium II Xeon and III Xeon | 64 bits |
| Itanium | 64 bits |

### 5.1.3   Control Signals

Control signals usually travel on the address bus. The signals determine the actions of the addressed components. (Control signals are sometimes referred to as the control bus even though they are not a separate physical bus.)

Control signals have three primary functions:

- **Device arbitration**—The control signal identifies which device has control of the bus and prevents collisions.

- **Data-flow direction**—The control signal identifies the direction of the bus cycle, read or write, and indicates when the cycle is complete.

- **Memory addressing type**—The control signal identifies whether the operation being performed is for memory or I/O.

Some control signal notations generated by the processor or other device include the following:

- **W/R**—Write/read
- **IRQ**—Interrupt requests
- **BCLK**—Bus clock
- **DRQ**—DMA requests

Many of these signals are point to point. Point-to-point signaling is intended for only one device on a dedicated line.

## 5.2   Bus Performance

Communication between the major subsystems occurs by reading and writing data across the buses in the system. Buses are designed with distinct standards applied throughout the system to move the data between subsystems effectively and to avoid or minimize bottlenecks.

Devices that require more than two clock cycles to respond to processor requests slow down the system during the time the processor is accessing those devices.

### 5.2.1   Bus Speed

Bus speed is the number of bus cycles that occur per second. It is measured in *hertz* (Hz). Bus speed is also called *frequency*.

Just as the bus width differs between buses, the bus speed can also be different between buses within the same system. Each subsystem in a server has its own operating frequency and communicates based on timing rules.

To communicate and transfer data between each component, the timing among components must be synchronized to a system heartbeat. The buses must also adhere to this timing rule and must be able to synchronize to the bus clock. The bus clock is controlled by the chipset and is a submultiple of the system clock frequency.

### 5.2.2   Bus Cycles

A bus cycle is the transfer process a component such as a processor, chipset, or bus master device uses to communicate or move data across a bus.

The bus activity required to transfer information includes first, a sequence of control signals and addresses on the address bus, and second, a movement of data on the data bus.

The basic types of bus cycles include memory reads, memory writes, I/O reads, and I/O writes.

All data transfers occur as a result of one or more bus cycles. A bus cycle is performed each time the processor or bus master needs code or data from memory or an I/O device.

In a standard bus cycle, the processor sends an address to memory on one clock tick and the memory returns the data from that address on a second clock tick. Each bus cycle takes a total of two clock ticks.

Memory can take longer than one clock tick to get the data on the data bus. When this happens, the processor must wait for the data. This is known as a *wait state*.

### 5.2.3   Maximum Transfer Rate

The amount of data that can flow across a bus during a period of time is called the *maximum transfer rate*. Maximum transfer rate is one way of measuring the performance of a server.

**Figure 5–2**

*Maximum transfer rate calculations.*

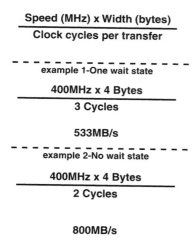

**Figure 5–3**

*Ways to increase performance.*

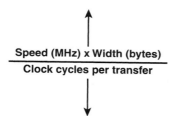

The transfer rate is given in bytes transferred per second. It is determined by this formula: Maximum transfer rate = [speed (MHz) × width (bytes)]/number of clock cycles per transfer.

Figure 5–2 shows the maximum transfer rates for a 400MHz bus, with a width of 4 bytes (32 bits) given a single wait state and a zero wait state.

As indicated by the master transfer rate formula, you can increase performance by either increasing the numerator (speed x width) or decreasing the denominator (clock cycles per transfer), as shown in Figure 5–3.

### 5.2.3.1 INCREASING THE NUMERATOR

You can increase the numerator in the maximum transfer rate formula by any of the following methods:

- Increase the speed at which bus cycles take place. This usually means increasing the clock speed of the processor.

- Increase the speed at which devices, especially system memory, can communicate with the processor. This involves implementing high-speed memory or adding a cache.

- Increase the width of the data bus to increase the amount of information passed in a single bus cycle.
- Implement modified bus cycles, such as a burst cycle.
- Add concurrent processes, such as dual independent buses or multiprocessing.

### 5.2.3.2 INCREASING DEVICE SPEED

As mentioned previously, one way to increase performance is to increase the speed of the devices in the system. These types of changes are common. As new processors are introduced, for example, they often feature support for higher bus speeds. It is important to remember that both the processor and the bus must be able to support the higher rate. Putting a faster processor on a slow bus will not increase performance.

Another way to increase performance is to widen the bus. A wider bus means there are more electrical traces on which data can travel.

### 5.2.3.3 IMPLEMENTING BURST CYCLES

Beginning with the 80486 processor family, all Intel processors support burst cycles for any data request that requires more than one data cycle.

**Address time is not usually included in this transfer rate.**

In a standard zero wait-state bus cycle, the address is sent on one bus cycle and data sent on the next. That means data is transferred on every other clock tick, as shown in Figure 5–4.

In a zero wait-state burst cycle, the first address is sent and a series of four data transfers occur one after another, as illustrated in Figure 5–5. A second address is sent at the same time that the fourth data transfer occurs. On the very next cycle, the data at the second address is transferred back followed by an additional three transfers. As a result, after the first address is sent, data is transferred on every clock cycle.

**Figure 5–4**

*Zero wait state.*

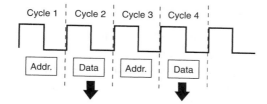

**Figure 5–5**

*Burst transfer.*

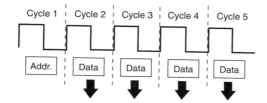

**Figure 5–6**

*Calculating the burst transfer rate.*

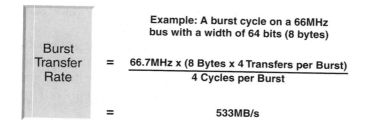

At a minimum, a burst transfer requires two clock cycles for the first data transfer (A1 + D1) and can be followed by up to three subsequent data transfers (D2 + D3 + D4). Throughput during a burst cycle might vary depending on many factors.

**5.2.3.3.1   BURST TRANSFER RATE** • Calculate the burst transfer rate by taking the total amount transferred in the total burst and dividing it by the total data time, as shown in Figure 5–6.

The address time is not included in the transfer rate calculated by this formula.

### 5.2.3.4   IMPLEMENT BUS MASTERING

A bus master is a device connected to the bus that communicates directly with other devices on the bus without going through the processor.

Bus mastering is the protocol used when the processor gives control of the bus to an I/O device. Bus mastering allows the I/O device to transfer data directly to memory. The processor does not have to act as a mediator on the bus, which frees the processor to perform other tasks and increases the speed of the data transfers.

The components that can serve as the bus master are the processor, the DMA controller, the memory refresh logic, and the EISA/PCI bus master card.

### 5.2.3.5   IMPLEMENT BUS ARBITRATION

If multiple bus master devices request a bus simultaneously, a bus controller acts as the arbitrator. Bus controllers determine which component gets control of the bus at any given time.

Each bus has its own bus controller. For system buses, such as the memory bus and local I/O buses, the controllers are located in the chipset. For expansion devices, the controller can be located in another *application-specific integrated circuit* (ASIC) on the system board or located on an expansion card.

## 5.3   PCI-Based Buses

PCI is a standard type of I/O bus commonly found in many computers, including HP ProLiant servers. The PCI protocol has gone through several iterations and more are planned.

Figure 5–7 shows a diagram representing a standard PCI bus system.

The PCI bus specification was introduced in 1992 as an industry-standard independent bus. The first PCI specification defined a 32-bit bus running at 33MHz. In 1994, the 2.1 specification defined a 66MHz and 64-bit PCI.

The following table shows the evolution of the PCI protocol through the years.

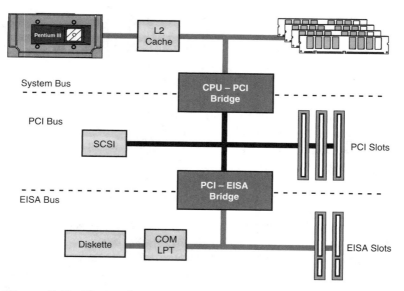

**Figure 5–7**  *The PCI bus.*

| Width | Speed | Throughput | Specification |
|---|---|---|---|
| 32-bit card | 33MHz | 133MB/s | 1.0 |
| 32-bit card | 66MHz | 267MB/s | 2.1 |
| 64-bit card | 33MHz | 267MB/s | 2.01 |
| 64-bit card | 66MHz | 533MB/s | 2.2 |
| 64-bit card | 100MHz | 800MB/s | PCI-X |
| 64-bit card | 133MHz | 1066MB/s | PCI-X |

## 5.3.1   Features of the PCI Bus

The main features of the PCI bus include the following:

- Full independence
- Plug-and-play architecture
- IRQ sharing
- Multiplexing
- Device loads
- PCI bus burst transfers
- 32- and 64-bit, 33 and 66MHz cards

### 5.3.1.1 FULLY INDEPENDENT BUS

PCI is fully independent of the processor local bus. As a result, PCI can be found in a variety of platforms, including Intel-based systems, Alpha-based systems, and Apple computers.

The host-to-PCI bridge is a fundamental part of the PCI design. It connects the PCI bus to the frontside bus of the processor. The bridge supports data buffering. This enables activity to take place on the PCI bus at the same time as processor-to-memory bus activity. The bridge makes the activity independent from processor signals and ISA and EISA I/O bus signals.

### 5.3.1.2 PLUG-AND-PLAY ARCHITECTURE

Plug and play is autoconfigured by the system BIOS or the System Configuration utility in legacy ProLiant servers. System resources are assigned automatically. PCI expansion cards do not need a configuration file because the card tells the computer which resources it requires. As a result, there is a greatly reduced chance of resource allocation conflicts.

### 5.3.1.3 IRQ SHARING

PCI allows shared IRQ lines. PCI uses INT lines rather than IRQ lines, which are then routed to IRQ lines or directly routed through the *advanced programmable interrupt controller* (APIC) bus of the processor (full table mode). IRQ sharing is mandatory only for cards complying with specifications for the PCI 2.1 or later.

### 5.3.1.4 MULTIPLEXING

The PCI standard reduces cost by using a multiplexed address/data bus that reduces the pin count and the size of the PCI slots.

### 5.3.1.5 DEVICE LOADS

The PCI protocol supports up to 256 devices per bus and 256 buses per system. The actual number of peripheral devices the bus can handle is based on loads, which relate to inductance, capacitance, and other electrical characteristics. Electrical loading reduces the number of slots per bus to 10. The PCI chipset requires three slots, leaving seven for peripherals. Controllers built on the system board use one load, and controllers that plug into an expansion slot use 1.5 loads. Using PCI/PCI-bridges allows for multiple PCI buses and thus for dozens of slots.

### 5.3.1.6   PCI BUS BURST TRANSFERS

The PCI bus executes all data transfers as burst transfers. Bursts can be either to memory or to the I/O space.

A 32-bit PCI bus running at 33MHz has a peak transfer rate of 133MB/s (33.3 million transfers × 4 bytes). Each PCI device has a latency timer that defines the maximum period of time that a device is allowed to use the bus when another PCI device wants to use the bus.

### 5.3.1.7   32- AND 64-BIT, 33 AND 66MHZ

PCI can be built either as a 32-bit bus or a 64-bit bus, running at 33 or 66MHz.

**5.3.1.7.1   32-BIT PCI AT 33MHZ** • PCI 33MHz/32-bit systems can move up to 90MB/s of data on the standard PCI bus. The rest is spent on overhead and latency resulting from poor bus utilization.

**5.3.1.7.2   64-BIT PCI AT 66MHZ** • A 64-bit PCI bus running at 66MHz achieves a peak transfer rate of 533MB/s. A 64-bit PCI bus has better bus utilization and double the bandwidth of a 32-bit PCI bus. The 64-bit address space is enormous (4 billion × 4GB). 32-bit PCI cards can support 64-bit addresses by using two consecutive 32-bit PCI cycles known as *dual address cycle.*

**5.3.1.7.3   32- AND 64-BIT, 33 AND 66MHZ CARD RULES** • The rules that govern the usage of PCI cards are as follows:

1. 66MHz PCI cards can be used on a 33MHz PCI bus.
2. A 33MHz card in a 66MHz PCI bus automatically operates at 33MHz.
3. 32-bit PCI cards can be installed in a 64-bit PCI slot.
4. 64-bit cards can be installed in a 32-bit slot and will work in 32-bit mode.

## 5.3.2   *PCI Bus Performance Planning*

A PCI bus can be so heavily used that it becomes a performance bottleneck. HP recommends that you plan for optimal performance when configuring the PCI devices.

Before beginning the configuration, consider the following:

- The PCI buses and slots available in the server
- The PCI protocols supported by the devices to be configured
- The expected amount of data sent to and from each of the devices (throughput)

Throughput does not include PCI bus interrupts or PCI protocol over-head but will yield reasonable bus planning results.

The following rules provide optimal configuration.

### 5.3.2.1 RULE 1. MATCH 66MHZ SLOTS WITH 66MHZ DEVICES

If you have 66MHz slots but no 66MHz devices, treat the 66MHz slots like 64-bit slots.

If you have 66MHz devices but no 66MHz slots, treat the devices like 64-bit devices.

If you have 66MHz slots and devices, place the 66MHz devices with the highest throughput in the 66MHz slots. Any remaining devices will be treated like 64-bit devices.

### 5.3.2.2 RULE 2. MATCH 32-BIT SLOTS WITH 32-BIT DEVICES

If you have 32-bit slots and devices, place the 32-bit devices with the highest throughput in the 32-bit slots. Any remaining devices will be placed in 64-bit slots. Be aware that some 32-bit slots are on 64-bit buses and should be treated appropriately.

If you have 32-bit devices but no 32-bit slots, the 32-bit devices must be placed in 64-bit slots.

### 5.3.2.3 RULES FOR REMAINING DEVICES

If you have available 32-bit slots, place the minimum number of 64-bit devices in the 32-bit slots, using the devices with the lowest throughput.

If you still have more devices than available 64-bit slots, the 66MHz slots will have to run at 33MHz (64-bit).

Distribute the remaining devices among the available 64-bit slots. You must double the throughput of the 32-bit devices because they use only half of the data transfer bits. Use these guidelines:

1. Place the unassigned device with the highest throughput on the bus with the fewest slots.
2. Of the remaining unassigned devices, place the device with the highest throughput on the next bus with the fewest slots. Again, double the throughput of 32-bit devices.
3. Continue assigning the device with the highest throughput on the next available bus, using all the buses in round-robin fashion. Do not be concerned if you run out of slots on a bus before all devices have been assigned.

### 5.3.3  PCI Bus Frequency Arbitration

PCI bus frequency is arbitrated during server initialization and cannot change without a server reboot. The arbitrated bus frequency is either the slowest PCI device or the maximum PCI bus speed, whichever is slower. All 32-bit and 64-bit devices can operate on the same 64-bit PCI bus without limitations; 32-bit devices use 32 bits of the data bus, but 64-bit devices use all 64-bits of the data bus. A hot-plugged PCI device must support the arbitrated PCI protocol—a nonsupported device will not initialize.

### 5.3.4  PCI Bus Number Assignments

Each PCI bus is assigned a bus number and each slot on the bus is also assigned a number. Requests to a device are addressed to the bus and slot number.

Some PCI cards contain a PCI controller on the card itself. When a card like this was installed in a PCI slot in older ProLiant servers, it caused bus numbers to change, preventing requests from reaching the right PCI device.

Newer ProLiant servers have preassigned PCI bus numbers for every slot. This preassignment ensures that the PCI bus numbers do not change when a card with a PCI bridge is installed.

### 5.3.5  PCI Hot Plug Support

PCI Hot Plug enables you to replace and install new PCI cards without powering down the system. PCI Hot Plug was developed by Compaq and has been accepted as an open industry standard.

The benefits of PCI Hot Plug include the following:

- **Uninterrupted service**—You can add or replace a network or other I/O controller board with the system up and operating. This can be accomplished through hot insertion or hot removal.

- **Broad, current compatibility**—PCI Hot Plug technology addresses compatibility concerns by using standard PCI adapters. A hot-plug system requires a hot-plug platform, a hot-plug operating system, and hot-plug adapter drivers. A system can include any combination of hot-plug and conventional versions of each of these components, including a mix of both hot-plug and conventional adapter drivers. However, a particular adapter can be hot plugged only if all three components for that adapter support hot-plug operation.

■ **Hot Plug Reservation**—Three PCI Hot Plug Reservation configurations are available, but they require that PCI Hot Plug Reservation be enabled:

- **Hot replacement**—Replacing an existing PCI adapter
- **Hot removal**—Removing an existing PCI adapter
- **Hot upgrade**—Adding a new PCI adapter

The hot-plug electronics designed by HP consist of two separate elements: the hot-plug controller and the slot-specific power control. The hot-plug controller manages the following components.

### 5.3.5.1 PCI BUS

The controller communicates with isolation devices on the PCI bus to electrically isolate a single PCI slot from the rest of the system. Slot isolation permits insertion or removal of an adapter without interruption to the server or other active adapters.

### 5.3.5.2 POWER

The controller receives a command from the operating system to power up or power down a single PCI slot. To perform this function, the controller uses the slot-specific power control. The slot-specific power-control electronics allow the proper power sequencing on the PCI bus and guarantee safe control of the power to the individual PCI adapters.

### 5.3.5.3 SLOT LED INDICATORS

The hot-plug controller also governs the slot LEDs. In the HP implementation of hot-plug hardware, each slot has a green and an amber LED to indicate slot status. The green LED indicates power to the slot and flashes while performing a power state change; the amber LED indicates that the slot requires attention.

### 5.3.5.4 PCI HOT PLUG BUTTON

This button is pressed to signal the software to initiate a power state change. Although the button is more convenient, the same functionality is provided through the software interface. Each slot has its own button to indicate which slot is to be addressed by the supporting software.

### 5.3.6  Adding a Hot-Plug Device to an Empty Slot

To add an adapter to an empty slot, follow these steps when the system is running:

1. Prepare the slot for installation of the adapter by opening the appropriate slot release lever and removing the expansion slot cover.
2. Install the adapter into the appropriate expansion slot.
3. Close the slot release lever.
4. Use the PCI Hot Plug button or the software user interface to notify the operating system that power can be applied to the slot. The green LED flashes when the operating system performs the power state change.

The operating system enables power to the slot and either automatically locates and loads the appropriate device driver or prompts the administrator to locate and load the driver.

## 5.4  PCI-X

PCI-X is a compatible extension of the existing PCI bus, jointly developed by Compaq, HP, and IBM. It is fully backward compatible with the PCI 2.1 protocol. PCI-X enables the design of systems that can operate at frequencies up to 133MHz using a 64-bit bus width, providing burst transfer rates higher than 1GB/s.

Figure 5–8 shows an illustration of the PCI-X architecture.

The PCI-X specification is an open industry standard available from the PCI Special Interest Group as an addendum to the PCI Local Bus 2.2 specification.

PCI-X enhancements to the PCI bus include the following:

- **Backward compatibility**—Because PCI-X is backward compatible with PCI, existing PCI cards work in a PCI-X environment. In fact, you can use both PCI-X and PCI cards on the same bus. However, the PCI-X bus defaults to the speed of the slowest card on the bus.

- **Forward compatibility**— PCI-X cards can be designed as universal cards, which means they can plug into either 3.3V I/O slots (66MHz and faster) or 5V I/O slots (33MHz). However, the added functionality and speed of a PCI-X card is not fully realized if it is used on an existing PCI bus.

- **Speed**—PCI-X is a 64-bit bus that runs at speeds up to 133MHz. Several other design improvements increase bus efficiency, leading to even more I/O throughput. Compared to the performance of a typical 32-bit/ 33MHz PCI implementation, PCI-X delivers up to a 10x improvement in performance.

- **Number of slots**—Because of stringent electrical requirements, PCI systems at 66MHz can support only one or two slots. PCI-X solves this limitation because it can support four or more slots at 66MHz.

The 64-bit PCI-X architecture runs at speeds up to 133MHz, providing burst transfer rates greater than 1GB/s. This critical I/O bandwidth is needed for industry-standard servers running enterprise applications such as Gigabit Ethernet, Fibre Channel, Ultra3 SCSI, and cluster interconnects.

In addition to performance improvements, PCI-X also increases the fault isolation of the PCI bus by helping the operating system work more effectively with adapters to better manage error conditions.

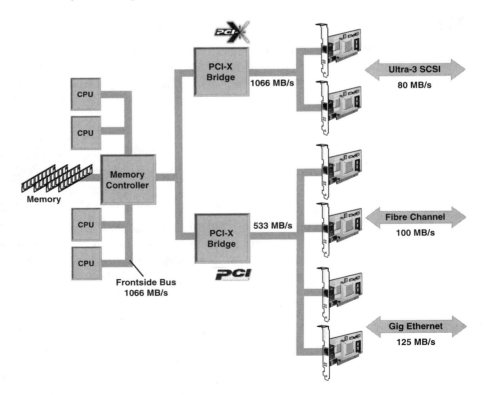

**Figure 5–8** *PCI-X architecture.*

PCI-X offers both added performance and flexibility, minimizing the trade-off between PCI slots and bus speed.

> **EXAMPLE**
>
> Based on preliminary simulation testing, a 66MHz four-slot implementation of PCI-X shows more than a 25% increase in I/O performance over a conventional PCI bus running at its maximum configuration (64 bits/ 66MHz). It is also possible to use multiple PCI-X buses at different speeds, providing a combination of ultra-high performance and maximum slot capacity.

As an open specification, PCI has been the foundation of continuous innovation throughout the industry. But the evolution of computing is driving I/O bandwidth requirements beyond the capacity of PCI 2.2, PCI-X, or any multidrop parallel bus architecture.

## 5.4.1  PCI-X Performance

Based on preliminary simulation testing, a 66MHz PCI-X implementation shows an increase of more than 30% in I/O performance over a conventional PCI bus running at its maximum configuration of 64 bits, 66MHz. This performance improvement is shown in Figure 5–9.

Using a 4KB block size typical of Gigabit Ethernet or Ultra3 SCSI controllers, the PCI-X protocol improved performance by up to 34% over the conventional PCI protocol. This improvement assumes an ideal memory controller with a 32-byte processor cache line and ideal 64-bit PCI adapters.

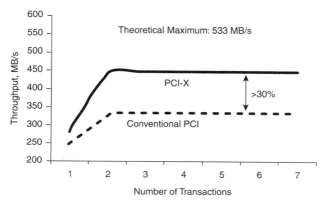

**Figure 5–9**  *PCI-X performance compared to conventional PCI.*

PCI-X achieves higher performance as a result of two primary differences between conventional PCI and PCI-X. First, PXI-X features higher clock frequencies made possible by a register-to-register protocol rather than an immediate protocol. Second, PCI-X includes new protocol enhancements such as attribute phase, split transactions, optimized wait states, and standard block-size movements

> **More information about PCI-X performance is available at the PCI Special Interest Group Web site at http://www.pcisig.com.**

### 5.4.2 PCI-X Hierarchical Structure

It is possible to use multiple PCI-X buses operating at different speeds to increase performance and gain more slots. Figure 5–10 illustrates how this can be accomplished.

A PCI-X bus running at 133MHz can support multiple slots at different speeds through PCI-X to PCI-X bridges as shown in this diagram.

PCI-X supports up to 256 bus segments. Each segment is initialized separately so that different operating frequencies can be used.

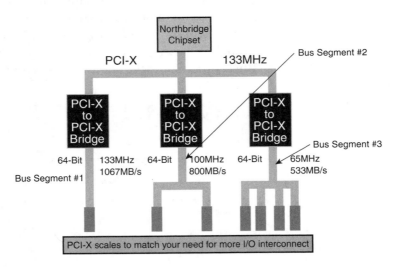

**Figure 5–10** *PCI-X bridges allow PCI to link up to 256 bus segments.*

### 5.4.3 PCI-X System Flexibility

In addition to increased performance, PCI-X offers flexibility of system design. For solutions that require maximum connectivity, PCI-X can support four expansion slots operating at 66MHz. For maximum speed, PCI-X can support a single slot at 133MHz.

The following table shows performance and slot comparison between PCI and PCI-X.

| Bus Width | Bus Frequency | Bus Bandwidth | PCI Slots | PCI-X Slots |
|---|---|---|---|---|
| 32 bits | 33MHz | 133MB/s | | N/A |
| 64 bits | 33MHz | 267MB/s | | |
| 64 bits | 66MHz | 533MB/s | or | |
| 64 bits | 100MHz | 800MB/s | N/A | |
| 64 bits | 133MHz | 1067MB/s | N/A | |

**PCI-X is fully backward compatible with conventional PCI systems. PCI-X requires no device driver or operating system modification for existing hardware. Changes to the device drivers are required only to take advantage of the new features such as transaction byte count.**

### 5.4.4 PCI Compared to PCI-X

The PCI-X register-to-register protocol provides better performance than the PCI protocol through the use of technological advances, such as the following:

- Timing enhancements
- Attribute phase
- Split transaction report
- Optimized wait states
- Standard block-size movements

### 5.4.4.1   PCI PROTOCOL

With conventional PCI, the time available to decode a transaction decreases as the bus frequency increases from 33MHz to 66MHz.

The conventional PCI bus uses an immediate protocol. With a conventional PCI device, the following steps occur when the device switches a control signal, as illustrated in Figure 5–11:

1. On the rising clock edge, the device switches the signal to a high or low state on the PCI bus.
2. The signal propagates across the bus (propagation delay).
3. During the same clock cycle, the receiving device decodes the signal to determine whether the signal is for the receiving device and whether it must respond by switching one of its outputs.
4. The receiving device responds immediately, that is, in the next clock cycle.

With a 33MHz clock frequency, the time allocated for the decode logic is 7ns of the total 30ns clock cycle time. At 33MHz, this is sufficient time for the

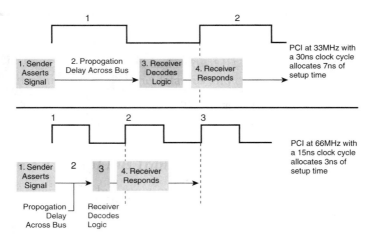

**Figure 5–11**   *How a PCI device switches a control signal.*

receiving device to respond on the next rising clock edge. However, when the bus frequency is doubled to 66MHz (with a clock cycle time of 15ns), the time available to perform this logic is reduced to 3ns.

These time constraints of the conventional PCI specification make it difficult to design a conventional PCI bus or adapter for 66MHz.

### 5.4.4.2 PCI-X REGISTER-TO-REGISTER PROTOCOL

In comparison to PCI, the PCI-X register-to-register protocol functions as shown in Figure 5–12.

With the PCI-X register-to-register protocol, the following steps occur:

1. On the rising clock edge, the device switches the signal to a high or low state on the PCI-X bus.
2. The signal propagates across the bus.
3. The signal is sent to a register, or flip-flop, that holds the signal state until the next clock cycle.
4. The receiving device has a full clock cycle to decode the signal and determine the appropriate response.
5. The receiving device responds two full clock cycles after the sending device first switched the signal.

PCI-X eases the timing constraints by allowing an entire clock cycle for the decode logic to occur. The net difference is that PCI-X transactions generally require one clock cycle more than conventional PCI transactions. A write transaction that completes in nine clock cycles for conventional PCI will complete in ten clock cycles for PCI-X.

### 5.4.4.3 TIMING DIFFERENCES

Figure 5–13 illustrates the actual time difference between the PCI and PCI-X protocols for a typical write transaction.

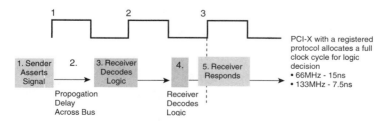

**Figure 5–12** *The PCI-X protocol allows an entire clock cycle for the decode logic to occur.*

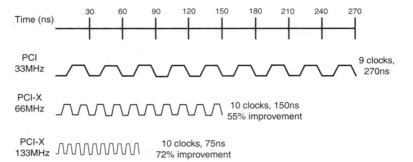

**Figure 5–13**  *Time differences between PCI and PCI-X for a write transaction.*

With the timing constraints reduced, it is much easier to design adapters and systems to operate at 66MHz and greater. System designers can benefit from the eased timing constraints by choosing maximum performance with a single PCI-X slot at 133MHz or maximum connectivity with additional slots on the PCI-X bus.

If a system designer chooses to increase the bus frequency, the actual time required to complete the transaction is greatly reduced, even though a clock cycle has been added. A transaction that takes 9 cycles at 33MHz will finish in 270ns. A PCI-X transaction that takes 10 cycles at 133MHz will finish in 75ns, which is a 72% reduction in transaction time.

If a system designer chooses to keep the frequency at 66MHz, slots can be added to the bus segment. Because more time is budgeted for a signal to propagate from one device to another, the signal can traverse a longer path across multiple slots.

### 5.4.4.4  ATTRIBUTE PHASE

The PCI-X protocol includes a new transaction phase called the *attribute phase* that uses a 36-bit attribute field that describes bus transactions in more detail than the conventional PCI specification allows. It follows immediately after the address phase and contains several bit assignments that include information about the following:

- The size of the transaction
- Ordering of transactions
- Cache snooping requirements
- Identity of the transaction initiator

The following enhancements are included within the attribute phase:

- Relaxed ordering
- Non-cache-coherent transactions
- Transaction byte count
- Sequence number

### 5.4.4.5 SPLIT TRANSACTION SUPPORT

The conventional PCI protocol supports delayed transactions. With a delayed transaction, the device requesting data must poll the target to determine when the request has been completed and its data is available.

With a split transaction as supported in PCI-X, the device requesting the data sends a signal to the target. The target device informs the requester that it has accepted the request. The requester is free to process other information until the target device initiates a new transaction and sends the data to the requester. Thus, split transactions enable more efficient use of the bus.

### 5.4.4.6 OPTIMIZED WAIT STATES

Conventional PCI devices often add extra clock cycles, or wait states, to their transactions. The wait states are added to stall the bus if the PCI device is not ready to proceed with the transaction, which can slow bus throughput dramatically.

PCI-X eliminates the use of wait states, except for initial target latency. When a PCI-X device does not have data to transfer, it removes itself from the bus so that another device can use the bus bandwidth. This removal provides more efficient use of bus and memory resources.

### 5.4.4.7 STANDARD BLOCK-SIZE MOVEMENTS

With PCI-X, adapters and bridges (host-to-PCI-X and PCI-X-to-PCI-X) are permitted to disconnect transactions only on naturally aligned 128-byte boundaries. This encourages longer bursts and enables more efficient use of cache line-based resources such as the processor bus and main memory. It also facilitates a more pipelined architecture within PCI-X devices.

## 5.4.5 Adapter Card Selection

PCI-X cards perform in current PCI systems just like conventional 66MHz cards, as illustrated in Figure 5–14.

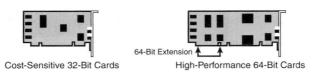

Cost-Sensitive 32-Bit Cards    64-Bit Extension    High-Performance 64-Bit Cards

**Figure 5–14** *How PCI-X cards can be used in current PCI systems.*

### 5.4.5.1 CARD SLOT SUPPORT

Many PCI cards and PCI slots operate at a single voltage only, either 5V or 3.3V. PCI slots and cards are keyed so that a 5V card cannot be inserted into a dedicated 3.3V slot and a 3.3V card cannot be inserted into a dedicated 5V slot.

Universal PCI cards are universally keyed. They can operate at either voltage and fit into either a 5V slot or a 3.3V slot.

PCI voltages have changed with each newer specification:

- All PCI slots use 5V for power, therefore the voltage listed for a card refers to the voltage used for its signaling lines.

- PCI 2.1 specification uses 5V signal lines with 3.3V signal line support optional. A PCI 2.1-compliant system board (chipset) might not have physical 3.3V signal lines because of the optional support and are keyed to only accept cards that support 5V signal lines.

- PCI 2.2 specification required using 3.3V signal lines. 3.3V signal lines are required on all 66MHz, 100MHz, or 133MHz PCI slots.

- PCI-X slots use only 3.3V signal lines.

You can use 32-bit/33MHz PCI cards in PCI-X slots if they are universal voltage—that is, if they work with both 5V and 3.3V voltages. PCI card and slot keys are meant to match signaling voltages. The 5V-only PCI cards are keyed so that they cannot be installed in a PCI-X slot. Some PCI-X cards work only with 3.3V voltage, so they are keyed so that they cannot be installed in a 5V slot.

If a 32-bit/33MHz 3.3V card is installed on the PCI-X bus, it automatically forces all the cards in the same PCI-X bridge to work at 32-bit/33MHz speed.

| | | Conventional PCI Cards | | PCI-X Cards | |
|---|---|---|---|---|---|
| | | 33MHz (5V or Universal) | 66MHz (3.3V or Universal) | 66MHz (3.3V or Universal) | 133MHz (3.3V or Universal) |
| Conventional System | 33MHz | 33MHz | 33MHz | 33MHz | 33MHz |
| | 66MHz | | | | 66MHz |
| PCI-X System | 66MHz | | 66MHz | 66MHz | |
| | 100MHz | | | | 100MHz |
| | 133MHz | | | | 133MHz |

**Figure 5–15**  *PCI and PCI-X interoperability matrix.*

### 5.4.5.2   INTEROPERABILITY MATRIX

Figure 5–15 illustrates how PCI and PCI-X cards function in a conventional system or a PCI-X system.

A PCI-X device can run at speeds from 33 to 133MHz. In a PCI-X system, the system runs at the speed of the slowest device. Because of backward-compatibility requirements, all PCI-X devices must be able to run at lower speeds to work in older systems or in PCI-X systems with a slower device or PCI device.

The PCI-X bus can accommodate only one PCI-X device at 133MHz, two devices at 100MHz, and four or more devices at 66MHz.

## 5.4.6   PCI Hot Plug Support in PCI-X

PCI-X technology supports PCI Hot Plug and offers a great deal of latitude in the design of hot-pluggable controllers. Certain considerations affecting hardware and software must be taken into account when migrating to PCI-X.

The hot-pluggable controller must

- Provide the hot-pluggable system driver with the means to check the PCIXCAP pin to identify PCI-X adapters.
- Drive the PCI-X initialization pattern on the bus with the proper timing before the rising edge of RST# for that slot.
- Coordinate with the arbitrator for bus ownership during hot insertion.

The hot-pluggable system driver must read the M66EN and PCIXCAP pin on the inserted card to ensure that the inserted adapter supports the bus frequency and operating mode of the bus.

| 5.5 | |
|---|---|

## Upcoming PCI Bus Technologies

This section provides a glimpse of the newest PCI specifications, PCI-X 2.0, and PCI Express.

### 5.5.1 PCI-X 2.0

Figure 5–16 shows how bus technologies have evolved over time.

The PCI-X 2.0 specification was released in July 2002. PCI-X 2.0 has four times the bandwidth of PCI-X without increasing its pin count. It is backward compatible with the hardware and software of PCI and PCI-X. Figure 5–16 shows how aggregate bandwidth has increased with the introduction of new bus technologies.

The PCI-X 2.0 specification defines two new versions of PCI-X add-in cards.

The PCI-X 266 runs at speeds up to 266MT/s, enabling sustainable PCI bandwidth of more than 2.1GB/s.

The PCI-X 533 runs at speeds up to 533MT/s, enabling bandwidth of more than 4.2GB/s.

Such throughput rates are more than sufficient to handle current applications and also support future high-bandwidth add-in card connections to 10 Gigabit Ethernet, 10 Gigabit Fibre Channel, Serial Attached SCSI, Serial ATA (SATA), InfiniBand, RAID, and cluster interconnects for servers and workstations.

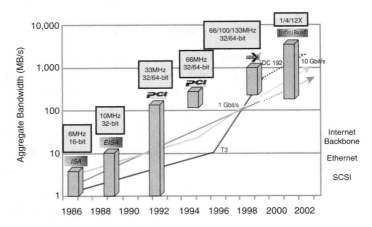

**Figure 5–16** *Evolution of bus technologies.*

PCI-X 2.0 leverages the protocol enhancements used in the widely adopted PCI-X 1.0 specification, such as byte counts and split transactions, enabling maximum operational efficiency with host bridges, PCI-to-PCI bridges, and main memory.

The PCI-X 2.0 specification also incorporates error checking and correction, ensuring end-to-end data integrity. Additionally, the bus per slot provided with PCI-X 2.0 delivers excellent fault isolation and improved performance guarantees for advanced levels of reliability.

PCI-X 2.0 is fully backward compatible with previous generations of PCI, which means that system board designers and system designers can immediately deploy products that accommodate existing PCI cards, and at the same time support present and future low-cost, high-bandwidth PCI-X 2.0 devices. In addition, PCI-X 2.0 adapter cards will be able to plug into any PCI slot and operate at the maximum speed of that slot.

### 5.5.2   PCI Express

The PCI Express specification was also released in July 2002. PCI Express defines a packetized protocol and a load/store architecture. Its layered architecture enables attachment to copper, optical, or emerging physical signaling media. It can be used for chip-to-chip and add-in card applications to provide connectivity for adapter cards, as a graphics I/O attach point for increased graphics bandwidth, and as an attach point to other interconnects such as InfiniBand.

PCI Express is a fully serial interconnect with links that use multiple, point-to-point connections called *lanes*. Its initial speed of 2.5Gb/s per direction provides two unidirectional 200MB/s communication channels that represent roughly three times the speed of classic PCI. By adding more lanes, bandwidth can be easily scaled.

PCI Express is designed with long-term scalability in mind. Key features include the following:

- Higher bandwidth per pin
- Low overhead
- Low latency
- Embedded clock architecture

Embedded clock timing and differential signaling enables PCI Express performance to scale to the limits of copper signaling, which are expected to be in the 10 to 15Gb/s range for high-volume copper technology.

The embedded clock architecture requires fewer pins than parallel architectures, which simplifies routing. This helps minimize costs and allows wider flexibility for component, motherboard, adapter, and system design. Fewer signals also means that systems can be designed using less board space and smaller connectors, which, in turn, supports smaller and more innovative form factors.

PCI Express is compatible with the current PCI software environment. PCI Express eventually might replace PCI, but InfiniBand architecture and PCI Express will be able to coexist because the primary focus of each is complementary:

- The focus of the InfiniBand architecture is on shared I/O in a multi-computer environment using a robust message-passing architecture.
- The focus of PCI Express is cost-effective local I/O, using a load/store architecture.

PCI Express is building on the electrical layer and silicon building blocks of the InfiniBand architecture. This is a key enabler toward future convergence of the two I/O architectures.

I/O requirements will be driven beyond the current capabilities and cost-effective scalability potential of the PCI bus by technology advances, including the following:

- Processor speeds in excess of 10GHz
- Faster memory speeds
- Higher-speed graphics
- 1Gb and 10Gb LANs

PCI Express is important to developers because it creates a high-performance, highly scalable, general-purpose I/O architecture. Additionally, it will be designed to serve as a long-term, general-purpose I/O interconnect to meet the requirements of desktop, mobile, server, communications, embedded, and other emerging and future applications.

## 5.6 USB

The *Universal Serial Bus* (USB) is a peripheral bus standard developed by the computer and telecommunications industries. This standard lets you hot plug peripheral devices without restarting or reconfiguring the system. USB devices are automatically configured as soon as they are physically attached.

With USB you can connect many peripherals simultaneously. Many computers come with two USB ports. Special USB peripherals, called *USB hubs,* have additional ports that enable you to connect multiple devices in a daisy chain.

USB also distributes electrical power to many peripherals. It enables the computer to automatically sense the power required and deliver it to the device. This feature eliminates those clunky power-supply boxes.

USB features include the following:

- **Broad industry support**—Computer and telecommunications leaders established the standards.

- **Ease of use**—Peripheral devices are automatically configured and hot pluggable.

- **Flexibility**—You can attach a variety of devices to the computer through the same connector simultaneously.

USB specifications include the following:

- 12Mb/s low-cost data transfer rates
- Support of up to 127 devices
- Both isochronous and asynchronous data transfers
- Up to 5m per cable segment

## 5.6.1   USB Connectors

USB connectors ship in two distinct varieties, Series A and Series B, as shown in Figure 5–17.

They are identical in function, but have differences to prevent connections that violate the USB architecture topology.

### 5.6.1.2   SERIES A

The Series A connector has a flat rectangular shape and plugs into the downstream port receptacles on the USB host or hub.

Both male connector and female receptacle have all four contact positions inline. The Series A connector is intended for all USB devices. In most cases, a USB cable will be captive (molded in) to its peripheral.

### 5.6.1.3   SERIES B

The Series B connector, roughly square with beveled corners, plugs into upstream receptacles on a USB device or hub.

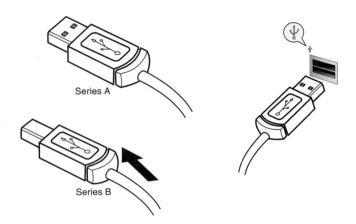

**Figure 5–17** *USB connections.*

Both the male connector and female receptacle have four contacts stacked two over two. There are some cases where a captive cable is restrictive. The Series B connector was created for such applications.

USB class drivers and *Windows Driver Model* (WDM), provided in Windows 98 and Windows 2000, support devices that comply with the particular device class specification. Devices can use the generic class drivers provided with the operating system, or manufacturers can create drivers or WDM minidrivers (depending on the device class) to exploit any additional unique hardware features.

### 5.6.2 USB 2.0

USB 2.0 extends the capabilities of the interface from 12Mb/s (200 × 56Kb/s) to between 120 and 240Mb/s.

## ▲ Summary

This chapter first discussed bus architecture and explained the functions of the address bus, the data bus, and the control signals.

The discussion then focused on the factors that increase bus performance. Several key bus performance concepts were explained, including bus speed measurement, bus cycles, and maximum transfer rate.

The architecture and characteristics of PCI and PCI-X buses were described and contrasted. Emerging PCI bus technologies were then discussed. Finally, an overview of the USB was provided.

## ▲ LEARNING CHECK

1. *What is bus width?*
   A. The number of bus cycles that occur per second
   B. The number of electrical lines in a bus
   C. The process used to transfer data
   D. The amount of data that can flow across a bus during a period of time

2. *Over what system bus are control signals usually sent?*

3. *What is the formula for maximum transfer rate of a bus?*
   A. (Speed × Width)/Clock cycles per transfer
   B. (Speed × Clock cycles per bus cycle)/Width
   C. (Width × Clock cycles per bus cycle)/Speed
   D. Speed/(Clock cycles per bus cycle × Width)

4. *What are four fundamental adjustments that can improve system performance?*

5. *What is a bus master device?*

6. *How many expansion slots operating at 66MHz can a PCI-X bus segment support?*

7. *How long does PCI-X allow for the decode logic to occur?*

8. *Match the following terms and descriptions:*

   | | |
   |---|---|
   | PCI Express | Incorporates error checking and correcting |
   | PCI-X 2.0 | Defines a packetized protocol and a load/store architecture |
   | USB | Enables you to hot plug peripheral devices without restarting or reconfiguring the system |

S I X

# Server Storage

After studying this chapter, you will be able to do the following:

- Explain the technical concepts behind ATA/IDE, ATAPI, and emerging ATA-based technologies.

- Explain the three major SCSI standards evolutions (SCSI-1, SCSI-2, and SCSI-3).

- Explain and describe key SCSI characteristics, including SCSI protocol compatibility, SCSI addressing, SCSI communication, and SCSI bus transactions.

- List the steps you would take to troubleshoot common SCSI problems.

- Compare and contrast SCSI with parallel ATA/IDE.

- Describe new and upcoming SCSI technologies, including iSCSI and Serial SCSI.

**111**

Two popular types of hard drive technology are currently offered in the server systems industry: ATA/IDE and SCSI.

ATA/IDE is a disk drive configuration that integrates the controller on the hard drive rather than on an expansion card. With this configuration, interface costs are reduced and firmware implementations are simplified.

SCSI is the leading technology to connect various devices to servers.

Both of these storage technologies are explained in this chapter.

## 6.1 ATA/IDE Hard Drive Technology

ATA was developed as a device attachment interface for the original IBM AT computer. HP, CDC, and Western Digital developed the original ATA interface and disk drives in the 1980s. In the late 1980s, the ATA interface design was set as an *American National Standards Institute* (ANSI) standard.

The ATA interface is the drive controller interface and the standard that defines the drive and how it operates. IDE is the actual drive and the 40-pin interface and drive controller architecture designed to implement the ATA standard.

### 6.1.1 ATA/IDE in Servers

Traditionally, ATA/IDE hard drives have been used in desktops and portable computers, but they have not been common in servers. However, low-cost ATA/IDE hard drives are an emerging opportunity for specific environments in which server duty cycle is relatively low and low price is the motivating force.

ATA/IDE hard drive technology offers several basic advantages, including the following:

- Lowest dollar per gigabyte
- Lowest power consumption
- Lower thermals
- Entry-level reliability

ATA/IDE is also known as *parallel ATA*. Because of the recent development of the serial ATA standard, parallel ATA is the now preferred term because it distinguishes between the two standards.

## 6.1.2 ATA/IDE Standards

Each version of ATA is backward compatible with the previous versions. Newer versions of ATA are built on older versions. With just a few exceptions, new versions can be thought of as extensions of the previous versions. The ATA standards are described in Table 6.1.

**Table 6.1** *ATA Standards*

| Standard | Description |
| --- | --- |
| ATA-1 | Defines the original ATA interface, which is an integrated bus interface between disk drives and host systems based on the ISA bus. |
| ATA-2 | Includes performance-enhancing features such as *programmed input/output* (PIO) and *direct memory access* (DMA) modes. EIDE is an extension of ATA-2 and builds on both the ATA-2 and *ATA Packet Interface* (ATAPI) standards. |
| ATA-3 | Improves the reliability of PIO mode 4; offers a simple password-based security scheme, more sophisticated power management features, and *Self-Monitoring Analysis and Reporting Technology* (S.M.A.R.T.). ATA-3 is backward compatible with ATA-2, ATAPI, and ATA-1 devices. |
| ATA-4 (Ultra-ATA/33) | Provides high-performance bus mastering at burst data rates up to 33MB/s using DMA data transfers. The implementation of Ultra-ATA is usually called Ultra-DMA/33 or UDMA/33. Implementing an Ultra-ATA drive system requires an Ultra-ATA drive, controller, and supporting BIOS. |
| ATA-5 (Ultra-ATA/66) | Supports high-performance bus mastering with burst data rates up to 66MB/s using DMA data transfers. This implementation of Ultra-ATA is usually called *Ultra-DMA/66* or *UDMA/66*. An Ultra-ATA/66 drive requires a controller, cable, and supporting BIOS. |
|  | The signal cable is a specially designed 40-pin/80-conductor cable for Ultra-ATA/66 or Ultra-ATA/100. It is fully backward compatible with previous ATA standards, but will not provide the UDMA performance with a standard 40-pin cable. The operating system must be DMA-capable, and the DMA mode must be activated. |
| ATA-6 (Ultra-ATA/100) | Provides backward compatibility with existing EIDE/UDMA hard drives, removable media drives, and CD-ROM and R/RW drives. Ultra-ATA/100 drives, also called *Ultra-DMA/100* or *UDMA/100*, are capable of 100MB/s data burst rates, which is a design modification originally created by Intel, Quantum, and Seagate. |
|  | A sensing mechanism allows the host to detect the 80-conductor cable and determine whether to enable Ultra ATA/66/100 transfer rates. Ultra ATA/100 requires the same 80-conductor cable as Ultra ATA/66. The Ultra ATA/33 requires a 40-conductor cable. |
| ATA-7 (Ultra-ATA/133) | Raises the ATA interface speed to 133MB/s and aligns the interface rate with the PCI bus data rate. Introduced by Maxtor, it was built on the double-edge clocking technology and cyclical redundancy checking of Ultra ATA/33 and the 80-conductor cable introduced with the Ultra ATA/66 interface. Backward compatible with all parallel ATA devices, it uses the same 80-conductor, 40-pin cable currently deployed for ATA/100. |

### 6.1.3   ATAPI

*ATA Packet Interface* (ATAPI) is an extension of the ATA interface, designed to allow devices other than hard drives to plug into an ordinary ATA/IDE port.

ATAPI is a standard, packet-based interface that derives its command set from SCSI. It provides the commands needed for devices such as CD-ROMs and tape drives that plug into an ordinary ATA/IDE connector. ATAPI also runs other removable storage devices, such as the LS-120 super-disk drives and internal Iomega Zip and Jaz drives.

The ATAPI specification was first defined under ATA-2, which is now obsolete. The current version of ATAPI was defined as part of ATA-4 specification.

### 6.1.4   Emerging Technologies—Serial ATA

Serial ATA technology enables the industry to move to the lower voltages and lower pin count required for efficient integration in future chipsets. Serial ATA is a point-to-point interface in which each device is directly connected to the host, using a dedicated link. As with parallel ATA, Serial ATA was designed only as an internal storage interface.

Serial ATA offers improvements and capabilities over parallel ATA, including the following:

- **No drive jumpers**—Eliminates the primary/secondary interaction between devices. Each device has the entire interface bandwidth dedicated to it.

- **Lower voltage**—Serial ATA reduces the signaling voltages from 5V to approximately 250 millivolts.

- **Pin efficiency**—The ATA interface has 26 signal pins going into the interface chip. Serial ATA uses only 4 signal pins, improving the pin efficiency.

- **Improved cable and connector**—The serial ATA cable length is 1 meter, which is considerably longer than the 18-inch maximum for parallel ATA. The current parallel ATA cable and connector is an 80-conductor ribbon cable and 40-pin header connector. Serial ATA uses much thinner cables with only 7 pins and smaller redesigned cable connectors.

- **Hot-plug capability**—Serial ATA includes all the mechanical and electrical features necessary to allow devices to be inserted directly into receptacles when the system is powered, and the protocol ensures that device discovery and initialization are handled.

- **Compatibility**—Serial ATA is compatible at the register level with the current parallel ATA. Serial ATA supports all existing ATA and ATAPI devices.
- **Scalability**—The current parallel ATA interface does not have scalability to support several more speed doublings. Serial ATA defines a road map starting at 1.5Gb/s and migrating to 3Gb/s, then to 6Gb/s.
- **Reliability**—Serial ATA uses a special encoding scheme called *8B/10B* to encode and decode data sent along the cable. This guarantees steady streamed voltage signal pulses on the circuits to increase reliability.

### 6.1.4.1   SERIAL ATA II

In the first quarter of 2002, the formation of the Serial ATA II Working Group was announced. The group's charge is to develop a Serial ATA II specification that will enhance the existing Serial ATA specification for the server and networked storage market segments, as well as deliver second-generation signaling speed.

## 6.2   Introduction to SCSI

SCSI is the dominant I/O technology in the open systems world. Because it is difficult for new storage technologies to be integrated into the wide variety of products sold, new I/O technologies, such as Fibre Channel, are often based on some form of SCSI to facilitate rapid development.

SCSI is a set of evolving ANSI-standard electronic interfaces that allow computers to communicate with peripheral hardware devices over a parallel bus.

Although there have been recent changes to include serial connections, SCSI is still considered to be primarily a parallel bus. A diagram of the SCSI configuration architecture is shown in Figure 6–1.

For more information on SCSI technology, refer to *The Book of SCSI, Second Edition: I/O for the New Millennium*, by Gary Field and Peter M. Ridge; and Chapter 1, "The Network Storage Landscape," in *Building Storage Networks*, by Mark Farley.

**Figure 6–1**

*SCSI block diagram.*

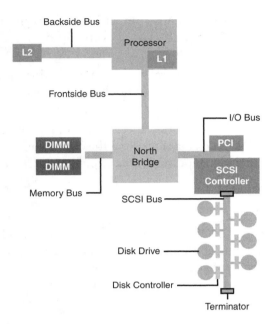

SCSI has evolved through three major standards beginning in 1986:

- **SCSI-1**—The original SCSI standard, approved by ANSI in 1986, defined the first SCSI bus.

- **SCSI-2**—SCSI-2 was approved in 1994 as an extensive enhancement to the original standard that defined support for many advanced features.

- **SCSI-3**—SCSI-3 was approved in 1996. SCSI-3 is a group of specifications that define the implementation of SCSI protocols on different physical layers.

### 6.2.1  SCSI-1

The original SCSI standard defined the first SCSI bus in terms of cable length, signal characteristics, commands, and transfer modes.

The default speed for SCSI-1 was 5MB/s. It had an 8-bit parallel bus that transferred a single byte of data with each bus cycle. The features included support for two devices, asynchronous mode, and a single-ended interface.

Regular and narrow conventions are no longer mentioned in the SCSI protocol names.

## 6.2.2   SCSI-2

SCSI-2 was approved in 1994. SCSI-2 was an extensive enhancement that defined support for many advanced features, including the following:

- **Synchronous mode**—Used command queuing to send 256 commands to 1 device.
- **10MB/s transfer rate**—Offered twice the throughput of the previous standard.
- **Fast SCSI**—High-speed transfer protocol doubled the speed of the bus to 10MHz.
- **Wide SCSI**—Widened the original 8-bit SCSI bus to 16 bits to permit more data throughput at a given signaling speed. The Fast-Wide SCSI-2 offered data transfer rates up to 20MB/s.
- **More devices per bus**—Supported 16 devices on Wide SCSI buses, as opposed to 8 using Narrow SCSI.
- **Better cables and connectors**—Defined a new high-density 68-pin B cable and connectors.
- **Active termination**—Provided a more reliable termination of the bus.

SCSI-2 also maintained backward compatibility with all SCSI devices.

## 6.2.3   SCSI-3

SCSI-3 was approved in 1996. SCSI-3 is a group of specifications that define the implementation of SCSI protocols on the following physical layers:

- SCSI-3 parallel interface
- High-performance serial bus
- Fibre Channel
- Serial storage architecture

Each physical layer has different performance characteristics and uses different hardware. Other documents in the SCSI-3 standard continue to be developed. Currently, the SCSI-3 standard includes the SCSI-2 performance and functionality enhancements plus the following:

- **Ultra SCSI**—Doubles the bus speed to 20MHz and the transfer rate to 20MB/s, using an 8-bit data pathway.
- **Wide-Ultra SCSI-3**—Doubles the Ultra SCSI transfer rate to 40MB/s, using a 16-bit data pathway.

- **Improved cabling**—A new 68-pin P cable replaces the B cable for use with Wide SCSI.

> HP has extensively tested and integrated the Wide-Ultra SCSI-3 technology into HP servers and storage options because this technology allows the highest available performance in a SCSI host interface. In addition, backward compatibility provides investment protection for HP customers.

### 6.2.3.1 WIDE-ULTRA2 SCSI-3

As the power of applications, processors, and storage devices increases, users seek ways to increase system performance. Wide-Ultra2 SCSI-3 products provide the speed, flexibility, and compatibility required to optimize workstations and servers.

Figure 6–2 shows how the evolution of the SCSI standards have improved data transfer rates over the years.

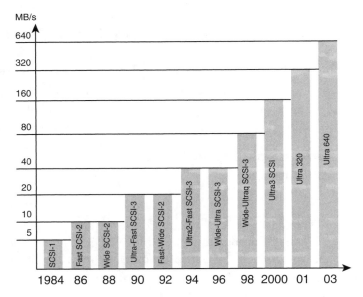

**Figure 6–2** *Data rate transfer speeds*

The Wide-Ultra2 SCSI-3 card uses *low-voltage differential* (LVD) technology and features the latest SCSI specifications. The Wide-Ultra2 SCSI-3 protocol

- Doubles the data burst of Wide-Ultra SCSI to 80MB/s, providing greater system throughput.

- Quadruples the maximum cable length of a Wide-Ultra SCSI-3 bus to 12m, allowing increased flexibility when adding external storage or configuring clustered servers.

- Maintains backward compatibility, allowing all previous SCSI implementations to be used on the same bus.

### 6.2.3.2   WIDE-ULTRA2 SCSI-3 CONNECTOR

Conventional attachment protocols that use separate power and data cables do not work well in high-end server environments. In addition to the more common cabling systems, high-end drives, usually Wide-Ultra or Ultra2 SCSI, can be set up to use a special connection system that replaces the power cable, data cable, and normal device ID assignment methods.

*Single Connector Attachment* (SCA), which was developed for servers and other high-end systems, replaces the conventional cabling scheme with a backplane system that uses a single 80-pin connector, as shown in Figure 6–3.

This connector replaces the standard 68-pin Wide SCSI cable and the standard 4-wire D-shaped power connector. It also includes signals for setting the device IDs for individual drives.

*Single Connector Attachment-2* (SCA-2) connectors are an improved version of the original SCA connector. The major difference is that the SCA-2 connector is designed so that 2 of the 80 pins on the connector are always connected first when attaching a drive and disconnected last when removing a drive. This improves reliability by ensuring that the drive remains grounded.

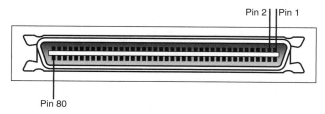

**Figure 6–3**   *SCA-2 80-pin connector.*

Multiple hard drives can be used together on high-end workstations and servers to increase performance and improve reliability. This typically is done using RAID, and in many cases, the hard drive subsystem is designed to allow hot swapping, which means that failed hard drives can be replaced without powering down the system. SCAs are hot-swappable.

### 6.2.3.3   ULTRA3

The strategy for universal storage devices that span all ranges of storage systems is based on the industry-leading Wide-Ultra3 SCSI-3 technology. The Wide-Ultra3 SCSI-3 drives and options provide twice the speed of previous versions with data transfer rates up to 160MB/s. This SCSI specification is also known as *Ultra160*. The Ultra160 feature set is widely supported by HP and other industry-leading systems manufacturers as well as SCSI drive and component suppliers.

As ratified by the SCSI Trade Association, the Ultra3 name refers to a product that incorporates any of the following features.

**6.2.3.3.1   DOUBLE TRANSITION CLOCKING** • Both Wide-Ultra2 and Wide-Ultra3 use a 40MHz bus speed on a 16-bit wide bus. However, Wide-Ultra3 doubles the rate at which data is sampled during a given cycle. Therefore, Wide-Ultra3 has a maximum data transfer rate of 160MB/s. Figure 6–4 shows the Ultra2 data transfer with the normal clock cycle. Compare this with Figure 6–5, which shows the Ultra3 data transfer cycle using double-transition clocking.

**6.2.3.3.2   CYCLICAL REDUNDANCY CHECK (CRC)** • With faster transfer rates, the need for data reliability increases. CRC treats data as long binary numbers and divides the binary numbers by a prime number. Both the transmitter and receiver of the data perform the calculation. The remainder from the

**Figure 6–4**

*Ultra2 data transfer with normal clocking.*

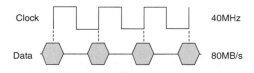

**Figure 6–5**

*Ultra3 data with double-transition clocking.*

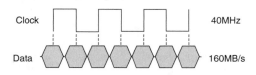

division is compared. In previous SCSI protocols, parity checking could detect only single-bit errors. CRC can detect single- and double-bit errors, an odd number of errors, and error bursts of up to 32 bits.

**6.2.3.3.3 DOMAIN VALIDATION** • The host controller attempts to negotiate a data transfer rate until a successful connection is made to the target device or until all possible slower speeds have been attempted. During the negotiation process, the host controller sends certain data to a target device at a particular speed. If the target device returns identical data, the negotiated speed is used. Otherwise, the host controller attempts a reduced transfer rate until the connection is successful.

With previous SCSI standards, devices that could not use a negotiated speed might have been inaccessible.

For more information on Wide-Ultra3 technology, visit http://www.ultra160-scsi.com.

For more information on HP ProLiant servers that support Wide-Ultra SCSI-3, visit http://www.compaq.com/smb/servers.

For more information on Wide-Ultra3 SCSI, visit http://www.compaq.com/products/storageworks/ultra3/index.html.

### 6.2.3.4 ULTRA320

Ultra320 SCSI, the next step in the SCSI evolution, introduces additional technologies, including protocol changes that reduce overhead and improve performance. These changes allow data to transfer safely and reliably at 320MB/s.

Ultra320 SCSI includes the following key features:

- **Double transfer speed**—Doubles the transfer rate across the SCSI bus to a burst rate of 320MB/s, enabling higher transfer rates across the SCSI bus and increasing the disk drive saturation point. This results in increased performance, especially in environments that use extended transfer lengths or have many devices on a single bus.

- **Packetized SCSI**—Includes support for packet protocol. Packetized devices decrease command overhead by transferring commands, data, and status using dual transition data phases instead of slower asynchronous phases. This improves performance by maximizing bus utilization and minimizing command overhead. Packet protocol also enables multiple commands to be transferred in a single connection.

- **Quick arbitration and selection**—Reduces the overhead of control release on the SCSI bus from one device to another, maximizing bus utilization.

- **Read and write data streaming**—Minimizes the overhead of data transfer by allowing the target to send one data stream *LUN Q-TAG* (LQ) packet followed by multiple data packets. In a nonstreaming transfer, there is one data LQ packet for each data packet. Write data streaming performance is also increased because the bus turnaround delay (from DT data in to DT data out) is not incurred between each LQ and data packet.

- **Flow control**—Allows the initiator to optimize its prefetching of data during writes and flushing of data FIFOs during reads. The target will indicate when the last packet of a data stream will be transferred, which will allow the initiator to terminate the data prefetch or begin flushing data FIFOs sooner than was previously possible.

Ultra320 SCSI maintains backward compatibility with previous versions of SCSI, even with the new added features. It also maintains compatibility with existing LVD SCSI technology, enabling customers to mix new and old technologies without interruption. For example, packetized SCSI is compatible with nonpacketized parallel SCSI. As a result, packetized SCSI devices can reside on the same bus as nonpacketized SCSI devices.

The computer industry can continue to look forward to new and faster SCSI technology. Ultra640 is already in development.

**6.2.3.4.1   ULTRA320 SCSI COMPLEMENTS PCI-X** • The faster Ultra320 SCSI I/O performance saturates the standard 66MHz PCI host bus that allowed for a maximum transfer rate of 533MB/s across a 64-bit bus, requiring PCI-X bus performance to take full advantage of Ultra320. Disk drive media data rates increase, exceeding 40MB/s. This required improvements over Ultra160 SCSI standard to support sustained throughput from the average number of drives in a server.

With Ultra160 SCSI, two SCSI channels on a single device achieve a maximum transfer rate of 320MB/s, leaving sufficient overhead before saturating the PCI bus. However, at 320MB/s, two SCSI channels can achieve 640MB/s, which saturates a 64-bit/66MHz PCI bus.

In addition to PCI-X doubling the performance of the host bus from 533MB/s to a maximum of 1066MB/s, there are protocol improvements so that efficiency of the bus is improved over PCI. Together PCI-X and Ultra320 SCSI provide the bandwidth necessary for current applications.

**6.2.3.4.2   PRECOMPENSATION** • Ultra320 SCSI speeds require new signaling technologies to maintain the high reliability required by server designs. Ultra320 SCSI signals on the SCSI bus are twice the frequency of Ultra160

SCSI signals, but cable requirements have not changed. Point-to-point connections can be 25 meters long, and multiple load systems can be 12 meters long. Doubling the maximum signal switching frequency in Ultra320 SCSI has pushed the SCSI bus into a frequency range that has greater signal attenuation in SCSI bus cables and has also required the signal slew rate to increase. The doubling of signal frequency has resulted in smaller amplitude signals and more reflections (undesired high frequency noise) on the SCSI bus.

In addition to the attenuation problem, the effects of *inter-symbol interference* (ISI) in Ultra320 SCSI causes the bit edges of digital signals to be distorted from their true position. ISI is caused by long periods of the signal being at one voltage level, which charges the cable much like a capacitor.

Skew compensation is required to address both the attenuation and ISI problems. In addition, Ultra320 SCSI requires precompensation (precomp) features in the SCSI output drivers to minimize attenuation and ISI. When precomp is enabled, the SCSI outputs switch to their maximum drive capability when there is a transition from 1 to 0 (or 0 to 1). The drive level is reduced on following bits when there is no transition. The reduction in drive level helps reduce the charging of the SCSI bus when the data bits contain a string of 0s or 1s, thereby reducing the ISI problems associated with an isolated 1 or an isolated 0.

**6.2.3.4.3   ADJUSTABLE ACTIVE FILTER** • An option to use an *adjustable active filter* (AAF) to address the attenuation and ISI problem is included in Ultra320 SCSI. Precomp works to correct problems at the transmission end of the SCSI bus. AAF corrects problems on the receiving end of the bus.

The purpose of adding an AAF to the SCSI receivers is to increase the signal-to-noise ratio of the SCSI signals. The AAF compensates for high-frequency attenuation in the cable and filters out the frequencies that are higher than the maximum Ultra320 SCSI signal frequency. The AAF automatically adjusts its high-frequency gain for the SCSI bus and calibrates itself during the training period so the high-frequency AAF gain (at 80MHz) cancels the high-frequency cable loss at 80MHz. Because Ultra320 SCSI has SCSI bus signals with switching frequencies up to 80MHz only, the AAF filters attenuates the unwanted frequencies (noise) more than 80MHz.

Both precomp and AAF devices can reside on the same SCSI bus. However, when precomp is active, AAF is not required. If AAF is active, precomp is not required.

The negotiation as to which technology is used occurs in the initialization process of the SCSI bus and is transparent to the user.

### 6.2.4  SCSI Standards Summary

The following table summarizes the characteristics of each the 11 SCSI device types.

| Type | Transfer Rates | SCSI Standard | Bus Width | Devices per Bus | Connectors |
|---|---|---|---|---|---|
| SCSI-1 | 2–4MB/s | SCSI-1 | 8 | 7 | 25-pin |
| SCSI-2 | 5MB/s | SCSI-2 | 8 | 7 | 50-pin |
| Wide SCSI-2 | 10MB/s | SCSI-2 | 16 | 15 | 68-pin |
| Fast SCSI-2 | 10MB/s | SCSI-2 | 8 | 7 | 50-pin |
| Fast-Wide SCSI-2 | 20MB/s | SCSI-2 | 16 | 15 | 68-pin |
| Ultra SCSI-3 | 20MB/s | SCSI-3 | 8 | 7 | 50-pin |
| Wide-Ultra SCSI-3 | 40MB/s | SCSI-3 | 16 | 15 | 68-pin |
| Ultra2 SCSI-3 | 40MB/s | SCSI-3 | 8 | 7 | 50-pin |
| Wide-Ultra2 SCSI-3 | 80MB/s | SCSI-3 | 16 | 15 | 68-pin |
| Ultra3 | 160MB/s | SCSI-3 | 16 | 15 | 68-pin |
| Ultra320 | 320MB/s | SCSI-3 | 16 | 15 | 68-pin |

*Bus widths of 8 bits are referred to as narrow and bus widths of 16 bits as wide.*

## 6.3  SCSI Characteristics

The SCSI standards have several key characteristics that are critical for you to understand and apply as an Accredited Integration Specialist, including the following:

- SCSI protocol compatibility
- SCSI addressing, which includes configuring SCSI IDs, SCSI device ID guidelines, and logical unit numbers
- SCSI communication
- SCSI bus transactions, which includes negotiation, disconnect and reconnect, tagged command queuing, and electrical signaling systems

### 6.3.1  SCSI Protocol Compatibility

SCSI protocols were designed to provide backward compatibility, so current host adapters should work with older SCSI peripherals and current peripherals should work on older host adapters. However, the variety of SCSI protocols makes it impossible to guarantee that any particular combination of devices will be compatible.

Consider the following guidelines when grouping SCSI devices:

1. Any SCSI device should work on any SCSI bus, but its operation is not guaranteed unless you are buying a completely tested system, including host adapter, peripherals, and cabling, from a single vendor.
2. The greater the difference in age between the devices, the more likely that there will be compatibility issues.
3. Narrow and wide devices can be mixed on the same bus, but this is more difficult to arrange than using all narrow or all wide. The greater the discrepancy in the types of SCSI being used, the more difficult it will be to make the bus work properly. Only wide devices will use the extra bandwidth. However, in most cases, you must terminate the wide and narrow part of the bus, or the wide devices might not function properly.
4. Never mix single-ended and *high-voltage differential* (HVD) SCSI unless you are using adapters to ensure that all the devices on the bus are one or the other.

**One of the major design criteria in the creation of SCSI-2 was backward compatibility with SCSI-1. In most cases, SCSI-2 devices will work with older SCSI-1 devices on a bus. This is not always practiced because older devices cannot support the SCSI-2 enhancements and faster transfer protocols.**

## 6.3.2    SCSI Addressing

Each device must have a unique target ID to enable the SCSI bus to distinguish the devices. For an 8-bit bus, a maximum of 8 targets is possible, using the 8 data channels on the bus. Narrow SCSI devices are numbered 0 through 7. For wide buses, the maximum number of target devices is 16. Wide SCSI devices are numbered 0 through 15. Wide devices that support 16 IDs use a 4-bit jumper block.

The SCSI device ID settings are shown in Figure 6–6.

**The host adapter is a SCSI device that requires an ID.**

| ID | Bit 3 | Bit 2 | Bit 1 | Bit 0 |
|----|-------|-------|-------|-------|
| 0  | OFF | OFF | OFF | OFF |
| 1  | OFF | OFF | OFF | ON |
| 2  | OFF | OFF | ON | OFF |
| 3  | OFF | OFF | ON | ON |
| 4  | OFF | ON | OFF | OFF |
| 5  | OFF | ON | OFF | ON |
| 6  | OFF | ON | ON | OFF |
| 7  | OFF | ON | ON | ON |
| 8  | ON | OFF | OFF | OFF |
| 9  | ON | OFF | OFF | ON |
| 10 | ON | OFF | ON | OFF |
| 11 | ON | OFF | ON | ON |
| 12 | ON | ON | OFF | OFF |
| 13 | ON | ON | OFF | ON |
| 14 | ON | ON | ON | OFF |
| 15 | ON | ON | ON | ON |

| ID | Bit 2 | Bit 1 | Bit 0 |
|----|-------|-------|-------|
| 0 | OFF | OFF | OFF |
| 1 | OFF | OFF | ON |
| 2 | OFF | ON | OFF |
| 3 | OFF | ON | ON |
| 4 | ON | OFF | OFF |
| 5 | ON | OFF | ON |
| 6 | ON | ON | OFF |
| 7 | ON | ON | ON |

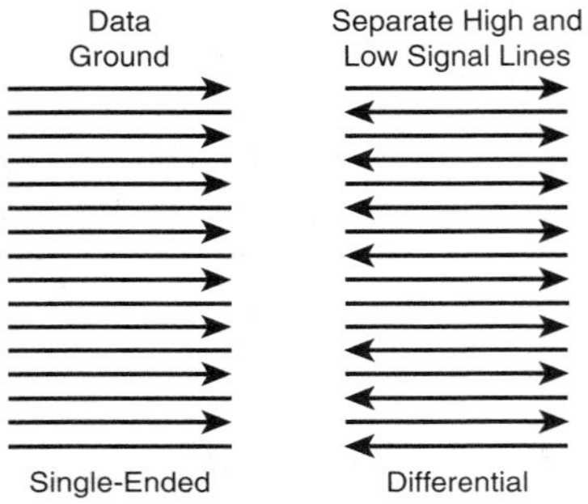

**Figure 6–6** *SCSI device ID settings.*

Some older host adapters can be strict about device IDs and will only start from a hard drive if it is set to device ID 0. Newer hardware has corrected this limitation.

The higher the SCSI target ID, the higher the priority of the device. In the event of arbitration between devices, the device that has the highest SCSI ID will win.

**EXAMPLE**

Information on a disk device should be more readily accessible (has a higher priority) than data from a backup tape. Therefore, a *Self-Monitoring Analysis and Reporting Technology* (S.M.A.R.T.) disk controller should have a higher target ID number than the tape controller. This system has led to the unofficial standard of using SCSI ID 7 for the host adapter.

On a Wide SCSI bus, the lower eight IDs have higher priorities than the higher eight IDs. This makes the priority order of target IDs on a Wide SCSI system 7, 6, 5, 4, 3, 2, 1, 0, 15, 14, 15, 12, 11, 10, 9, and 8.

A Narrow SCSI device cannot communicate with a SCSI device with a target ID larger than seven. Do not move the target ID of the SCSI host adapter to a number higher than seven.

### 6.3.2.1   CONFIGURING SCSI IDS

The method of configuring the ID depends on the specific piece of hardware. Many devices use hardware switches, jumpers, or a rotary dial on the back of the device enclosure to set the device ID. More sophisticated devices, especially the more modern SCSI host adapters, use software utilities.

Plug-and-play SCSI allows for automatic assignment of device IDs on the bus to eliminate simultaneous use of a single ID on multiple devices. SCA systems, introduced with SCSI-3, use a special single connector to provide power and data to each hard drive and to allow the controller to set the device ID of each drive.

### 6.3.2.2   SCSI DEVICE ID GUIDELINES

The SCSI device ID guidelines include the following:

1. Although both Wide and Narrow SCSI host adapters reliably support up to seven SCSI devices, some Wide SCSI devices do not support more than seven target IDs. With the advent of LVD SCSI, HP added support for 15 devices to its original 7-device support on Wide SCSI controllers.
2. IDs are set automatically with HP hot-swappable hard drives. The HP reserved and available SCSI ID numbers for SCSI devices are as follows:

   - **0**—Usually reserved for the bootable hard drive
   - **1 through 6**—Available on both narrow and wide implementations
   - **7**—Usually reserved for the SCSI host adapter
   - **8 through 15**—Available for wide devices that support 16 IDs

3. Every SCSI chain or circuit must be terminated at both ends by using the termination feature on the device or by using a terminated cable.
4. SCSI devices that do not have terminating jumpers must use cable terminators.
5. Before powering on the computer, power on the external SCSI device, so the system board controller can recognize the external SCSI device and automatically reset.
6. For HP implementations, all SCSI hard drives on a single SCSI bus must be either internal or external, but never both. However, the storage system accommodates a combination of other internal and external SCSI devices, such as SCSI tape and CD-ROM drives. Devices that can be mixed on the same SCSI bus can vary depending on the machine type. Check the specifications of a SCSI controller before mixing internal and external devices on the same SCSI channel.

**Note**

HP restricts the number of devices on a bus because some wide controller implementations support only seven devices on a wide channel. However, wide SCSI generally accepts up to 15 devices in addition to the controller.

### 6.3.2.3   LOGICAL UNIT NUMBERS

Each SCSI ID device can be broken down into logical unit numbers (LUNs). The number of LUNs available depends on the number of available data lines, as follows:

- 8 (LUNs 0 to 7) for Narrow SCSI
- 16 (LUNs 0 to 15) for Wide SCSI

Each disk in a device can be addressed independently through LUNs (a four-disk CD jukebox could be assigned LUN 0 to 3).

**EXAMPLE**

A CD-ROM storage system that contains six individual CD-ROM drives is addressed logically as a single SCSI device and requires only one SCSI ID. The individual CD-ROM drives are addressed using LUNs. Consequently, it is possible to daisy chain up to 7 (15 for Wide) CD-ROM expansion units (containing a total of 42 CD-ROM drives) on a single SCSI bus.

### 6.3.3 SCSI Communication

When SCSI devices communicate on the bus, one device acts as an initiator and the other device acts as a target.

The initiator is a SCSI device capable of starting an operation and is typically an adapter or controller in the host computer. The initiator starts an operation and is responsible for target selection and for providing commands and data.

The target is a SCSI device that performs the operation. SCSI storage devices have a fixed role, usually as a target. Information transfer on the SCSI bus is allowed between only two SCSI devices at a time. The target manages the commands provided by the initiator and performs the operations.

All activity on the SCSI bus occurs in one of eight SCSI bus phases. The bus phases determine the direction of the transfer and the type of information that is placed on the data lines.

The first four phases are collectively known as the *negotiation phase* because they are used by a SCSI device to obtain permission to use the SCSI bus. The last four phases are collectively known as the *information transfer phase* because they are used to transfer data or control information. The information transfer phase does not have a specified order.

**The SCSI bus cannot be in more than one phase at a time.**

The following table describes the SCSI bus phases and their functions.

| Bus Phase | Description |
|---|---|
| *Negotiation Phase* | |
| Bus free | This phase indicates that no SCSI device is actively using the bus. Before a SCSI device can begin an arbitration phase, the SCSI bus must be free. |
| Arbitration | This bus phase allows a SCSI device to gain control of the bus so that it can assume the initiator or target role. After an initiator recognizes that the bus is free, it asserts the BSY signal and its own ID on the bus. After a delay, the initiator checks the data bus and clears itself from arbitration if a higher ID device is on the bus. |

*continued*

| Bus Phase | Description |
|---|---|
| *Negotiation Phase* | |
| Selection | This phase allows the initiator to select a target to perform a function, such as a read or write command. It does this by asserting the SEL line, the data bus with the desired target ID, and an initiator ID. The initiator then releases the BSY signal so that the target can assert a BSY signal on the bus. |
| Reselection | During this phase, the target that won arbitration reconnects to the initiator so it can resume a previously started transaction. |
| *Information Transfer Phase* | |
| Command | This phase allows the target to request command information from the initiator. The command information is a collection of bytes grouped into a data packet called the command descriptor block. This might require that more information be transferred between the devices. If this is the case, the additional information is transferred during a data in or data out phase. |
| Data | The data in phase allows the target to request a data transfer to the initiator. The data out phase allows the target to request a data transfer from the initiator. |
| Status | This phase allows the target to request that status information be transferred to the initiator. The target can tell the initiator whether the command was successfully completed. |
| Message | The message out phase allows the initiator to tell the target device which part of the target should act on a command. The message in phase allows the target to request that a message be sent to the initiator. This phase is used to indicate errors and abort commands or to warn an initiator that a target device will disconnect. |

SCSI uses an arbitration or requesting technique to control the bus. Arbitration is a priority system that grants control of the SCSI bus to the highest priority SCSI device that is requesting use of the SCSI bus.

With SCSI, a bus master priority is established as each device arbitrates for control of the bus. After an initiator recognizes that the bus is free, it asserts a bus-busy signal and its own ID on the bus. After the arbitration delay, the initiator checks the data bus and clears itself from arbitration if a higher ID device is on the bus.

Information transfers on the data bus are asynchronous and conform to a request/acknowledgment handshake, followed by 1 byte of data.

### 6.3.4 SCSI Bus Transactions

Certain SCSI bus functions are assigned to the initiator and target. The initiator arbitrates for the SCSI bus and selects a target. The target requests the transfer of command, data, status, or other information on the data bus, and in some cases, the target arbitrates for the SCSI bus and reselects an initiator to continue an operation.

**Figure 6–7**

*SCSI bus transaction process.*

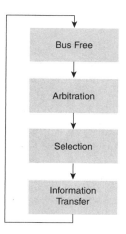

This process is illustrated in Figure 6–7.

### 6.3.4.1 NEGOTIATION

Negotiation is the process in which the controller agrees on a transfer rate with each connected device during the initialization phase. During negotiation, the decision to operate in Fast-Wide mode during the data transfer phase is made on a drive-by-drive basis between the controller and drive during the command setup phase.

> **! IMPORTANT**
>
> The controller and drive negotiate individually for the highest data transfer speed they can handle. This is important if 8- and 16-bit SCSI devices share a bus.
>
> Do not disable negotiation, setup, or jumpers unless a SCSI device fails to respond during the negotiation phase. It is possible for a Fast SCSI controller to communicate with both Fast SCSI-2 hard drives and Fast-Wide SCSI-2 hard drives. A Fast-Wide SCSI-2 controller can be used with either type of hard drive.

> **! IMPORTANT**
>
> The maximum transfer rate between the SCSI controller and each disk drive on the bus is determined by the native protocol of the slowest device.

### 6.3.4.2   DISCONNECT AND RECONNECT

When a SCSI device receives a request, it disconnects temporarily from the bus when it processes the data internally. The SCSI device reconnects with the bus after it has processed the request, which enables seven devices to operate simultaneously on a single bus. The data presented by the individual devices is then transferred across the bus in an interleaved mode.

Connect and disconnect times are a function of the SCSI controller as well as the SCSI devices. The ability of the SCSI host and devices to disconnect rapidly from the SCSI bus enhances performance. Disconnect times are continually decreasing as technology progresses.

### 6.3.4.3   TAGGED COMMAND QUEUING

Tagged command queuing (TCQ) enables a drive to receive many commands and perform those commands without involving the SCSI bus. This allows other devices to use the bus. The drive indicates when it has completed the commands, when its buffers are full, and when it is ready to transfer information. This technique increases the efficiency of a bus that can have only one target active at a time.

A SCSI device that supports TCQ can accept up to 256 SCSI commands to optimize command execution.

> **EXAMPLE**
>
> A hard drive accepts 10 write commands and 5 read commands, then sorts them to optimize head positioning. This increases throughput by almost 30% or more.

A tag uniquely identifies each I/O request. The operating system uses the tag to see which I/O in the device driver queue is reported as complete by the device. An initiator can add or delete commands from the queue. When adding commands to the device queue, the initiator can specify a fixed order of execution or specify the next command to be executed. Otherwise, all commands are executed in the order received.

Implementing TCQ is optional for SCSI-2. Modern SCSI devices, particularly magnetic drives, support TCQ, which allows the device to have multiple I/O requests outstanding at the same time. Because the device is intelligent, it can optimize operations, such as head positioning, based on its own request queue.

On SCSI devices such as RAID arrays, the TCQ function takes advantage of the inherent parallelism of the device.

Some operating systems also support presorting data to reduce head positioning, but in RAID systems, this type of presorting is optimized for access to the logical drive, not the physical drive. This can actually lead to an increase in head movements. Therefore, TCQ is essential at the hardware level. TCQ requires device driver support.

TCQ belongs to the set of optional SCSI commands and is not supported by some drive manufacturers. If an unsupported drive is connected to the bus, TCQ must be disabled completely, which leads to degraded performance.

All HP SCSI hard drives support TCQ.

#### 6.3.4.4   ELECTRICAL SIGNALING SYSTEMS

Signal integrity on the bus is always a concern. The longer the cables, the more problems there can potentially be with signal degradation or interference. The faster the bus runs, the more difficult it is to keep the signals clean.

SCSI has defined two electrical signaling systems: single-ended SCSI and differential SCSI. Differential SCSI includes both *high-voltage differential* (HVD), and *low-voltage differential* (LVD).

A comparison between these two electrical signaling systems is shown in Figure 6–8.

**6.3.4.4.1   SINGLE-ENDED SCSI** • On a single-ended interface, data travels over a single wire known as the *signal line*. There is a corresponding ground wire for the signal line. However, voltage is carried only on the signal line. A positive voltage is a 1 and ground voltage is a 0.

Single-ended SCSI is the most common type of SCSI because it offers the most flexible and cost-effective solutions. However, the cable length of the bus is extremely limited. A single-ended SCSI bus uses signals that are either 5V or 0V and are relative to a common ground reference. A single

**Figure 6–8**

*SCSI electrical signaling systems.*

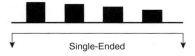

Single-Ended

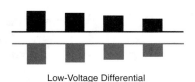

Low-Voltage Differential

ended 8-bit SCSI bus has approximately 25 ground lines, which are all tied to a single rail on all devices.

The signals in the parallel signal lines can interfere with each other. Therefore, single-ended SCSI allows only short cables. HP uses only single-ended SCSI because this configuration uses inexpensive cabling and operates reliably when all the SCSI rules are observed.

A standard single-ended bus has a maximum length of 6m. If the same bus is used with Fast SCSI devices, the maximum length allowed decreases to 3m. Fast SCSI means that on a narrow channel, instead of 5MB/s, the bus allows 10MB/s transfers. On a wide channel, it allows 20MB/s. Ultra SCSI and Ultra2 allow for 20MHz and 40MHz, respectively. Therefore, Ultra is 20MB/s on an 8-bit bus and 40MB/s on a 16-bit bus. For Fast-20, the maximum bus length is 1.5m, and for Fast-40, the maximum bus length is 12m.

**If some devices on the bus use Ultra SCSI or Ultra2 to communicate, the bus must adhere to the length restrictions for fast buses.**

**6.3.4.4.2  DIFFERENTIAL SCSI** • Differential SCSI uses a paired plus and minus signal level to reduce the effects of noise on the SCSI bus. Each signal is carried on a twisted pair of wires. A 1 is represented by a positive voltage on one wire and an equal but opposite negative voltage on another wire. A 0 is electrical ground, or zero voltage, on both wires. Any noise injected into the signal would be present in both a plus and minus state and would be canceled out. This concept is illustrated in Figure 6–9.

**Figure 6–9**

*How differential SCSI cancels noise.*

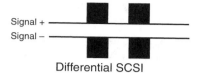

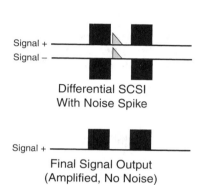

Using two conductors per signal makes the signal more resilient and less likely to be corrupted, enabling the use of much longer cabling than single-ended SCSI. This does increase the cost, however.

Conventional differential SCSI is now referred to as *HVD*. A differential SCSI bus has a maximum length of 25m. A single-ended Fast SCSI bus has a maximum length of 3m.

Differential interfaces use a twisted-pair cable for every SCSI signal. The signal integrity is verified at the cable end before the data is passed to the drives, so it is used in external applications.

Differential signals give a greater noise margin. Differential buses normally will be used for intercabinet connections. Because of the lower cost, single-ended SCSI typically is used for shorter buses.

**EXAMPLE**

If the original signal is at 5V, then the other line has the inverse signal of –5V. The differences are amplified, and the difference between the two lines is 5V – (–5V) = 10V. The second line is subtracted from the first line because the difference is being used.

A noise spike or other electrical noise on the lines would occur at the same time and at approximately the same amplitude.

> **EXAMPLE**
>
> If a 1V noise spike occurred, then both lines would have the 1V spike at the same time. The difference is 1V – 1V = 0V, and the spike is canceled out by the differential amplifier. This is called *common-mode rejection* because signals that are common, or in phase, are rejected.

Transfer rate protocols are defined for potential use in each of these signaling systems. This does not mean that all of the different protocols are readily available in both single-ended and HVD SCSI. HVD SCSI is used far less often and is much more expensive.

**High-Voltage Differential**—A differential interface uses signal transmitters and receivers to drive the signal over longer distances and create greater noise immunity than single-ended buses. The signal is split into positive and negative components and transmitted over cable pairs. Five volts is carried on both wires. The signal is recombined at the receiving device. Greater noise immunity allows substantially longer SCSI cables of up to 25m, compared to 6m or less for single-ended devices. It also produces a faster data transfer rate. Differential and single-ended SCSI are not compatible on the same bus without an electronic device, such as a SCSI converter, to convert between differential and single-ended configuration.

**Warning**

Single-ended and HVD SCSI are incompatible at the electrical level. Do not mix single-ended and HVD SCSI devices on the same bus or physical damage to equipment could result.

**Low-Voltage Differential**—This interface uses 3.3V and differential modes of operation to increase cable length up to 12m, although using 80MB/s transfer effectively eliminates line noise. Therefore, this interface is both faster and more reliable than existing single-ended SCSI configurations. LVD was created to reduce costs associated with HVD.

LVD SCSI is a technology that is the best choice in configurations in which Fibre Channel is too costly and single-ended SCSI is not viable because of its cable-length constraints. The lower voltage also means lower radiation of electromagnetic signals.

Single-ended and LVD devices can be used on the same bus, but the entire SCSI bus will then run with single-ended speeds.

### 6.3.4.5 CABLES

The type of SCSI cable used depends on the protocol and configuration. Cable selection can be confusing because SCSI has a variety of protocols and configurations and differential and single-ended SCSI devices look identical.

Figure 6–10 shows cable lengths that can be used with different SCSI standards.

Although single-ended cables are more common, both single-ended and differential cables share the following characteristics:

- **A cable**—The standard 50-wire cable, which is used either by itself for the Narrow, 8-bit SCSI or in combination with a B cable for Wide, 16-bit SCSI. The connector at each end of the cable depends on whether the device is internal or external.

- **B cable**—The B cable was added in SCSI-2 to enable Wide SCSI. This cable has 68 connectors and was used in parallel with the A cable. Because this combination was cumbersome, the B cable has been replaced by the P cable.

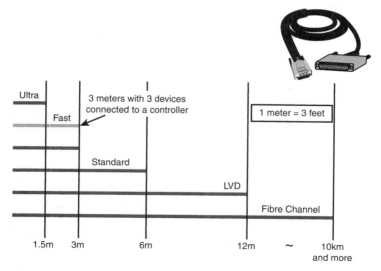

**Figure 6–10** *SCSI cable lengths.*

- **P cable**—This cable is the current standard 68-wire cable used in all Wide SCSI implementations. P cables use the same connectors for internal and external connections.

The SCSI bus width dictates the cable type, and the bus speed dictates the cable length. Faster SCSI buses that have more problems with signal corruption over longer distances are restricted to using shorter cables when using single-ended SCSI. Differential SCSI allows longer lengths regardless of speed.

**6.3.4.5.1 CABLING CONSIDERATIONS** • The cables used for single-ended and HVD SCSI look the same. Verify the cable type before installation. Converters between single-ended and HVD SCSI are available. Single-ended and HVD SCSI signaling methods, device cabling, and electrical characteristics are not compatible, except with special adapters. Matching the type of devices used with a SCSI host adapter is important.

HP has certified 4m (12-ft) cables in Fast, Fast-Wide, and Wide-Ultra rack solutions.

Two-meter (6-ft) cables are certified for tower solutions. HP overcame the Fast SCSI and Ultra SCSI cable length restrictions by using specially designed expander chip technology. An expander chip is a device that joins independent SCSI bus cables, so the cables seem as a single SCSI bus to all attached devices.

The expander chip technology allows the data signal to be powered at the same strength as the previous SCSI protocol, but allows the data bandwidth to function at the faster protocol. The result is that cables are qualified by HP to support a combination of 2m and 4m cable length and the faster data protocol from Wide-Ultra SCSI-3. The only cable with the 1.5m (4.5-ft) restriction is the daisy chain cable for the HP SCSI Storage Expander.

### 6.3.4.6  SCSI CONNECTORS

The table on the following page provides examples of SCSI connectors.

Electrical signals travel across wires in a manner similar to physical waves traveling across a string. When the signals reach the end of the wire, the signals reflect and travel back across the wire. If this happens, the reflected signals interfere with the other data on the bus and cause signal loss and data corruption. To ensure that this does not happen, you must terminate each end of the SCSI bus. Special components are used to catch any signals that make it to the end of the bus and prevent them from reflecting.

| SCSI Type | Bus Width (bits) | Bus Speed (MHz) | Maximum Transfer Rate (MB/s) | Connector |
|---|---|---|---|---|
| SCSI-1 | 8 | 5 | 5 | Centronics 50-pin connector |
| Fast SCSI-2 | 8 | 10 | 10 | 50-pin external connector<br>50-pin internal connector |
| Fast Wide SCSI-2 | 16 | 10 | 20 | Wide 68-pin connector (internal and external) |
| Wide-Ultra SCSI-3 | 16 | 20 | 40 | Wide 68-pin connector (internal and external) |
| Wide-Ultra2 SCSI-3 (LVD) | 16 | 40 | 80 | Wide 68-pin internal connector<br>VHDCI 68-pin external connector |
| Wide-Ultra3 SCSI-3 (LVD) | 16 | 40 | 160 (Double-Transition Clocking) | Wide 68-pin internal connector<br>VHDCI 68-pin external connector |

**Figure 6–11**

*Active termination.*

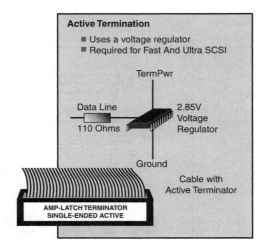

SCSI buses use two kinds of termination, which differ in the electrical circuitry used to terminate the bus:

- **Active termination**—The minimum required for any of the faster-speed SCSI buses. Adding voltage regulators enables more reliable and consistent termination of the bus. Active termination is illustrated in Figure 6–11.

- **Forced perfect termination (FPT)**—A more advanced form of active termination in which diode clamps are added to the circuitry to force the termination to the correct voltage. This termination eliminates any signal reflections or other problems that could occur and provides for the best form of termination of the SCSI bus.

**6.3.4.6.1 TERMINATOR POWER •** Terminators need power to operate properly. On the SCSI bus, a line is dedicated to this purpose. TERMPWR is a 5V signal used to power the termination logic. Usually the controller delivers this voltage. Each device can provide its own terminator power through integrated terminator sockets. When using HP equipment, always set the TERMPWR jumper to TERMPWR = OFF.

When a device supplying integrated terminator power to the SCSI bus line is intentionally or inadvertently powered off, the bus is no longer terminated.

When external terminators are mixed with integrated terminators on the device, the system can be accidentally configured with terminators in locations other than the end of the bus or with terminators in addition to the required two per bus. This configuration causes system failures or errors.

Initiators are devices that start actions on the bus and supply terminator power. All SCSI devices are allowed, but are not required, to supply terminator power.

To allow for unpowered devices on a bus, the terminator power must be supplied to the bus through a diode, preventing a backflow of current to unpowered devices.

The terminator power is usually fused. A blown fuse can lead to a nonfunctional bus. If multiple devices supply terminator power, a single blown fuse will not make the bus inoperable. External terminators sometimes have an LED indicator that shows whether terminator power is present. Newer designs sometimes use autorestoring fuses that reset themselves.

Although there are four methods for terminating single-ended SCSI cables, the ANSI committee has approved only passive and active, and passive is no longer used on modern HP systems. Passive and active termination also require termination from both sides of the cable. In this rapidly changing area, better terminating techniques are discovered that improve overall signal quality and provide better grounding capability. Additionally, all signals not defined as RESERVERS, GROUND, or TERMPWR will be terminated.

## 6.4  SCSI Troubleshooting

The following list provides solution guidelines for the most common SCSI problems.

- Check for loose connectors and cables.
- Verify the location and number of the terminators.
- Ensure that the bus has at least one supplier of terminator power, especially with external terminators.
- Verify that no two devices share the same ID.
- Ensure that all external devices are powered on before system startup.
- Make a minimal bus configuration with as few devices as possible.
- Configure the host adapter to use slower bus speeds, if possible.

## 6.5 SCSI Compared to Parallel ATA/IDE

SCSI hard drive technology has been the industry standard because of its reliability and superior protocol features. HP provides unique values for SCSI hard drive technology, such as the following:

- Universal architecture
- Optimized firmware
- Superior testing and quality standards

Customers generally choose SCSI hard drive technology for its hot-plug capability in addition to higher data integrity, performance, and reliability.

ATA/IDE hard drive technology in server environments offers the lowest price per gigabyte and lowest power consumption per drive. It also provides the reliability needed in light-duty environments. ATA/IDE customers are looking for basic server functionality, such as static Web page delivery, entry-level file/print, or shared Internet access.

The following table lists the basic differences between parallel ATA and SCSI.

| Attributes | Parallel ATA | SCSI |
|---|---|---|
| Performance | 8ms seek times | 5ms seek times |
| Spindle speed | Up to 7,200 rpm | Up to 15,000 rpm |
| Transfer rate | 100MB/s | 160MB/s (Ultra 3) |
| Scalability | 2 drives per channel | 15 drives per channel |
| Maximum cable length | 19-inch parallel cable | 20 ft |
| Reliability (*mean time between failure*, MTBF) | 300—500K hours | 1M hours |
| Ability of service | Non-hot-pluggable | Hot-pluggable |
| Manufacturers warranty | 3-year | 3-year |
| Design power on hours (5-year life span) | 3,000h/year | 8760h/year |
| Design operating temperature | 35°C (95°F) | 55°C (131°F) |
| Generations per year (average) | 2 | 1 |
| Queuing | Allows only one transaction at a time | Allows multiple, simultaneous transactions |
| Disconnect/reconnect | No; transaction ties up the bus until complete | Yes; bus disconnects after request and reconnects when the data is available |

*Serial ATA reduces the gap between the ATA and SCSI interfaces.*

**6.6**

## Newer SCSI Technologies

SCSI technology is continuing to evolve. Two important new SCSI technologies are iSCSI and Serial SCSI.

### 6.6.1 iSCSI

Internet SCSI (iSCSI) is a new storage protocol for native Ethernet/TCP/IP storage networks. iSCSI transports storage blocks across networks and the Internet.

iSCSI is similar to Fibre Channel, but the data transmission differs. The SCSI storage protocol is layered on top of the IP protocol, which allows data to be sent over a network or the Internet.

HP uses iSCSI to extend a consolidated *storage area network* (SAN) and to enable IP tunneling to and from remote sites. This iSCSI tunneling will be an alternative to the remote site replication protocols currently being used.

During iSCSI tunneling, the following process occurs:

1. User or an application requests data, a file, or an application.
2. The SCSI commands and data request are processed by the operating system.
3. The commands are encapsulated or encrypted, and a packet header is added. These packets are then transmitted over an Ethernet connection.
4. The packet is received and disassembled or decrypted. The SCSI commands and requests are separated.
5. The SCSI commands and data are sent to the SCSI controller, then to the SCSI storage device.

Data can be returned in response to the request. iSCSI is bidirectional.

### 6.6.2 Serial SCSI

Serial SCSI is also known as *IEEE 1394*, the name of the standard, or as the Apple brand name *FireWire*. It is a high-performance serial bus and provides a versatile, high-speed, low-cost method of interconnecting a variety of computer peripherals, storage systems, and consumer electronics devices. Serial SCSI characteristics include the following:

- **Fast**—100, 200, or 400Mb/s; or 12.5, 25, or 50MB/s
- **Guaranteed**—Both isochronous and asynchronous transfers
- **Consumer-friendly**—Small connectors, hot-pluggable, auto ID, and auto termination
- **Expandable**—63 devices (16 daisy chained), 4.5m flexible cable

The IEEE 1394 serial bus is also

- **A digital interface**—There is no need to convert digital data into analog and tolerate a loss of data integrity.
- **Physically small**—The thin serial cable can replace larger and more expensive interfaces.
- **Hot-pluggable**—You can add or remove 1,394 devices with the bus active.
- **Inexpensive**—It is priced for consumer products.
- **Scalable**—Currently you can mix 100, 200, and 400Mb/s data rates on one bus, with an 800Mb/s and multi-GB/s upgrade path.
- **Flexible**—The topology supports daisy chaining and branching for true peer-to-peer communication.

### 6.6.2.1 SERIAL SCSI CABLES

Instead of a 68-wire cable, Serial SCSI uses a 6-wire cable, as shown in Figure 6–12.

**Figure 6–12**

*IEEE 1394 cable cross-section.*

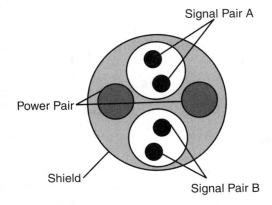

Signal Pair A

Power Pair

Shield

Signal Pair B

Because signal management using IEEE 1394 technology is limited to a single data line, it supports isochronous data transfer, which provides guaranteed data transport at a predetermined rate. Serial SCSI is ideal for multimedia I/O delivery, such as streaming video and audio.

### 6.6.3 Parallel/Serial SCSI Comparison

In a parallel SCSI interface, data is transmitted 8 or 16 bits at a time, in parallel. Serial SCSI transmits one bit at a time. The distinction between parallel and serial SCSI is similar to the difference between the serial and parallel ports.

The SCSI bus bandwidth is directly proportional to its width. The change from 8- or 16-bit data transfer widths to one bit at a time might seem like a step backward, but the dramatic increases in speed allowed by serial communication reverses this bandwidth loss.

Improved technology increases the demand for bandwidth. The demand for increased speed has driven the SCSI bus from the original, to Fast, then Ultra SCSI. However, each time a faster bus is created, it becomes more difficult to manage the complex signaling and prevent data corruption.

When you send signals across a parallel bus, there is no guarantee that they will all arrive at their destination at the same time. They might become scrambled on different signals because data transfer is asynchronous. Serial SCSI supports both asynchronous and isochronous data transfers.

Isochronous (guaranteed bandwidth) data transfer ensures that data flows at a preset rate so that an application can handle it in a timed way.

Single-ended parallel SCSI has certain restrictions that do not apply to serial SCSI:

- To ensure data integrity, the maximum cable length for single-ended SCSI decreases by half each time the signal speed doubles.
- The 20MHz of Ultra SCSI is the highest achievable transmission frequency using the older, single-ended bus.

## ▲ Summary

This chapter provided a detailed overview of the two main types of hard drive technologies currently used in industry-standard servers: ATA/IDE and SCSI.

The following key concepts explained in this chapter are critical for HP Accredited Integration Specialists to understand:

- The advantages and disadvantages of ATA/IDE
- The differences between ATA/IDE and SCSI
- The different versions of ATA/IDE
- The attributes of SCSI-1, SCSI-2, and SCSI-3, and the differences between the versions
- Compatibility between different SCSI protocols
- How SCSI addressing works, including device IDs and LUNs
- SCSI cables, connectors, and termination
- How to troubleshoot problems with SCSI devices

The next chapter introduces concepts relating to drive arrays.

## ▲ LEARNING CHECK

1. *Define ATA and IDA, and explain the differences.*

2. *What are the three major SCSI standards?*

3. *What is the main difference between a single-ended and differential SCSI interface?*

4. *Which one of the following terms identifies the process in which the controller agrees on a transfer rate with each connected device during the initialization phase?*

    A. Disconnect/reconnect

    B. Tagged command queuing

    C. Negotiation

    D. None of the above

5. *What is the purpose of tagged command queuing?*

6. *How many terminators should be on a SCSI bus and where should it/they be placed?*

7. *What are the three new features included with Wide-Ultra3 SCSI-3?*

# Disk Array Technologies

After studying this chapter, you should be able to:

- Define drive array and explain the concept of logical drives.
- Define RAID, list RAID benefits, and describe the key features and capabilities of RAID.
- Explain the differences between software- and hardware-based RAID.
- Explain the advantages that hardware-based RAID has over software-based RAID.
- Explain how RAID 0 works and list its advantages and disadvantages.
- Explain how RAID 1 works and list its advantages and disadvantages.
- Explain how RAID 1+0 works and list its advantages and disadvantages.
- Explain how RAID 3 works and list its advantages and disadvantages.
- Explain how RAID 5 works and list its advantages and disadvantages.
- Explain how RAID ADG works and list its advantages and disadvantages.
- Compare and contrast the current-industry RAID levels.

**147**

A drive array is a set of hard disk drives or physical drives grouped together as a single, larger drive. An array is comprised of one or more subsets called *logical drives* (or *logical volumes*) that are spread across all physical drives in the array.

## Drive Array Technologies

Operating systems address a logical drive as a single, contiguous storage space, although it is made up of several physical drives. Assembling drives together in an array quickly and reliably provides access to many gigabytes of data to users.

The advantages of a drive array implementation are as follows:

- Effective high-speed data transfer rates
- Ability to handle simultaneous multiple requests
- Increased storage capacity
- Flexibility in configuring data
- High reliability

Drive array technology can access data from multiple drives faster than from any one physical drive and enables the arrayed drives to service multiple requests simultaneously.

Drives within a drive array can have different sizes. All disks will adjust their size to the capacity of the smallest disk. The excess capacity of all larger drives is not accessible.

### 7.1.1 Number of Disks in an Array

You can increase the I/O bandwidth of an array by adding drives. This addition allows data to be read from or written to a large number of drives simultaneously.

Many customers buy a few large-capacity drives as opposed to a larger number of low-capacity drives because of cost and management concerns and because they do not understand performance implications. Performance can suffer when there are insufficient drive spindles.

The RAID level and the number of drives affect the available I/O bandwidth for a given disk configuration. You must have enough drives (regardless of the drive capacity) to sustain the I/O rates of the application.

## 7.1.2   *Logical Drives*

A logical drive is a subset of an array that is presented to the operating system as a single drive. The operating system cannot see the individual disks and assumes there is only one disk per logical drive.

An example is shown in Figure 7–1. This graphic shows that seven physical drives could be configured as one logical drive of 127GB (top right) or as three logical drives of 42.5GB each. (Other logical drive configurations would also be possible.)

Figure 7–2 shows a situation where three physical drives are configured as three logical drives, and each logical drive spans a portion of the physical drive.

Drives with different sizes, speeds, and SCSI protocols can be mixed within an array. The configuration might result in wasted space and performance degradation, but it will work.

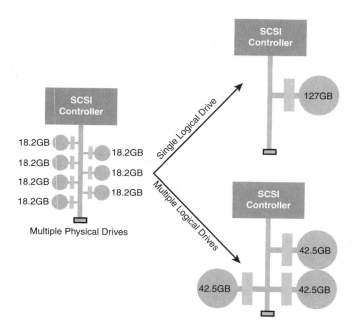

**Figure 7–1**   *Logical drive configurations of multiple physical drives.*

**Figure 7–2**
*Logical drives spanning physical drives.*

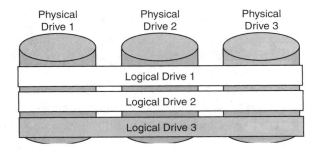

### 7.1.3   Drive Array Features

Drive arrays provide the following features:

- **Data striping across multiple drives**—A file is divided into a selected number of sectors and then written across a series of drives. The process of writing or reading a file across multiple drives is much faster than the same process on a single drive.

- **Multiple channels**—The drive array uses multiple channels simultaneously (depending on the controller used), thereby increasing performance.

- **Request processing**—Because multiple commands can be issued across multiple channels, all commands can be processed at the same time. The requests are processed in the most logical order using *tagged command queuing* (TCQ).

#### 7.1.3.1   TAGGED COMMAND QUEUING

TCQ allows a device to accept multiple commands from a host I/O controller and organize them for the most efficient operations on the disk drive. The host I/O controller and the device keep track of the I/O requests by using numbered tags.

TCQ offers better performance gains with randomly accessed I/O traffic. With sequentially accessed data, an implied sorting is already being applied so the performance gain will be minimum.

## 7.2   RAID Technology Overview

RAID is an acronym for redundant array of independent disks. RAID is a group of disk drives that the host system sees as a single large device. The purpose of RAID is to set up fault-tolerant and fast disk arrays.

RAID technology is based on the theory that a group of smaller drives is more efficient than one large drive. The basic premise of fault-tolerant RAID is that an intelligent drive controller, or manager, can handle a drive array so that it can withstand the failure of any individual drive in the array without losing data.

RAID storage offers major benefits over nonarrayed storage systems, including the following:

- **Performance**—The RAID system distributes data and I/O requests among all members of the drive array. Each drive in the array helps process the I/O requests, which increases concurrency and can increase overall performance.

Fault-tolerant RAID configurations incur a performance penalty based on how the fault tolerance is configured.

- **Data availability and reliability**—The RAID system enables you to employ a fault-tolerant configuration that duplicates portions or all of the stored data, protecting the information against loss because of a failed disk. Many RAID solutions can automatically recover from a disk failure, and often provide continuous I/O service to the hosting environment.

- **Dynamically increased storage capacity**—A RAID system can expand storage capacity well beyond the capacity of a single disk system. Many RAID solutions are dynamic, enabling you to add disks to expand the array.

- **Simplified storage management**—The RAID system combines many smaller disk drives into one or more virtual disks with the desired capacity, data availability, and performance. This allows management of mass storage consolidated into a single array.

## 7.2.1 JBOD

*Just a bunch of disks* (JBOD) is a storage option that connects one or more standalone disk drives to the RAID controller or other drive controller of a server. This option increases capacity and is used for noncritical business data.

The JBOD drive does not become part of a RAID array, but it is made available to the server on the same interconnect bus as the other devices controlled by the RAID controller. The JBOD disk drive has no data redundancy or striping.

## RAID Implementation

Two different levels of RAID technology exist: software-based RAID and hardware-based RAID.

In software-based RAID, the array management functions are implemented by software executing in a host environment, such as the operating system.

With hardware-based RAID, the array management functions are implemented by hardware and firmware within a RAID controller. The RAID controller orchestrates read and write activities in the same way a controller for a single disk drive does, and treats the array as if it were a single or virtual drive. This level is transparent to the host software and is self-contained within the storage solution. It does not interfere with the primary function of the host, which translates into higher overall performance and potential for advanced RAID capabilities.

Figure 7–3 contrasts software RAID and hardware RAID.

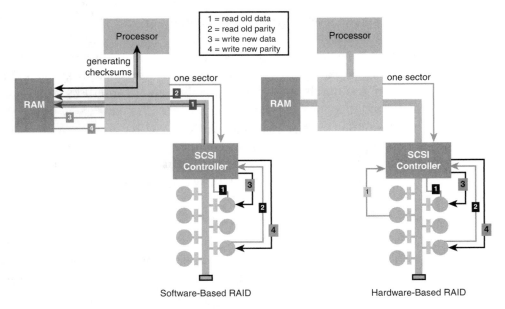

**Figure 7–3** *Software-based RAID vs. hardware-based RAID.*

**Note** The ability to use online spares is available with hardware-based **RAID**. Online spares are extra drives that are automatically brought online when a drive fails in a **RAID** set.

The advantages of software-based RAID are as follows:

- The ability to span multiple storage subsystems or even hosts
- Lower cost

The disadvantages of software-based RAID are as follows:

- Lower performance than hardware RAID
- No boot capability from RAID 5 protected arrays (Microsoft Windows)
- No support for RAID 1+0 or RAID ADG
- No support for RAID 5 support under Novell NetWare
- No support for PCI Hot Plug for RAID 5 protected arrays (Windows)
- No support for online spare drives
- Increased processor load
- Configuration utilities not user-friendly
- Operating system interface required when starting a rebuild

In a software RAID solution, each sector requires an extra transfer of three sectors across the I/O bus. This requires 256 transfers on the I/O bus. The memory bus and the processor bus also have to execute extra cycles for parity generation.

After a drive failure, a hardware protected RAID 5 logical drive is several times faster than a software-protected drive, due to the overhead of reconstructing data of the failed drive from the remaining drives.

In a hardware RAID solution, after the data has reached the array controller there is no extra activity on the I/O bus, the memory bus, or the frontside bus. All RAID-related activities are local to the array SCSI bus. For a single sector that is written to the disk, 64 transfers are executed on a 64-bit PCI bus.

The advantages of HP hardware-based RAID are as follows:

- Safe write caching through the array accelerator
- Superior manageability, such as multiple volumes with different RAID levels

- High flexibility such as separation of I/O into different disk volumes
- Hardware RAID, automatic recovery, PCI Hot Plug capability, and online spares
- Automatic data distribution and I/O balancing across multiple disk drives
- Superior performance and I/O optimization

## 7.3.1  Mean Time Between Failure

*Mean time between failure* (MTBF) is the expected time after the initial burn-in phase that it takes a hardware component to fail because of normal wear and tear. For disk drives, MTBF is calculated from the theoretical steady state failure rate from a large population of drives tested in volume manufacturing.

The actual individual drive MTBF depends on the drive usage and environmental conditions. Stressing a drive beyond normal usage can significantly reduce the predicted MTBF of the drive.

The MTBF of an array is equal to the MTBF of an individual drive divided by the number of drives in the array. The number lowers because there are more physical spindles that are subject to failure. This is a good reason to use RAID configurations that support fault tolerance.

> **EXAMPLE**
>
> If the MTBF of a single drive is 200,000 hours, the MTBF of an array with 5 similar drives is calculated as 200,000 divided by 5, for a total array MTBF of 40,000.

It is important to note that as the number of drives increases in a RAID configuration, the efficiency of the array increases but does not change the MTBF of each drive predicted by the drive manufacturer.

### 7.3.1.1  EXTENDING MTBF

To offset the increased probability of drive failure resulting from increasing the number of drives by using drive arrays, an online spare can be added to any of the fault-tolerant RAID levels. An online spare further decreases the probability of logical drive failure to about a thousandth of the previous level.

In addition, HP ProLiant servers provide full-spectrum fault management. ProLiant servers employ a unique set of high-availability technologies for handling faults and providing fault prevention, fault tolerance, and rapid recovery.

## 7.3.2 Striping Factor

Striping unites multiple physical drives into a single logical drive. The logical drive is arranged so that blocks of data are written alternately across all physical drives in the logical array. The number of sectors per block is referred to as the *striping factor.*

Depending on the array controller in use, the striping factor can be modified, usually with the manufacturer's system configuration utility. Many of the Smart Array controllers can be modified with the *Array Configuration Utility* (ACU).

## 7.3.3 RAID Levels

Industry-standard RAID levels are listed in the following table.

| Level | Description |
| --- | --- |
| RAID 0 | Data striping without parity |
| RAID 1 | Disk mirroring |
| RAID 1 | Disk duplexing |
| RAID 2 | Complex error correction |
| RAID 3 | Parallel-transfer, parity drive |
| RAID 4 | Concurrent access, dedicated parity drive (data guarding) |
| RAID 5 | Concurrent access, distributed parity (distributed data guarding) |
| RAID 1+0 | Disk mirroring and data striping without parity |
| RAID ADG | Distributed data guarding with two sets of parity |

**RAID levels 2 and 3 are no longer used in the industry.**

## RAID 0—Disk Striping

RAID 0 is not fault tolerant and is often used in situations that are not mission-critical, where performance and capacity are more important than uptime. RAID 0 is the only non-fault-tolerant RAID level supported by HP.

RAID 0 is illustrated in Figure 7–4.

RAID 0 is known as stripe sets because data is striped, or distributed, across all the drives in the array. Instead of filling each drive to capacity in sequential order, only a small amount of data, called a block or a chunk, is stored on each drive before allocation advances to the next drive. The size of each block (chunk size) is called the striping factor and the collection of blocks at the same location on each physical drive is called a stripe.

Data is broken into stripes (or chunks) and then written across multiple disks, greatly improving the disk latency (the time a disk head has to wait for the target sector to move under the head). In addition, 100% of the disk space is available for data and overall disk performance is improved.

By definition, RAID 0 requires two or more drives for a true stripe set. However, with Smart Array controllers, a RAID 0 logical volume can be created with a single drive.

Because RAID 0 has no overhead associated with duplication of information, it provides the highest performance. Both read and write requests can use all member disks simultaneously.

The limitations of RAID 0 include the following:

- Data striping is faster than conventional file writing to a single disk; however, there is no fault protection should a drive fail.

- When more drives are added to the array, the potential for logical drive failure rises.

**Figure 7–4**

*RAID 0.*

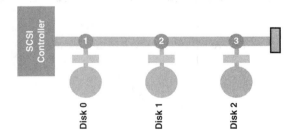

## RAID 1—Disk Mirroring

RAID 1 is used in mission-critical environments where performance and fault tolerance are a requirement for smaller data sets, such as system disks, root master files, and database journals.

The implementation of RAID 1 is shown in Figure 7–5.

### 7.5.1   Disk Mirroring

Disk mirroring uses two disk drives of identical size. Data is written to one drive and an exact copy is written on the second disk. If one drive fails, the mirrored drive ensures data is not lost and read-write operations continue to be served. As a result of the duplication of all data, available disk space is 50% of raw capacity.

All HP Smart Array controllers support hardware-based mirroring. Software-based mirroring does not require drives of identical size, but it does require operating system support. Data is written to partitions of equal size.

### 7.5.2   Disk Duplexing

Disk duplexing works like mirroring. However, disk duplexing uses two disk controllers rather than one, which increases fault tolerance. The logical drive is available even in the case of a controller failure. As a result of the duplication of all data, available disk space is 50% of raw capacity.

**Duplexing must be handled by the operating system. (This is also true for duplexed HP Smart Array controllers.)**

**Figure 7–5**

*RAID 1 implementation.*

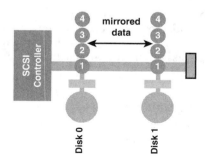

**Figure 7–6**

*Disk mirroring and disk duplexing.*

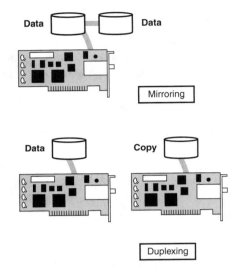

Disk mirroring and disk duplexing are illustrated in Figure 7–6.

### 7.5.3   RAID 1 Performance

In a multidisk configuration, RAID 1 mirrors each pair of disks to each other. These disk pairs can then be striped to create a virtual disk. RAID 1 can tolerate multiple disk failures if no two disks forming a mirrored pair fail. Some RAID implementations support *n*-way mirroring, where the original data is duplicated *n* times on *n* disks.

The performance in read environments is high, especially when the array controller takes advantage of split seeks (choosing one disk over the other based on lower seek times). RAID 1 incurs a slight write penalty caused by duplication of the write requests.

 The HP implementation of drive mirroring is accomplished with hardware. Drive mirroring also can be implemented in software at the operating system level. Software mirroring adds additional overhead to the processor and is often less efficient than hardware mirroring.

The limitation of RAID 1 is that it is an expensive solution because it requires twice as much drive storage to store duplicate data. Only 50% of the total disk space is available for data storage.

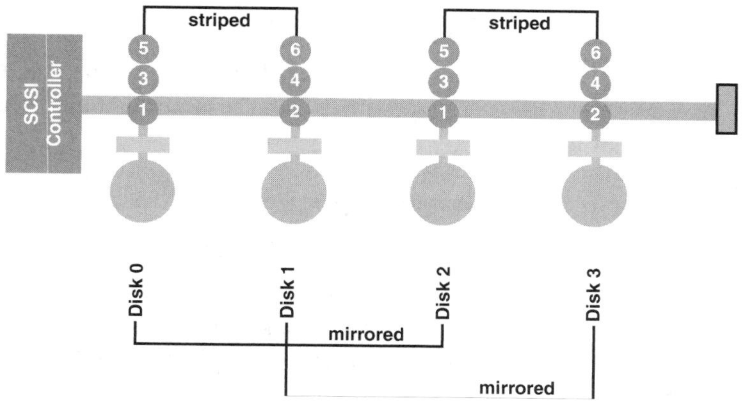

**Figure 7–7**   *RAID 1+0.*

**7.6**   ## RAID 1+0—Striped Mirror Sets

The most expensive of RAID configurations, RAID 1+0 combines RAID 1 mirroring with RAID 0 striping. The drives are first mirrored and then striped across the member disks. RAID 1+0 has good performance, no write penalties, and excellent redundancy.

RAID 1+0 is illustrated in Figure 7–7.

This array configuration can lose several disks as long as they do not belong to the same mirrored pair. If two disks in the same mirrored pair fail, the data is lost. This means that RAID 1+0 cannot guarantee protection against a two-disk failure.

RAID 1+0 process involves the following sequence:

1. Disk 0 is mirrored to disk 2.
2. Disk 1 is mirrored to disk 3.
3. Disk 0 and disk 1 are striped together.
4. Disk 2 and disk 3 are striped together.

In a RAID 1+0 configuration, all HP RAID controllers can

- Sustain multiple drive failures.
- Sustain an entire bus failure if the drives are equally distributed across buses.
- Service I/O requests to all operational drives in a degraded condition.
- Survive $n/2$ drive failures, where $n$ is the number of drives in the array, as long as one member of each mirrored pair survives.

### 7.6.1 RAID 1+0 Performance

Performance characteristics of RAID 1+0 are the same as RAID 1. RAID 1+0 can tolerate multiple disk failures as long as no two failed disks are mirrored to each other.

#### 7.6.1.1 READ PERFORMANCE

For read operations in a RAID 1+0, the disk controller can use only half of the disk drives because the other half contains the same information. This has a slight negative impact on performance compared to RAID 0. The number of disk drives (spindles) available for read request processing is reduced by 50%.

This negative impact on read performance is offset in the process of reading data from the drives; the requested data nearest to the read/write heads will be read.

#### 7.6.1.2 WRITE PERFORMANCE

For write operations, the disk controller must generate the same write request twice. The same data must be written to both sets of mirrored disk drives causing the array controller to perform twice as many write operations, which generates a substantial amount of overhead.

## 7.7   RAID 2—Data Sector Striping with ECC

RAID 2 arrays stripe data across groups of drives, with some drives relegated to storing error checking and correcting (ECC) information. Because most hard drives now embed ECC information within each sector, RAID 2 offers no significant advantages over RAID 3.

**RAID 2 is an outdated technology and is not supported by HP.**

## RAID 3—Parity Check

RAID 3 leverages the basic organization of RAID 0, but adds an additional disk to the stripe width to hold the parity data. Like RAID 0, RAID 3 divides the data into stripes and the parity disk contains corresponding blocks that contain the computed parity for the data blocks on each member of the stripe unit, as shown in Figure 7–8.

RAID 3 handles large quantities of sequential I/O at a relatively low cost. Bulk I/O is normally requested in large increments and RAID 3 performance is maximized for sequential I/O. RAID 3 has been popular in the supercomputing arena.

However, RAID 3 does not work well for random access I/O, including most database management system workloads. Random access suffers under RAID 3 because of the physical organization of a RAID 3 stripe—every write to a RAID 3 volume involves accessing the parity disk. RAID 3 uses only one parity disk and it becomes the bottleneck for the entire volume.

**HP does not support RAID 3, because the clock circuit synchronizes the platter/spindles and because each drive is on a dedicated bus to the controller (multiple chips, one per SCSI bus).**

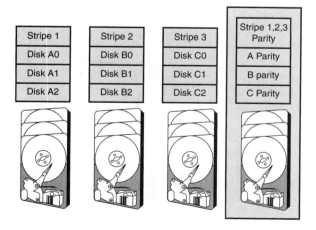

**Figure 7–8**  *Effects of RAID 3 on performance.*

## RAID 4—Data Guarding

RAID 4 uses data striping in combination with a dedicated parity drive, as shown in Figure 7–9. Three or more disks are required for a RAID 4 disk set.

If one drive fails, data from the failed disk can be reconstructed from the other drives in the array. Because only one drive is used for storing checksums, available disk space is higher than with mirroring. The more disks there are in the logical drive, the better the performance, because all drives can be accessed individually. Several operations (even mixed read and write operations) can take place at the same time. RAID 4 stores parity information for each data stripe on a single disk. RAID 4 can tolerate only a single disk failure.

**RAID 4 drives can share the same bus.**

**Because RAID 4 can tolerate the failure of one drive without losing data, it is considered fault tolerant. RAID 4 can support RAID memory.**

**Figure 7–9**

*RAID 4—data guarding.*

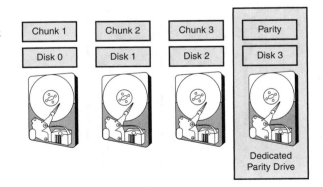

### 7.9.1  RAID 4 Limitations

In write-intensive environments, the parity update operations are serialized to a single disk. Because every write operation requires that data be written to the parity disk, this disk can become a performance bottleneck. Consequently, the use of RAID 4 has rapidly declined.

**7.10**

## RAID 5—Distributed Data Guarding

RAID 5 distributed data guarding, also referred to as stripe sets with parity, breaks data up in chunks, calculates parity, and then writes the data chunks in "stripes" to the disk drives, saving one stripe on each drive for the parity data. The total amount of disk space used for redundancy (parity data) is equivalent to the capacity of a single drive.

RAID 5 distributes the parity information among all disk members. By doing so, it eliminates the performance bottleneck at the parity disk, and if one drive fails, the failed disk can be re-created after it is replaced. This is illustrated in Figure 7–10.

RAID 5 is based on the RAID 4 principle of generating new checksums when write operations occur. Unlike RAID 4, parity data is not stored on a dedicated drive but is distributed evenly across all drives.

RAID 5 requires a minimum of three drives. Available disk space is the sum of the size of all disks minus the size of one disk. Five 9GB disks produce a logical drive size of $(5 - 1)$ times 9GB, which is 36GB.

A disadvantage of RAID 5 is that only a single drive can fail at one time without loss of data. If a second drive fails, before the failed drive has been replaced and recovered, the data will be lost.

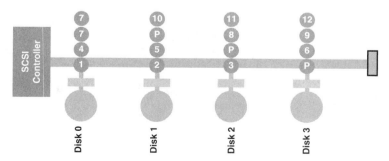

**Figure 7–10**  *RAID 5—distributed data guarding.*

## 7.10.1 RAID 5 Performance

RAID 5 is the most cost-effective of the fault-tolerant RAID solutions, but is slower in performance than RAID 1+0 and loses additional performance when a member disk is missing.

RAID 5 performs well in environments where the I/O profile consists predominately of read requests. Read operations can occur in parallel and because of distributed parity, all drives are available to service read operations. RAID 5 is often used in database transaction processing and multiuser file services environments.

Because the array controller needs to perform an average of four I/O operations for each write request, RAID 5 has a write overhead penalty that slows the overall performance of the system. For multiple write operations, parity updates can occur in parallel because of the interleaved parity.

These four I/O operations, illustrated in Figure 7–11, are as follows:

1. The controller must read the old data block (the data block that is about to be overwritten).
2. The controller must read the old parity block. (This parity block must be updated to reflect the new data.)
3. The controller must recalculate and write the new parity information.
4. The controller must write the new data block.

**Figure 7–11**

*RAID 5—I/O operations.*

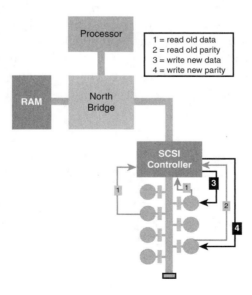

Where RAID 1 mirroring requires a 100% increase in capacity to protect the data, RAID 5 requires as little as 50% (2 + 1), and commonly only 20% (5 + 1). The larger the RAID 5 set, the more burdensome it is to manage and the more readily performance could suffer.

## 7.11    RAID AD—Advanced Data Guarding

RAID advanced data guarding (ADG) delivers high fault tolerance similar to RAID 1, but keeps capacity utilization high, as with RAID 5. It protects data from multiple drive failures with an ability to withstand two simultaneous hard drive failures without data loss or downtime.

RAID ADG uses two sets of parity striped across the disks, as shown in Figure 7–12. This method results in protection for an array with as many as 56 drives and requires the capacity of only two drives to store parity information.

### 7.11.1    RAID ADG Performance

ADG employs two independent parity schemes. Two sets of parities must be modified for each logical write operation, which requires six physical transfers—three reads and three writes.

After the existing data and both sets of parity are read from the physical drives, each set of parity is modified by operating on the existing data, the data to be written, and the old parity. The new data and both sets of modified parity data are then written to the physical drives.

Although RAID ADG provides the dual advantages of increased fault tolerance and high capacity, it does so at the cost of performance that is less than that of other RAID levels.

Performance equals that for RAID 5 when reading data, but is slower when writing because of the extra parity data.

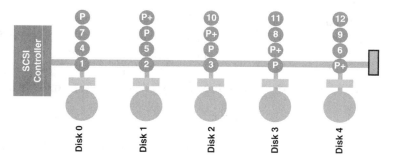

**Figure 7–12**    *RAID ADG.*

### 7.11.2 When to Use RAID ADG

RAID ADG delivers high fault tolerance similar to RAID 1+0, but keeps capacity utilization high, as in RAID 5. This higher level of protection is ideal where large logical volumes are required.

Advantages of ADG include the following:

- It safely protects an array of up to 56 total drives; extensibility increases the number of parity drives to provide greater fault tolerance.
- It can tolerate two simultaneous drive failures without downtime or data loss.
- It has greater fault tolerance than RAID 4, RAID 1+0, or RAID 5.
- It offers lower implementation cost than RAID 1 or RAID 1+0.
- It supports online spare drives.
- It supports online RAID level migration from RAID 1, RAID 1+0, or RAID 5.
- It is ideal for applications requiring large logical drives with many physical drives.

RAID ADG is best implemented under the following criteria:

- When protecting mission-critical data
- When greater capacity utilization is needed
- For applications requiring larger storage volumes
- When better capacity than RAID 1 or RAID 1+0 is needed
- When higher fault tolerance than RAID 1, RAID 1+0, or RAID 5 is necessary

### 7.11.3 HP ADG Support

For ADG support on a ProLiant server, use the HP Smart Array 5304/128 controller with at least four disk drives, or use the HP Smart Array 5302 controller with a minimum of 64MB cache and the ADG upgrade kit.

HP recommends RAID ADG or RAID 1+0 for more than 8 disks. RAID 5 is recommended for up to 8 disks (maximum of 14).

### 7.11.4 RAID ADG Fault-Tolerance Comparison

Figure 7–13 shows the relative probability of logical drive failure for different RAID settings and different logical drive sizes, assuming no online spares are present.

**Figure 7–13**

*Logical drive failure probability for different RAID configurations.*

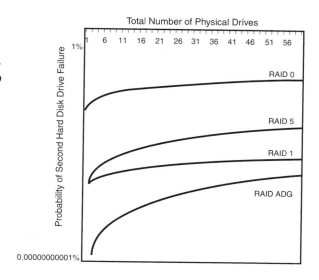

With growing numbers of individual disk drives needed in a single logical volume on a single controller, RAID ADG provides higher data reliability and has a superior fault tolerance when compared to RAID 5 or RAID 1.

With RAID 0, the logical drive fails if one physical drive fails.

With RAID 5, the logical drive fails if two physical drives fail.

With RAID 1 or 1+0, the maximum number of hard drives that can fail without failure of the logical dive is *n*/2. However, a RAID 1+0 logical drive fails if only two hard drives fail, if they are mirrored to each other.

With RAID ADG, three hard drives must fail before data loss is incurred.

For RAID 5, HP recommends that no more than 14 (8 is optimal) physical drives be used per logical drive. However, logical drive failure is much less likely with RAID ADG, and HP supports the use of up to 56 physical drives per drive array when running this fault-tolerance method.

## 7.12 RAID Level Performance Comparison

Figure 7–14 shows a decision tree to assist you in selecting the right level of RAID for your situation.

### 7.12.1 RAID 0

RAID 0 shows the best overall performance. However, all data is lost if a single drive in the array fails. No storage space is required for fault tolerance.

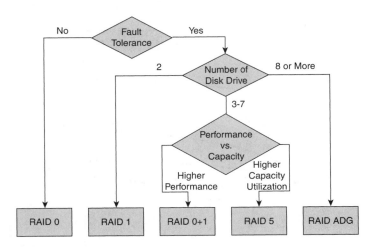

**Figure 7–14** *RAID level decision tree.*

RAID 0 should not be used in servers. RAID 0 can make sense in workstations that require fast disk access. Data should be backed up as often as possible.

### 7.12.2 RAID 1 and RAID 1+0

RAID 1 or RAID 1+0 is tolerant of multiple drive failures when more than two disks are configured for an array. It uses the most storage capacity for fault tolerance of all the RAID levels. RAID 1 or RAID 1+0 has a higher write performance than RAID 5.

### 7.12.3 RAID 4

RAID 4 should not be used because RAID 5 is faster for reads and writes and offers the same available space and fault tolerance. RAID 4 is supported only in later Smart Array controllers if migrated from older controllers supporting RAID 4.

### 7.12.4 RAID 5

RAID 5 can handle a single drive failure and uses the least amount of storage capacity for fault tolerance. The read performance is almost as good as with RAID 0 and RAID 1. The write performance, however, is usually lower than RAID 1 write performance.

## 7.12.5   RAID ADG

RAID ADG delivers high fault tolerance similar to RAID 1, but keeps capacity utilization high as with RAID 5. RAID ADG protects data from multiple drive failures, but only requires the capacity of two drives to store parity information. This higher level of protection is ideal where large logical volumes, with a large number of physical drives, are required.

## 7.12.6   RAID Failed Drive Recovery Time

When a drive fails, the data recovery time is influenced by the following factors:

- Type and size of the drive
- RAID level
- Workload on the system
- Controller type
- HP Smart Array Accelerator setting
- HP Smart Array drive-recovery priority level

If the system is in use during the drive rebuild, recovery time can depend on the level of activity. Most systems should recover in nearly the same amount of time with moderate activity as they would with no load. RAID 1 implementations would be only marginally affected. RAID 5 is much more sensitive to system load during the recovery period because of the considerably heavier I/O requirements of the failed system.

> **! IMPORTANT**
>
> If you are running a mission-critical application that cannot tolerate any outages caused by disk failures, consider using online spare drives supported by HP Smart Array controllers. An online spare is a drive the controller uses when a drive failure occurs. If a drive fails, the controller rebuilds the data that was on the failed drive on the online spare. The controller also sends data that it would normally store on the failed drive directly to the online spare.

## 7.12.7   Optimizing the Stripe Size

Selecting the appropriate stripe (chunk) size is crucial to achieving optimum performance within an array. The stripe size is the amount of data that is read or written to each disk in the array as data requests are processed by the array controller.

> The terms *chunk, block,* and *segment* are used interchangeably. Chunk is used more often when discussing storage.

The following table lists the available stripe sizes and their characteristics.

| Fault-Tolerance Method | Available Stripe Sizes (KB) | Default Size (KB) |
|---|---|---|
| RAID 0 | 128, 256 | 128 |
| RAID 1 or 1+0 | 8, 16, 32, 64, 128, 256 | 128 |
| RAID 5 or RAID ADG | 8, 16, 32, 64 | 16 |

The default stripe size gives good performance in most circumstances. When high performance is important, you may need to modify the stripe size.

Using the incorrect stripe size can have one of two negative impacts. If too large, there will be poor load balancing across the drives. If too small, there will be a lot of cross-stripe transfers (split I/Os) and performance will be reduced.

Split I/Os involve two disks; both disks seek, rotate, and transfer data. The response time depends on the slowest disk. Split I/Os reduce the request rate because there are fewer drives to service incoming requests.

| Type of Server Application | Suggested Stripe-Size Change |
|---|---|
| Mixed read/write | Accept the default value. |
| Mainly read (such as database or Internet applications) | Larger stripe sizes work best. |
| Mainly write (such as image manipulation applications) | Smaller stripes for RAID 5, RAID ADG. Larger stripes for RAID 0, RAID 1, RAID 1+0. |

## ▲ Summary

Understanding of disk array technologies is a critical skill for an AIS. This chapter explained the following critical topics with which you should be very familiar in preparation for the AIS exam:

- The advantages of a drive array implementation.
- The various RAID levels, how they differ one from another, and the situations in which each level is best implemented.
- How performance varies, depending on which level of RAID is selected.
- RAID levels supported by HP.

The next chapter introduces concepts relating to Fibre Channel technologies.

## ▲ LEARNING CHECK

1. *What are four major benefits of RAID storage that are offered over nonar-rayed storage systems?*

2. *What are the two major types of RAID implementations?*

3. *Which RAID level obtains the highest read and write operations?*

4. *Which features are supported by hot-pluggable hard drives? (Select three.)*
    A. Replacement of a failed drive in a fault-tolerant array
    B. Addition of drives and arrays
    C. Expansion of arrays
    D. Replacement of an array controller when the machine is online

5. *RAID 1 is considered to be an inexpensive solution providing complete fault tolerance.*
    ❏ True
    ❏ False

6. *RAID ADG will support how many simultaneous drive failures without loss of data?*

# Introduction to Fibre Channel

After reading this chapter, you should be able to do the following:

- Explain the core concepts and architectural features behind Fibre Channel.

- List and describe the benefits of Fibre Channel.

- Define the terminology of the Fibre Channel architecture.

- Diagram how Fibre Channel connects server components together and explain the function of each component, including host bus adapters, gigabit interface converters, gigabit link modules, array controllers, hubs, switches, tape libraries, and cables.

- Describe each of the three main Fibre Channel topologies—point to point, FC-AL, and FC-SW.

- Describe Fibre Channel Asynchronous Transfer Mode.

- Describe IP over Fibre Channel.

**173**

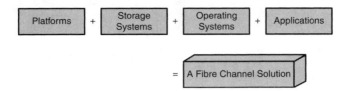

**Figure 8–1**  *StorageWorks Fibre Channel solution.*

Fibre Channel is an integrated set of standards developed by the *American National Standards Institute* (ANSI). Fibre Channel technology is an industry-standard interconnect serial data transfer architecture that delivers a high level of reliability, throughput, and distance flexibility for the server industry.

Fibre Channel uses fiber optics to provide an interconnection scheme among devices. It enables rapid delivery of large amounts of data by supporting high-performance protocols, such as *Fiber Distributed Data Interface* (FDDI) and *Small Computer System Interface* (SCSI).

As shown in Figure 8–1, a complete Fibre Channel solution includes hardware platforms, storage systems, operating systems, and applications.

A Fibre Channel solution is hardware-intensive and operates among only a few devices with predefined addresses. Data communication on a Fibre Channel system occurs over a direct or switched point-to-point connection between the communicating devices. As a result, Fibre Channel systems transport data at a high speed with low overhead.

In comparison, computer networks handle a more extensive range of tasks than Fibre Channel systems because the operating system translates and converts data across several layers of the network. Because a network is software-intensive, it has a relatively high overhead.

## 8.1    Fibre Channel Benefits

Fibre Channel provides benefits in performance, availability, scalability, flexibility, and distance between nodes.

### 8.1.1    Performance

The current Fibre Channel throughput standard is 100MB/s net user payload. ANSI has defined Fibre Channel throughput standards for 200MB/s and 400MB/s.

Fibre Channel technology provides the fundamental building blocks of *storage area networks* (SANs), *Enterprise Network Storage Architecture* (ENSA), and many high-availability and clustering implementations.

> **Note**
>
> These rates are for half-duplex transmission. Full-duplex transmission doubles throughput.

### 8.1.2 Availability

Fibre Channel also provides the following availability advantages:

- Hot-swappable support
- Built-in robustness (error detection and correction through the 8-bit/10-bit encoding/decoding), which allows for inexpensive implementation and low protocol overhead
- Wide industry support

### 8.1.3 Scalability

Fibre Channel technology enhances scalability by providing the following:

- Increased storage capacity per expansion slot
- 126 nodes on a *Fibre Channel arbitrated loop* (FC-AL)
- 16 million nodes on a *Fibre Channel switched fabric* (FC-SW)

### 8.1.4 Flexibility

Fibre Channel technology greatly enhances flexibility by providing the following advantages:

- Protocol independence
- Flexible wiring and small connectors
- No bus termination necessary
- Multiple topologies (point to point, arbitrated loop, and switched fabric)
- Unification of networking and I/O channel data communications
- Flexible transmission service
- Dedicated bandwidth
- Multiplexed transmission with multiple source or destination ports with acknowledgment
- Best-effort multiplexed datagram transmission without acknowledgment

### 8.1.5 Distance

Fibre Channel provides the following:

- 30m between nodes with copper cabling
- 500m between nodes with multimode cabling and shortwave lasers
- 10km between nodes with single-mode cabling and longwave lasers (Enhancements currently under development or already available can increase this distance.)

For more information on Fibre Channel standards, access the Fibre Channel Industry Association Web site at http://www.fibrechannel.org.

## 8.2 Fibre Channel Terminology

To fully understand the methods employed by Fibre Channel technology, a solid comprehension of the most common Fibre Channel terms is essential. Following are the key terms with which you need to be familiar:

- **Node**—Fibre Channel devices are called nodes. A node can be a computer (host), adapter, or any device containing one or more Fibre Channel ports.
- **Node ID**—The node ID is a unique identifier for a node.
- **Port**—Each node must have at least one port to provide access to other devices if it is connected to a Fibre Channel topology. The port on the node is known as an *N_port*. In the port-naming convention, *N* designates node, *L* designates loop, and *F* designates fabric. The Fibre Channel port names, types, topologies, and descriptions are listed in the following table.

| Port | Type | Topology | Description |
|------|------|----------|-------------|
| N_port | Node | Point to point or fabric | The port on a specific node |
| NL_port | Node | Arbitrated loop | The node connected to an arbitrated loop |
| F_port | Fabric | Switched fabric | The fabric port |
| FL_port | Fabric | Switched fabric | The fabric connected to an arbitrated loop |
| L_port | Loop | Arbitrated loop | The hub port on an arbitrated loop |

- **Link**—Each Fibre Channel port uses a pair of optical fibers. One of the fibers carries information into the receiver port; the other fiber carries information out of the transmitter port. This pair of fibers is called a *link*.

- **Topology**—A Fibre Channel topology is an interconnection scheme that connects two or more Fibre Channel N_ports. The three Fibre Channel topologies are point to point, FC-AL, and FC-SW.

For more information on Fibre Channel technology, review A. F. Benner's book *Fibre Channel: Gigabit Communication and I/O for Computer Networks*.

## 8.3   Fibre Channel Hardware Components

As shown in Figure 8–2, the hardware components of a Fibre Channel implementation can include the following:

- Host bus adapters (HBAs)
- Gigabit interface converters (GBICs)
- Gigabit link modules (GLMs)

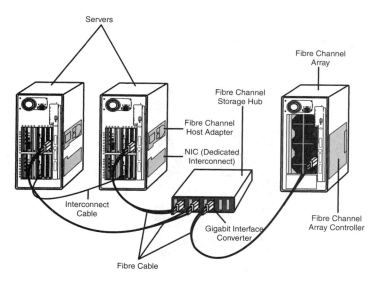

**Figure 8–2**   *RA4X00 configuration.*

- Storage and Fibre Channel drive arrays
- Fibre Channel array controllers
- Fibre Channel hubs and switches
- Tape libraries
- Fibre Channel cables

### 8.3.1   Host Bus Adapters

A *Fibre Channel host bus adapter* (HBA), shown in Figure 8–3, translates SCSI commands into serial data that can then be converted to light by GBICs. A GBIC is a transceiver that converts serial electrical signals to and from serial optical signals. In a network, a GBIC is used to transmit data across Fibre Channel media.

Most Fibre Channel HBAs use GBICs or GLMs. Like GBICs, GLMs convert electrical signals to and from optical signals, but they also convert serial signals to and from parallel signals.

A typical HBA uses the PCI bus, which in turn uses a highly integrated *application-specific integrated circuit* (ASIC) for processing the Fibre Channel protocol and managing the I/O with the host.

Each server can have one or two HBAs. The number of HBAs that can be configured in each node limits the maximum number of storage arrays.

**Figure 8–3**

*Fibre Channel host bus adapters.*

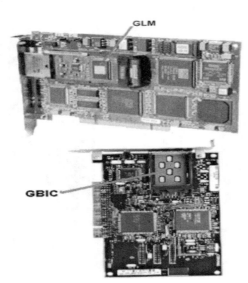

The operating system detects the HBA as a SCSI controller, not as a Fibre Channel *network interface card* (NIC). Therefore, it should be configured using the operating system, just as other SCSI controller cards are configured.

### 8.3.2 Gigabit Interface Converters

The GBIC translates the electrical impulse into the optical signal used with the fiber-optic medium. It contains a device that emits an optical signal used for transmission along the fiber-optic cable.

Each Fibre Channel link requires two GBICs, one at each end of the fiber-optic cable, as shown in Figure 8–4.

The GBIC module installs in a special receptacle on the following components:

- HBA
- Fibre Channel controller
- Fibre Channel storage hub
- Fibre Channel switch

The GBICs have two channels, one for each optical fiber within the cable (link). Therefore, each GBIC module is a full-duplex transmission device.

**Figure 8–4**

*GBICs attached to a fiber-optic cable.*

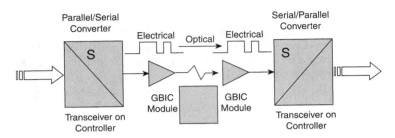

**Figure 8–5** *How GBICs work.*

### 8.3.2.1 HOW GBICS WORK

A GBIC converts serial electrical signals to and from serial optical signals for transmission of data across the Fibre Channel media.

When using Fibre Channel as the communication medium, the signal must go through two types of conversion: parallel to serial, and electrical to optical.

With parallel to serial, the parallel signals generated by the host or the target storage device must be converted into serial (Fibre Channel) signals.

With electrical to optical, the electrical signal generated by the host or the target storage device must also be converted into an optical signal used by the optical Fibre Channel medium.

### 8.3.2.2 GBIC SHORTWAVE

*GBIC shortwave* (GBIC-SW) is a shortwave version of the GBIC module that supports the multimode fiber. The following table shows the GBIC-SW specifications.

| Feature | Details |
| --- | --- |
| Compliance | Fibre Channel FC-PH-2 physical layer option 100-M5-SN-I |
| Baud rate | 1062.5MB/s |
| Fiber shortwave | 50µm diameter (preferred) or 62.5µm multimode fiber |
| Laser wavelength | 780nm (non-OFC) |
| Optical connector interface | Dual SC |
| Distance | 50m: 2 through 300m per link (International) 62.5m: 2 through 500m per link (North America) |

### 8.3.2.3 GBIC LONGWAVE

*GBIC longwave* (GBIC-LW) is a longwave version of the GBIC module that supports the single-mode fiber. GBIC-LWs have the following specifications.

| Feature | Details |
| --- | --- |
| Compliance | Fibre Channel FC-PH-2 physical layer option 100-M5-SN-I |
| Baud rate | 1062.5MB/s |
| Fiber longwave | 9μm single-mode fiber |
| Laser wavelength | 1250nm |
| Optical connector interface | Dual SC |
| Distance | 10km per link (maximizes cable length per FC-AL to 25km) |

### 8.3.3   Gigabit Link Modules

*Gigabit link modules,* or GLMs, are highly integrated fiber-optic transceivers that provide high-speed, bidirectional continuous throughput. They are similar to GBICs because they convert electrical signals to and from optical signals. However, GLMs also convert serial signals to and from parallel signals. Figure 8–6 shows a typical GLM.

One GLM at each end of a point-to-point duplex configuration plugs into a host card such as an HBA or a Fibre Channel hub or switch. The 64-bit/33MHz HBAs use GLMs rather than GBICs.

Either single-mode or multimode Fibre Channel SC duplex connectors can be inserted into the ports of the GLM.

Like GBICs, GLMs are available in both longwave and shortwave configurations.

**Figure 8–6**   *Gigabit link module.*

### 8.3.4 Fibre Channel Hubs

Hubs link individual elements together to form a loop with shared bandwidth. They share the following characteristics:

- Enable the connection of multiple arrays to a single host adapter, which greatly increases the amount of storage available to the server
- Interconnect loop devices in a physical star topology, in which all workstations are networked to a central computer, providing more convenient wiring and cable management
- Integrate easily and are relatively low in cost
- Implement an FC-AL topology
- Provide connection to a shared 100MB/s FC-AL (half duplex between servers and disks, all sharing bandwidth)
- Provide more complex error recovery because of loop initializations
- Detect all traffic that passes between other nodes

Hubs perform several functions:

- Provide support for single-mode or multimode optical cables
- Enable hot-swapping of cable interconnects for service or repair
- Provide increased fault isolation in case of a cable or node failure
- Provide failure status and traffic monitoring capability
- Enable implementation of a SAN

### 8.3.5 Fibre Channel Switches

A switch interconnects multiple nodes. A network of switches in a Fibre Channel environment, which can include as many as 16 million nodes, is referred to as a *fabric*. Nodes connect to this fabric to access other nodes.

A switch typically uses packet switching. The switch divides each message into small sections called *packets* and adds the network address of the sender and destination to each packet. The packets can take any route to the destination and are reassembled for delivery.

The primary function of a switch is to receive frames from a source node and route them to a destination node. Each node has a unique Fibre Channel address, which the switch uses to route frames. The switch relieves each individual port of the responsibility for station management. Each node manages only a simple point-to-point connection between itself and the switch. Nodes can be servers, storage devices, or another device that communicates through the network.

Here are some key points to remember about a Fibre Channel switch:

- A switch implements FC-SW.
- It provides support for optical cables as long as 500m (10km with long-wave GBICs).
- It enables hot-swapping of cable interconnects for service or repair.
- It provides increased fault isolation in case of a cable or node failure.
- It enables implementation of a storage network through Fibre Channel technology.
- A switch can cascade and make large topologies.
- A switch uses *Simple Network Management Protocol* (SNMP) for management and control.
- It provides a full-duplex 100MB/s point-to-point connection to the Fibre Channel fabric, allowing the servers to use loops (results in improved scaling of loops for optimized performance).
- It isolates individual nodes from the reconfiguration and error recovery of other nodes within the fabric.
- It has built-in intelligence.
- It offers room for growth.
- It provides multiple methods for switch management.

### 8.3.5.1 FIBRE CHANNEL SWITCH ZONING

Zoning is a method of segregating storage I/O traffic between groups of servers and their associated storage subsystems.

The zoning types are as follows:

- **Soft zoning**—The Fibre Channel switch provides filtering to mask ports belonging to a zone from ports that do not belong to a zone.
- **Hard zoning**—Hard zoning is hardware implemented and physically blocks access to the zone from outside nodes.
- **Port zoning**—Often port zoning and hard zoning are considered to be the same. However, port zoning is a software implementation that allows unauthorized external access.
- **Broadcast zoning**—Broadcast zoning filters broadcast messages so that they are not sent to specified ports.

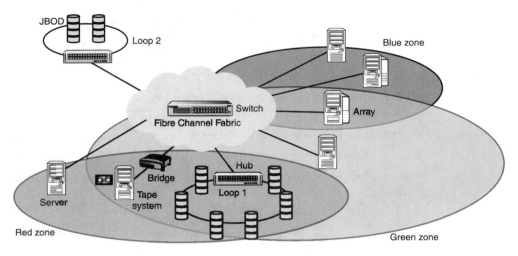

**Figure 8–7** *Fibre Channel switch zoning.*

Each zone has a member list consisting of one or more zone members. Members of a zone can be specified through node *World Wide Name* (WWN), port WWN, or switch domain ID and port number. A Fibre Channel switch-zoning configuration is shown in Figure 8–7.

A device can be a member of multiple zones. However, when zoning has been enabled, every device in the fabric must be part of a zone or zones.

When zoning has been implemented in a SAN, the zoning information will need to be changed each time a server or storage subsystem is added or removed. HBA replacement also requires a zoning information update.

### 8.3.6   Comparing Hubs and Switches

Until recently, hubs have been the entry-level devices for connectivity because they are relatively low in cost and simple to integrate.

Switches are just as easy to install as hubs, but offer superior connectivity. Fibre Channel switches provide scalable systems of almost any size, unlike hubs that have a 127-node limit. Figure 8–8 shows placement of hubs and switches.

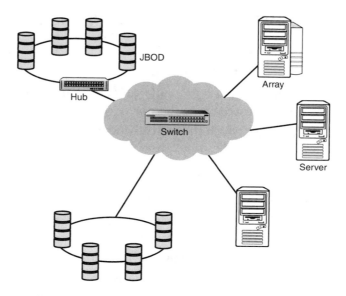

**Figure 8–8** *Placement of Fibre Channel hubs and switches.*

The following table compares the use of hubs and switches in Fibre Channel networks.

| Hubs | Switches |
| --- | --- |
| Implement an FC-AL topology with shared bandwidth among all devices. | Implement an FC-SW topology, with ports for either fabric devices or arbitrated loop devices. |
| Provide connection to a shared 100MB/s FC-AL, single 100MB transfer at a time. | Provide 100MB/s point-to-point connection between devices, multiple 100MB transfers at a time, no multiple device arbitration time. |
| Performance decreases as nodes are added because of additional arbitration time. | No performance reduction as additional nodes are added. |
| Nodes on the Fibre Channel loop see all traffic going between other nodes. | Nodes on the Fabric Channel detect only data destined for themselves. |
| More complex error recovery because of loop initializations. | Individual nodes are isolated from reconfiguration and error recovery of other nodes within the SAN. |
| More chances for traffic disruption on reconfiguration and errors because of loop initializations. | Fewer chances for traffic disruption on reconfiguration and errors because control features manage loop initialization events. |
| HP 12-port hubs have optional management. | Provide management control of the Fibre Channel infrastructure. |
| Seven-step *loop initialization process* (LIP). If a device encounters an error, it initiates a LIP. Loop is unavailable for data transfer during the error recovery. | Provide greater stability during error recovery. |

### 8.3.7 Guidelines for Choosing Between Switches and Hubs

Use hubs in the following situations:

- Applications with one to four servers
- Cost-sensitive Microsoft Windows 2000 applications with a homogeneous platform and operating system environment
- Applications in which the shared bandwidth of an arbitrated loop configuration is not a limiting factor

Use switches in these situations:

- Applications with more than four servers
- Multinode cluster configurations in which traffic disruption because of reconfiguration or repair is a concern
- "Clusterlike" configurations in which expansion is anticipated
- Heterogeneous platform and operating system applications
- High-bandwidth applications in which a shared arbitrated loop topology is not adequate

## 8.4  Fibre Channel Cabling and Cable Concepts

The Fibre Channel specification allows for two types of cabling: copper fiber and optical fiber.

Copper fiber is typically used for shorter distances measured in meters (as opposed to kilometers). Copper fiber uses electrical pulses rather than light and is less expensive than optical fiber.

> **! IMPORTANT**
>
> HP does not support copper cable. Current HP Fibre Channel implementations use fiber optic cabling.

Optical fiber cable is composed of two active elements, the core and the cladding, as shown in Figure 8–9.

The core is the inner, light-carrying member. It carries about 80% of the light. The cladding is the middle layer. It confines the light to the core because it has a higher reflective index than the core.

The outer layer of the optical fiber is known as the buffer or coating. It serves as a shock absorber to protect the core and cladding from damage.

Optical fiber can be either single-mode or multimode. The main distinction between single-mode fiber and multimode fiber is the physical diameter of the core.

### 8.4.1  Single-Mode Optic Fiber

Single-mode fiber has the highest bandwidth and lowest loss performance. The core is so small that only a single mode of light can enter it. Therefore, the chromatic and modal dispersion are greatly reduced or eliminated. Single-mode fiber is shown in Figure 8–10.

The information-carrying capabilities of the single-mode fiber are infinite. Single-mode fiber supports speed of tens of gigabits per second and can carry many gigabit channels simultaneously. Each channel carries a different wavelength of light without any interference.

Single-mode fiber is the preferred medium for long-distance telecommunications. It is also useful in networks for interbuilding runs and high-speed backbones. Applications for single-mode fiber to the desk are not anticipated.

**Figure 8–9**

*Optical fiber components.*

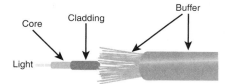

**Figure 8–10**

*Single-mode fiber.*

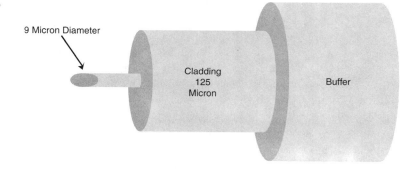

Networking and data communications use a single-mode step-index fiber to carry communications.

## 8.4.2 Multimode Fiber

The diameter of multimode fiber is large enough to allow multiple streams of light to travel different paths from transmitter to receiver. Shortwave lasers are used with multimode fiber for transmitting over medium distances. Multimode fiber is shown in Figure 8–11.

The following are the most popular multimode fibers for networking, FDDI, and Ethernet:

- 50μm/125μm (primarily used in Europe and most common worldwide)
- 62.5μm/125μm (primarily used in the United States)

Multimode fiber carries information at 100MB/s (1062.5Mb/s) and up to 500m.

The two types of multimode fiber are step-index fiber and graded-index fiber.

### 8.4.2.1 MULTIMODE STEP-INDEX OPTIC FIBER

Step-index fiber has a high modal dispersion. See Figure 8–12 to understand how step-index fiber works.

The core material (n1) is not graded, so it does not focus the light beam to follow the axis (axial transmission) of the core. Different light rays leaving the source simultaneously reach the destination at significantly different times, reducing the bandwidth of the fiber and its distance.

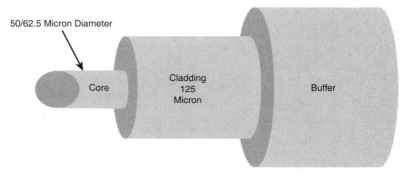

**Figure 8–11** *Multimode fiber.*

Step-index fiber has the following characteristics:

- It is relatively inexpensive.
- It decreases bandwidth and distance.
- It has a higher modal dispersion than graded-index fiber.
- It is seldom used in networking and data communications.

### 8.4.2.2  MULTIMODE GRADED-INDEX FIBER

Grading of the fiber-optic core focuses the light beam closer to the axis of the core. The light rays travel closer to the axis, which reduces travel distance and synchronizes arrival rates.

Figure 8–13 shows multimode graded-index fiber.

Grading is achieved by varying the chemical composition of the core material ($n1$).

Key characteristics of graded-index fiber include the following:

- It is more expensive than step-index fiber. Manufacturing advances and wide adoption of fiber-optic cabling have significantly reduced its manufacturing costs.
- It increases bandwidth and distance.
- It has a lower modal dispersion than step-index fiber because it provides more accurate signal transmission.

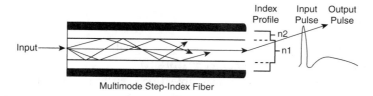

**Figure 8–12**  *How multimode step-index fiber works.*

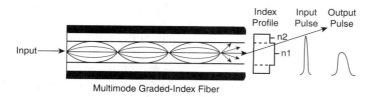

**Figure 8–13**  *How multimode graded-index fiber works.*

- It is frequently used in networking and data communications. (Nearly all multimode fibers used in networking have a graded index.)

With graded-index fiber, data input slows down when the data enters the cable and accelerates when it exits the cable.

Additional information about graded-index fiber can be found at http:/www.fibrechannel.org.

### 8.4.3   Cable Safety Requirements

Because the light produced from the laser has the potential to damage the eye, there are established regulations for the amount of optical power that can be used. For example, the Class 1 laser safety standard mandates the amount of allowable safety levels.

The Fibre Channel industry has adopted the Open Fiber Control technology to meet these safety requirements. Open Fiber Control is the ability of line driver components to reduce the laser power output when they recognize that their light circuits are broken.

 **Because of their signaling differences, Open Fiber Control cables and non-Open Fiber Control cables are not compatible.**

### 8.4.4   Attenuation

Attenuation is the loss of power as a signal travels over a distance. It is measured in *decibels per kilometer* (dB/km).

For commercially available fibers, attenuation ranges from approximately 0.5dB/km for single-mode fibers to 1000dB/km for large-core plastic fibers.

Attenuation is lessened with higher-quality, more-expensive, single-mode fibers, and it is greater with lower quality, less expensive, multimode fibers.

Power loss can result from any of the following conditions:

- Light absorption caused by material impurities
- Light scattering caused by material impurities, defects at the core/cladding interface, or scattering of the molecules of the medium (silica)

- Macro bends (cable bends past the specified radius) and micro bends (cable wrapping or squeezing)
- Scattering and reflection at cable splices

Attenuation varies with the wavelength of light. There are three low-loss windows, measured in nanometers:

- **780 to 850nm (HP recommends 790nm)**—Most widely used because 780 to 850nm devices are inexpensive (shortwave)
- **1200 to 1300nm (HP recommends 1250nm)**—Lower loss, but a modest increase in cost for LEDs (longwave)
- **1550nm**—Mainly of interest to *very long-distance* (VLD) telecommunications applications

Attenuation in optical fiber is mainly the result of scattering and absorption within the core material. Dirty or poorly made connections will also diminish the light intensity. Therefore, loss occurs over long distances and at connections. Any connection, regardless of quality, will induce an insertion loss.

### 8.4.5 Macro Bending

Macro bending is the physical bending of the fiber cable past the specified radius (1.25 to 1.50 inches). Figure 8–14 illustrates this concept.

As the fiber exceeds the specified radius, the light loses some particles and attenuation increases.

### 8.4.6 Micro Bending

Micro bending losses occur when the beam does not follow an entirely linear path, such as when a cable is wrapped with a tie or the cladding is squeezed, as illustrated in Figure 8–15.

**Figure 8–14**

*Macro bending.*

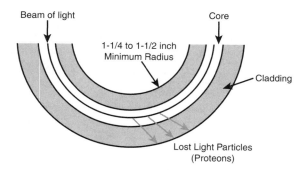

Beam of light

Core

1-1/4 to 1-1/2 inch Minimum Radius

Cladding

Lost Light Particles (Proteons)

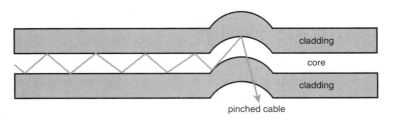

**Figure 8–15**   *Micro bending.*

Micro bends in the axis of an optical fiber can dramatically reduce the transmission of light through it.

## 8.5   Fibre Channel Topologies

Fibre Channel supports the following three topologies:

- Point to point
- FC-AL
- FC-SW

To understand the discussion in this section, you must be familiar with the various Fibre Channel port types as defined in the following table. Refer back to this table as needed during the discussion of the three topologies.

| Port | Type | Associated Topology |
|------|------|---------------------|
| N_port | Node | Point to point or fabric |
| NL_port | Node | Node connected to an arbitrated loop |
| F_port | Fabric | Fabric port |
| FL_port | Fabric | Fabric connected to an arbitrated loop |
| L_port | Loop | Hub port on an arbitrated loop |
| L_C_F | Loop | *Link Control Facility* (L_C_F) is a hardware facility that attaches to each end of the link and manages transmission and reception of data. It is located within each port, contains a transmitter and receiver, and provides the logical interface to the node. |
| Rx | | The *receiver* (Rx) is the portion of the link control facility dedicated to receiving an encoded bit stream from the media, converting this bit stream into transmission characters, and decoding these characters using the rules specified by FC-PH. |
| Tx | | The *transmitter* (Tx) is the portion of the link control facility dedicated to converting valid data bytes and special codes into transmission characters using transmission code rules. The Tx then converts these characters into a bit stream and transmits the bit stream into the transmission media, which is either optical or electrical. |
| G_port | | This is a generic switch port that operates in either E_port mode or F_port mode. |
| E_port | | This interswitch expansion port is used to connect to an E_port of another switch to build a larger fabric. |

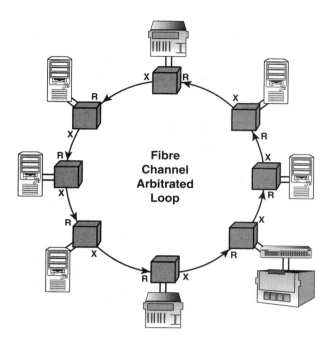

**Figure 8–16** *Fibre Channel arbitrated loop topology.*

## 8.5.1 Fibre Channel Arbitrated Loop Topology

By connecting nodes to a Fibre Channel hub, you can create an FC-AL, as shown in Figure 8–16.

FC-AL adds capacity (support for up to 126 nodes on a single loop) but not performance. The bandwidth is shared among all active nodes on the loop.

This topology allows a single connection between one pair of ports at any point in time. After a session (two devices communicating) is started, the other devices connected to the loop must wait until the connection ends.

Devices participating in the arbitrated loop share access, but the active link has the full bandwidth. Only one pair of nodes can be communicating on the loop at the same time.

The arbitrated loop topology permits several devices to share the bandwidth of a single loop of fiber running between them. The FC-AL standard is implemented by modifying an N_port to be an NL_port. Each NL_port is attached to one link. The information flows in one direction around the arbitrated loop.

An arbitrated loop is a logical loop and a physical star. In Figure 8–16, $X$ represents the output of one node, and $R$ represents the receiver port of another node. The transmitter port on one node is connected to the receiver port on another node. Notice that information flows in one direction around the loop.

In an arbitrated loop topology, the routing function is distributed to each loop port. The separation of the transmit and receive fibers associated with each port makes this possible.

### 8.5.2   Switched Fabric Topology

A network of switches in a Fibre Channel environment is referred to as a *fabric*. Nodes connect into this fabric to access other nodes, as illustrated in Figure 8–17. A wide-open architecture uses intelligent switches to connect many ports.

The Fibre Channel fabric was designed as a generic interface between a node and the physical layer. By adhering to this interface, Fibre Channel nodes can communicate over the fabric with other nodes without knowing about that node.

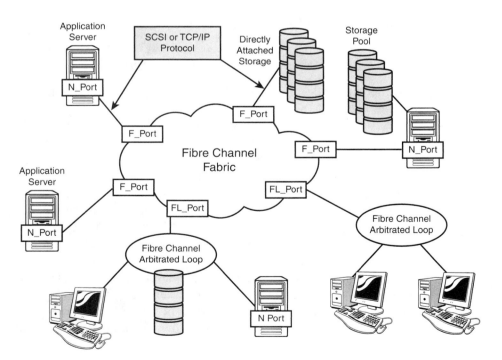

**Figure 8–17**   *Fibre Channel switched fabric topology.*

A fabric is often referred to as a switch topology. Frames are routed through various switches by having the fabric elements interpret the destination address identifier in a frame when it arrives at each fabric element.

Ports on one node can communicate with ports on other nodes connected to the same fabric. With the fabric topology, many connections can be active at the same time.

The any-to-any connection service and peer-to-peer communication service provided by a fabric is fundamental to Fibre Channel architecture. Fibre Channel can support both channel and network protocols simultaneously.

The class of service used influences frame routing. The class of service request is generated in the start of frame delimiter of each frame.

The key advantages of the switch fabric topology include the following:

- Support for up to 16 million nodes
- Switches that act like routers (with only those ports communicating seeing the traffic)
- High-aggregate bandwidth (with multiple paths enabled concurrently)
- Electrical and logical isolation
- More expensive than FC-AL

A switched fabric works as follows:

1. A direct connection to the fabric in the host is through an interface that supports the NL_port protocol.
2. The switch itself has F_ports to which the cable from another device connects. A whole FC-AL group can attach to a switch through an FL_port.
3. Most FC-AL groups attach to a switch through their hub; the FL_ports for some switches allow the loop to attach directly without a hub.

### 8.5.2.1 FABRIC ELEMENT

In the fabric topology, at least one active element (such as a switch, ring, or hub) must be placed between ports. This element is responsible for functions such as responding to fabric login requests, managing class of service for the fabric, and assigning addresses.

A fabric element can

- Attach N_ports.
- Attach arbitrated loops.
- Serve as the root element for distributed fabric elements.

A fabric element is the smallest entity that can function as a complete fabric topology. It must have at least three F_ports or FL_ports to make routing decisions.

When multiple fabric elements are interconnected, they form a cooperative unit that is still a fabric. The term *heterogeneous fabric* refers to the variations in function that are possible with multiple fabric elements.

### 8.5.3 Point-to-Point Topology

The simplest Fibre Channel topology is point to point, in which a single link connects only two ports. This topology is inexpensive because no hub is required.

To create larger point-to point configurations, you can provide multiple N_ports on each node.

Each point-to-point connection provides the full bandwidth supported by the N_ports. Depending on the type of link (multimode or single-mode fiber), the two nodes can be separated by up to 500m (multimode fiber) or 10km (single-mode fiber).

## 8.6     Asynchronous Transfer Mode

*Asynchronous Transfer Mode* (ATM) is a method of digital communication that is capable of very high speeds. It is used to transport voice, video, data, and images. ATM can be used as the basis for both LAN and WAN technologies.

Separate networks are often used to carry voice, data, and video information, largely because these traffic types have different characteristics. With ATM, separate networks are not required. ATM is the only standards-based technology designed from the beginning to accommodate the simultaneous transmission of data, voice, and video.

In an effort to combine LAN communications with telecommunications, ATM is gaining increasing favor. ATM, which is also the prevailing wide area backbone technology in public data networks, provides the potential for creating a single set of hardware and communications protocols for both.

Standard ATM communication was based on a small (53-byte) packet size that posed a significant technical challenge when used to transfer data files. Additionally, ATM packet dropping, which had no serious consequences when transferring voice or video data, was not acceptable for data communication.

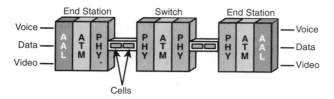

**Figure 8–18** *Asynchronous Transfer Mode.*

To address these issues, a variation of ATM—Asynchronous Adaptation Layer 5—was designed to provide scalable system-to-system communication for computer data.

A gateway interface connects Fibre Channel switches to an ATM network to extend the distance of the fabric between local and remote sites. ATM is available at various speeds from megabit to gigabit.

ATM is illustrated in Figure 8–18.

## 8.7 Fibre Channel over IP

Fibre Channel over IP, also known as *Fibre Channel tunneling* or *storage tunneling*, is an IP-based storage networking technology developed by the Internet Engineering Task Force. It enables Fibre Channel information to be transmitted by tunneling data between SAN facilities over IP networks. This capacity facilitates data sharing over a geographically distributed enterprise.

IP communications between nodes over Fibre Channel is achieved by creating a unidirectional exchange. For the receiving node to respond (bidirectional interaction), another exchange must be created.

Because IP addresses are 4 bytes and Fibre Channel address identifiers are 3 bytes, an *Address Resolution Protocol* (ARP) server must be available to allow mapping between the two addresses. Normally, the ARP server is implemented at the fabric level and has its own address (x 'FF FFFC').

An IP packet set is handled at the Fibre Channel level as a sequence. The maximum IP packet size is 65,280 bytes, which allows the packet and its 255 bytes of overhead to fit within a 64KB buffer.

If a frame error occurs, the default exchange error policy (abort, discard a single sequence) is to discard the packet with no retransmission. Subsequent sequences are not affected. Retransmission, if needed, is handled at the *Internet Protocol* (IP) and *Transmission Control Protocol* (TCP) levels and is transparent to the Fibre Channel.

## ▲ Summary

This chapter provided a basic overview of Fibre Channel technologies. The implementation of Fibre Channel technologies in HP server products is explained in greater detail in later chapters.

Critical AIS knowledge covered in this chapter includes the following:

- Fibre Channel terms and concepts
- Fibre Channel hardware components, including host bus adapters, gigabit interface converters, gigabit link modules, hubs, and switches
- Fibre channel cabling, and cabling concepts such as cable types and cable safety
- Fibre channel topologies and their advantages and disadvantages
- Asynchronous Transfer Mode
- Fibre Channel over IP

This chapter concludes the discussion of key industry technologies.

## ▲ LEARNING CHECK

1. *Which of the following is not a part of a complete Fibre Channel solution?*
   A. Hardware platforms
   B. Storage systems
   C. Operating systems
   D. Applications
   E. Bus termination

2. *Match the Fibre Channel term with its definition:*

   | | |
   |---|---|
   | Node | A pair of optical fibers. One of the fibers carries information into the receiver port; the other fiber carries information out of the transmitter port. |
   | Node ID | A connection point between each node that provides access to other devices. |
   | Port | An interconnection scheme that connects two or more Fibre Channel N_ports. |
   | Link | Unique identifier. |
   | Topology | A Fibre Channel device. |

3. *Fibre Channel is an industry-standard interconnect and high-performance serial I/O protocol that can deliver a new level of reliability, throughput, and distance flexibility for the server industry.*

   ❏ True

   ❏ False

4. *Which one of the following are the three Fibre Channel topologies?*

   A. Parallel to serial, SCSI IDs, and switched fabric

   B. Point to point, arbitrated loop, and switched fabric

   C. Point to point, arbitrated loop, and RAID 0

   D. Point to point, fabric arbitrated loop, and storage fabric

5. *What is a gigabit interface converter (GBIC)?*

6. *Which Fibre Channel topology uses Fibre Channel hubs?*

7. *What is the function of an E_port on a Fibre Channel switch?*

8. *What are the two types of Fibre Channel cabling?*

9. *Which one of the following best describes attenuation?*

   A. The bending of a cable past a specific radius

   B. The loss of power over a distance

   C. The ratio of velocity in a vacuum

10. *What is the name for a network of switches in a Fibre Channel environment?*

11. *What is the only standards-based technology designed from the beginning for simultaneous data, voice, and video transmission?*

    A. ATM

    B. Fibre Channel

    C. IP over Fibre Channel

    D. Multimode Fiber

    E. Point-to-Point topology

12. *What technology enables Fibre Channel information to be transmitted over the network between SAN facilities?*

# HP Server Technologies

**A**n HP Accredited System Engineer should understand the HP server product line and other HP products related to the enterprise.

Part 2 of this book explains the HP server product line, HP rack technologies, and HP power technologies.

Here is an overview of the chapters in Part 2.

**Chapter 9**   # The HP ProLiant Server Line

Chapter 9 provides an overview of the HP ProLiant family of servers. This chapter explains how HP servers are designed and how HP servers are categorized by line and series. In addition, this chapter describes the characteristics of each HP server series.

**Chapter 10**   # HP Rack and Power Technologies

Chapter 10 explains the advantages and features of HP rack and power technologies, and the tools that are provided by HP to configure and optimize rack and power solutions.

# The HP ProLiant Server Line

After studying this chapter, you will be able to do the following:

- Explain the factors that influence the overall design of an HP ProLiant server.

- Explain how HP ProLiant servers are categorized by line, and describe the characteristics of the ML, DL, and BL server lines.

- Explain how HP ProLiant servers are categorized by series, and describe the characteristics of the 300 series, the 500 series, and the 700 series.

- Explain what the term *generation identifier* means, and explain how ProLiant servers implement generation identification.

This chapter explains how the HP ProLiant line of servers is categorized, organized, and structured.

## 9.1 Basic Server Design

Many factors influence the design of an HP server, including the customer profile (small/medium business or enterprise) and server function (the projected role of the server).

### 9.1.1 Customer Profile

HP recognizes that one server size, price, or performance level does not fit all customer requirements. Therefore, HP designs a full range of servers so customers can choose the right server solution.

HP offers a range of industry-standard servers for small, medium, and enterprise businesses. This range includes ProLiant servers, which offer the functionality to meet most industry requirements. ProLiant servers can be categorized as general-purpose servers, small-business servers, and enterprise servers.

## 9.2 The HP ProLiant Server Family

HP positions ProLiant servers by two criteria—line and series—to help customers choose the server that best fits their requirements. The relationship between line and series is illustrated in Figure 9–1.

The ProLiant server line is designated by the ML, DL, or BL prefix. This prefix designation indicates the type of customer environment for which the server is best suited.

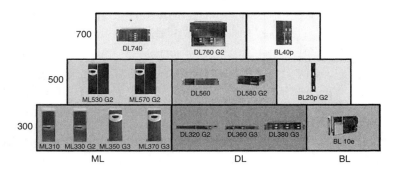

**Figure 9–1** *The ProLiant server family line.*

### 9.2.1   ML Line

The ProLiant ML server line is maximized for internal system expansion. ML servers are designed so that customers can maximize their computing power by adding additional components, such as PCI expansion cards and disk drives, inside the chassis. They are available in both rack and tower models. The highly flexible, configurable design of the ML line enables them to be used in a wide variety of customer environments, including remote sites, branch offices, and data centers.

ProLiant ML servers also provide high-availability features to ensure maximum uptime, resulting in price and performance flexibility for the customer. The ProLiant ML330 Generation 3 server is shown in Figure 9–2, and the ProLiant ML530 Generation 2 server is shown in Figure 9–3.

**Figure 9–2**
*ProLiant ML330 Generation 3 server.*

**Figure 9–3**
*ProLiant ML530 Generation 2 server.*

### 9.2.2 DL Line

The ProLiant DL server line is density-optimized for rackmount environments. The ProLiant DL line incorporates embedded components that provide a rich feature set at the same time as reducing the chassis size. This makes the servers ideal in dense, space-constrained, and multiserver environments.

Available only as rack models, the servers provide the following:

- Maximum computing power in small, space-saving designs
- Integrated and embedded options
- Efficient clustering

The ProLiant DL360 Generation 3 server is shown in Figure 9–4.

### 9.2.3 BL Line

The ProLiant BL server line is comprised of ultra-dense server blades optimized for rapid deployment. The ProLiant BL line is designed to help corporate customers and service providers adapt to changing market requirements. The tool-free modularity of the BL architecture conserves limited human and technology resources, maximizes efficiencies, and enables rapid response to customers in a dynamic business climate. ProLiant BL server blades enable rapid deployment, which simplifies and standardizes multiserver deployments.

The ProLiant BL line has two classes of products, the BL e-Class and the BL p-Class.

The BL e-Class servers offer power-efficient performance for front-end applications by integrating an enterprise-class chipset, ultra-low voltage processor, and other power-saving components in an ultra-dense design. Up to 280 power-efficient edge server blades can fit in a standard rack, providing maximum utilization of data center space.

**Figure 9–4** *ProLiant DL360 Generation 3 server DL line.*

The BL p-Class servers provide high performance and availability for multitiered environments. The BL p-Class infrastructure has centralized, redundant power and offers enhanced management capabilities. Compared to the BL e-Class, the BL p-Class offers higher performance with less density.

The ProLiant BL10 e-Class server blade is shown in Figure 9–5, and the ProLiant BL40 p-Class server blade is shown in Figure 9–6.

**Figure 9–5**  *ProLiant BL10 e-Class server blade.*

**Figure 9–6**  *ProLiant BL40 p-Class server blade.*

## 9.3 Series Classifications

Each ProLiant server line is divided into three series classifications. Each series is defined by performance level and server availability. Figure 9–7 shows the relationship between performance and availability and how it relates to the series designation.

### 9.3.1 100 Series

The 100 series offers an affordable server optimized for

- Clustered solutions for high-performance technical computing applications.
- Demanding workloads.
- Very large memory applications.

### 9.3.2 300 Series

The servers in the 300 series are best suited to performing applications, such as

- File/print and domain servers.
- Web server functions.
- Small databases and infrastructure applications.

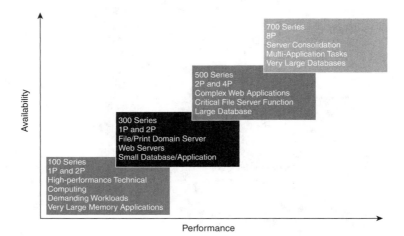

**Figure 9–7** *ProLiant server series performance/availability matrix.*

### 9.3.3 500 Series

The servers in the 500 series offer increased levels of availability and performance, making them ideal for

- Complex Web applications.
- Large databases.
- Critical file server applications.

### 9.3.4 700 Series

The servers in the 700 series offer the maximum in performance and availability, which enables them to handle

- Very large databases.
- Server consolidation solutions.
- Multi-application environments.

## 9.4 Generation Identifier

When ProLiant servers transition from one generation to the next, there is a need to visually identify which generation of server is being serviced. To ensure that the correct documentation, options, and parts are used, a 1-square-centimeter label is affixed to the server to identify Generation 2 (G2) and subsequent generations.

On rack servers, the label is located in the left rack screw opposite the Intel logo.

In tower servers, the label is located in the top-left chassis behind the door or bezel.

The identifier is used in technical documentation when the generation difference is relevant. The identifier is used in several formats, depending on constraints, such as available space in a database field.

The identifier might not be used in certain marketing documentation, such as brochures and pictures. It will not be applied retroactively, but will be implemented with new generations of servers in the future.

Note

The generation identifier is not an indication of any specific technology. A G2 server can be just as current a product as a related G3 server. It identifies the hierarchy of the server in the technology evolution and distinguishes between legacy and new servers.

## ▲ Summary

It is vital for an AIS to be able to clearly explain how the HP ProLiant server line is organized, classified, and categorized.

The following key concepts were explained in this chapter:

- The factors that influence the selection of an HP ProLiant server.
- How HP ProLiant servers are categorized by line, and the distinguishing characteristics of the ML, DL, and BL server lines.
- How HP ProLiant servers are categorized by series, and the distinguishing characteristics of the 300 series, the 500 series, and the 700 series.
- How generation identifiers are used in ProLiant servers

## ▲ LEARNING CHECK

1. *What are the two criteria by which HP servers are positioned?*

2. *Which server is best suited to act as a file and print server that can grow as the number of saved documents grows?*
    - A. ML370
    - B. DL320
    - C. DL560
    - D. DL760
    - E. BL10e

3. *Which server is best suited to handle a large database and allow for future internal system expansion?*
    - A. ML370
    - B. DL320
    - C. ML570
    - D. DL760
    - E. BL10e

# HP Rack and Power Technologies

After reading this chapter, you will be able to do the following:

- Describe the advantages of HP racks, and list the features of the HP Rack 9000 series racks and the HP Rack 10000 series racks.

- Describe the rack options available from HP, including the following:
  - Security and monitoring options
  - Monitors and keyboards
  - Console switches
  - Cable management kits
  - Shelving and stabilizing kits

- Explain how Rack Builder Online is used and list its key features and advantages.

- Explain service considerations for HP racks.

- List the features and advantages of HP *power distribution units* (PDUs).

- List and describe the features and functions of HP *uninterruptible power supplies* (UPSs).

- Explain service considerations for HP UPSs.

- Describe HP Power Management software features.

**211**

The HP enterprise-class rack and power product line provides a full range of products that protect and manage computer systems, from individual workstations to distributed enterprises.

HP offers a wide range of rack, rack options, and power products designed with the latest innovative technologies.

## 10.1    HP Racks

HP racks provide a common, integrated platform for mounting all enterprise hardware, including servers, workstations, networking, and storage products. All HP rack-mountable products are designed to fit industry-standard 19-inch-wide racks.

HP industrial-strength racks feature a universal design that accommodates all HP equipment, including ProLiant severs, AlphaServer systems, StorageWorks, UPSs, and PDUs, in addition to select third-party equipment.

HP racks have perforated front and back doors with solid side panels. This construction ensures environmental integrity by allowing for high airflow and cooling.

In addition, a variety of options are available to customize ProLiant racks to suit the business requirements of most customer environments.

For more information on rack options, visit http://h18004. www1.hp.com/products/servers/proliantstorage/rack-options/list.html.

### 10.1.1    HP Rack 10000 Series

With a loading capacity of 200 pounds and a depth of 1 meter, the 10000 series rack ships in metallic graphite. The HP Rack 10000 series is shown in Figure 10–1.

**Figure 10–1**

*The HP Rack 10000 series.*

The HP Rack 10000 series is an enterprise-class rack cabinet system that combines next-generation structural integrity and ease-of-use capabilities to deliver industry-leading performance. It is ideal for onsite assembly of rack-mountable products.

The HP Rack 10000 series is available in 14 to 47U heights at 1 meter deep with loading capacities up to 2000 lbs. Solid side panels ensure environmental integrity, and perforated front and back doors enable high airflow and cooling.

## 10.2 HP Rack Options

A variety of options are available to customize ProLiant racks to suit the business requirements of most customer environments. The option categories include the following:

- Monitors and keyboards
- Cable management
- Shelving and stabilizing
- Console switches

For more information on rack options, visit http://h18004.www1. hp.com/products/servers/proliantstorage/rack-options/list.html.

### 10.2.1 Monitors and Keyboards

HP racks feature an optional flat-panel *thin film transistor* (TFT) monitor that provides a full 17-inch viewing screen when needed and tucks away in 1U of rack space when not being used. The monitor is designed to allow a switchbox to mount behind it on the rails, further maximizing rack space.

Figure 10–2 shows the HP TFT5110R rack-mounted flat-panel monitor.

**Figure 10–2**

*HP TFT5110R rack-mounted flat-panel monitor.*

**Figure 10–3**

*HP integrated rack keyboard and drawer.*

**Figure 10–4**

*HP cable management system.*

Figure 10–3 shows the HP integrated keyboard and drawer

To provide maximum flexibility, the integrated keyboard and drawer also tucks away when not in use. The unit is ideal for small remote sites as well as high-density data centers.

### 10.2.2   Cable Management

The space-saving design of HP racks facilitates cable management, as illustrated in Figure 10–4. Optional cable management kits are available to further reduce cabling requirements.

A cable management arm ships in the rack kit with the server, and includes hook-and-loop straps that are used to secure multiple server and peripheral cables to the arm, as shown in Figure 10–5. It allows secure extraction of the server from the rack, without the risk of removing a cable.

### 10.2.3   Shelving and Stabilizing

Shelving, mounting, and grounding kits are available for HP racks. These kits allow you to

- Optimize rack configuration.
- Improve accessibility.
- Minimize use of floor space.

**Figure 10–5**

*HP rack cable management arms.*

Stabilizer options kits increase stability and support, and improve safety factors.

## 10.2.4   Console Switches

A console switch is a device that eliminates the need for a separate keyboard, mouse, and monitor for every server. It routes the capabilities of those devices through a single keyboard, mouse, and monitor set. Recently introduced *keyboard, video, and mouse* (KVM) designs use networking technology to connect to and remotely manage systems.

The HP console switch uses interface adapters and Cat 5 cabling technology to connect the keyboard, video, and mouse ports on a server, and the IP console switch provides local and remote management functions using a LAN.

### 10.2.4.1   LEGACY SERVER CONSOLE SWITCH

A legacy HP server console switch is a device that provides a direct connection to multiple computers and enables you to logically switch a single KVM among those systems, as shown in Figure 10–6.

Server console switches can be connected in a tiered fashion to increase server access from 4 or 8 servers to as many as 64.

### 10.2.4.2   HP CONSOLE SWITCHES

HP offers 8-port, single-user and 16-port, two-user versions of its console switches, as shown in Figure 10–7. Both versions use Cat 5 cables and RJ-45 connections. PS/2 connections are available for local users.

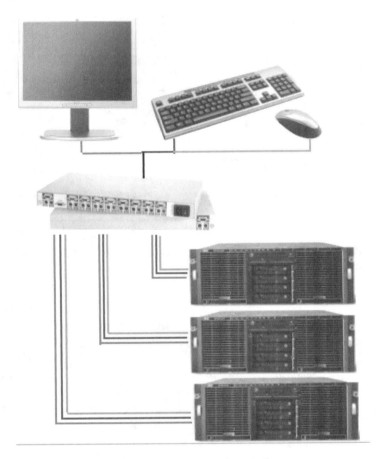

**Figure 10–6** *HP legacy server console switch.*

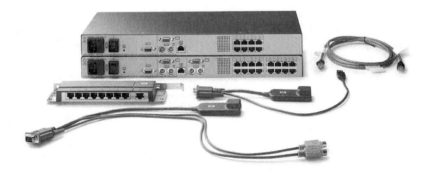

**Figure 10–7** *HP console switches.*

These analog KVM switches reduce cabling problems, feature improved scalability, and enable seamless integration with existing HP KVM switches.

Eight servers can be tiered on each switch port through an expansion port. Interface adapters connect unshielded Cat 5 cables to the standard PS/2 and USB connections on servers or legacy Compaq KVM switches.

### 10.2.4.3   IP CONSOLE SWITCHES

Like a server console switch, an HP IP console switch allows access to the rack console and attached servers. However, the IP console switch also provides this access through a network. Remote users can access applications and screens as if they were standing in front of the rack.

The HP IP console switch provides KVM connections to 16 direct attached servers. IP console switches do not require the installation of specific software on the attached servers, enabling users to connect a single switch to servers running a variety of operating systems.

Figure 10–8 shows an HP IP console switch.

The IP console switch connects to any type of server that has a standard PS2 or USB KVM connection.

Figure 10–9 shows how HP IP console switches can be connected to a network.

**Figure 10–8**   *HP IP console switch.*

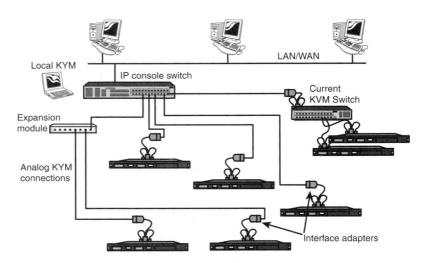

**Figure 10–9** *IP Console switches connection diagram.*

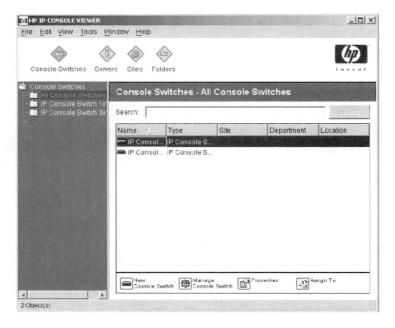

**Figure 10–10** *HP IP Console Viewer interface.*

**10.2.4.3.1 HP IP Console Viewer** • The HP IP Console Viewer software, shown in Figure 10–10, enables users to discover switches and to configure interface adapters and cascaded legacy switches.

Before the IP console switch can be used over the network, you must install the IP Console Viewer software on the system you will use to manage the switch.

**This viewer is not Web-based; you must install it on each machine that will use it.**

## 10.3    HP Enterprise Configurator Custom Builder

The HP Enterprise Configurator utility, shown in Figure 10–11, is the replacement for the Rack Builder Online utility as of February 2004. The Enterprise Configurator offers new and enhanced Web-based services for configuring one or multiple racks through the Custom Builder configuration tool.

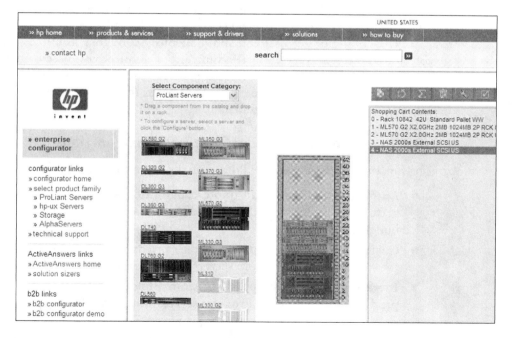

**Figure 10–11** *HP Enterprise Configurator interface.*

Using a simple guided interface, you can create rack configurations for HP ProLiant servers and StorageWorks products. The Custom Builder configuration tool has two user modes:

- **Let Me Build a New Solution Myself**—For experienced users who are familiar with the HP product line and with applicable functional and regulatory requirements. This mode does not perform any of the calculations necessary for automatically selecting and sizing rack components.

- **Help Me Build a New Solution**—For users who would like help in selecting and sizing racks and rackmount components. This mode directs you through the HP Enterprise Configurator using a simplified user interface, which includes an interview session. This mode automatically performs the calculations necessary to properly size power components in accordance with functional and regulatory requirements.

The rack configurations are created using a complete and current database that includes all HP rack-mountable products.

The Custom Builder tool helps to manage the increasing complexity of high-density environments by enabling users to preconfigure racks for more efficient management of their data center.

The configuration tool can simultaneously configure multiple racked solutions of HP servers and HP storage and connectivity based on user requirements, and quote an estimated price for each configuration. After a rack is built, you can still make changes as long as the Rules for Racks system is met.

### 10.3.1 Custom Builder Configuration Tool Functions

The functions of the Custom Builder configuration tool include the following:

- **Automatic configure and quote capabilities**—Each component displays a list price, and the tool calculates a total configuration and budgetary quote.

- **Customizable server options**—You can configure accessories within the server and place custom servers within a rack.

- **Increased product support**—Custom Builder provides current HP product information for ProLiant servers and StorageWorks products.

- **Simplified custom manufacturing instructions**—You can add customer intent notes to individual components for specific factory configurations.

- **Online configuration assistance from HP Contact Centers**—Click the phone icon to send the configuration to an HP Contact Center inside sales representative, who will contact you with pricing information.

- **Timely support of new server, storage, and option components**—New product information is updated when products are launched. Hyperlinks embedded in the pages provide immediate access to information and QuickSpecs from the HP Web site.

- **Rack configuration validation**—The automatic validation functions ensure that rack configurations are operationally complete with all necessary accessories.

- **Configuration-specific power protection**—The power-sizing function calculates the appropriate power protection based on components included in the configuration.

- **Graphic representations of rack configurations**—You can view rack configurations and drag and drop individual components to specific locations quickly and easily to customize configurations.

- **Reporting and exporting options**—You can choose from multiple report formats such as Microsoft Excel, Word, and others.

The Custom Builder replaces the Rack Builder Online. You can find more information about the Enterprise Configurator and Custom Builder at http://h30099.www3.hp.com/configurator.

## 10.4 HP Rack Service Considerations

The following service considerations should be taken into account when handling HP racks:

- If installing a single rack, ensure that the rack is level and has been stabilized before installing the components. Stabilizing feet are not required on the back of a standalone rack. To reduce risk of personal injury, attach HP rack stabilizing feet to all standalone racks.

- There is a leveling foot at each corner of the rack, which should be fully extended, screwed down, and locked in place with a locking nut before any component is installed on the rack. To reduce the risk of damage to the casters, ensure that the full weight of the rack rests on the leveling feet rather than the casters. The casters are designed only as an aid in moving the rack into position.

- Join multiple racks with a coupling kit to increase stability. Position the racks and install the coupling kits before populating the racks with components.
- When installing the various components, mount the heaviest components first in the bottom of the rack. The UPS should always be on the bottom.
- Do not simultaneously extend more than one component from the rack. Doing so can cause the rack to become unstable and tip.
- Rack-mountable ProLiant servers draw in cool air through the front door and exhaust warm air out the rear. Therefore, the front door must be adequately ventilated to allow ambient room air to enter the cabinet, and the rear door must be adequately ventilated to allow the warm air to escape from the cabinet.
- Blanking plates should be used to cover any spaces where components are not mounted. Blanking plates are essential for correct airflow. When servicing a customer's rack system, if you notice that blanking plates are missing, ask the customer to install them.
- In the event of a lost key for a rack, contact a locksmith for assistance. Replacement key lock assemblies can be ordered from HP.

## 10.5   HP Power Distribution Units (PDUs)

PDUs provide power to multiple objects from a single source. In a rack, the PDU distributes power to the servers, storage units, and other peripherals. Figure 10–12 shows a rack PDU.

**Figure 10–12**   *Module PDUs in 0U and 1U configurations.*

PDU systems (1) address issues of power distribution to components within the computer cabinet, (2) reduce the number of power cables coming into the cabinet, and (3) provide a level of power protection through a series of circuit breakers.

The architecture of the modular HP PDU line is designed for customers who want to maximize power distribution and space efficiency.

Modular PDUs consist of two essential building blocks. The control unit distributes single-phase input power into four single-phase branch outputs. Extension bars provide up to 32 outlets or receptacles.

HP offers a low-voltage model to connect to the HP low-voltage UPSs and the 16A model that connects to the HP high-voltage UPSs. The 16A model, with its detachable input power-cord feature, offers increased flexibility and adaptability by enabling customers to use country-specific input power cords.

For mission-critical environments with UPSs, HP offers a fault-tolerant dual-input PDU. This PDU automatically switches over to a secondary input source if the first source fails.

All PDUs ship with 1U/0U mounting brackets, which are required to mount the PDUs in HP Rack 10000 series units. The extension bars mount directly to the rack frame.

Benefits of the modular PDUs include the following:

- Increased number of outlet receptacles
- Modular design
- Superior cable management
- Flexible 1U/0U rack mounting options
- Easy accessibility to outlets
- Limited three-year warranty

For more information, refer to the HP UPS/PDU compatibility matrix at http://h30140.www3.hp.com/page/prodinfo.html.

## 10.6 HP Uninterruptible Power Systems

A UPS can provide several key benefits to a computing infrastructure. Planning and selecting the proper UPS system ensures

- Maximum system backup time in the event of a power loss.
- Consistent power voltage levels.
- Protection from damaging power spikes.

**Figure 10–13**

*HP T1000XR UPS.*

- Increased power efficiency, reducing power loss through heat and harmonic frequencies.
- Power management capabilities of your power protection system.

HP offers a wide range of UPSs from 500VA to 12,000VA in both tower and rack form factors. Figure 10–13 shows an HP T1000XR UPS.

An HP UPS contains batteries that protect against power disturbances—natural or man-made—and circuitry that filters and enhances utility power to provide a more stable voltage. If a UPS determines that the utility voltage is within the nominal operating range, the UPS supplies the utility power to the output receptacles. If the utility voltage is outside the nominal operating range, or has failed, the UPS supplies battery power to the output receptacles.

HP UPSs are bundled with HP power management software, which includes HP Power Manager and HP Rack and Power Manager. This software uses load segment control to schedule startups and shutdowns of less-critical devices, which extends the operation of the mission-critical devices. The bundled power management software continuously manages and monitors HP UPSs.

### 10.6.1    UPS Options

To scale capacity, connect additional UPSs to the original UPS through the UPS card slot. These options add value and leverage control of the IT investment.

### 10.6.1.1    EXTENDED RUNTIME MODULE (ERM)

The ERM extends the capability of the UPS to power equipment during a failure. At the recommended 80% load, one ERM can extend the available UPS run time up to 30 minutes.

Acting as an extra battery for a UPS, an ERM attaches to a power receptacle located on the UPS rear panel. A UPS can support up to two ERMs. You must install an ERM at the bottom of a rack, with the UPS directly above it.

The ERM Configurator ensures that accurate runtime predictions are reported to any network software communicating with the UPS. Network software uses runtime information to conduct a timely shutdown of attached servers.

> **! IMPORTANT**
>
> A licensed electrician should wire the ERM to the UPS.

### 10.6.1.2    SNMP/SERIAL CARD

The SNMP/Serial Card provides *Simple Network Management Protocol* (SNMP) functionality, including power event alerts, network power diagnostics, and remote UPS rebooting and testing. The card can also provide simultaneous network and out-of-band (modem) communications.

### 10.6.1.3    MULTI-SERVER UPS CARD

The Multi-Server UPS Card allows up to three servers to be connected (depending on the number of load segments the UPS has), regardless of the server operating system. Each load segment functions as a separate UPS with individual shutdown schedules and load segment configurations. If the network is down, the HP Multi-Server UPS Card can still conduct prioritized shutdowns. The HP Multi-Server UPS Card is intelligently manageable through HP Power Management software.

## 10.6.2    *Enhanced Battery Management*

Batteries that are constantly trickle-charged (a constant voltage feeding a low current to the battery) reach the end of their useful life in less than half the time of those charged using advanced techniques such as enhanced battery management technology.

HP enhanced battery management incorporates an advanced three-stage battery charging technique that doubles battery service life, optimizes battery recharge time, and provides up to a 60-day advanced notification of the end of useful battery life.

### 10.6.2.1  INTELLIGENT BATTERY CHARGING

The HP UPS uses a three-stage charging process that doubles battery service life. First, the HP UPS rapid charges the battery to 90%. A constant voltage (float charge) continues until the battery reaches full capacity. The charger is then turned off and the HP UPS goes into a rest mode, enabling the battery to be preserved for future power failures.

Most manufacturers use a trickle-charging method, which dries the electrolytes and corrodes the plates, reducing potential battery life by up to 50%.

### 10.6.2.2  ADVANCE NOTIFICATION OF BATTERY REPLACEMENT

Because UPS batteries are valve-regulated, sealed, lead-acid cells, there has not been a practical way to provide users with advance notification of battery failure. The only way to determine that batteries needed replacement was to wait until the power failed, taking the servers and computers down with it.

Enhanced battery management is the only technology available that reliably provides advance notification of battery failure. A microprocessor tracks the charge and discharge characteristics of the battery and compares these characteristics to an ideal battery state. By monitoring the battery, the user receives advance notice when battery replacement is necessary.

### 10.6.2.3  SUPERIOR VOLTAGE REGULATION

Most UPSs correct input voltage variations as low as −25%, but transfer to battery when a surge or sag must be filtered in the system. This type of voltage regulation shortens the battery service life of the UPS.

Innovative HP buck/double-boost voltage regulation ensures consistent input voltage to the load by automatically "bucking" it if it is too high, or "boosting" it if it is too low. Voltage variations as low as −35% or as high as +20% of nominal voltage are corrected—without transferring to the battery. As a result, the number of charge/recharge cycles is reduced, and the life of the HP UPS battery is extended.

### 10.6.3 Using the UPS Sizing Tool

HP offers a UPS Sizing tool, shown in Figure 10–14, to help you determine the appropriate UPS solution.

The UPS Sizing tool is available at http://www.upssizer.com/. To use the Sizing tool, go to the HP Web site and follow these steps:

1. Specify a group of devices you need to protect. Ensure that all devices within the group are close together so that their power can be supplied by the UPS. Any devices that are not in close proximity should become part of another group. Use the UPS selector to find a solution for each group of devices separately.
2. Specify the UPS requirements, such as input voltage, runtime (length of time you want the UPS to power your group of devices), and provisions for future growth. Click View Solution.
3. The UPS Sizer recommends the best solution and shows the specifications of the recommended UPS. You can print or e-mail this information.

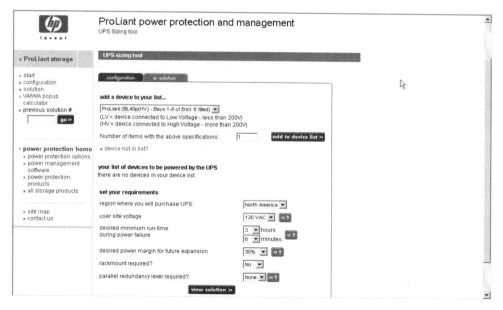

**Figure 10–14** *HP UPS Sizing tool.*

## 10.6.4    Power Manager

The HP Power Manager is an advanced, customizable UPS utility that provides information about power conditions, health, and status of a UPS and power environment. Figure 10–15 shows the Power Manager interface.

Designed for the business-class environment, Power Manager provides an easy-to-use browser interface for managing and monitoring serially attached HP UPSs.

Features of the Power Manager include the following:

- A familiar browser interface enables novice users to configure and manage power protection settings.
- The standalone software does not require complex management systems, simplifying deployment, configuration, and management of UPS-protected environments.
- Increased stability and security with automated policies based on power and environmental alarms.
- Management of single, serially attached UPSs in business-class environments is simplified.

### 10.6.4.1    USING THE POWER MANAGER UTILITY

Use the Power Manager utility to

- Support serially attached devices.
- Monitor, manage, and control a single UPS device.
- Autodiscover and autoreconnect devices.

**Figure 10–15**  *HP Power Manager.*

- Provide detailed system logs and UPS diagnostics.
- Provide secure remote access (up to 128-bit *Secure Sockets Layer* [SSL]).
- Control independent UPS load segments.

The Power Manager is ideally suited for customers who need

- To run diagnostics on power management devices to ensure availability of adequate battery power.
- To monitor and manage a single, serially attached power protection device.
- Power protection for offices and small data rooms.
- Power failure settings that are easy to use and configure.

Power Manager is available on the HP Power Management CD and from the HP Web site.

For more information, visit http://h18004.www1.hp.com/products/servers/proliantstorage/power-protection/software/powermanager/index.html.

**HP Rack and Power Manager is different from HP Power Manager. HP Rack and Power Manager is an enterprise-class, Web-based application that is used for large-scale deployments, and it is not covered in this book.**

### 10.6.5   Power Calculators

HP developed automated tools to help you manage the size and scope of a solution environment. The following sizing tools are available for ProLiant BL server products:

- ProLiant BL p-Class Power Calculator
- ProLiant BL e-Class Power Calculator

Based on performance data on HP servers running Microsoft products, the utilities are flexible, graphical tools that provide valuable information to help plan for delivery and installation of ProLiant BL systems. ProLiant Power Calculators are macro-driven Microsoft Excel spreadsheets developed to (1) review server loading to determine the number of power supplies required to provide redundancy, and (2) approximate the electrical and heat load per server for facilities planning.

Based on configuration criteria, these utilities generate site-planning information, such as power distribution requirements and environmental specifications. You can configure each server blade with appropriate options, choose interconnects for each enclosure, and enter power information. Enter information based on your environment and equipment requirements to calculate the following:

- Power specifications
- Summary of server blade components in the rack
- Number of power supplies and power enclosures needed for configuration entered
- System weight

### 10.6.5.1 PROLIANT BL E-CLASS POWER CALCULATOR

Use the drop-down menu to configure the system by selecting Line Input Voltage; the number of power supplies; amount of memory; and the number of processors, expansion cards, and hard drives. Then watch for error messages and correct as necessary.

### 10.6.5.2 PROLIANT BL P-CLASS POWER CALCULATOR

To configure each enclosure, follow these steps:

1. Click the Configure Enclosure X button.
2. Enter information on the Configurator page; then click Done to return to the main page.
3. Use the drop-down menu to configure the system by selecting interconnect switches, type of blades, the number of processors, and the amount and type of hard drives, network cards, and memory. Also select the line voltage and number of line phases.
4. View the results and repeat as necessary.

The BL p-class Power Calculator generates an equipment list that can be copied to another spreadsheet.

The ProLiant BL10e and ProLiant BL p-Class System Power Calculators can be downloaded from http://activeanswers.compaq.com/configurator/.

### 10.6.5.3  POWER CALCULATOR FEATURES AND BENEFITS

No other blade calculator in the industry matches the ProLiant BL series Power Calculators features. For example

■ Every value used in the calculator is an actual measured value, not an extrapolation from a formula.

■ The calculators were written in Excel, ensuring widespread compatibility and portability.

■ No macros were incorporated into the worksheet, ensuring accurate information even for customers who disable Microsoft macros.

Additional benefits include the following:

■ Summary of the entire rack at a glance, including the following:
  • Power consumption for the entire rack
  • Part numbers for selected rack components
  • Individual server blade configuration

■ Support for mixed server blades on the same enclosure

■ Support for mixed patch panels on different enclosures

## 10.7  Service Considerations for All UPSs

A self-test can be run on any HP UPS by pressing the Test/Alarm/Reset button for three seconds. This button also resets an audible alarm when pressed for two seconds.

Access to the hot-swappable batteries is through the front panel. These batteries are to be replaced by service personnel only.

An optional Multi-Server UPS Card can be added that facilitates direct communication with up to three servers through the serial ports. The Scalable Card option enables three HP UPSs to work together as a virtual UPS.

Other than the hot-swappable batteries and add-on cards, the 700, 1000, 2000, and 3000 series are whole-unit replaceable. The 3000XR and 6000 have a replaceable electronics module. HP UPSs ship with a 3-3-3 warranty.

The sleep mode function is enabled by default, causing the UPS to shut itself down in approximately five minutes when it does not detect a minimum load for 5% to 10% attached to the UPS ports. This shutdown occurs independently of any software shutdown settings. Sleep mode is designed to save battery power. To prevent the sleep mode function from enabling with minimal load, disable it by following the steps outlined in the UPS user guide.

All HP UPSs make a clicking sound when the internal relay makes a switch from a buck-to-boost status or from a boost-to-buck status. This is a normal occurrence. If the UPS is clicking repetitively, run a self-test by following the steps outlined in the UPS user guide. If a problem is detected, an audio alarm sounds and an LED illuminates. If the self-test passes, have a qualified electrician test the A/C utility power for input voltage variations.

A high concentration of hardware connected to the same source of primary AC power through a UPS can cause damage to hardware or electrical shock to the user. Be sure to configure rack-based solutions in compliance with safety standards and electrical codes.

Moving a Multi-Server UPS Card or Scalable Card from an R3000 UPS (or earlier) into an R6000 UPS will produce the following error message:

```
Communications Failure with UPS.
```

To eliminate the error, upgrade the UPS option card to the latest firmware version.

For the Multi-Server UPS Card ROM, use spares kit 341260-001.

For the Scalable Card ROM, use spares kit 105998-001.

When configured with an HP UPS and running HP Power Management agents, a Novell NetWare 5.x server with the multiprocessor option enabled may lose communication with the UPS and display an error message similar to the following at the console:

```
09/09/00 10:59am. Communications failure with UPS
```

To eliminate the error, update UPSBASE.NLM of the HP Power Management agents for NetWare 1.70, available as Softpaq SP12978.

Do not connect laser printers to a UPS because the printers pull an extensive load when powered on.

**Never modify a UPS or the UPS power cord. Doing so could void the UPS warranty.**

## ▲ Summary

This chapter explained key skills and concepts relating to HP rack and power technologies, including skills necessary to perform basic troubleshooting on power technologies.

As an *Accredited Integration Specialist* (AIS), you should be able to properly position HP rack and power technologies and recommend an appropriate solution for a given customer situation.

## ▲ LEARNING CHECK

1. *What hardware component managed through HP Power Management software is required to manage multiple platforms with one UPS?*

2. *If a UPS is beeping every five seconds, what problem could be indicated?*

3. *What should you do with an HP UPS that is clicking repeatedly?*

4. *Match each of the following to the correct description:*

   | | |
   |---|---|
   | Leveling feet | Provides a direct connection to multiple servers |
   | Coupling kit | Required for standalone racks |
   | Console switch | Rack configuration tool |
   | Stabilizing feet | Take the full weight of the rack |
   | Rack Builder Online | Required for multiple rack configurations |

# HP Storage Technologies

**A**n HP Accredited System Engineer should understand the storage technologies that are used in, or used with, HP ProLiant servers.

Part 3 of this book explains the HP storage products and technologies.

Here is an overview of the chapters in Part 3.

## Chapter 11   HP SCSI Implementation

Chapter 11 provides an overview of the HP SCSI implementations that ensure high performance, scalability, and compatibility across the HP server product family. Key topics explained include HP StorageWorks SCSI adapters, HP SCSI drives, and hot-plug capabilities of HP SCSI drives.

## Chapter 12   HP ProLiant Storage

Chapter 12 explains key network storage technologies, such as *direct-attached storage* (DAS), *network attached storage* (NAS) and *storage area networks* (SANs). In addition, the HP *Enterprise Storage Architecture* (ENSA) is explained, and the HP StorageWorks MSA Disk family of products is described.

## Chapter 13   HP Array Technologies

Chapter 13 contains information that is absolutely vital for Accredited Integration Specialists. This chapter discusses the key advantages, features, and capabilities of HP Smart Array controllers. In addition, the utilities used to configure and optimize these utilities are explained. Finally, ATA RAID is discussed.

# HP SCSI Implementation

HP has developed SCSI implementations that ensure high performance, scalability, and compatibility across the HP product family. These innovations are fully integrated and tested with all HP storage solutions and ProLiant servers.

This chapter covers the following topics:

- HP StorageWorks SCSI adapters
- HP SCSI drives
- Hot-plug capabilities of HP SCSI drives

| 11.1 | **HP StorageWorks SCSI Adapters** |

All HP SCSI adapters are fully integrated and tested with the entire line of ProLiant servers and management software. HP adapters use *tagged command queuing* (TCQ) to improve performance by accepting commands simultaneously, sorting efficiently, and minimizing response time.

HP StorageWorks adapter products provide a range of connectivity alternatives for SCSI-based solutions, including non-hot-swappable SCSI hard drives and secondary tape storage and backup solutions.

HP SCSI adapters feature the following:

- Data transfer rates of up to 160MB/s per channel for 64-bit/66MHz dual-channel products
- 64-bit/66MHz dual-channel Wide-Ultra3 SCSI adapter
- Data transfer rates of up to 80MB/s per channel for 64-bit dual-channel products
- Tape array installation for 64-bit/66MHz dual-channel products
- 66MHz and 33MHz PCI support for 66MHz products
- Dual independent channels for up to 28 device connections
- Backward compatibility with most earlier SCSI protocols, including Wide-Ultra SCSI, Fast-Wide SCSI-2, and Fast SCSI-2 devices

| 11.2 | **HP SCSI Drives** |

HP drives differ from the original drives supplied by the manufacturer. The hardware is generally identical, but HP has modified the firmware to support extra features, including the following:

- Reorganization of the drive geometry
- Self-monitoring of performance characteristics
- Support for HP Prefailure Warranty
- Added functions
- Enhanced diagnostics
- Enhanced error detection and correction

This chapter explains how HP has added value to the traditional SCSI drives.

### 11.2.1   HP Wide-Ultra2 and Wide-Ultra3 drives

HP Wide-Ultra2 and Wide-Ultra3 drives use a drive carrier that features a strong mechanical design and improved drive cooling. Greater packaging density allows more than a 25% increase in packaging drives in servers and storage enclosures.

HP Wide-Ultra2 and Wide-Ultra3 drives are not backward compatible with drive cages and storage expansion units designed for Fast and Wide-Ultra SCSI. A drive height converter is required if a 1-inch disk drive is installed in a 1.6-inch drive bay to comply with cooling requirements.

Universal disk drives can be used in Intel- and Alpha-based systems. The firmware is the only difference between a standard drive and a universal drive. They may be 7,200, 10K or 15K rpm. Universal drives have a blue stripe on the swing arm label.

### 11.2.2   10K and 15K RPM Drives

A 10K rpm drive offers high performance. In file and print server environments, the performance increase can be as high as 40% compared to 7,200 rpm drives.

First-generation 10K drives should be installed only in systems with hot-plug support because of their higher power consumption. First-generation 10K drives must not be used when the ambient temperature is higher than 30 degrees C.

A 15K rpm drive offers extremely high performance. In file and print server environments, the performance increase can be as high as 30% compared to 10K drives and 60% compared to 7,200 rpm drives.

**When using third-party drives, you might have problems such as time-outs and general data corruption. The firmware of drives supplied by HP has been optimized for RAID environments and supports prefailure warning mechanisms and advanced diagnostics.**

**11.3**      ## Hot-Plug SCSI Drives

All HP drives that are mounted on a hot-plug drive carrier can be removed and installed during system operation.

The SCSI ID of hot-pluggable drives is assigned automatically. The bay position of the drive automatically determines the SCSI ID. The IDs are hard-coded on the backplane board. The SCSI ID is assigned to the drive bay and not to the drive itself; so when you remove a hot-pluggable drive, it will lose its SCSI ID.

The SCSI controller, not the drives, controls HP hot-pluggable drive LEDs. If you use a third-party controller, you will have no support for the LEDs.

### 11.3.1 Hot-Plug Drive Support

Several of the advantages provided by Smart Array controllers require hot-pluggable SCSI drives. Without hot-pluggable drives, the following operations cannot be completed with the drive online:

- Replacement of a failed drive in a fault-tolerant array
- Addition of drives and arrays
- Expansion of arrays

Although HP supports non-hot-pluggable drives on all of its array controllers, they are not recommended. One of the primary advantages of array controllers is the ability to recover fully from a drive failure without taking the server offline. This capability requires the use of hot-pluggable drives in conjunction with an array controller.

### 11.3.2 Hot-Pluggable Drive LEDs

The HP Smart Array controller firmware is enhanced so that when the controller detects that an attached hot-pluggable hard drive has entered a degraded status, the amber LED on the hard drive flashes. This enhancement allows easier detection and replacement of the affected physical hard drive, especially when reported by a system management utility such as Insight Manager 7. The affected hot-pluggable hard drive remains online and displays the LED combinations listed in the following table.

Figure 11–1 shows the various meanings of the LED indicators.

The following table explains LED indicators.

| Status | Condition |
|---|---|
| Online | On |
| Drive Access | On, off, or blinking |
| Drive Failure | Blinking amber |

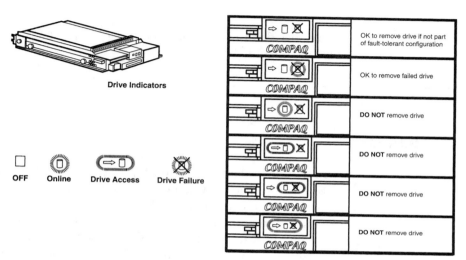

Drive Indicators

| | | |
|---|---|---|
| □ | OFF | |
| Online | | |
| Drive Access | | |
| Drive Failure | | |

OK to remove drive if not part of fault-tolerant configuration

OK to remove failed drive

DO NOT remove drive

DO NOT remove drive

DO NOT remove drive

DO NOT remove drive

**Figure 11–1**   *Drive LED indicators.*

This feature is not supported in a non-fault-tolerant RAID 0 configuration. The controller must be in a fault-tolerant configuration: RAID 1, RAID 1+0, RAID 5, or RAID *advanced data guarding* (ADG).

## 11.3.3   Replacing Hot-Pluggable SCSI Drives

Built-in hot-plug drive support enables you to insert or remove drives in fault-tolerant configurations with the system running.

If the hard drive LED activity light is on or flashing while the online light is also on, it indicates that the drive is online and being accessed. If a predictive failure alert is received when the online and drive access lights are on simultaneously (provided that the array is configured for fault tolerance and all other drives in the array are online), you can replace the drive online. Remove the drive only if the replacement drive is immediately available.

A drive can be hot-plugged during normal activity. When a drive is hot-plugged, the subsystem will no longer be fault tolerant until the removed drive is replaced and the rebuild operation is completed.

If another drive fails when replacing a hot-pluggable disk drive, the entire array will be lost.

## ▲ Summary

Chapter 11 added the HP layer on top of the industry-standard SCSI concepts you learned back in Chapter 6 by explaining how HP has added value to the SCSI implementation in HP ProLiant servers.

This chapter discussed the architecture of HP StorageWorks SCSI adapters and the features and benefits of HP SCSI drives.

Finally, this chapter explained HP hot-plug support with SCSI drives, how to interpret the SCSI drive LED indicators, and the rules for swapping hot-plug drives.

## ▲ LEARNING CHECK

1. *What technology is implemented in HP SCSI adapters to accept commands simultaneously, sort them efficiently, and minimize response time?*

2. *List the ways that HP drives differ from original manufacturer drives.*

3. *What determines the SCSI ID of a hot-pluggable SCSI drive?*

4. *What does a flashing amber light mean on a hot-plug SCSI drive?*

# HP ProLiant Storage

This chapter explains the following topics:

- Network storage technologies, such as direct-attached storage (DAS), network attached storage (NAS), and storage area networks (SANs)
- HP Enterprise Storage Architecture (ENSA)
- The HP StorageWorks MSA Disk family of products

IT infrastructures need speed and flexibility to adapt to dynamic markets. The HP approach to delivering storage enables a business to be competitive in the following areas:

- Physical resources serve as highly available data repositories.
- Virtualization capabilities simplify storage management and extend the span of management of physical storage resources.
- Resource-level storage management capabilities serve to configure, provision, control, and maintain storage.

**243**

## 12.1    HP StorageWorks

HP StorageWorks products for small and medium-size businesses include a complete line of disk systems and *modular SAN array* (MSA) systems, designed to achieve greater agility for changing business needs.

Storage requirements have evolved beyond the type and capacity of drives attached to a single server. As a result, the need for a high-speed connection between servers and storage devices has become critical to business performance. Storage solutions that are designed to meet these requirements include the following:

- Direct-attached storage (DAS)
- Network attached storage (NAS)
- Storage area network (SAN)
- HP Enterprise Network Storage Architecture (ENSA)

The key features of DAS, NAS, and SAN, are shown in Figure 12–1.

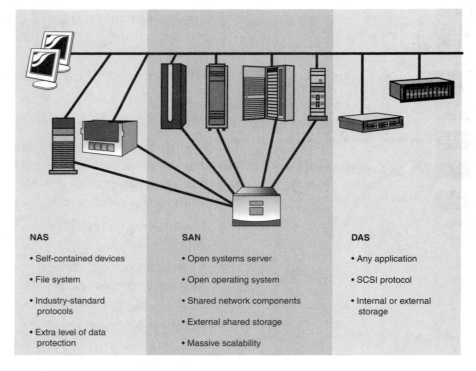

**Figure 12–1** *Comparison of storage solutions.*

### 12.1.1 Direct-Attached Storage

A DAS solution consists of an open-system server running any customer application and with dedicated internal or external storage subsystems using the SCSI protocol. This type of technology provides dedicated storage for multiple clients with a one-to-one server-to-storage ratio.

DAS offers the easiest way to deploy incremental amounts of storage as needed without extensive upfront planning. Because RAID inside the server is becoming less expensive, DAS is growing in popularity. Currently more than 70% of all storage deployed is DAS.

Smart Array controllers in a DAS configuration provide the ideal platform for high-performance applications such as databases, e-mail and messaging, and other applications that benefit from high I/O performance.

Advantages of DAS include the following:

- High performance
- Easy deployment
- Relatively inexpensive to acquire, maintain, and expand
- Fast server-to-storage data transfer
- Easy migration to SAN solutions

Although many customers currently have separate storage systems with storage management software products that are connected to individual servers, this strategy produces islands of data dispersed throughout a distributed IT environment.

Disadvantages of the DAS method include the following:

- Inefficient use of resources
- Unnecessarily duplicated equipment
- Server-based management model

### 12.1.2 Network Attached Storage

NAS servers are self-contained, intelligent devices that attach directly to your existing LAN. A file system is located and managed on the NAS device and data is transferred to clients over industry-standard network protocols using industry-standard file-sharing protocols. This intelligence on the NAS device enables true data sharing among heterogeneous network clients.

### 12.1.3 Storage Area Network

A SAN solution can be described as open-system servers running customer applications on an open operating system. The solution includes shared external storage resources, network infrastructure components (Fibre Channel hubs and switches), and value-added software for enhanced storage and data management. This technology provides consolidated and virtualized storage with massive scalability and fault tolerance.

### 12.1.4 HP Enterprise Network Storage Architecture

ENSA brings SAN, NAS, and DAS together in an architecture that meets enterprise storage requirements. Described as storage virtualization, ENSA products create pools of virtual storage from local or remote physical disks. These scalable storage pools offer flexible capacity to applications, and hardware and software fault-tolerant technologies maximize availability of the storage pool.

For more information on HP StorageWorks products, visit http://h18006.www1.hp.com/storage/arraysystems.html.

## 12.2 StorageWorks Disk Systems

HP ProLiant storage utilizes HP StorageWorks products for small and medium-size businesses. HP StorageWorks products include a complete line of disk systems and MSA systems, designed to achieve greater agility for changing business needs.

The current HP StorageWorks MSA product line is examined in this chapter.

## 12.3 StorageWorks MSA20

The MSA20 enclosure is a SATA 1.5 Gb/s disk drive storage enclosure with Ultra320 SCSI host connectivity. The MSA20 is a 2U rack-mountable 12-drive SATA external enclosure that is for minimum I/O workloads such as reference data, archival, and disk-to-disk backup.

All models of the MSA20 enclosure family have the following features:

- Support for SATA 160GB and 250GB drives allows up to 3TB of raw storage capacity in a 2U enclosure.

- Supports up to 12 (1-inch) SATA 1.5 Gb/s Universal serial hard disk drives.

- Up to 24TB of raw storage capacity in 18U when deployed behind the MSA1500 SAN controller shelf.

- Houses up to 21 enclosures in one 42U rack for a single-rack storage capacity of up to 63TB of disk storage.

- Ultra320 (LVD) host support—compatibility with sixth generation Smart Array controllers.

- 128MB battery-backed write cache with 72hr battery life.

- Integrated Smart Array technology to minimize drive-rebuild time.

- Support for RAID 0, RAID 1, RAID 5, and *advanced data guarding* (ADG).

- Hot-pluggable disk drives, power supplies, and fans.

- Redundant fans and redundant power supplies.

- Integrated environmental monitoring—monitors environmental conditions within the enclosure and components, such as the power supply and fans.

- Easy removal of parts provides better serviceability. No tools are required.

## 12.4   StorageWorks MSA30

The MSA30 enclosure, shown in Figure 12–2, is a 3U, Ultra320 SCSI disk drive storage enclosure. The MSA30 is intended for use with servers delivering business-critical data and applications with requirements for high availability, performance, excellent serviceability, and large storage capacity.

**Figure 12–2**

*StorageWorks MSA30 enclosure.*

All models of the MSA30 enclosure family have the following features:

- 3U rack height.
- Supports up to 14 (1-inch) Ultra 2, Ultra3, or Ultra320 Universal hard drives.
- Provides storage capacity of up to 2.05TB per enclosure (using 146.8GB 1-inch disk drives).
- Houses up to 14 enclosures in one 42U rack for a single-rack storage capacity of up to 28.7TB of disk storage.
- Ultra320 (LVD) support, delivering maximum data transfer rates up to 320 MB/s per channel.
- Direct-connect drive carrier, which provides better cooling and reliability for 10K and 15K rpm drives.
- Hot-pluggable disk drives, power supplies, and fans.
- Redundant fans, redundant power supplies, and dual bus I/O module.
- Environmental monitoring unit (EMU) that monitors environmental conditions within the enclosure and components such as the power supply and fans.
- Easy removal of parts provides better serviceability. No tools are required.

## 12.5 StorageWorks MSA500 G2

The MSA500 G2, shown in Figure 12–3, is a 4U, Ultra320 SCSI storage enclosure. It supports up to 14 HP Universal disk drives and is expandable with an in-place upgrade to the MSA1000. The MSA500 G2 system adds support for four-node clusters and a combined cluster and storage-sharing environment.

Providing high data availability at SCSI economics, the MSA500 G2 offers superior data protection and increased uptime with redundant controllers, power supplies and fans, and the Smart Array Multipath software option to provide multiple I/O paths to the same logical volume.

**Figure 12–3**

*StorageWorks MSA500 enclosure.*

Because the MSA500 G2 is SCSI based, there are no Fibre Channel infrastructure requirements such as hubs, switches, and cables, allowing for significantly lower initial investment when compared to Fibre Channel SANs. Armed with DAS-to-SAN (DtS) technology, the MSA500 G2 adaptive infrastructure permits seamless conversion from SCSI protocol to the Fibre Channel-based HP StorageWorks MSA1000.

Key MSA500 G2 features include the following:

- Four-node clustering support
- High-bandwidth Ultra320 SCSI controllers and connectivity
- 256MB read/write cache standard, expandable to 512MB cache
- Double the performance for RAID 5 and RAID ADG environments
- Rapid drive-rebuild technology; 5x drive-rebuild acceleration
- Two Ultra320 SCSI adapters included in MSA500 G2 package; no additional HBA purchase necessary
- Scalable to 2TB with 146GB disk drives (upgrade to MSA1000 for 6TB)

## 12.6   StorageWorks MSA1000

The MSA1000, shown in Figure 12–4, is a 4U, 2Gb Fibre Channel storage system for the entry-level to midrange SAN. Designed to reduce the complexity, expense, and risk of SAN deployments, it provides the customer with a low-cost, scalable, high-performance storage system with investment protection.

The MSA1000 ships standard with a single high-performance controller. Options include a second controller; with the addition of two more drive enclosures, it controls up to 42 Ultra2, Ultra3, or Ultra320 SCSI drives, for 6TB capacity.

**Figure 12–4**

*StorageWorks MSA1000 enclosure.*

You can install an optional eight-port SAN switch in the MSA1000, which is a cost-effective and space-saving method of attaching this entry-level storage unit to a large SAN environment. This switch offers low-price-per-port connectivity and full interoperability with most external SAN switches from HP. An optional embedded three-port hub easily facilitates a basic two-node SAN at the lowest possible cost.

Key features and benefits of the MSA1000 include the following:

- **Versatility**—Supports Windows 2003 (32- and 64-bit), Windows 2000 and NT, NetWare, Linux (32- and 64-bit), and Tru64 UNIX or Open-VMS operating systems
- **Performance**—Provides transmission rate of up to 30K I/O per second (cache), throughput of up to 200MB
- **Compatibility**—Supports 14 1-inch drives and 1 or 2Gb Fabric Switches or hubs in a 4U rack space
- **Scalability**—Is easily expanded to 6TB using forty-two 146 GB hard drives in 10U of rack space
- **Integration**—Allows installation of an optional internal eight-port switch or three-port hub
- **Serviceability**—Supports hot-plug drives, controllers, fans, power supplies, switches, and hubs
- **Reliability**—Supports RAID ADG

**12.7**  ## StorageWorks MSA1500

The MSA1500 is a Fibre Channel SAN attached 2U controller shelf that connects to HP StorageWorks SATA and/or SCSI disk enclosures. The MSA1500 solution has been designed as a hardware foundation for which future solutions can be designed and implemented for investment protection.

The MSA1500 has capacity for up to eight attached SATA enclosures, which can provide the customer with up to 24TB (96 to 250GB SATA disk drives) of raw capacity. If the business needs SCSI reliability, then attach up to four SCSI enclosures for a raw capacity of 8TB (using 56 to 146GB SCSI disks).

The MSA1500 utilizes existing SCSI drive enclosures and MSA1000 controller technology, integrating low-cost SATA hard drives and enclosures. Key features include the following:

- **Capacity**—24TB (8 SATA shelves) using up to 96 to 250GB SATA disk drives.

- **Modular 2U rackmount disk array controller shelf**—Ability to attach SCSI and SATA enclosures.

- **Advanced data guarding (ADG)**—Highest level of fault tolerance, allocating two sets of parity data across drives and allows simultaneous write operations, this level of fault tolerance can withstand two simultaneous drive failures without downtime or data loss.

- **2Gb/1Gb Fibre connections to host**—Supports both 1Gb and 2Gb Fibre Channel fabrics to ensure your investment in 1Gb infrastructure is protected.

- **Hot-plug expansion and replacement support**—Hot-plug expansion and replacement of hard drives, redundant controllers, for simple, fast installation and maintenance. Fans and power supplies are also hot-plug replaceable.

- **Integrated configuration and management tools**—Uses standard ProLiant and MSA family management and utility software. These tools consistently lower the cost of ownership by reducing training and technical expertise needed to install and maintain the MSA1500.

## ▲ Summary

This chapter provided a high-level overview of network storage technologies, including direct-attached storage, network attached storage, storage area networks, and HP Enterprise Network Storage Architecture (ENSA). In addition, this chapter provided an overview of the HP StorageWorks MSA storage systems.

## ▲ LEARNING CHECK

1. *Where should first-generation 10,000-rpm drives be installed?*

2. *List three advantages of DAS.*

# HP Array Technologies

After studying this chapter, you should be able to do the following:

- List and describe the advantages of HP Smart Array controllers

- List and describe the utilities used to configure, optimize, and troubleshoot HP Array controllers.

- Explain the key technological advantages of HP Array controllers

- Describe ATA RAID, and explain how HP ProLiant servers support this drive array configuration

All HP Smart Array products use a standard set of technologies and management and utility software to facilitate storage management.

The array controller utilities discussed in this chapter include the following:

- Array Diagnostics Utility (ADU)
- Array Configuration Utility (ACU)
- Array Configuration Utility XE (ACU XE)
- Option ROM Configuration for Arrays (ORCA)

The array controller technologies discussed in this chapter include the following:

- Online spare drives
- Online drive array expansion
- Logical drive capacity extension
- Online RAID-level migration
- Online stripe-size migration
- HP hard drive failure prediction technology
- Dynamic sector repair (DSR)
- Hot-plug drive support
- Automatic data recovery
- Array accelerator (read/write cache)
- Data protection
- Array performance tuning

In addition, this chapter discusses HP's implementation of ATA RAID.

## 13.1 Advantages of HP Smart Array Controllers

As data storage requirements increase and computing needs change, flexibility within server configurations and in storage configurations becomes more important. The HP Smart Array controller family includes a standard toolset that you can use to configure array controllers, expand an existing array configuration by adding disk drives, or reconfigure an array by extending volume sizes.

Only select Smart Array controllers offer RAID *advanced data guarding* (ADG), which offers higher fault tolerance than RAID 5 with lower implementation costs than RAID 1+0 and greater usable capacity per U than RAID 1. Using patented HP technology, you can safely deploy large-capacity disk drives and create large storage volumes.

In a RAID 1+0 configuration, all HP Smart Array controllers can

- Sustain multiple drive failures.
- Sustain an entire bus failure if the drives are equally distributed across buses.
- Service I/O requests to all operational drives in a degraded condition.
- Survive $n/2$ drive failures, where $n$ is the number of drives in the array, as long as one member of each mirrored pair survives.

**RAID 1+0 can support multiple drive failures when multiple drives that fail are not in the same mirrored pair.**

For RAID 5, HP recommends that no more than 14 (8 is optimal) physical drives be used per logical drive. Because logical drive failure is much less likely with RAID ADG, however, HP supports the use of up to 56 physical drives per drive array when running this fault-tolerance method.

## 13.2    HP Array Controller Utilities

HP provides several utilities that are used to configure, optimize, and troubleshoot HP Array controllers. These utilities include the following:

- Array Diagnostics Utility (ADU)
- Array Configuration Utility (ACU)
- Array Configuration Utility XE (ACU XE)
- Option ROM Configuration for Arrays (ORCA)

### 13.2.1    Array Diagnostics Utility

HP provides an ADU to help you quickly identify such problems as the following:

- An incorrect version of firmware
- Drives installed in the wrong order
- Inappropriate error rates
- A failed battery on the array accelerator board

The ADU displays a detailed analysis of the system configuration. If the cause of a problem is still not apparent, the ADU can generate a full report that administrators can fax or e-mail to HP customer service for phone support.

Beginning with HP SmartStart and Support Software Release 4.10, ADU 1.10 replaced the Drive Array Advanced Diagnostics (DAAD) utility. The DAAD utility is no longer included on the SmartStart CD and has not been updated to support current Smart Array controllers.

To run ADU properly, boot the system from the SmartStart CD and select ADU from the System Utilities screen.

### 13.2.2  Array Configuration Utility

The HP ACU, shown in Figure 13–1, allows both online local and remote management and configuration of an array through a browser. The ACU simplifies array configuration by providing an interface to the intelligent features of HP Smart Array controllers. The ACU can be started from within the supported operating system or from the HP SmartStart CD.

ACU features include the following:

- Configuration wizards for optimized array configurations
- Express and custom initial configuration options
- Easy reconfiguration through capacity expansion, logical drive extension, RAID-level migration, and stripe-size migration tools
- Support for fault-tolerance RAID levels 0, 1, 1+0, 5, and RAID ADG
- User-selectable stripe sizes
- Variable cache read/write ratio and stripe size for tuning controller performance
- Set drive rebuild and capacity expansion priorities
- Online spare (hot spare) configuration
- Separate fault tolerance configuration on a logical drive basis
- Blinking drive tray LEDs for quick storage identification

ACU can manage all Smart Array controllers from one central location. It enables you to

- Perform online array expansions.
- Perform online logical drive capacity extensions.
- Perform online RAID-level migrations.
- Perform online stripe-size migrations.
- Perform configuration using configuration wizards.
- Perform drive and expansion priority changes.
- Perform stripe-size selection.
- Perform controller performance tuning through variable cache read/write ratios and stripe sizes.
- Perform storage identification with blinking drive tray LEDs.
- Configure online spares (hot spares).
- Configure the array accelerator.
- Configure RAID 0, 1, 1+0, 5, and ADG.
- Configure separate fault tolerance on a logical drive basis.
- Leverage express and custom initial configuration options.

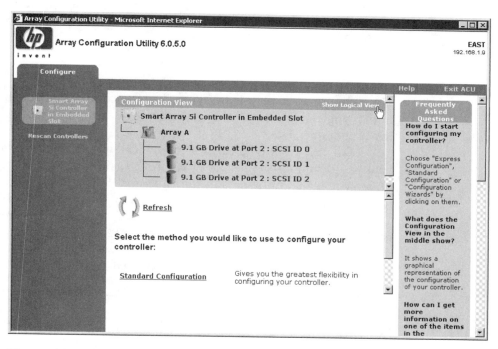

**Figure 13–1**  *Array Configuration Utility interface.*

ACU is compatible with Microsoft Internet Explorer 5.0 and later.

After you display the ACU, the utility will automatically begin detecting the controllers that are installed on your system. Based on your type of controllers, the following options display:

- **Express Configuration**—Allows the ACU utility to set up the optimum configuration for the controller automatically
- **Assisted Configuration**—Enables you to configure the controllers using the Configuration Wizard manually
- **Advanced Configuration**—Enables you to configure the controller manually

Download the ACU from the ACU home page at http://h18004. www1.hp.com/products/servers/proliantstorage/software-management/ acumatrix/index.html.

In most cases, all disk drives attached to a controller should be grouped into a single array. This configuration provides the most efficient use of RAID fault tolerance.

Using the ACU, you can assign physical drives to an array and designate up to four drives per array controller as online spares. All physical drives within an array should be the same size. If disks of higher capacity are installed within a single array, the extra capacity will not be available.

Up to 32 logical drives can be defined with any HP Smart Array controller. Some operating systems support fewer than 32 logical drives.

### 13.2.2.1 LOCATION OF ARRAY CONFIGURATION DATA

When the array configuration is saved from ACU, the information is stored on the *RAID information sector* (RIS) on each hard drive. This allows replacement of computer components without losing data. A set of drives can also be moved from one machine to another without losing data.

Changes to logical volume structure and RAID level are often data-destructive.

### 13.2.3   Option ROM Configuration for Arrays

ORCA executes out of the option ROM that is located on an array controller, including on the RAID LC2 controller. It is designed for users who have minimal configuration requirements. During *Power-On Self-Test* (POST), any array controller that supports ORCA will provide a prompt to the computer system console as part of the initialization process.

If there are no configured logical drives on the array controller, this prompt waits 10 seconds before bypassing ORCA and continuing with POST. If any logical drives are configured, the prompt waits 5 seconds. When a HP RAID controller with ORCA support is installed in the system, the controller-based option ROM prompts during POST for 10 seconds.

Press the F8 key to start ORCA.

The main features of ORCA include the following:

- Does not require disks or CDs to run
- Can be started when the server is powering up
- Creates, configures, and deletes logical drives
- Configures controller order
- Assigns an online spare for the created logical drives
- Specifies RAID levels
- Cannot set stripe size or controller settings
- Supports only English

#### 13.2.3.1   CONFIGURATION METHODS

Only the newest HP Smart Array controller models support ORCA. All other HP Smart Array controllers only support ACU. The HP RAID LC2 controller can be configured with ORCA only.

ORCA does not support drive expansion, RAID-level migration, or setting the stripe size.

| 13.3 | **Array Controller Technologies and Capabilities** |
|---|---|

Several key capabilities and technologies are implemented in HP array controllers, including the following:

- Online spare drives
- Array capacity expansion
- Logical volume extension
- Online RAID-level migration
- Online stripe-size migration
- Hard drive failure prediction
- Dynamic sector repair
- Hot-plug drive support
- Automatic data recovery
- Array accelerator (read/write cache)
- Data protection
- Array performance tuning

It is important for Accredited Integration Specialists to understand these technologies and features.

### 13.3.1   Online Spare Drives

The online spare drive acts as a temporary replacement for a failed drive, as illustrated in Figure 13–2. One online spare drive can be added to any fault-tolerant logical drive (RAID 0 is not supported). An online spare may be assigned to more than one array, if efficient use of drive capacity is important. The capacity of the online spare must be at least as large as that of the other drives in the array. All HP Smart Array controllers support up to four online spare drives.

When a data drive fails, the online spare drive automatically starts to rebuild the data of the failed drive. After the online spare drive has been completely rebuilt, the failure of a second drive can be handled without data loss. A second drive most likely will not fail until the online drive has been rebuilt; nevertheless, only ADG can handle two simultaneous drive failures in all cases.

As soon as the failed drive is replaced, data is automatically rebuilt on the new drive. After data has been completely rebuilt on the new drive, the online spare switches back to its role as an online spare drive. This avoids roaming online spare drives.

**Figure 13–2**

*How an online spare drive works.*

**RAID 5 Protected Logical Drive**

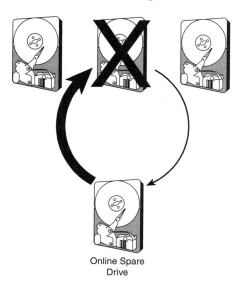

Online Spare
Drive

Data is rebuilt to the online spare at a rate of 10 to 20 minutes per gigabyte, depending on the priority assigned to rebuilding and the total number of drives in the array.

The online spare drive does not have to be partitioned or formatted. The online drive is always active and running, even when it is not in use.

Insight Manager 7 can monitor the online spare drive just like all the other active drives.

The online spare drive is available for RAID 1, RAID 1+0, RAID 4, RAID 5, and RAID ADG.

**! IMPORTANT**

Selecting a high rebuild priority results in reduced server performance while the rebuild is in progress. Setting the rebuild priority to low allows normal server performance, because rebuilding only occurs when the server is idle; rebuild time can be significantly longer depending on system activity.

### 13.3.2   Array Capacity Expansion

To perform an online array expansion, install a new drive in a hot-pluggable drive bay and use the ACU to add the new drive to an existing array. Figure 13–3 illustrates capacity expansion.

All data is relocated after the expansion process is started. Redistributing data across all the drives creates free space in each drive. These zones on all drives are then available to create a new logical drive or extend the capacity of an existing logical drive.

When the new logical drive is presented to the operating system after the expansion process, the operating system does not see a larger drive. It sees the old logical drive and a new logical drive. The expansion process is independent of the operating system. For example, if a 10GB logical volume is expanded from four drives to six drives, the operating system is unaware of this change.

**Note**

Physical drive expansion does not create a larger logical drive, but creates a new logical drive. It is visible to the operating system after the expansion process is completed.

Drive array expansion is performed at the array controller level, not at the logical drive level. In most cases, all disk drives attached to a controller should be grouped together into a single array. This provides the most efficient use of RAID fault tolerance. Using the ACU, you can assign physical drives to an array and designate up to four drives per array controller as online spares.

Up to 32 logical drives can be defined with any HP Smart Array controller. All drives within an array should be the same size. If disks of higher capacity are installed within a single array, the extra capacity will not be available. Some operating systems support fewer than 32 logical drives.

**Figure 13–3**

*How an online spare drive works.*

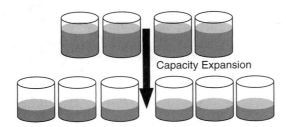

Capacity Expansion

Under Windows 2003, Windows 2000, Windows NT, Linux, and Novell NetWare, the ACU can be started online. The server does not have to be powered down when disks are configured.

The amount of time required to perform the online capacity expansion depends on several parameters, including drive speed, server processor speed, the amount of I/O work the server is doing, and the priority level of the capacity expansion.

The priority level can be changed from low (the default in ACU) to medium or high to expand the volumes as quickly as possible. Depending on these factors, the expansion process takes between 10 to 15 minutes per gigabyte.

All current HP Smart Array controllers support online array expansion without data loss. Data reallocation runs as a background process. It can be assigned a high, medium, or low priority depending on the performance required when the data is reallocated. RAID protection is maintained throughout reallocation. The time required for data reallocation depends on the size of the logical drive.

### 13.3.3   Logical Volume Extension

Performing a drive extension is the process of growing the size of a logical drive. In this case, the increased size of the logical drive is reported to the operating system. Volume extension is illustrated in Figure 13–4.

Only operating systems that support volume extension can use the added capacity without losing data.

**Figure 13–4**

*Logical volume extension.*

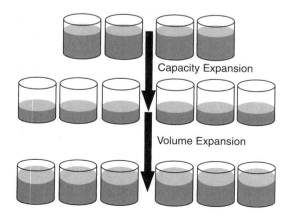

Not all operating systems support online logical drive extension through the ACU.

Windows, NetWare, and other advanced operating systems support volume and logical drive extension, which enables you to add additional drives to an existing RAID set and extend the logical drive so that it displays as free space at the end of the same drive presented to the operating system.

Linux only supports volume and logical drive extension at the operating system level. It is not supported through the logical drive extension on the array controller.

You can use the Diskpart.exe command line utility, included with Windows Server 2003 or the Windows 2000 Resource Kit, to extend an existing partition into free space.

HP OpenView Storage Volume Growth enables dynamic expansion of volumes on Microsoft Windows 2000 or Windows Server 2003 basic disks.

Third-party software vendors have created utilities that can be used to repartition disks without data loss. Most of these utilities work offline.

Some operating systems require updates or service packs to support volume or logical drive extension. For example, Windows 2000 requires at least SP3 if you are using dynamic disks. For basic disks, Windows does require SP3.

### 13.3.4 Online RAID-Level Migration

All current HP array controllers support RAID-level migration. You can easily migrate a logical drive to a new RAID level. There might need to be unused drive space available on the array for the migration to be possible, depending on the initial and final settings for the stripe size and RAID level.

Online RAID-level migration is illustrated in Figure 13–5.

In a Windows or NetWare architecture, this can be performed online without disrupting system operation or causing data loss. Offline migration can be performed with any operating system.

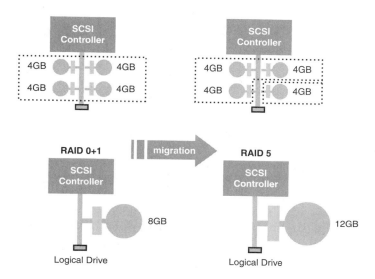

**Figure 13–5** *Online RAID-level migration.*

## 13.3.5 Online Stripe-Size Migration

All current HP array controllers also support stripe-size migration. You can easily change the stripe size of an existing logical drive using the ACU. In a Windows and NetWare architecture, this can be performed online without disrupting system operation or causing data loss. The default data stripe size for controllers differs depending on which fault-tolerant RAID is used.

## 13.3.6 Hard Drive Failure Prediction Technology

HP pioneered failure prediction technology for hard disk drives in the form of monitoring tests run by Smart Array controllers. Called *Monitoring and Performance* (M&P) or Drive Parameter Tracking, these tests externally monitor hard drive attributes such as seek times, spin-up times, and media defects (more than 20 parameters) to detect changes that could indicate potential failure.

The flowchart in Figure 13–6 illustrates the process used by drive failure protection technology.

HP worked with the hard drive industry to help develop a diagnostic and failure prediction capability known as *Self-Monitoring Analysis and Reporting Technology* (S.M.A.R.T.). Over the years, as S.M.A.R.T. matured, HP used both M&P and S.M.A.R.T. to support hard drive failure prediction technology for Prefailure Warranty replacement of hard drives.

**Figure 13–6**

*Drive failure prediction process.*

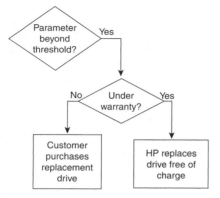

S.M.A.R.T. has now matured to the point that HP relies exclusively on this technology for hard drive failure prediction technology to support Prefailure Warranty.

Starting in 2001, HP has been shipping SCSI hard drives configured to disable M&P tests on the Smart Array controllers. This eliminates false failure predictions and improves performance by eliminating the hourly M&P controller-initiated tests.

S.M.A.R.T. improves failure prediction technology by placing monitoring capabilities within the hard disk drive. These monitoring routines are more accurate than the original M&P tests because they are designed for a specific drive type and have direct access to internal performance, calibration, and error measurements. S.M.A.R.T. uses internal performance indicators and real-time monitoring and analysis to improve data protection and fault prediction capability beyond that of the original M&P tests. In addition, HP Smart Array controllers proactively scan the hard drive media during idle time and deal with any media defects detected.

S.M.A.R.T. can often predict a problem before failure occurs. HP Smart Array controllers will recognize a S.M.A.R.T. error code and notify the system of an impending hard drive failure. Insight Manager will be notified whenever a potential problem arises. HP drives that fail to meet expected criteria are eligible for replacement under the unique HP Prefailure Warranty.

### 13.3.7   Dynamic Sector Repair (DSR)

Under normal operation, even initially defect-free drive media can develop defects. This is a common phenomenon. The bit density and rotational speed of disks is increasing every year, and so is the likelihood of problems. Usually a drive can internally remap bad sectors without external help using *cyclic redundancy check* (CRC) checksums stored at the end of each sector.

All Smart Array controllers perform a surface analysis as a background job when there is no other disk activity. Even a completely unreadable sector can be rebuilt and remapped by using the RAID capabilities of the controller.

DSR functions automatically with hardware-handled fault tolerance. DSR is unavailable when hardware fault tolerance is not used. It uses the fault tolerance of the drive subsystem to replace a bad sector with a spare sector. The correct data is written to the spare sector on the same drive.

DSR triggers automatically. The HP Smart Array controllers trigger DSR after 30 seconds of idle time.

When DSR detects a bad or a potentially bad sector, it relocates the data to a sector on a different track (as shown in Figure 13–7), just in case two sectors within the same track are bad.

DSR does not affect disk subsystem performance because it runs as a background task. DSR discontinues when the operating system makes a request.

**Figure 13–7**

*How DSR works.*

The disk drive activity LEDs flash when the DSR is running.

### 13.3.8  Hot-Plug Drive Support

Several of the advantages provided by Smart Array controllers require hot-pluggable SCSI drives. Without hot-pluggable drives, the following operations cannot be completed with the drive online:

- Replacement of a failed drive in a fault-tolerant array
- Addition of drives and arrays
- Expansion of arrays

Although HP supports non-hot-pluggable drives on all of its array controllers, they are not recommended. One of the primary advantages of array controllers is the ability to recover fully from a drive failure without taking the server offline. This capability requires the use of hot-pluggable drives in conjunction with an array controller.

#### 13.3.8.1  HOT-PLUGGABLE DRIVE LEDS

The HP Smart Array controller firmware has been enhanced so that when the controller detects that an attached hot-pluggable hard drive has entered a degraded status, the amber LED on the hard drive flashes. This enhancement allows easier detection and replacement of the affected physical hard drive, especially when reported by a system management utility such as Insight Manager. The affected hot-pluggable hard drive remains online and displays the LED combinations listed in the following table.

| Status | Condition |
| --- | --- |
| Online | On |
| Drive Access | On, off, or blinking |
| Drive Failure | Blinking amber |

This feature is not supported in a RAID 0 no-fault-tolerant configuration. The controller must be configured in a RAID 1, RAID 1+0, RAID 5, or RAID ADG fault-tolerant configuration.

### 13.3.9 Automatic Data Recovery

A Smart Array controller automatically detects whether a failed drive has been replaced. When the RAID level is set for 1, 1+0, 4, 5, or ADG, data is rebuilt automatically on the new drive. All you must do is replace the failed drive. In a system that supports hot-pluggable drives, this replacement can be done with the system up and running. The rebuild priority can be set and changed any time using the ACU.

When a drive fails, the following factors influence the data recovery time:

- Type and size of the drive
- RAID level
- Workload on the system
- Controller type
- HP Smart Array accelerator setting
- HP Smart Array drive-recovery priority level

If the system is in use during the drive rebuild, recovery time depends on the level of activity. Most systems should recover in nearly the same time with moderate activity as with no load, particularly RAID 1. RAID 5 is more sensitive to system load during the recovery period because of the considerably heavier I/O requirements of the failed system.

**! IMPORTANT**

Selecting a high rebuild priority results in reduced server performance when the rebuild is in progress. Setting a low rebuild priority allows normal server performance, because rebuilding occurs only when the server is idle; rebuild time can be significantly longer depending on system activity.

### 13.3.10   Array Accelerator (Read/Write Cache)

The array accelerator on the Smart Array controllers dramatically improves I/O performance. Depending on the controller, it can have a size of 4, 16, 32, 64, 128, or 256MB.

The array accelerator uses an intelligent read-ahead algorithm that anticipates data needs and reduces wait time. It detects sequential read activity on single or multiple I/O threads and predicts what requests will follow. The data is gathered and stored in the high-speed cache. As soon as the data is requested by the operating system, the data is delivered 100 times faster than a disk can deliver data.

Whenever random-access patterns are detected, read-ahead is disabled because reading ahead data under random I/O slows down the system instead of making it faster.

By default, the array accelerator cache capacity is equally divided between reads and writes. If your server application has significantly more reads than writes (or vice versa), you may need to change this setting to improve performance. This change can be accomplished online without rebooting the system. The optimal ratio setting is application-dependent.

If the disks are busy, new writes can be stored in the cache and written to the disk later when there is less activity (write-back). Some smaller blocks can usually be combined into larger blocks resulting in fewer but larger blocks written to the disk, thus improving performance.

The Smart Array 5300 controller is the only array controller family with upgradeable cache modules.

### 13.3.11   Data Protection

Data in a write cache demands special protection. Data protection provided by HP array controllers are battery backup, BBWC enabler, and recovery ROM.

#### 13.3.11.1   BATTERY BACKUP AND BBWC ENABLER

All Smart Array controllers with a *battery-backed write cache* (BBWC) feature a removable memory module and a BBWC enabler. A short cable connects the memory module and the enabler. In the event of a server shutdown, without using tools you can remove the memory module, the enabler, and the hard drives and install them in another ProLiant server that supports BBWC. When the new server is powered on, an initialization process writes the preserved data to the hard drives.

In the event of a general power outage, the BBWC enabler protects data in the memory module, which holds both the read cache and the write cache. You can allocate the size of each cache with the ACU.

The batteries in the BBWC enabler are recharged continuously through a trickle-charging process whenever the system power is on. The batteries protect data in a failed server for up to three or four days, depending on the size of the memory module. Under normal operating conditions, the batteries last for three years before replacement is necessary.

The BBWC enabler consists of the following components:

- A battery module, which includes a charger and status indicators
- A field-installable battery cable

Depending on the HP ProLiant server platform, there are several mechanisms for deploying a BBWC enabler. The enabler might be

- A standard feature.
- Available as an option.
- Bundled with a Smart Array 5i to 5i Plus controller upgrade.

For more information on the HP Smart Array controllers, visit http://h18004.www1.hp.com/products/servers/proliantstorage/arraycontrollers/.

### 13.3.11.2   RECOVERY ROM

Smart Array controllers feature recovery ROM, which provides protection against firmware corruption.

The controller maintains two copies of firmware in ROM. Previous working firmware is maintained when new firmware is flashed to the controller. The controller will roll over to standby firmware if corruption occurs.

Recovery ROM reduces the risk of flashing new firmware to the controller.

### 13.3.12 Array Performance Tuning

You can optimize the performance of an array in several ways, including the following:

- Choose a stripe size suitable for the type of data transfer common to the system.
- Change the fault-tolerance mode to one that requires less overhead.
- Enlarge the logical drive to span all four controller channels (depending on the controller).
- Change the read/write cache ratio in the Smart Array controller.

### 13.3.13 Disk Striping

To speed operations that retrieve data from disk storage, you can use disk striping to distribute volume segments across multiple disks. The most effective method is to distribute volume segments equally across the disks.

Striping improves disk response time by uniting multiple physical drives into a single logical drive. The logical drive is arranged so that blocks of data are written alternately across all physical drives in the logical array. The number of sectors per block is referred to as the *striping factor.*

Depending on the array controller in use, the striping factor can be modified, usually with the manufacturer's system configuration utility. Many of the HP Smart Array controllers can be modified online with online utilities that indicate the status of the logical drives and arrays and display the completion percentage of the rebuild process. For NetWare, this utility is cpqonlin.nlm and for Windows, it is the ACU. The ACU for Linux is installed along with the *ProLiant Support Paq* (PSP). You can enable the ACU through the Systems Management home page using the command **cpqacuexe.**

To access the System Management home page, go to https://127.0.0.1:2381.

**Warning**

On HP controllers released before the Smart Array 3100ES, changes to stripe size are data-destructive. In addition, any change to the logical volume geometry (such as striping factor, volume size, or RAID level) can be data-destructive.

RAID 0 striping improves volume I/O because you can read data and write data concurrently to each disk. If one of the disks fails, the entire volume becomes unavailable. To provide fault tolerance, implement some of the fault-tolerant RAID levels supported by Smart Array controllers.

### 13.3.14   Optimizing the Stripe Size

Selecting the appropriate stripe (chunk) size is important to achieving optimum performance within an array. The stripe size is the amount of data that is read or written to each disk in the array when data requests are processed by the array controller.

The terms *chunk*, *block*, and *segment* are used interchangeably. Chunk is used most often when discussing storage.

The following table lists the available stripe sizes and their characteristics.

| Fault-Tolerance Method | Available Stripe Sizes (KB) | Default Size (KB) |
| --- | --- | --- |
| RAID 0 | 128, 256 | 128 |
| RAID 1 or 1+0 | 8, 16, 32, 64, 128, 256 | 128 |
| RAID 5 or RAID ADG | 8, 16, 32, 64 | 16 |

To choose the optimal stripe size, you should understand how the applications request data.

The default stripe size delivers good performance in most circumstances. When high performance is important, you might need to modify the stripe size.

If the stripe size is too large, there will be poor load balancing across the drives.

If the stripe size is too small, there will be many cross-stripe transfers (split I/Os) and performance will be reduced.

Split I/Os involve stripes split onto two disks, causing both disks to seek, rotate, and transfer data. The response time depends on the slowest disk. Split I/Os reduce the request rate because there are fewer drives to service incoming requests.

| Type of Server Application | Suggested Stripe-Size Change |
|---|---|
| Mixed read/write | Accept the default value. |
| Mainly read (such as database or Internet applications) | Larger stripe sizes work best. |
| Mainly write (such as image-manipulation applications) | Smaller stripes for RAID 5, RAID ADG. Larger stripes for RAID 0, RAID 1, RAID 1+0. |

If you stripe disks on two or more SCSI controllers (called *controller multiplexing*), the operating system must calculate where to place data in relation to the striping, in addition to other calculations that contribute to processor overhead. For best performance, stripe disks only on the same controller or use an HP Smart Array controller with multiple channels and specific circuitry for handling these calculations.

A multichannel card uses only one interrupt. The HP Smart Array 5300 and 6400 series controllers feature two or more channels for enhanced performance and capacity.

## 13.4 ATA RAID

ATA RAID capabilities provide an extra level of fault tolerance, performance, and convenience over software RAID, without the added cost of a SCSI-based array controller. This technology is made possible with a combination of firmware and software.

The ATA RAID 0/1 PCI card mirrors data and boots drives on an ATA system. The operating system can be installed on a preconfigured mirror (RAID 1 volume). Regardless of which drive fails, recovery of the mirror after replacing the drive does not require user or operating system intervention. This is an improvement over software RAID implementations, which often require the reconfiguring of hardware and software settings and a manually forced rebuild to recover from a similar failure.

ProLiant ATA RAID is implemented through both software BIOS and hardware. Third-party ATA RAID is available as a hardware solution.

### 13.4.1   Integrated ATA RAID

Some ProLiant servers feature Integrated ATA RAID capabilities for increased fault tolerance.

An integrated dual-channel ATA-100 controller with integrated ATA RAID is embedded on the system board. The firmware on the controller interfaces with the MegaIDE driver to parse data and distribute it to the disks according to the RAID setting on the configuration sector.

Because it is enabled by the BIOS, ATA RAID supports the mirroring of boot drives. However, because it uses the system processor to perform the RAID functionality, it decreases a performance of the system in comparison to hardware RAID.

Integrated ATA RAID does not support RAID 5 capability. Integrated ATA RAID functionality is monitored through the standard management utility, Insight Manager 7, so the user receives any degradation notices that might occur.

### 13.4.2   Setting Up ATA RAID

You can access the integrated ATA RAID configuration utility, shown in Figure 13–8, by pressing F8 during POST. Because this utility resides in ROM, you can configure an ATA hard drive array before loading the operating system. You can use the utility to create a RAID 0 or 1 array and to assign drives to the array. This information is then written to a configuration sector on the drives.

Consider these suggestions when implementing ATA RAID:

- Connect one drive per channel with both drives configured as masters for optimum performance.
- Use the same type of drives or drives with similar speeds and capacities.
- Always use 80-conductor Ultra ATA cables.
- Do not connect any ATAPI devices (for example, CD-ROM, Zip drive, or LS120 drive) to the ATA controller.
- If you do not run the integrated ATA RAID configuration utility, the option ROM will automatically configure the drives to RAID 0.

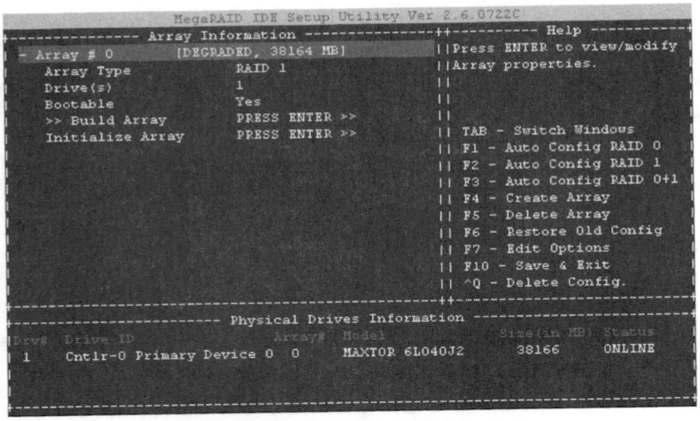

**Figure 13–8**

*Integrated RAID configuration utility interface.*

You cannot add drives or remove drives from an array that has already been configured. In addition, you cannot change the stripe size of an array that has already been configured.

Customers testing Windows Server 2003 need to be aware that Windows Server 2003 does not natively support the MegaIDE driver. You must install the driver from a disk or during a SmartStart assisted installation.

### 13.4.3   Integrated ATA RAID Management Utility

HP provides array monitoring through the integrated ATA RAID management utility. This utility runs automatically when the computer starts.

This utility provides a visual representation of array status using the Applications tray icon (Microsoft operating system only).

In addition, the ATA RAID management utility writes array status to a log file if you are running Linux or Microsoft operating systems.

The ATA RAID management utility also provides an automatic rebuild of preconfigured, online spares following a RAID 1 failure (Linux and Microsoft operating systems only).

### 13.4.4   Comparing RAID Implementations

Integrated ATA RAID provides an extra level of fault tolerance, performance, and convenience over software RAID, without the added cost of a SCSI-based array controller.

The requirements discussed in this section are specific to a two-drive implementation.

### 13.4.4.1   ATA RAID COMPARED TO SOFTWARE RAID

Software RAID, normally enabled by the operating system, enables you to mirror data files across two logical drives and uses the processor to perform the RAID functionality.

Software RAID will not allow you to set up a RAID 0 configuration on the operating system volume because it will not allow the operating system to be distributed across drives.

With integrated ATA RAID, the operating system can be installed on a preconfigured mirror (RAID 1 volume). Regardless of which drive fails, recovery of the mirror after replacing the drive does not require user or operating system intervention. This capability is an improvement over software RAID implementations, which often require reconfiguring of hardware and software settings and a manually forced rebuild to recover from a similar mirror failure.

ATA RAID provides better performance than software RAID. Software RAID normally causes system performance to decrease due to the processor being occupied by RAID-related activities. With ATA RAID, part of the RAID logic resides in the integrated dual-channel ATA-100 controller, which relieves the processor of some of the burden.

### 13.4.4.2   ATA RAID COMPARED TO SCSI RAID WITH SMART ARRAY TECHNOLOGY

SCSI RAID using Smart Array technology has several advantages over ATA RAID.

SCSI RAID using Smart Array technology will always be faster than ATA RAID because the Smart Array controller has a separate processor and can offload the distribution task from the system processor.

SCSI RAID using Smart Array technology supports RAID 5 capability. Integrated ATA RAID does not support RAID 5.

Both SCSI RAID and integrated ATA RAID can mirror the boot drive because they are invoked by the BIOS.

ATA RAID does have one advantage over SCSI RAID. It is generally less expensive than SCSI RAID, so some customers might be willing to sacrifice performance for price.

**Note**

Customers do not have to purchase the optional SCSI daughter card to enable SCSI RAID. They need only purchase the Smart Array controller.

## ▲ Summary

HP array technologies are key technological differentiators in the HP server portfolio.

As an Accredited Integration Specialist, you need to know the advantages, capabilities, and features provided by HP array technologies.

You need to know how to use the utilities used to configure, optimize, and troubleshoot HP array controllers: ADU, ACU, ACU XE, and ORCA.

Finally, ATA RAID provides advantages over software RAID, without the added cost of a SCSI-based array controller. You need to understand the pros and cons of ATA RAID, and when it can appropriately be recommended as a solution.

## ▲ LEARNING CHECK

1. *RAID ADG offers higher fault tolerance than RAID 5.*
   - ❏ True
   - ❏ False

2. *What is the maximum number of drives recommended by HP for a RAID 5 implementation?*
   - A. 6
   - B. 12
   - C. 14
   - D. 56

3. *What is the recommended maximum number of drives per array for a RAID ADG implementation?*

    A. 6

    B. 12

    C. 14

    D. 56

4. *Which array utility executes out of the option ROM that is located on an array controller, and is designed for situations that have minimal configuration requirements?*

    A. Array Diagnostic Utility (ADU)

    B. Array Configuration Utility (ACU)

    C. Array Configuration Utility XE (ACU XE)

    D. Option ROM Configuration for Arrays (ORCA)

5. *What is a potential disadvantage of setting a high rebuild priority when an online spare drive is implemented?*

6. *Which of the following LED statuses indicate that a drive has failed?*

    A. On

    B. Blinking

    C. Off

    D. Blinking amber

# Systems Integration

**A**n HP Accredited Integration Specialist should be able to evaluate the customer environment and make a recommendation for an appropriate solution. In addition, the AIS should be able to deploy an HP ProLiant server, from the time it arrives in the box at the site to the point where the server is put into production.

Here is an overview of the chapters in Part 4.

| Chapter 14 | **Evaluating the Customer Environment** |

Chapter 14 provides an overview of how the customer environment should be analyzed and evaluated, including how to conduct a needs analysis and a site survey. When the needs analysis and site survey are completed, the next step is to create a scope of work. Chapter 14 provides an overview of the content of a scope of work as well as resources available from HP to assist you in this process.

| Chapter 15 | **Installing, Configuring, and Deploying a Single Server** |

As an AIS, you should be able to deploy a single ProLiant server from the time when the components are pulled out of the box up to the point where the server is placed into production. This chapter provides an overview of the skills, tools, and techniques needed to accomplish this deployment. Particular emphasis is placed on the techniques for the initial server configuration and the procedures for landing the operating system on the server.

# Evaluating the Customer Environment

After reading this chapter, you will be able to do the following:

- Conduct a needs analysis
- Conduct a site survey
- Determine the business value and return on investment
- Build a statement of work
- Understand the resources and tools available to you from HP

An HP *Accredited Integration Specialist* (AIS) is expected to have the skills to assess customer needs and assist in planning the implementation and growth of the IT infrastructure.

Your ultimate objective is to apply your knowledge of the HP product line to recommend the best possible solution package to your customer. The recommendation you make comes together with the statement of work document. However, to get to the point where you can craft a solid statement of work document, you need to have a sound understanding of the needs, expectations, and environment.

In this chapter, you learn how to do the following:

- Conduct a needs analysis
- Conduct a site survey
- Determine business value and return on investment
- Create a statement of work document

To complete these activities, it is helpful to also understand the resources provided to you by HP. These resources are explained at the end of this chapter.

## 14.1   Conducting a Needs Analysis

Conducting a needs analysis is the first step in accurately determining a customer's requirements. Proper planning helps to avoid potential costly mistakes up front and lays the groundwork for an effective upgrade path in the future.

A needs analysis starts with an interview. During the interview, ask the customer questions to help determine the problems he is facing, if he has ideas about how to solve the problems, and what his future plans are. Understanding customer needs is crucial to developing a positive long-term relationship.

If the customer has experience with server technology, ask questions about intended solutions. If not, you may need to determine the answers to these questions yourself. Consider asking questions in the following categories:

### Future plans

- What are the business goals?
- What is the projected role of the server?

- What is the projected operating system?
- Will RAID be implemented?
- Will the server be connected to more than one network?

### Current environment

- How much storage currently is used?
- Have storage needs grown over the last 12 months?

### Business requirements

- What is the expected availability of the server?
- Is server price or functionality more important?
- Is a rack or tower configuration preferred?
- Will backups be performed?
- Is power protection needed?
- What kinds of system management tools are needed?
- Does the server need to be set up from the component level, or is it ready to be installed right out of the box?
- What level of maintenance and support is desired?

### Obstacles

- What is the biggest IT problem facing the business today?
- What does the customer feel are possible solutions?
- What are the barriers to the solution?

### Resources

- Is the customer willing to commit resources to achieving these goals?
- Is the customer willing to let technical professionals help guide the way?

Based on answers to these questions, you can make recommendations about which server components are required and which are optional. For example, if file and print is the projected role of the server, storage capacity and transfer rate are important selection factors. On the other hand, if the server is intended to be a database server, processor speed and memory must be considered.

| 14.2 | ## Conducting a Site Survey |

After the completing the needs analysis, you should conduct a site survey to assess the customer's facility. A site survey is a review of the facility and an evaluation of its suitability for the proposed IT environment. Factors to consider include the following.

- **Site/facility suitability**—Server room size, layout, limitations, and interference
- **Site services/utilities**—Power delivery, fire suppression, and environmental controls
- **Physical security**—Key locks and card access
- **IT integration**—Existing computing infrastructure
- **Applications/software**—Loads and availability
- **Human resources**—Ownership, internal or external support
- **Projected growth**—Computer, employee, and business expansion

To evaluate these factors, you can use survey questions like the following:

- How large is the facility?
- Does the facility currently have any *radio frequency interference* (RFI) problems?
- Is there any extra space?
- Will an existing space need to be modified?
- Are adequate utility outlets available in the proposed space?
- Is the electrical circuit of sufficient capacity?
- Is the electrical circuit shared or isolated?
- Are there extra electrical circuits available in the facility?
- What type of fire-suppression system is in place (if any)?
- If overhead sprinklers are installed, are they water- or halon-based?
- Is there adequate ventilation for the space?
- Is extra cooling capacity available?
- Is the proposed space in the interior of the building or does it have an outside window?
- Does the facility already use keypads, card readers, or other physical security devices to control access?

- How many workstations does the company have now?
- How many servers are in use?
- Is a recent inventory of company IT assets available?
- If there is an existing network, what is its topology?
- What kinds of IT equipment purchases are planned for the next 12 months?
- What kinds of software are used regularly?
- Is the software workstation- or server-based?
- What software purchases are planned for the next 12 months?
- How are IT support issues currently handled?
- Who is responsible for IT issues at the company?
- Will any IT staff be added?
- How many other employees will be added in the next 12 months?
- Does the company plan to open other offices in the next 12 months?

This is not a complete list, but is a guide to generate other questions pertinent to a particular environment. It also helps identify existing resources, such as network capacity or an inventory of IT assets, which are crucial to determining what additional resources to make available for the transition from old to new environment.

The availability of resources also affects the implementation timeline. For instance, if no network cabling exists in the facility, the plan must include time to install the wires. Although the plan can recommend simultaneous tasks, it is inefficient to have servers and workstations in place waiting for interconnectivity to complete their configuration. The number of hours needed to set up the server and the amount of time needed to address dependencies must be determined.

### 14.2.1  Applying the Site Survey Data to Server Selection

The information you have gathered during the site survey will be used to narrow down the choices for the server or servers that you will recommend to the customer.

Every server has storage, but factors for deciding on a RAID or non-RAID configuration are cost, storage availability, and fault tolerance. For a file and print server, a non-RAID configuration leaves data vulnerable to disk failure or data corruption. This would be less important to a firewall server, the focus of which is network-centric.

Depending on the existing network topology or the decision for a new topology, server networking capabilities must also be determined. Current corporate networks are at least 100Mb/s (Fast Ethernet), although corporate backbones can exceed 1Gb/s (Gigabit Ethernet) at the same time that remote offices are still at 10Mb/s (Ethernet).

Memory and processor technology components are equally important. Fault-tolerant memory or redundant processors are less crucial to a file and print server than they are to a database server, which primarily performs computations and requires temporary storage.

Determining the relative importance of server technologies, in conjunction with the server's projected role, will help narrow the focus to a server with the required capabilities.

The choice of operating system also has a direct effect on server components. As a general rule, the more recent (and thus more advanced) the operating system, the greater its demands will be on system hardware. This rule generally holds true for Microsoft products, but less so for Linux.

Linux has gained market share in both the corporate and consumer segments in recent years because of its open-source nature and lower demand on system resources. This allows organizations to save money by running an operating system that is available essentially free of charge on cheaper, less-powerful computers.

Certain operating system features can also steer the decision to a particular vendor. For example, the tight integration of the Microsoft Active Directory network structure in Windows Server 2003 makes it more attractive to those organizations that need that feature. As a result, however, potential server purchases must be made based upon careful consideration for meeting or exceeding the higher minimum system requirements.

## 14.3  Placing the ProLiant Server

There are two kinds of security to consider when deciding where to place your ProLiant server:

- **Physical**—Locks, codes, and location
- **Virtual**—Passwords, permissions, and access control lists

The two types of security relate to where a customer wants to locate the server and how will it be configured.

Deciding to place a server in an interior room with a locked door sufficiently addresses most physical security needs. Because the temperature and humidity in a windowless interior room remain relatively constant, there should be no need to keep the door open to enhance airflow. Keeping the door closed and locked ensures that only those individuals with authority and access can get in.

It is a good idea to be alert for physical and virtual security holes. When an employee leaves an organization, it is important to recover any keys and access cards. It might also be necessary to change locks and codes. Disabling the employee's user account and changing high-level passwords that the employee had access to is also good practice.

Setting up users, groups, and permissions addresses virtual security needs. Each user needs a password to gain access to project files stored on the server, and being a member of a particular group allows or denies access to other network resources. A good rule is to grant each user only as much access as he or she typically needs. In addition, all passwords should also be changed regularly; be a minimum length (as defined by the operating system); and contain a combination of letters, numbers, and special characters.

User-level security should not be confused with share-level security. User-level security allows or denies access to a particular resource based on who the user is and which group the user is a member of. Share-level security is decided at the resource level; that is, if a directory or printer is shared, anyone who knows the password can access it. Share-level security is most often used in peer-to-peer networks that lack an authentication server.

All of these procedures fit together to form an IT security policy. Procedures regulating physical access, virtual access, staffing changes, password changes, and user-level security must be integrated to form a policy that allows access without compromising security. A good policy is also scalable, so that as a business grows the policy can incorporate new procedures and security products.

HP partners with many industry-leading security providers to bring effective, appropriate, and affordable solutions to the workplace. HP also offers many of its own security products and services to enterprise-class customers.

## 14.4 Determining Projected Budget, Value, and Return

After you understand the customer's needs, you must determine the project budget and the expected value and return. By understanding the future plans, you can prepare the scope of work with an eye to the company's projected growth.

Some considerations will often include the following:

■ **Total cost of ownership**—Server cost does not end with purchase and delivery. Over its productive life, a server requires maintenance and upgrades. It must also be managed as part of an infra-structure. The total expense of components and services add up to the total cost of ownership.

■ **Performance**—Server system performance depends on a balanced design, where the computer bandwidth matches the memory bandwidth and the I/O bandwidth matches the demands of the software. If the memory system is dramatically slower than processor requests for instruction and data transfers, the processor becomes memory-starved and performance potential is wasted. A fast memory system on a slow processor shifts the bottleneck to the processor.

■ **Reliability**—Reliability is an important feature for all servers, affecting both total cost of ownership and performance. A reliable server is dependable and available almost all the time. A highly available server takes reliability to another level by incorporating fault-tolerant capabilities and features that enable the smooth replacement of failed components. A high-availability server is a class of server that must be able to run continuously. Certain reliability and high-availability baseline goals are desirable for each class of server.

■ **Capacity**—For many server applications, scalability and expandability become very important. Requirements related to components, such as RAM expansion capabilities and storage capacity, are considered to address scalability issues of a server.

■ **Ease of use and maintenance**—Two factors that strongly affect the total cost of ownership for servers are ease of use and ease of maintenance. Critical design criteria for these factors include the following:

• **Mechanical components**—The server components must be durable and of high-quality.

• **Thermal plan**—Sufficient airflow through the server is necessary to avoid deterioration of components or performance due to excessive heat.

• **Service accessibility**—The server chassis and internals must be accessible with the least amount of tools and disruption as possible.

■ **Third-party integration**—Industry-standard components must easily integrate into the system.

- **Management**—Hardware and software components must allow for alert notification and resolution.

- **Security**—Some businesses protect user data and control access to system components. The system designer must continually weigh cost against performance when working to meet security requirements and when supporting hardware design recommendations.

- **Failure recovery**—Server components should be modular to allow for easy replacement in the event of a failure. Modular replacement is more cost effective than replacing an entire system or subsystem. System components should have a level of integration that enables rapid recovery after a failure.

## 14.4.1  Using Third-Party Business-Value Tools

Two excellent tools are available to assist you in planning, determining business value, and *return on investment/total cost of ownership* (ROI/TCO). These tools are the Gartner IT HealthCheck TCO comparison tool and the Microsoft Rapid Economic Justification framework.

### 14.4.1.1  GARTNER IT HEALTHCHECK

The Gartner IT HealthCheck TCO comparison tool is used to input IT infrastructure data to determine TCO. Enter contact information, information about the distributed computing environment, and a selection of best practices implemented.

The Gartner IT HealthCheck TCO comparison tool is available at http://ithealthcheck.gartner.com/site/welcome.asp?b=valid.

### 14.4.1.2  MICROSOFT RAPID ECONOMIC JUSTIFICATION FRAMEWORK

The Microsoft *Rapid Economic Justification* (REJ) framework is a conceptual overview of IT planning. The REJ is a five-step process to help IT professionals analyze and optimize the economic performance of IT investments, and appropriate optimal resources and capital for IT projects.

Learn more about the REJ framework at http://www.microsoft.com/technet/treeview/default.asp?url=/technet/ittasks/plan/sysplan/wwww.asp.

## 14.5    Writing a Scope of Work

A scope of work is a document that captures the plan, timeframe, resources required, and completion milestone of a project. It is crucial for ensuring a mutual understanding between you and the customer. A scope of work is a preproject overview prepared for a proposal, and should not be confused with a statement of work, which is a final project overview prepared for billing.

Among other things, a scope of work must list resources critical to success. Essential to this is executive support; without leadership from management, implementing an IT project is more difficult.

Generally, a scope of work should have the following components:

- **Introduction**—A description of the type of work provided, the service provider, the customer, and key points about the document itself.

- **Assumptions**—A list of any assumptions made by the service provider about the customer.

- **Objectives**—A list of what the plan aims to accomplish. A key point of the document.

- **Customer responsibilities**—A statement of what the service provider and the customer agree on that the customer must do to implement the plan. A key point of the document.

- **HP services**—A list of what the service provider will do. A key point of the document.

- **Resources required**—A list of what resources the service provider and/or the customer must provide to implement the plan.

- **Location of work**—A statement that the work will be performed at the customer's address.

- **Project timeline**—A description that details when the plan will commence and how long it is expected to take. It can also include any mitigating statements, such as a delay in the start of the project of the customer does not receive or provide resources in a timely manner. A key point of the document.

- **Completion criteria**—A statement of a milestone indicating completion of the plan. This can be an achievement of the objectives, completion of the estimated consulting hours, or a date.

- **Change-management procedure**—It is important that any agreed-upon plan have a change-management procedure. This provides a formalized way to alter the project plan after the initial terms of the work statement have been accepted. Typically, it describes the vehicle for submitting the request (usually a form), a description of the change requested, a statement that all parties must agree to the change for it to be implemented, any costs associated with implementing the change, and any exceptions to the agreement that would automatically trigger a change form, such as the estimated hours required to complete the plan being exceeded by 20%.

- **Company contacts**—A list of the names, positions, telephone numbers, addresses, and e-mails of the responsible parties.

- **Costing schedule**—A key point of the document, the schedule lists and describes any fees estimated for the project. It should also describe what can be charged in the event of unforeseen problems, and the expected business hours.

## 14.6   Resources Available from HP

HP provides a wide variety of tools, informational resources, and services. The resources available to you from HP can be categorized as follows:

- HP online tools
- HP alliances and programs
- HP adaptive infrastructure framework
- HP product support programs and options

To be able to recommend the best solution to your customer, you need to be able to understand the content, purpose, and application of these resources and apply them to the customer situation.

### 14.6.1   HP Online Tools

The two main online tools available are the HP Web site and HP ActiveAnswers.

### 14.6.1.1 THE HP WEB SITE

One of the best places to find online information about ProLiant servers is the HP Web site. Depending on the size of the customer, choose the Small & Medium Business link or the Enterprise link, and then click Servers. Click Entry-Level tc Series and ML300 Series Servers to open the HP Entry Level Servers page where you can use the HP how-to guide for servers to research and choose from a variety of servers and options. These tools will help you understand how to size a server to suit specific business needs.

 See how-to guides, compare servers, and customize a model at http:// h18004.www1.hp.com/products/servers/platforms/index-tc.html.

Servers can also be customized online. Each server model page includes a customize link. Through this link you can add memory, drive controllers, hard drives, removable media bay devices, cables, monitor, modem, additional *network interface cards* (NICs), operating system, server management, CarePaq services, rack deployment options, hot-plug devices, ProLiant Essentials software, *uninterruptible power supplies* (UPSs), and printers.

 The degree to which a server can be customized depends on the line and series. Not all options are available for every server.

### 14.6.1.2 ACTIVEANSWERS

The HP ActiveAnswers Web site, shown in Figure 14–1, provides a set of tools, e-services, and information to help customers plan, deploy, and operate business solutions. Through the ActiveAnswers site, you can size a server and select options to match a particular enterprise environment. You can use the Configurator and Sizing tools to generate potential solutions and the corresponding bill of materials.

Although ActiveAnswers is designed for the enterprise market, using the sizers is a good way to learn about the positioning and value of the HP ProLiant lines.

You can use the Solutions link to select a category to research. For example, one of the ActiveAnswers Solution Sizers is for the Apache Web Server for Linux. This sizer helps you choose an entry-level, preconfigured, single-server solution suitable for small and medium-size businesses, or build your own solution based on customer requirements.

For more information on ActiveAnswers or to register, visit the ActiveAnswers home page at http://activeanswers.compaq.com.

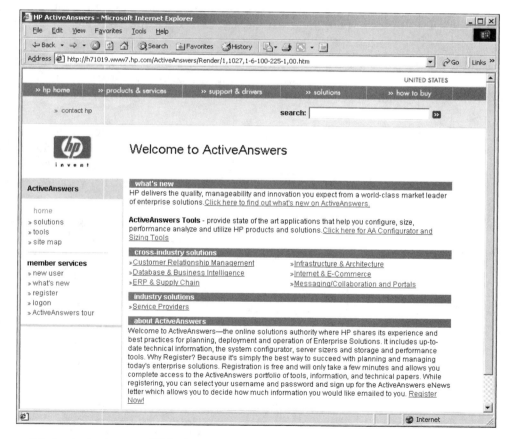

**Figure 14–1** *ActiveAnswers Web site.*

### 14.6.2 HP Alliances and Programs

HP partners with leading providers of software, services, and operating systems to enable success in the e-business environments of today and tomorrow. Working closely with partners such as Microsoft, Novell, Oracle, SAP, and many others, HP delivers products, services, and solutions for the computing challenges faced everyday. Using these proven solutions, deployments are fast and simplified, and ongoing management of systems easier than ever before. Benefits include the following:

- **Faster time-to-solution**—Proven partner solutions are engineered, tested, tuned, and optimized on HP platforms to enable fastest time-to-solution with reduced risk. And through the HP ActiveAnswers Web site, you can access a broad range of tools and information for quickly planning, deploying, and operating an HP and partner solution.

- **High availability**—HP is committed to providing industry-leading capabilities and to meeting the enterprise customer's complete spectrum of requirements for reliable, highly available platforms, software, and solutions.

- **Confidence**—Experience, enterprise technology leadership, and strategic industry partnerships place HP in a unique position within the IT market—providing customers unprecedented choice and confidence in the architecture and deployment of their network computing infrastructures.

- **Accelerating industry standards**—As a global enterprise leader, HP pushes the boundaries to drive peak customer value. HP provides the broadest range of mission and business critical solutions on standard platforms to give the customer the freedom of choosing the industry's leading applications.

- **Commitment to success**—HP partners with industry leaders to accelerate success. HP will continue to broaden its portfolio of industry-leading partnerships to provide greater choices and fastest time-to-solution.

### 14.6.3 Adaptive Enterprise

Adaptive Enterprise is the ultimate state of business fitness: business and IT synchronized to capitalize on change through the following:

- **Business solutions**—Deploy the solutions, services, and products that enable the business processes within an adaptive enterprise
- **Integration solutions**—Integrate business solutions and trading partners with enterprise integration solutions, services, and products
- **Infrastructure solutions**—Leverage infrastructure solutions, services, and products to serve as the foundation for business solutions
- **Management solutions**—Utilize management solutions, services, and products to provide instrumentation of business and infrastructure solutions

The HP Adaptive Enterprise is based on years of experience in delivering open and collaborative solutions and services. It tightens the link between customer IT and business objectives so that customers can anticipate and rapidly respond to new market requirements. As business strategies change and new business processes demand higher levels of service, an adaptive enterprise responds immediately and intelligently with the required services.

The Adaptive Enterprise is shown in Figure 14–2.

The HP Adaptive Enterprise architecture is based on a foundation of robust information technology and services to continuously align infrastructure resources as enterprise business requirements evolve. Evolving toward an Adaptive Enterprise requires a phased approach that

- Embraces an agility strategy and continuously assesses agility capabilities.

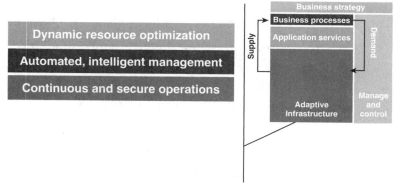

**Figure 14–2**  *HP Adaptive Enterprise.*

- Ensures that network architectures can accommodate the inclusion and removal of business systems, applications, lines of business, and all supporting hardware and software.
- Identifies and eliminates underpowered, underused, and overdeployed technologies.
- Consolidates assets into a scalable infrastructure where services are managed automatically and delivered on demand.

### 14.6.3.1 HP ADAPTIVE ENTERPRISE DIFFERENTIATORS

One of HP's key differentiators is its key design principles that promote the synchronization and integration of business and IT, including standardization, simplification, integration, and modularity.

These key differentiators are applied consistently across business processes, applications, and infrastructure.

## 14.6.4 Support Options

In addition to helping customers select a server, you must also help them plan for support. Customers might decide to have an outside contractor or someone in-house perform system support. Alternatively, they can select a support option from HP when customizing the server online. Customers also can contact HP Customer Care Centers or the HP Services network if they have any questions.

### 14.6.4.1 PRODUCT INFORMATION CENTER

The HP Product Information Center can help you obtain the following:

- Presales and post-sales product information for commercial and consumer, desktops, workstations, and portable units
- Part number, configuration, and upgrade information
- Authorized Reseller information
- Nontechnical support
- Customer satisfaction assistance

Most services are available 24×7, including holidays.

### 14.6.4.2   CUSTOMER SOLUTION AND SUPPORT CENTER

HP receives a large number of telephone calls daily for support and technical assistance. For the HP Technical Support Engineer to assist you, you must have complete information about the system, including serial numbers and problems for which you are requesting assistance. It is best to call from the location of the machine being serviced.

HP technical support for desktops, portables, professional workstations, and servers is available 24×7, including holidays.

For more information about HP Customer Care Centers, go to http://h30011.www3.hp.com/cust_care/support.html?pageseq=675379.

## 14.6.5   HP Services Network

HP Services provides a complete portfolio of services tailored to customer needs. Using a proven set of methodologies, HP partners closely with the customer to help design, build, integrate, manage, and evolve an adaptive infrastructure that responds effectively to business changes.

For more information about HP Services, go to http://www.hp.com/hps/servers/sr_proliant.html.

## ▲  Summary

As an AIS, your task is to take your customer from a heterogeneous mixture of un-networked workstations to the basics of an HP Adaptive Enterprise. After performing a needs analysis and site survey, in a scope of work you detail the steps necessary for the customer to undertake to update the facility and install the new server.

## ▲ LEARNING CHECK

1. *What information are you trying to gather during the needs analysis? (Select three.)*

    A. The types of problems the customer is experiencing

    B. How reliable a customer expects a server to be

    C. The customer's thoughts on solving his current IT problems

    D. The customer's existing physical environment

    E. The customer's physical security

2. *What information are you trying to gather during the site survey? (Select two.)*

    A. The types of problems the customer is experiencing

    B. How reliable a customer expects a server to be

    C. The customer's thoughts on solving his current IT problems

    D. The customer's existing physical environment

    E. The customer's physical security

3. *A customer was referred to you and tells you that his recently installed server is no longer working. After inspecting the server, you discover that the customer has placed the server under a desk and too near a wall, blocking the airflow through the server. Which of the following steps was likely omitted when you first talked to the customer about purchasing a new server?*

    A. Conducting a needs analysis

    B. Conducting a site survey

    C. Determining business value

    D. Choosing the right server

4. *Which of these might help you determine the business value of a server to a customer? (Select three.)*

    A. Reliability

    B. Performance

    C. Site survey

    D. Security

    E. RAID level

    F. Operating system

# Installing, Configuring, and Deploying a Single Server

This chapter explains the following key concepts:

- Installing ProLiant hardware components
- Installing an operating system on a ProLiant server
- Configuring the operating system to enable networking
- Addressing security requirements
- Validating and testing the solution

As an *Accredited Integration Specialist* (AIS), you are expected to be able to set up and configure an HP ProLiant server for many different customer environments. In this chapter, you will learn how to do the following:

- Install and configure server hardware and options.
- Use HP SmartStart to install Microsoft Windows Server 2003.
- Configure a basic network infrastructure.
- Validate and test the solution.

**301**

## 15.1    Installing ProLiant Hardware Components

Depending on how the server is ordered, it ships with options in separate boxes or preassembled with options. If the server arrives preassembled, installation involves only positioning it, connecting the cables, and powering it on.

Servers without preassembled options require installation of those components. You might need a Torx screwdriver to perform the installation. In a suitable work area, remove the chassis cover and note which components are already installed. As you open each component package, read the instructions carefully to ensure proper installation. Follow all guidelines, including rules for electrostatic discharge protection. When installation is complete, replace the chassis cover, position the server, connect all cables, and power on the server.

Observe the console of the server during the *Power-On Self-Test* (POST) for any errors. When you power on an unconfigured server, a variety of messages and errors might display on the screen. These errors typically relate to the following items:

- The BIOS is set to the defaults.

- The system date and time are not set.

- No array configuration is present although an array controller is installed.

After the server performs its autoconfiguration, you can launch the *ROM-Based Setup Utility* (RBSU) or *Option-ROM Configuration for Arrays* (ORCA) to make further changes or verify system settings.

### 15.1.1    Updating System and Option ROMs

Before configuring a ProLiant server, you must verify that the system and option ROMs are the latest version. If they are not, you must upgrade them.

You can identify the system ROM family and version for your server in two ways.

First, if the server is offline (operating system not running), you can use one of these techniques:

- Reboot the server. The POST information shows the ROM family and the ROM version.

- Use the RBSU to identify the family and ROM version.

- Use the HP Diagnostics and Inspect Utility.

Second, if the server is online (operating system is running), you can use one of these techniques:

- Use the HP Insight Diagnostics Survey utility.
- Use HP Insight Manager 7 or HP Systems Insight Manager.
- Select System Info from the main menu of the Integrated Management display.

Flashing the ROM is the process of upgrading system, array controller, or options firmware on a target server with a new ROM image that supports new features or has been modified to fix problems in the previous version. You can flash the ROM in either offline or online mode.

> **! IMPORTANT**
>
> Do not reboot the target server while the ROM upgrade is in progress. You do not need to restart the target server before the system or option ROM flash upgrade begins. When the flash upgrade is complete, you must restart the target server for system and option ROM upgrades to take effect.

## 15.1.2   System Startup Behavior

After you have installed the server components and updated system and option ROMs, the next step is to configure the installed hardware. You may configure ProLiant servers when you start them for the first time or you may use startup defaults. You can reconfigure the default settings later if necessary.

ProLiant servers have various indicators for monitoring system status. These indicators typically are integrated into the front panel of the server and are grouped together for easy reference. The most obvious indicator is the power LED. Other front-panel LEDs include the hard drive activity LED, the network activity LED, the internal health LED, and the unit ID LED.

Some components have their own indicators, either on the front of the component or in the back or inside. Hot-plug drives, for example, have three LEDs on the front of the drive that indicate power, access, and fault. Internal (non-hot-plug) drives usually just have an activity LED on the front bezel of the server. Removable media drives (disk, CD-ROM, and other drives) have their own LEDs that activate when system power is started or when media in the drive is being accessed.

When a system is powered on, all the LEDs briefly light up, and then return to the behavior normal for each indicator. Recognizing normal indicator behavior is crucial to recognizing when the LEDs are indicating an abnormal condition.

As the server goes through the POST process, system video activates and system messages display on the console. Typically, these are the RAM count, BIOS date, HP name, processor description, array controller (if present), and any POST errors. The information displayed will vary depending on the options installed. The POST process must complete before any autoconfiguration can occur.

In legacy ProLiant servers, the System Configuration Utility was used to configure the BIOS. Currently shipping ProLiant servers (except the 100 series), use RBSU. To configure the array controller, you can use either ORCA or the online *Array Controller Utility* (ACU).

When you start up your server the first time, RBSU automatically configures the system without any intervention during the POST process. After the system configuration is complete and the server restarts, if an array controller is present, ORCA automatically configures your array to a default setting based on the number of drives connected to the controller.

You can manually execute RBSU, which is contained in the system ROM, during POST by pressing F9 when prompted. After the server has been configured using RBSU, the system restarts. To configure, you can then change the primary array controller (if present) by pressing F8 when prompted to execute ORCA.

**You will not be prompted for ORCA if you do not have an array controller installed in your server.**

After the system restarts again, you can install the operating system and any necessary applications.

In the rare case that the lithium battery that backs up the nonvolatile memory (NVRAM) fails, all system configuration data will be lost. Replacing the battery and powering on the server will cause it to go through the same automatic configuration process.

### 15.1.3   ProLiant Setup Configuration Flow

Figure 15–1 shows the sequence of events that occurs when a ProLiant server is powered on.

#### 15.1.3.1   DEFAULTS

The RBSU has two default settings. The default operating system is Windows 2000/Windows .NET, and the default language is English.

**Press the F9 key when prompted during the boot process to change the server settings, such as the settings for language, operating system, and primary boot controller, using RBSU.**

The ORCA disk configuration is set to a default based upon number of drives in array. If there are fewer than two drives in the server, the disk configuration is set to RAID 0. If two drives are in the server, the configuration is RAID 1. If three to six drives are installed, the default is RAID 5. If more than six drivers are installed, there is no automatic default configuration.

**Figure 15–1**

*ProLiant Server power-on sequence.*

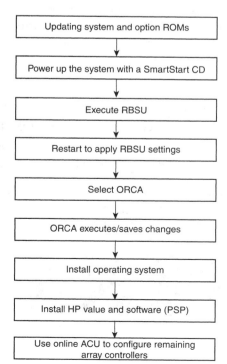

Updating system and option ROMs

↓

Power up the system with a SmartStart CD

↓

Execute RBSU

↓

Restart to apply RBSU settings

↓

Select ORCA

↓

ORCA executes/saves changes

↓

Install operating system

↓

Install HP value and software (PSP)

↓

Use online ACU to configure remaining array controllers

Long timeouts for both operating system and disk configuration defaults might occur. If any data has ever been written to the drive, ORCA will not configure the drive automatically.

For more advanced configurations, run ACU from the **SmartStart CD** or from within an operating system.

### 15.1.3.2 BOOT OPTIONS

After the autoconfiguration process is complete or after the server restarts upon exit from the RBSU, the POST sequence runs and the boot option screen displays, as shown in Figure 15–2.

This screen is visible for several seconds before the system attempts to boot from either a bootable CD or disk or the hard drive.

During this time, the menu on the screen enables you to (1) install an operating system by inserting the operating system CD or the SmartStart for Servers CD, or (2) make changes to the server configuration by pressing an industry-standard function key:

- **F8 for ORCA**—To configure the array controller
- **F9 for RBSU**—To make changes to the server configuration
- **F10 for the System Maintenance menu**—To run ROM-based utilities
- **F12 for PXE boot**—To turn a *preboot execution environment* (PXE)-enabled *network interface card* (NIC) into a bootable device

If you take no action, the system attempts to start using the default boot order before starting from the hard drive. The default boot order is (1) disk, (2) CD, (3) hard drive, and (4) PXE.

```
System currently configured for Microsoft Windows 2000/Windows Server 2003.
Press "F9" key for ROM-Based Setup Utility
Press "F10" key for System Maintenance Menu
Press "F12" key for PXE boot
```

**Figure 15–2** *Boot options screen.*

### 15.1.3.3 SERVER ROM FUNCTIONALITY

The server ROM is the system component that stores most of the basic server functionality. ProLiant server ROMs come in two sizes: 2MB or 4MB.

The base functionality with 2MB ROM includes dynamic setup support (boot driver and ROM), an embedded Setup Utility, and an embedded Diagnostic Utility.

The 4MB ROM includes all the functionality of the 2MB version plus an embedded Inspect Utility.

ProLiant G2 servers and later have RBSU embedded in the system ROM.

> On some systems, ROM-based enhancements are available that automatically configure ORCA and RBSU. Refer to your server-specific user documentation, which will mention these features if they are available. For more information on using the ROM-based enhancements, refer to the ROM-Based Setup Utility User Guide located on the server documentation CD or at www.hp.com/smartstart.

### 15.1.3.4 DYNAMIC SETUP SUPPORT

The operating system-specific drivers in ROM include storage drivers and new boot drivers that feature support for these operating systems:

- Windows Server 2003
- Linux 2.4.x
- Red Hat (Linux)
- SuSE (Linux)
- Novell NetWare 6

### 15.1.3.5 SYSTEM MAINTENANCE MENU

The System Maintenance menu, shown in Figure 15–3, displays the following options:

- **Setup Utility**—Runs RBSU
- **Inspect Utility**—Runs the embedded Inspect Utility
- **Diagnostic Utility**—Runs the embedded Diagnostic Utility

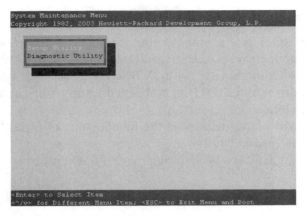

**Figure 15–3** *System Maintenance menu.*

This menu, embedded in the system ROM, replaces the legacy system-partition functionality supported on some ProLiant servers.

To access the System Maintenance menu, press F10 when prompted from the boot option screen.

The Inspect Utility is available only on a ProLiant server with 4MB ROM.

## 15.1.4   RBSU

The purpose of RBSU is to help you configure server hardware settings and prepare a server for an operating system installation. RBSU enables you to view and establish server configuration settings during the initial system startup, and to modify them after the server has been configured.

The ROM on ProLiant servers currently shipping contains the functionality provided by the system partition utilities on legacy ProLiant servers. RBSU replaces the SCU that shipped on legacy ProLiant servers. RBSU provides the same functions, eliminating the need for a system partition on the primary drive and the use of a boot disk. Figure 15–4 shows the RBSU interface.

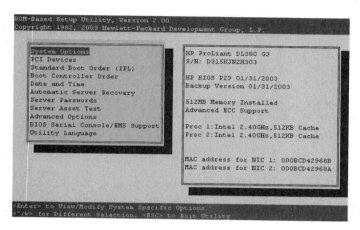

**Figure 15–4** *RBSU interface.*

The following table describes some of the differences between RBSU and the SCU.

| ROM-Based Setup Utility | System Configuration Utility |
|---|---|
| Saves changes to NVRAM when they are made. | Must save changes before exiting. |
| Silent conflict resolution. | Displays warnings when conflicts are resolved. |
| Embedded in system ROM; does not use disk. | Disk-based; can be installed on system partition. |
| Customized for each server resulting in smaller, faster utility. | Comprehensive utility—one version supports all servers. |
| Configuration-oriented and table-driven. | Device-oriented and file-driven. |
| Replication utility support with configuration information in RBSU table. | No direct replication utility support except through configuration backup. |
| Utility update through RBSU ROM flash or physical ROM change. | Utility update through new version of the software. |
| Advanced Options is a menu selection. | Advanced mode accessed by pressing Ctrl+A. |

**Warning**

RBSU is not available on some older HP servers. Do not flash an RBSU ROM image on a system initially configured with SCU. Reflashing a server configured with the SCU with an RBSU ROM image can result in potential loss of data, system lockup, and other unpredictable results.

### 15.1.4.1   STARTING AND EXITING RBSU

Press F9 to access RBSU when prompted during the POST sequence to modify component configuration settings without a SmartStart CD or disk.

RBSU configures the server automatically if the server is in an unconfigured or erased state. After configuring the server, you must exit RBSU to restart the server with the new settings.

Pressing Esc at the main menu displays a confirmation to exit, as shown in Figure 15–5. The current boot controller also displays for reference purposes.

To exit, press F10. The server powers up with the new configuration settings.

### 15.1.4.2   RBSU MAIN MENU

From the RBSU main menu, you can select which configuration setting to view or modify. Some selections bring you directly to configuration functions. Others lead to submenus that expand the available choices.

The main menu, located on the left side of the screen, enables you to select which configuration setting to view or modify. The selection choices are as follows:

- System Options
- PCI Devices
- Standard Boot Order (IPL) (applies only to 32-bit servers)
- Boot Controller Order
- Date and Time

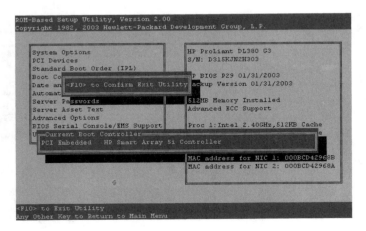

**Figure 15–5**   *Confirm RBSU exit.*

- Automatic Server Recovery (ASR)
- Server Passwords
- Server Asset Text (and IMD Text—applies only to 64-bit servers)
- Advanced Options
- BIOS Serial Console/EMS Support (applies only to 32-bit servers)
- Utility Language

A window on the right side of the RBSU screen displays basic information about the server. This information includes the server model, serial number, BIOS version, backup BIOS version, and memory and processors installed.

Pressing F1 when any menu option is highlighted enables you to view a description of that option.

### 15.1.4.3   RBSU ADVANCED OPTIONS

The Advanced Options menu of the main RBSU menu enables you to configure options normally set by default and not user modified, such as hot-plug resources and processor correction marking.

The POST F1 Prompt option is a toggle setting that enables you to set the configuration options for errors on POST. By default, you must press F1 when an error is detected before the POST process will continue. From this menu, you can choose to delay or disable this feature.

If you select Delayed and an error occurs, the system pauses for 20 seconds at the F1 prompt, and then continues to boot the operating system.

If you select Enabled and an error occurs, the system stops booting at the prompt until you press the F1 key.

The **POST F1 Prompt** setting is enabled by default in ProLiant ML and DL servers, and delayed by default in BL servers.

### 15.1.4.4   PROCESSOR HYPER-THREADING AND ADVANCED MEMORY PROTECTION OPTIONS

The Advanced Options menu also offers the Processor Hyper-Threading option, which is a toggle setting that enables you to enable or disable Intel Hyper-Threading technology. It is enabled by default.

Hyper-Threading technology enables multithreaded applications to execute threads in parallel on each processor. This technology boosts system performance without going to a higher clock rate or adding more processors.

When multiple instruction streams, called *threads*, are simultaneously available to a single processor, they allow the processor to better schedule the use of internal resources. Hyper-Threading technology is available in ProLiant servers that use Intel Xeon processors.

Advanced memory protection is also available on most ProLiant servers. HP offers three levels of advanced memory protection to increase the fault tolerance of HP ProLiant servers:

1. OnLine spare memory
2. Hot-plug mirrored memory
3. Hot-plug RAID Memory

### 15.1.4.5 EMBEDDED ERASE OPTION

The Advanced Options menu also provides two embedded erase options to erase the NVRAM, as shown in Figure 15–6.

The Erase Non-volatile Memory option resets the nonvolatile memory of the server to an initial, factory state. When you select Yes, Select to Erase, the following pop-up message displays:

```
Are you sure you want to erase NVRAM? You will lose all
System Configuration Settings. {Y/N}
```

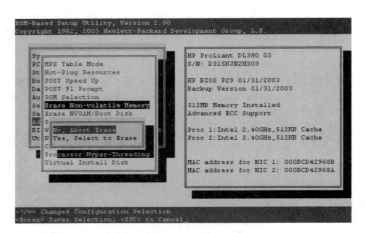

**Figure 15–6** *Erase options.*

The Erase NVRAM/Boot Disk option erases the system configuration by resetting the NVRAM, but it completely erases the boot disk. Use this option only when you are redeploying a server and are required to erase the NVRAM and boot disk to reinstall the operating system. User selectable options are as follows:

- Clear NVRAM only
- Clear NVRAM and Drive 80h

The Erase Non-volatile Memory option is a standard component of both the 2MB and 4MB system ROMs. If the Erase NVRAM/Boot Disk option is available for your server, it is listed under the Advanced Options menu of the main RBSU menu.

### 15.1.4.6   EMBEDDED DIAGNOSTIC UTILITY

The Diagnostic Utility provides a preboot method for quickly checking the validity of the three major server subsystems needed to start an operating system—memory, CPU, and boot disk, as shown in Figure 15–7.

This utility augments the version of server diagnostics available on the legacy system partition supported on some ProLiant servers.

The purpose of the ROM-based Diagnostic Utility is to provide critical support diagnostics only. The Diagnostics Utility is available only in English.

The Memory Test option tests all memory in the system. The CPU Test evaluates all processors in the system. The Boot Disk Test checks the boot drive for its readiness to boot.

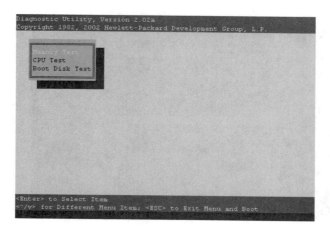

**Figure 15–7** *Diagnostic Utility interface.*

### 15.1.4.7 EMBEDDED INSPECT UTILITY

The ROM-based Inspect Utility displays system configuration information and saves it to a file on a disk. This utility replaces the version of the Inspect Utility available on the legacy system partition supported on some ProLiant servers.

To run the utility, select Inspect Utility from the System Maintenance menu. The Inspect Utility is a standard component on all ProLiant servers with 4MB ROM.

## 15.1.5 ORCA

The newest HP Smart Array controllers, including the RAID LC2, are configured using ORCA. Other HP Smart Array controllers are configured using the ACU. Figure 15–8 shows the ORCA interface.

**The RAID LC2 controller can be configured with ORCA only.**

ORCA is similar to the ACU but does not require the use of disks or CDs. Instead, ORCA executes out of the Option ROM that is located on the array controllers. It is designed for users who have minimal configuration requirements.

```
Option Rom Configuration for Arrays, version  2.02
Copyright 2002 Compaq Information Technologies Group, L.P.

Controller: HP Smart Array 5i, slot 0
Direct-Attached Storage




                         Main Menu
              Create Logical Drive
              View Logical Drive
              Delete Logical Drive





<Enter> to create a new logical drive
<UP/DOWN ARROW> to select main menu option; <ESC> to exit
```

**Figure 15–8** *ORCA interface.*

ORCA lets you create and delete logical drives, set interrupts, and set boot controller order.

 **Note**

> ORCA does not support drive expansion, RAID-level migration, or setting the stripe size.

ORCA is executed by pressing F8 when prompted during the boot process. After using ORCA, the server restarts if any changes were made.

During POST, any array controller that supports ORCA provides a prompt to the computer system console as part of the initialization process. If there are no configured logical drives on the array controller, this prompt waits 10 seconds before bypassing ORCA and continuing with the POST sequence. If any logical drives are configured, the prompt waits five seconds. When an HP RAID controller with ORCA support is installed in the system, the controller-based option ROM prompts during POST for 10 seconds.

The main features of ORCA include the following:

- Does not require disks or CDs to run
- Can be started when the server is powering up
- Can create, configure, and delete logical drives
- Can configure controller order
- Can assign an online spare for the created logical drives
- Can specify RAID level (0, 1, 1+0, 5)
- Cannot set stripe size or controller settings
- Supports only English

### 15.1.5.1 CONFIGURATION METHODS

ORCA default disk configuration depends on the number of drives present at initial configuration, as follows:

- Fewer than 2 drives = RAID 0
- Two drives = RAID 1
- Three to six drives = RAID 5
- More than six drives = No default configuration. You must use ACU to configure the drives.

If an array drive is not empty or there are more than six drives connected to the RAID controller, ORCA does not configure the array automatically. If this occurs, run ORCA to configure the array manually. For more information on running ORCA, refer to the server-specific setup and installation guide.

### 15.1.6   ACU

The ACU, shown in Figure 15–9, simplifies array configuration by providing a user-friendly interface to intelligent features of HP Smart Array controllers. You can start the ACU from within the operating system, from the SmartStart CD, or from a bootable disk.

ACU features include the following:

- Configuration wizards for optimized array configurations
- Express and custom initial configuration options
- Easy reconfiguration through capacity expansion, logical drive extension, RAID-level migration, and stripe-size migration tools

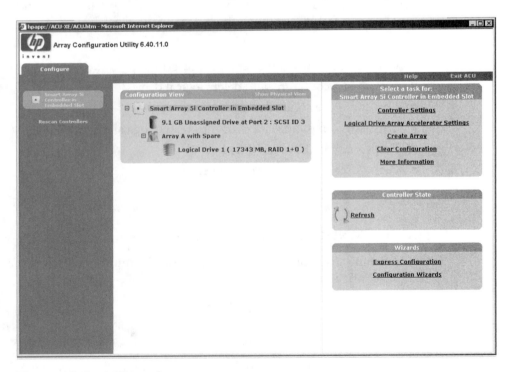

**Figure 15–9**   *ACU interface.*

- User-selectable stripe sizes
- Support for fault-tolerant RAID levels 0, 1, 1+0, 5, and RAID *advanced data guarding* (ADG)
- Variable cache read/write ratio and stripe size for tuning controller performance
- Drive rebuild and capacity expansion priority settings
- Online spare (hot spare) configuration
- Separate fault tolerance configuration on a logical drive basis
- Blinking drive-tray LEDs for quick storage identification

## 15.1.7 ProLiant Essentials Software

ProLiant essentials software, shown in Figure 15–10, is a critical part of the HP solution. These tools and utilities enable you to easily and quickly set up, configure, deploy, and manage ProLiant servers. This optional software extends the functionality of the HP adaptive infrastructure to address specific business problems and needs.

**Figure 15–10** *ProLiant essentials.*

Insight Management tools, along with other key management products, are packaged as ProLiant essentials value packs. These software tools enhance solutions and services and are designed to meet specific customer needs.

### 15.1.8 ProLiant Essentials Foundation Pack

The primary component of ProLiant essentials software is the foundation pack (previously distributed as the ProLiant Server Setup and Management Kit), shown in Figure 15–11.

The foundation pack ships with every ProLiant server and includes the essentials needed to install, configure, and manage ProLiant servers, including the following:

■ SmartStart for reliable and consistent server deployment
■ Insight Manager 7 for simple yet powerful Web-based server management

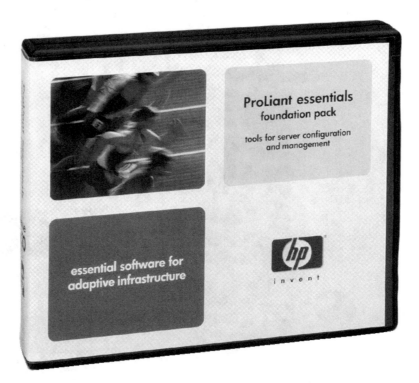

**Figure 15–11** *ProLiant essentials foundation pack.*

- System Management Homepage, which includes management agents for predictive fault management, version control agents for predictive fault management, and the Survey Utility for configuration analysis and troubleshooting.
- ActiveUpdate for proactive notification and delivery of the latest software updates
- Support software and utilities, such as the ACU, *ProLiant Support Packs* (PSPs), ROMpaqs, and Diagnostics

**Note** SmartStart (32-bit) is not included with the ProLiant DL590/64 server. This server uses a default configuration and RBSU to prepare for a 64-bit operating system installation.

## 15.1.9 Value Packs

ProLiant essentials value packs are optional software offerings available for purchase that extend the functionality of the foundation pack software. The value packs available from HP include the following:

- **Performance Management Pack**—An integrated management software solution that detects and analyzes hardware bottlenecks on ProLiant servers.
- **Rapid Deployment Pack (RDP)**—An integrated HP and Altiris solution that automates the process of deploying servers remotely.
- **Recovery Server Option Pack**—Enables an active-standby configuration of two servers where one server acts as the primary or active server and the second is the recovery server in a passive or pre-initialization mode.
- **Integrated Lights-Out Advanced Pack**—Holds the license key to switch on the advanced feature set of the *Integrated Lights-Out* (iLO) solution.
- **Workload Management Pack**—Enables easy management of complex environments, improving overall server utilization and providing Windows customers with a method to deploy multiple applications on a single multiprocessor ProLiant server. It features *Resource Partitioning Manager* (RPM) 2.0.

The Performance Management Pack with one license is included on the management CD in the foundation pack. It is also available as a value pack with flexible licensing options.

ProLiant essentials value packs are offered in a variety of licensing packages suitable for single copy through large volume acquisitions. Two licensing choices are available for each value pack product: the Flexible Quantity License Kit and the Master License Agreement.

### 15.1.9.1    FLEXIBLE QUANTITY LICENSE KIT

The Flexible Quantity License Kit allows customers to purchase a single software package, and provides one copy of the documentation and installation media (where applicable) and a single license key that is able to activate the exact number of licenses desired.

### 15.1.9.2    MASTER LICENSE AGREEMENT

The Master License Agreement is available for customers who want a single key for licenses of a value pack product that they plan to purchase incrementally over time.

## 15.1.10    Choosing a Deployment Method

If you need to deploy a single ProLiant server, SmartStart is the preferred deployment tool. If you need to deploy multiple ProLiant servers, the two primary solutions are SmartStart Scripting Toolkit and *Rapid Deployment Pack* (RDP). Figure 15–12 shows these options.

Both SmartStart and the SmartStart Scripting Toolkit are powerful yet easy-to-use tools. Each solution is designed to meet specific customer requirements.

The SmartStart Scripting Toolkit is available for download from http://h18013.www1.hp.com/products/servers/management/toolkit/index.html

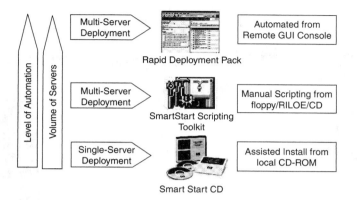

**Figure 15-12**  *ProLiant server deployment options.*

## 15.1.11   SmartStart

The SmartStart and Support Software CD contains the SmartStart setup program, shown in Figure 15–13, which is the integration tool that optimizes platform configurations and simplifies the setup and installation of HP servers.

SmartStart performs the following functions:

- Configures HP hardware
- Loads optimized drivers
- Assists with software installation
- Integrates operating systems on HP servers to optimize reliability and performance

The SmartStart software is easy to use for single-server deployment. SmartStart requires user attention throughout the process and can be performed on only one server at a time. Not all operating systems that are supported by the server can use the SmartStart installation.

The SmartStart CD is delivered in the ProLiant essentials foundation pack. It supports all HP ProLiant ML and DL servers except the DL590/64 and 100 series of servers. SmartStart is a very useful tool for both novice and advanced users.

The SmartStart CD contains optimized drivers and utilities that provide maximum performance on all leading operating systems.

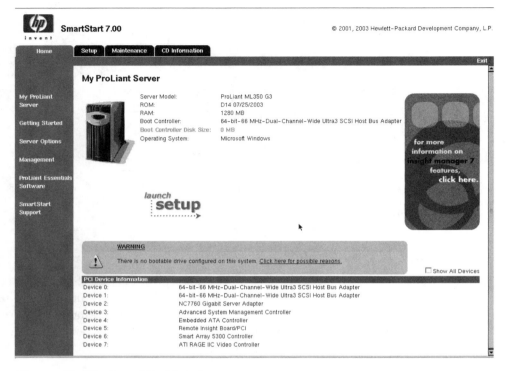

**Figure 15–13** *SmartStart interface.*

### 15.1.11.1 PROLIANT SUPPORT PACKS

PSPs are operating system–specific bundles of HP server support software. Each PSP includes multiple self-installable components known as *smart components* (optimized drivers, management agents, and utilities) for Microsoft Windows, Linux, and Novell NetWare.

### 15.1.11.2 SMARTSTART CD UTILITIES

The following utilities are also included with SmartStart:

- **Array Configuration Utility (ACU)**—Enables you to configure newly added array controllers and associated storage devices

- **Array Diagnostics Utility (ADU)**—Performs device tests on HP array controller hardware

- **Insight Diagnostics**—Performs tests on system components and displays information about the hardware and software configuration of a server

- **Erase Utility**—Provides options to clean different areas of the system such as attached drives, unattached drives, BIOS, and NVRAM.

SmartStart 6.00 and later offers an assisted installation path only. The assisted installation prepares the server hard drives by erasing the drives, creating a boot partition, preparing for the file system, and installing server support software, including the PSP.

For manual installations, use vendor-supplied operating system media and the RBSU and ORCA ROM-based utilities.

Server systems that support RBSU and ORCA feature maintenance utilities and automatic configuration operations that enable you to boot from the operating system CD to install the operating system, and then manually install server support software from the SmartStart CD or obtain the PSP.

### 15.1.12   System Erase with SmartStart 5.x

Use the System Erase Utility to erase all previous hardware and software configurations, including the network operating system, before using Smart-Start 5.x to initialize a server. The System Erase Utility can be run from SmartStart 5.x. The System Erase Utility erases system configuration information from NVRAM, from the hard drives, and from the Smart Array controllers present in the system.

When reinitializing a system using SmartStart, be sure to use the System Erase Utility.

The System Erase Utility is destructive to all data. If you start a previously configured server with SmartStart and it prompts you to run the System Erase Utility, do not run the System Erase Utility unless you want to clear all existing server configuration and data. The System Erase Utility destroys all configuration information and data by completely erasing all hard drives.

### 15.1.13   System Erase with SmartStart 6.x

SmartStart 6.x and later also includes the System Erase Utility, which provides options to clean various areas of the system, including attached drives, unattached drives, BIOS, and NVRAM.

Unlike previous versions of SmartStart, the System Erase Utility for SmartStart 6.x and later does not erase the Smart Array controllers.

For legacy systems, the Erase Utility is still available for download.

To access the latest release of the Erase Utility, go to Software and Drivers Download at http://www.hp.com.

## 15.2   Installing an Operating System on a ProLiant

This section provides the necessary steps to install Windows, Linux, or NetWare on a ProLiant server. Before installing an operating system, make sure that you complete the following steps:

1. Check the ProLiant certified operating systems list to ensure that the operating system you want to install is supported.

A list of supported operating systems is available at http://h10018.www1.hp.com/wwsolutions/index.html.

2. If the operating system you want to install is supported, search for a white paper about the operating system implementation. The white paper will provide detailed information on installation procedures and any open issues.

White papers are available at http://h18004.www1.hp.com/products/servers/technology/whitepapers/index.html.

3. If the server is not new, use the System Erase Utility to erase all previous hardware and software configurations before you reconfigure the server for a new installation. You can access the System Erase Utility through SmartStart or you can download it from the HP Web site.

### 15.2.1   Implementing Microsoft Windows Server on a ProLiant Server

Windows Server 2003 is an extension of the Windows 2000 operating system environment developed to enhance the customer experience and to improve overall usability and deployment. With few exceptions, application code developed for use under Windows 2000 will work with the Windows Server 2003 family of operating systems.

Windows Server 2003 should load and run on any ProLiant server that meets the recommended hardware configuration established by Microsoft.

### 15.2.1.1 INSTALLATION PROCEDURE FOR MICROSOFT WINDOWS SERVER 2003

Beginning with SmartStart 6.30, deployment of Microsoft Windows Server 2003 has become consistent and easy with the use of ROM-based utilities. This is true whether you choose a SmartStart assisted installation or a manual operating system installation.

To fully optimize the performance of your hardware platform, a SmartStart assisted installation walks you through the entire operating system installation process. Using an assisted installation, SmartStart prepares the server for installation, enables you to install the operating system using the vendor-supplied CDs, and provides automated installation of server support software using PSPs.

To use the SmartStart process to install Windows Server 2003, follow these steps:

1. Insert the SmartStart CD and boot the server.
2. When SmartStart has finished loading, select your language.
3. Acknowledge the license agreement.
4. Launch the setup program from the server home page.
5. Choose the operating system.
6. Configure the boot partition size.
7. Enter the operating system configuration information.
8. Follow the remaining prompts to guide you through the attended installation.
9. After installing the PSPs, deploy the operating system service packs or patches.
10. Redeploy the PSPs before restarting the server.

For more information about the Windows Server 2003 operating system, go to http://h18001.www1.hp.com/partners/microsoft/windows server2003/support.html or http://www.microsoft.com.

## 15.2.2 Implementing Red Hat Enterprise Linux 3 on a ProLiant Server

HP supports Linux on a wide range of ProLiant server models. The ProLiant server certification matrix identifies, by model, the ProLiant servers that have been certified for Linux, the Linux distribution and version each supports, and the status of HP support for each.

> To view this matrix, go to http://h18000.www1.hp.com/products/servers/linux/hplinuxcert.html.

Installing Linux on a new server can be more involved than installing Windows Server 2003 because a SmartStart assisted installation is not supported. After you have prepared the server and started it for the first time, configure the hardware as described in the preceding Windows Server 2003 section.

Using the RBSU (and ORCA, if applicable), select Linux as the operating system instead of Windows. Then use the vendor-supplied operating system media to begin the manual installation process. Unlike an attended SmartStart installation that performs an interview before beginning the operating system installation, a manual installation requires you to make choices about options and configurations during the installation process.

### 15.2.2.1 INSTALLATION PROCEDURE FOR RED HAT ENTERPRISE LINUX

HP recommends that customers wanting to install Red Hat Enterprise Linux 3 on ProLiant servers also install Update 1 (2.4.21-9.EL kernel) or later.

> You can find the most recent updates at http://rhn.redhat.com/errata/RHSA-2004-017.html.

To install Red Hat Enterprise Linux 3, follow these steps:

1. If the server contains drive arrays, configure them using ORCA or the ACU to create the logical drive.
2. Configure the server using RBSU:
   a. When prompted, press F9 during POST.
   b. Select System Options, and set the operating system selection to Linux.
   c. Set the controller boot order, if applicable.
   d. Press F10 to save the configuration and exit RBSU.
3. Insert the Red Hat Enterprise Linux 3 CD 1 into the CD-ROM drive and start the operating system from the CD.
4. Follow the instructions detailed in the Red Hat Linux installation guide.

**You can find the Red Hat Linux installation guide at www.redhat.com/docs/manuals/linux/3.**

5. After installing the operating system, upgrade your drivers by running the PSP.

**For additional information, go to http://h18000.www1.hp.com/products/servers/linux/index.html.**

## 15.2.3   Implementing Novell NetWare 6.5 on a ProLiant Server

NetWare has been proven on ProLiant servers through HP quality and assurance processes. In addition, ProLiant servers have completed the Novell certification process.

HP delivers a variety of information and tools for the deployment of NetWare. An HP migration tool helps you plan a NetWare deployment. In addition, numerous white papers, product bulletins, tools, and industry information help ensure the fastest time-to-implementation.

Designed to combine the stability of the business network and the global standard of the Internet, NetWare delivers tools and services for IP connectivity and management. NetWare also delivers high-performance and industry-standard support for application development.

Novell NetWare 6.5, the latest release of the NetWare 32-bit operating system, is built on the Novell NetWare 6 code base. NetWare 6.5 focuses on the end user by providing OneNet access from anywhere and any device. Applications currently supported on NetWare 6 are also supported on NetWare 6.5.

### 15.2.3.1 INSTALLATION PROCEDURE FOR NOVELL NETWARE 6.5

The ProLiant server certification matrix identifies, by model, the ProLiant servers that have been certified for NetWare 6.5.

To view the ProLiant server certification matrix, go to ftp://ftp.compaq.com/pub/products/servers/os-support-matrix-310.pdf.

SmartStart 7.0 supports attended installations of NetWare 6.5. After the hardware configuration and software interview process, you are guided through the operating system installation.

Using RBSU and ORCA, if applicable, select NetWare as the operating system. An attended installation is straightforward after the software interview process is completed. During the NetWare installation process, you must make choices about operating system options and configurations.

To install Novell NetWare 6.5, follow these steps:

1. If the server contains drive arrays, configure them using ORCA or ACU to create the logical drive.
2. Configure the server using RBSU:
   a. When prompted, press F9 during POST.
   b. Select System Options, and set the operating system selection to Novell NetWare.
   c. Set the controller boot order, if applicable.
   d. Press F10 to save the configuration and exit RBSU.
3. Insert the SmartStart CD and boot the server.
4. When SmartStart has finished loading, select your language.
5. Acknowledge the license agreement.

6. Launch the setup program from the server home page.
7. Select the operating system.
8. Configure the boot partition size.
9. Follow the remaining prompts to guide you through the attended installation.
10. After installing the PSPs, deploy the operating system service packs or patches.
11. Redeploy the PSPs before restarting the server.

For more information, refer to specific white paper at http://h18004.www1.hp.com/products/servers/technology/whitepapers/os-techwp.html.

**15.3** ## Using ProLiant Support Packs

The PSP is used after installing the operating system to update drivers and install HP utilities and agents on ProLiant servers. The PSP Web site is shown in Figure 15–14.

PSPs are operating system-specific bundles of HP server support software. Each PSP includes multiple self-installable components known as *smart components* (optimized drivers, management agents, and utilities).

One of the reasons why the individual PSP components are called *smart* is that each component checks the system for its installation dependencies (including hardware, software, firmware, and operating system) before installing the software. If the dependencies are not met, the smart component does not install. This design improves and simplifies operating system integration, flexibility, and system configuration.

PSP deployment utilities are hardware setup and software maintenance tools that provide an efficient way to manage routine software maintenance tasks. PSP deployment utilities are available for Microsoft Windows NT 4.0, Windows 2000, Windows Server 2003, Novell NetWare, and Linux server environments.

PSPs and the PSP deployment utilities integrate with other software maintenance, deployment, and operating system tools. They provide the information and flexibility needed to efficiently install, upgrade, and manage system software and reduce server maintenance costs.

Figure 15–14  *ProLiant Support Packs Web site.*

### 15.3.1  *PSP Software Maintenance Benefits*

The PSP deployment utilities provide the following software maintenance benefits to system administrators using Windows, NetWare, and Linux platforms:

- Self-installable components with easy-to-understand software update descriptions
- Components that can be installed individually or as part of a support pack
- Installation logic and version control that automatically checks for hardware, software, firmware, and operating system dependencies, installing only the correct software updates and latest drivers for optimal system configuration
- Silent command-line options and return codes that enable scripting and enhanced integration of the PSP deployment utilities with Insight Manager (Windows only) and the SmartStart Scripting Toolkit

- Common log files that provide easy access to a consolidated view of software installation history on target servers
- Content in ready-to-run native operating system file formats that save time by installing directly from a CD or from a shared network drive

Some legacy applications or documents might refer to Compaq Support Paqs, but in all cases, the terms *Compaq Support Paq, CSP, ProLiant Support Pack,* and *PSP* should be regarded as equal.

The PSP deployment PSPs and utilities can be obtained as follows:

- Through the HP Web site
- By downloading the PSP through the Version Control Repository Manager (VCRM)
- Using HP CD media

### 15.3.2 Deploying ProLiant Support Packs in Microsoft Windows

HP provides the following tools for configuring components and deploying PSPs for Windows:

- Remote Deployment Utility (RDU) for Microsoft Windows
- Remote Deployment Console Utility for Microsoft Windows

Some of the Smart Components included as part of a PSP must be configured before being deployed.

**! IMPORTANT**

Components only need to be configured once. The configuration information is stored inside each smart component so that it is available when the component is installed. You do not need to configure components each time they are deployed. However, configuration is independent of the target computer you select. If you change the configuration of a component after you have deployed it, you must redeploy the component.

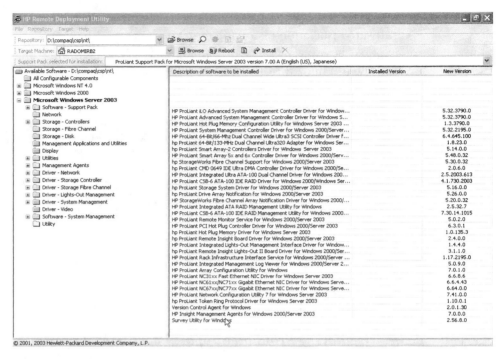

**Figure 15–15** *Remote Deployment Utility main control window.*

Configurable components include, but are not limited to, Insight Management Agents and Version Control Agent.

> **! IMPORTANT**
>
> The Web-based management portion of the Insight Management agents requires that a user ID, password, and trust level be configured in the smart component before installation if this is the first time the agents are being installed. If the agents are being updated and are already configured on the target system, the new agent component does not need to be configured before being deployed.

### 15.3.2.1 DEPLOYING COMPONENTS OR PSPS

The RDU allows local and remote nonscripted deployments only.

The Remote Deployment Console Utility for Microsoft Windows is a command-line version of the RDU. The functionality of the command-line-based Remote Deployment Console Utility is identical to the graphical RDU but enables unattended scripted deployment.

In some instances, you might want to install a single component manually, rather than install an entire support pack. To install a single component on your local system, follow these steps:

1. Double-click the filename of the component to be installed, for example cpxxxxxx.EXE, where the X's represent the component number. A screen similar to the one shown in Figure 15–16 displays.
2. Click the Install button. A screen similar to the one shown in Figure 15–17 displays.
3. Click the Install button, and then follow the instructions on the screen to complete the installation.

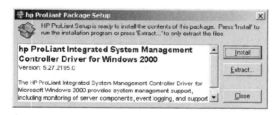

**Figure 15–16** *Component installation screen.*

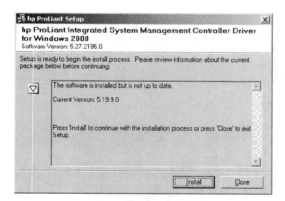

**Figure 15–17** *Component installation confirmation screen.*

### 15.3.3 Deploying ProLiant Support Packs in Novell NetWare

HP has developed the ProLiant Deployment Utility for Novell NetWare to provide enhanced PSP deployment capabilities. Using a console interface, the utility enables you to deploy and maintain PSP software on a local server.

To download the Deployment Utility for Novell NetWare, go to http://www.hp.com/support/files.

The utility has two modes of operation:

- **User interface mode**—Provides a Novell User Technologies-based graphical interface to guide the installation of a PSP or a subset of components in the PSP
- **Command-line mode**—Enables nongraphical command-line installation of a PSP or individual components

The Deployment Utility for Novell NetWare supports local deployments only.

### 15.3.4 Deploying ProLiant Support Packs in Linux

HP provides the HP ProLiant *Linux Deployment Utility* (LDU) for deploying the PSPs for Linux.

HP developed the LDU to provide an easy and efficient way to upgrade and manage system software. The utility enables you to deploy and maintain PSP software on local servers through use of the terminal window and on remote servers through use of the secure shell utility. Figure 15–19 shows the LDU main window.

To download the LDU with PSPs for Linux, go to http://www.hp.com/support/files.

**Figure 15–18**  *ProLiant Deployment Utility for Novell NetWare main window.*

! IMPORTANT

Root access is required for the LDU. If you do not have root access, the installation will not proceed.

The utility has two modes of operation:

- **Terminal window mode**—Enables nongraphical terminal window installation of a PSP or individual components. The terminal window mode is divided into three modes: silent, no user interface, and single-step.

- **Graphical mode**—Provides a graphical interface to guide the installation of a PSP or a subset of components in the PSP.

The LDU supports deployment on the local server only. Although the deployment can be executed from a secure shell to a remote server, it can be deployed only on the server that contains the PSP and the LDU.

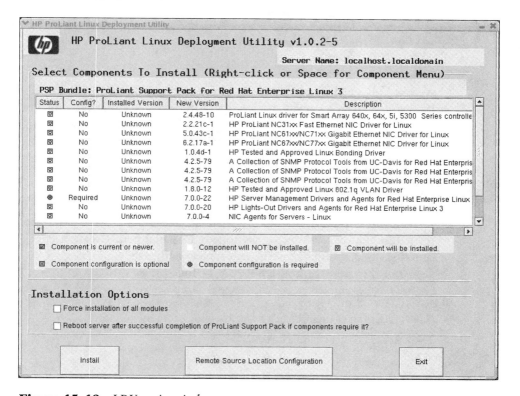

**Figure 15–19**  *LDU main window.*

Some components may require optional configuration settings. Configuration parameters can include information necessary to set up the component correctly or passwords required for software installed by the component.

The three methods for configuring a component are as follows:

- Using graphical installation mode
- Using terminal window installation mode
- Using a scripted installation

If the optional configuration data for a component is not provided and the component has not been installed previously, it will use default values for that configuration data. If the component has been previously installed and configured, the existing configuration information will be preserved if no changes are made to the configuration data.

Starting with ProLiant Support Pack 7.00, the HTTP server passwords no longer default to **compaq** if you do not specify them. If you do not set the HTTP server passwords, connectivity to the HTTP server will fail.

If you need more information on configuring and installing PSPs on ProLiant servers using different operating systems, refer to the PSP user guide. This guide is available on the SmartStart CD in the \compaq\csp folder, or you can download it from the HP Web site (http://www.hp.com).

## 15.4 Validating and Testing the Solution

After all of the components are installed, configured, and complete, you must test that everything works together as planned. Create a checklist of functions that adequately represent typical daily usage.

For the user, you must validate the following:

- Server log in
- Access to project data
- Access to server resources
- Access denied to restricted resources

For the administrator, you must validate the following:

- Server log in
- Determining access to project data
- Determining access to server resources
- User and group creation and modification
- System modification
- System log access

The successful completion of these tasks indicates that the solution delivered is what was promised. Although this work is over, it is important to maintain the relationship with the customer by describing the ways that HP can still provide value to the business.

## 15.5  Troubleshooting a Failed Installation

Not all upgrades go as planned. For example, unforeseen software incompatibilities and user error may cause an unsuccessful installation. It is important to gather all relevant system information and follow all instructions when planning and installing additional hardware.

Other reasons why upgrades fail include the following:

- Hardware not supported
- Hardware problem (power, cable, and so forth)
- Software not supported

The first step to recovering from the failure is to review the system information and the installation instructions. Questions to ask include the following:

- Was the right part ordered for the computer?
- Were the hardware installation instructions followed correctly?
- Were all cables or accessories connected properly?
- Did the hardware activate at system power-on?
- Did the computer display an error during the POST process?
- Were the software installation instructions followed correctly?
- Were any known incompatibilities addressed?
- Did the operating system or software display an error?

You can use logic to eliminate possibilities. For instance, if all procedures were followed properly, but the device remains unresponsive or unacknowledged, it is likely that the part is defective. The operating system or software may or may not display an error if a part is faulty. Always check the documentation included with the part for help or information on any known issues or last-minute errata.

Replacing the newly installed but suspect part with another one is the easiest way to determine or verify where the fault lies. This is also true in most cases of an installed part that fails, such as a fan in a power supply. However, replacement is not always practical because of inventory costs or time constraints. In such cases, eliminating as many failure points as possible can expose the true cause of the problem.

A repeated failure in one area of the system can be a symptom of a problem in another area. For example, if PPMs repeatedly fail, it could be that there is nothing wrong with the PPM, but actually a problem with the processor board, power supply, or even line voltage.

### 15.5.1 Recovering from a Failed SmartStart Installation

Often, sudden power failures can be disruptive. Unless the system has power protection, some work may be lost or corrupted. On an existing system, this is an inconvenience. When it happens during a SmartStart installation, it can be a much bigger problem. A power failure is one way the SmartStart process can fail.

Recovering from a failed SmartStart installation depends on the following:

- The installation path chosen
- The operating system being installed
- The point in the process at which the interruption occurs

An interrupted manual installation of Linux, for example, must be restarted from the beginning. A complete restart is necessary because in manual installations there is no SmartStart involvement after the hardware is configured until after the operating system installation is complete.

If the interruption occurs during the early phase of an attended installation, where SmartStart is copying files to a temporary partition on the hard disk, the whole process also must be restarted, beginning with a system erase, because not all the drivers or operating system setup files have been copied. This is true for both Windows and NetWare at this stage.

If the interruption occurs after SmartStart has finished the file copying process and the server has restarted, the operating system might be able to pick up from where it left off, especially if it is a Windows product. If recovery is not possible, the whole process must be restarted, beginning with a system erase.

## ▲ Summary

This chapter discussed the basics of deploying a single-server ProLiant solution. The key distinction between the *Accredited Integration Specialist* (AIS) designation and the *Accredited Systems Engineer* (ASE) designation is that the AIS focuses on the small- to medium-size business, whereas the ASE focuses on the enterprise. Therefore, skills relating to deploying single-server solutions are positioned at the AIS level.

As an AIS, you should be able to deploy a single ProLiant server from the time when the components are pulled out of the box up to the point where the server is placed into production. This chapter provided an overview of the skills, tools, and techniques needed to accomplish this deployment, including the following:

- Initial server power-on
- Updating system and option ROMs
- Server configuration tools and utilities, including RBSU, Inspect Utility, and ORCA.
- The available deployment methods and how to select the correct method
- HP SmartStart
- How to install an operating system.

This chapter concludes Part 4. Part 5 provides key concepts on HP systems management.

## ▲ LEARNING CHECK

1. *Name the utility that RBSU replaces.*

2. *During the system startup process, what should you press to access RBSU?*
    A. F8
    B. F9
    C. F10
    D. F12

3. *List three differences between RBSU and the SCU.*

4. *Which utility delivers enhanced functionality for the 4MB ROM?*
    A. Embedded Inspect Utility
    B. RBSU
    C. ORCA
    D. ROM-Based Diagnostics Utility

5. *What is ORCA?*

6. *What are three differences between ORCA and the ACU?*

7. *Which of the following is not a function of ORCA?*
    A. Testing logical drives
    B. Creating logical drives
    C. Setting interrupts
    D. Setting boot controller order

8. *List three server deployment solutions from HP.*

9. *What does PSP stand for?*

10. *What is a difference between the Remote Deployment Utility (RDU) and Remote Deployment Console Utility?*

# Systems Management

**O**ne of HP's long-standing differentiating benefits has been its strength in server and system management technologies. Part 5 provides the information that an Accredited Integration Specialist needs to know about these technologies.

Here is an overview of the chapters in Part 5.

## Chapter 16   Introduction to HP Systems Management

Chapter 16 provides an introduction to the technologies involved in HP systems management, including systems management agents, management applications, and management platforms.

HP Insight Management agents are a particular focus of Chapter 16, because they enable well-known HP server differentiating features, including HP Prefailure Warranty and Automatic Server Recovery.

## Chapter 17   HP Lights-Out Management Technologies

A second layer of HP systems management is comprised of the HP Lights-Out management technologies, including *Integrated Lights-Out* (iLO) and *Remote Insight Lights-Out Edition* (RILOE II).

Lights-Out management provides virtual on-site management capabilities. Rather than calling the remote site to have another person issue keyboard commands and listening to the other person describe the response from the server, you can view server operations and manage the server directly.

An Accredited Integration Specialist will have a fundamental understanding of the HP Lights-Out management technologies, when to recommend them, and how to implement them.

# Introduction to HP Systems Management

After reading this chapter, you should be able to do the following:

- List and describe the key HP technologies enabled by the HP Insight Management agents.
- Describe the HP Prefailure Warranty program, and explain how the HP Insight Management agents provide the technical foundation for this program.
- Describe the HP Automatic Server Recovery features and explain how the HP Insight Management agents provide the technical foundation for this technology.
- Explain how to connect to the Systems Management home page for a managed HP ProLiant server.
- Describe how point management works, and explain the conditions when it provides an effective management solution.
- Explain the difference between a management application and a management platform.
- Describe HP Insight Manager 7 and its functions and features.
- Describe HP Systems Insight Manager.
- Describe the features and functions of the HP OpenView portfolio and explain the four levels of integration provided by HP OpenView.
- Describe the HP Survey Utility, its functions and features, and how to use the Survey Utility to gather and analyze system management information.

HP Insight Management *agents* form the foundation of the HP systems management strategy. The Insight Management agents enable the following core HP technologies:

- HP Prefailure Warranty
- Automatic Server Recover
- HP Systems Management home page
- Point management

*Management applications* are software programs that run on a server and work with agents to

- Provide necessary information about the network.
- Set parameters and thresholds for elements and agents.
- Execute any needed management commands across the network.

The management application you choose does most of the work that is required to manage your systems, including interpreting, organizing, presenting, and manipulating system information. A management application also performs these tasks:

- Queries agents for information and displays it in a format that can be easily interpreted by the system administrator.
- Monitors and reports alerts received from agents. The application can either forward the alerts to another application or notify the administrator by pager.
- Enables the administrator to set parameters in agents, such as the threshold at which an agent delivers an alert.

A *management platform* is a broader concept for software that allows vendors to accomplish two main functions:

- Publish *Management Information Bases* (MIBs) that can be compiled into the management system without the need to run the vendor's management application
- Design management applications that fit into the management system

Management platforms enable administrators to use the available tools to manage each component on the network.

This chapter discusses the following HP management applications:

- Insight Manager 7
- HP Systems Insight Manager
- HP OpenView
- HP Survey Utility

## 16.1  Insight Management Agents

HP Web-enabled management agents are the key piece of the HP remote management strategy. They provide direct access to in-depth instrumentation built in to HP servers, workstations, desktops, and portables. After they are installed on a network device, these software components read the device's instrumentation, evaluate it, and use industry-standard protocols to report device status or to transmit system alerts to a management console such as HP Systems Insight Manager.

HP management agents monitor more than 1,000 parameters on system and subsystem elements such as the disk, processor, memory, and fans. In the event of subsystem failures or abnormal instrumentation readings, these agents initiate alerts to the management console.

HP management agents work with the *Simple Network Management Protocol* (SNMP), a widely used industry-standard management protocol. SNMP uses standard and extended MIBs to define the types of information that can be retrieved from a device. HP makes its MIBs freely available to enable integration of HP management agents with a wide variety of management platforms.

For a complete list of available agents and supported operating systems, go to http://www.hp.com/support/files.

## 16.2  Prefailure Warranty

The HP management agents also form the foundation for HP's Prefailure Warranty program. If the HP management agents detect problems that require replacement of a disk, processor, or memory within the server's warranty period, HP will replace these components free of charge.

The process of predicting an event requires monitoring, detecting, and analyzing. Monitoring entails looking at the operating parameters of the system components. Detecting means that the server finds the required events as they occur. Analyzing ensures that the severity or frequency of the occurrence is understood; and if the analysis indicates an impending failure, the system alerts the system administrator.

The combination of the HP management agents and the HP Prefailure Warranty program helps system administrators prevent unnecessary downtime by providing advance notice of potential server failures and by facilitating rapid and proactive replacement of failing parts.

## 16.3    Automatic Server Recovery

Automatic Server Recovery (ASR) is a feature that causes the server to restart when a catastrophic operating system error occurs, such as a blue-screen, ABEND (abnormal end), or panic. A system fail-safe timer, the ASR timer, starts when the System Management driver, also known as the health driver, is loaded.

After the HP Server Health Driver is loaded, it sets the ASR timer to the ASR timeout value. (The default is 10 minutes, but can be changed in the *ROM-Based Setup Utility* [RBSU].) If the timer is not reset within this specified time, it is presumed that an operating system fault has occurred. After the timer has expired, it will trigger an interrupt, which initiates a system reboot.

The HP Server Health Driver also monitors the system temperature and the system fans. If a fan fails or the temperature of the system exceeds the caution level, the operating system invokes an auto-shutdown sequence to prevent data loss.

If the driver is not loaded, or the thermal shutdown has been disabled in the RBSU, the power will be immediately switched off without a proper shutdown of the operating system to avoid hardware damage.

## 16.4    Systems Management Home Page

Along with the management agents, HP provides an HTTP server that is viewable using a standard Web browser through port 2301 or 2381. From the agent home page on this HTTP server, IT administrators have access to all Web-enabled HP management software active on the HP device. The

HTTP server enables administrators to view system status and to manage their systems from anywhere using a standard Web browser.

Figure 16–1 shows a typical systems management home page.

If you are using a Windows-based system, you can monitor your server locally with this address: https://127.0.0.1:2381 or https://localhost:2381.

To monitor your server remotely, use this address: https://*machine*:2381 (where *machine* is the IP address or the computer name under *Domain Name System* [DNS]).

The 2381 that follows the URL represents the port or socket number that the Insight Management agents use to communicate with the browser. If this number is not specified, the browser might attempt to connect to another Web page if the managed server is running a Web server.

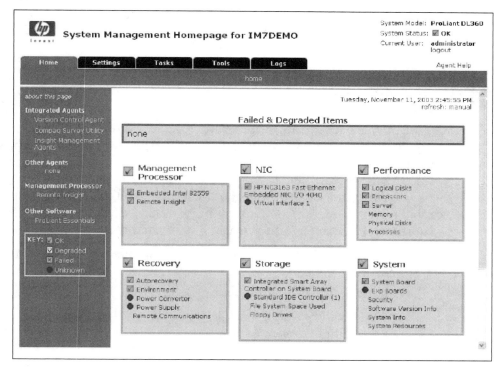

**Figure 16–1** *Typical systems management home page.*

If you are using a non-Windows operating system, use this address to monitor your server locally: http://127.0.0.1:2301 or http://localhost:2301.

To monitor your server remotely, use http://*machine*:2301 (where *machine* is the IP address or the computer name under DNS).

### 16.4.1   Point Management

Point management uses the browser to establish point-to-point connections with each manageable device in the network. Each device displays one or more HTML pages that show the overall status of the device and its subsystems. The browser interface enables the administrator to use a single console to display information about multiple devices.

Other hyperlinks can be created on these pages to enable the administrator to gather more information from various sources, such as CD-ROMs, online databases, or Help files.

Point management is an ideal solution for small networks with fewer than a hundred devices because of the low entry cost and ease of use. However, point management does not work as well across larger networks. In addition, you cannot use this solution to manage devices that use different management protocols or standards.

## 16.5   Insight Manager 7

Insight Manager 7, shown in Figure 16–2, is a Web-based management application that monitors HP servers, clusters, desktops, and portables. It can also manage third-party devices compliant with any of these standards: HTTP, SNMP, MIB, and DMI.

With a single click from the home page, you can view information about these devices. Communicating with the software agents installed during server setup, Insight Manager 7 automatically

- Discovers all of the servers and management processors in your environment.
- Shows summary health status for each device.
- Provides one-click access to management resources such as
  - Insight Management agents.
  - Version Control.

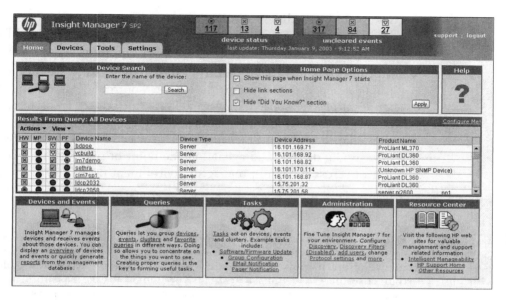

**Figure 16–2**   *HP Insight Manager 7 interface.*

## 16.5.1   *Insight Manager 7 Functions*

Insight Manager 7 aggregates important management information, such as device status and asset configuration, from managed devices throughout the IT environment. It ships with the capabilities described in this subsection:

- **Integrated database installation**—During installation, you can choose to install *Microsoft SQL Server 2000 Desktop Engine* (MSDE) database or point to an existing SQL Server database containing performance, asset, and configuration data.

- **Autodiscovery and identification**—You can configure Insight Manager 7 to automatically discover and identify HP platforms as well as other HTTP-, SNMP-, and DMI-instrumented devices attached to the network. By default autodiscovery is set to run daily.

- **Discovery filters**—Discovery filters enable you to control the type of devices (servers, clients, management processors, and so on) added to the Insight Manager 7 database.

- **E-mail and paging notification**—Insight Manager 7 can send both e-mail and paging notifications based on the receipt of a specified event or a change in device status. This eliminates the need to constantly monitor a management console and helps maximize the productivity of IT personnel.

- **Group configuration**—Administrators can manage groups of devices simultaneously. Specified configuration settings can be extracted from a reference system, edited, and copied to multiple target systems.

- **Multiple-system version control and system software update**—Insight Manager 7, together with Version Control agents and the *Version Control Repository Manager* (VCRM), introduces an architecture for version managing and updating HP system software. The software maintenance architecture enables you to select a baseline set of software (BIOS, drivers, and agents) as the point of reference for version control across the entire managed environment or a selected portion of it.

*ProLiant Support Paqs* (PSPs) are sets of drivers, utilities, and management agents that have been ordered and tested for optimal performance and reliability on ProLiant servers. Although HP recommends that customers use PSPs to establish system software baselines, the VCRM also enables the creation of custom groupings of system software.

- **Management agent integration**—Insight Manager 7 automatically discovers the management agents and any other Web-based management application running at a set of predefined HTTP ports. Hardware status reported by the management agents displays in the device list.

### 16.5.1.1 ADDITIONAL BENEFITS

Insight Manager 7 also serves as the central launching point for other ProLiant Essentials products such as Lights-Out devices and ProLiant Essentials *Performance Management Pack* (PMP).

As the foundation for the PMP, Insight Manager 7 SP2

- Displays server performance status.
- Provides in-context launch of the PMP console.
- Receives performance events from managed systems.

Insight Manager 7 ships with standard tasks and queries to discover and report on your systems from the moment of installation.

To download the latest Insight Manager 7 updates, PSPs, and MIBs, go to http://www.hp.com/servers/manager.

**16.6**

## HP Systems Insight Manager

A new technology for 2004, HP Systems Insight Manager is the one management tool you need for ProLiant systems. It merges the best of premerger HP and premerger Compaq systems-level tools: HP Servicecontrol Manager, HP Insight Manager 7, and HP TopTools.

HP Servicecontrol Manager is a Web-based and command-line interface, multisystem application that provides a single point of administration for managing multiple HP-UX or Linux systems, configuration, and workload management.

HP Insight Manager 7, described previously in this chapter, is a Web-based enterprise management application that manages HP servers, clusters, storage, printers, desktops, workstations, and portables (see Figure 16–3). It provides a pro-active, automated, and cost-effective solution for managing and checking the health status of distributed systems.

HP TopTools is a collection of applications and agents that identify and diagnose network and HP system problems quickly using a Web-based interface.

HP Systems Insight Manager replaces Insight Manager 7 on ProLiant servers.

**Figure 16–3**

*HP Systems Insight Manager 7 interface.*

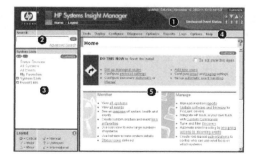

**HP OpenView**

The HP OpenView portfolio contains about 50 products. Most OpenView products have integration capabilities built in. Integration with one Open-View product is fairly simple. However, as the industry challenge moves up from network management to *integrated network and system management* (INSM), to service management, and ultimately to business process management, multiple products must play together to realize that higher goal. An *independent software vendor* (ISV) might integrate with just one product, or might integrate with multiple OpenView products, depending on the objective.

Figure 16–4 shows the HP OpenView Operations Manager interface.

HP OpenView integrations can be divided into four general types:

- Fundamental integration
- Strategic integration
- Extended integration
- Service management integration

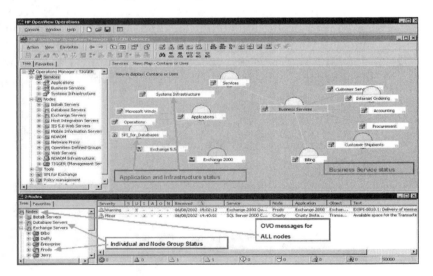

**Figure 16–4** *HP OpenView Operations Manager interface.*

### 16.7.1 Fundamental Integration

*Network Node Manager* (NNM) is the foundation of the fundamental integration category.

NNM is map-oriented and supplemented by an event browser. It is focused on (and restricted to) network infrastructure management, with rich data about the devices in the network and their relationships (network topology). System or application management is possible with NNM via SNMP, but NNM is not ideal for this purpose.

It is inaccurate to state that a fundamental integration is simple; it can actually be very elaborate.

### 16.7.2 Strategic Integration

*OpenView Operations* (OVO) is the foundation of this integration category.

OVO is event-oriented and focused on an event browser containing rich information about alerts from diverse sources. It is strategic because it is the foundation for all other higher-value solutions: Systems management, applications management, and service management all begin with an OVO integration. OVO is highly extensible, through its built-in capabilities or by supplementing it with other OpenView or ISV products.

OVO is designed for large-scale operations, multiple operators, and diverse message sources.

### 16.7.3 Extended Integration

OVO is also the foundation of this integration, but it offers much more. Typically called a *Smart Plug-In* (SPI ), an extended integration is an OVO integration plus integration with one or more other OpenView products, packaged for portability. It can be plugged into existing OpenView environments to instantly increase value to the customer. There are few limits for this kind of integration.

### 16.7.4 Service Management Integration

The pinnacle of OpenView integrations today, the service management integration has a three-product foundation: OVO, Service Navigator, and Service Desk.

Together, these three products define, present, and monitor services rather than just components. They use the combined events from component devices, systems, and applications to deduce and present the health of the services that those components support. Like the other integrations, the service management integration can be extended in many ways by the addition of other OpenView and ISV products. An ISV seeking to contribute to a service-oriented management model must understand this particular combination of OpenView products, how they work together, and how to add information into (and get information from) the OpenView service model.

## 16.8  HP Survey Utility

The Survey Utility is an online, information-gathering agent that runs on ProLiant servers. It is designed to enhance serviceability and maximize server availability by streamlining the configuration analysis and troubleshooting processes.

Figure 16–5 shows a typical HP Survey Utility interface.

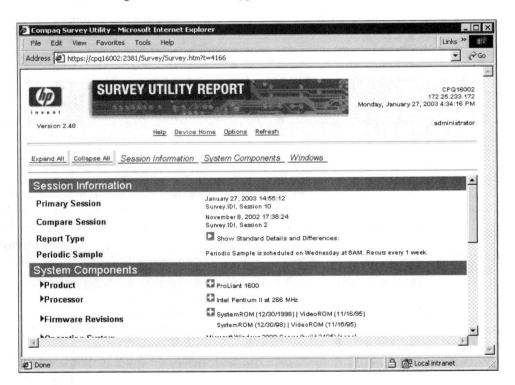

**Figure 16–5** *HP Survey Utility interface.*

In addition to management tools, service tools can be invaluable to help resolve server issues. When a service call is placed, the correct information must be available. The primary information requirement, and the one that provides the greatest insight into server problems, is the system configuration.

In relation to system configuration, the Survey Utility provides the following:

- Comprehensive configuration captures
- Automatic identification and comparison of configuration changes
- A configuration history log

The information is saved automatically as a history of multiple sessions in a downloadable file. This critical information helps to troubleshoot server problems and streamline the service process by enabling quick and easy identification of the server configuration.

Survey Utility interprets and reports various types and levels of information, which you can specify. For example, you can view the active session or, because the Survey Utility stores multiple configuration sessions, you can generate a report that automatically compares any two sessions.

The Survey Utility compares the sessions and highlights any differences. This feature proves useful for identifying the source of server problems. It helps you to identify (1) the history of events, (2) the order of changes, and (3) when specific changes were made to the system.

You can install the Survey Utility on a ProLiant server running Windows, NetWare, or Linux.

For the latest versions of Linux supported by HP ProLiant servers, visit the operating system matrix at this Web site: ftp://ftp.compaq.com/pub/products/servers/os-support-matrix-310.pdf.

Insight Diagnostics is the replacement for the Survey Utility on ProLiant ML/DL G2 and later systems running Windows and Linux. You should continue to use the Survey Utility for pre-G2 systems and systems running Novell NetWare.

### 16.8.1   Using the Survey Utility

At this time, only Classic Survey is available for use online. This version of Survey has been around for years, and is available by individual SoftPaq, autoloaded by the PSPs, the System Management home page, and other sources. It is available for Windows, Linux, and NetWare.

Online Insight Diagnostics is available from the System Management home page, Insight Manager 7, through the Start menu from the Windows desktop, and from HP Systems Insight Manager.

HP plans to retire Classic Survey with the release of SmartStart 7.1. And although it might still be available, it will not be updated with new product support and will be replaced with the Online Insight Diagnostics Survey Utility. In fact, only the Survey Utility will be available with Online Insight Diagnostics when it first announces with SmartStart 7.1.

Except for support for new products and the *graphical user interface* (GUI), Online Insight Diagnostics Survey will provide comparable information to Classic Survey. Offline Survey is available only with Offline Insight Diagnostics by booting from the SmartStart CD and going to the Maintenance home page. The information provided by Offline Survey is comparable to that formerly provided by the Inspect Utility.

In addition to supporting Windows environments, Online Insight Diagnostics is scheduled to include support for Linux environments with the release of SmartStart 7.1. Classic Survey will continue to be updated with new products for NetWare environments.

In the modern business environment, servers run increasingly critical and complex applications. Because the success of these businesses depends on continuous server operation, server availability is an important requirement.

### 16.8.2   Survey Utility Features

The Survey Utility addresses availability and serviceability requirements with a comprehensive set of features.

- **Online installation and operation**—Online installation and operation eliminates the need to restart the server or take it offline when installing or running the utility. This is an improvement over the HP Inspect Utility, which provided similar information, but required a server restart.

- **Comprehensive configuration capture**—The comprehensive configuration capture function gathers detailed hardware and system configuration information using a single tool.

- **Automatic configuration audit trail**—The automatic configuration audit trail feature maintains a configuration history for the server. It provides a detailed record of the configuration history by storing multiple configuration snapshots and highlighting changes and differences.
- **Integration with Lights-Out devices**—By integrating with HP Lights-Out devices, the Survey Utility enables you to view information about a server that has lost power, which is critical to bringing the server online as soon as possible.

This combination of features simplifies the service process and minimizes server downtime.

### 16.8.3   Survey Utility Architecture

The Survey Utility agent resides on each managed server and communicates with various operating system–specific components to capture detailed information. These components include the following:

- File systems
- System BIOS
- SCSI drivers
- Windows *hardware abstraction layer* (HAL)
- Disk array drivers
- Windows Registry
- NetWare *application program interfaces* (APIs)
- Health driver

This architecture enables the Survey Utility agent to identify both hardware and operating system information within the same polling process. When a configuration snapshot is initiated, the Survey Utility agent polls all of these sources for the most current information and view of the system.

### 16.8.4   Sessions

A session is a description of the configured state of a server at a specific point in time. When installed on a server, the Survey Utility maintains up to ten distinct sessions.

For Windows and NetWare systems, the session information is maintained in the survey.idi file, which is located in the same directory as the executable portion of the program. This file contains all binary information captured for every session. It can be analyzed locally at the management console by the Survey Utility or sent to HP or another location, such as a help center, to generate custom reports.

For Windows and NetWare systems, the sessions are organized as three distinct types:

1. **Original**—The original session is the first session recorded (referenced as session number 2). The Survey Utility treats this session as a master configuration and never overwrites it.
2. **Checkpoint**—The checkpoint sessions (referenced as session numbers 3 to 10) are the next eight samples that differ significantly from the original session.

   - A checkpoint is made only when there has been a configuration change that would not occur under normal operation of the server. Therefore, not all changes generate checkpoints.
   - The significance of a checkpoint is determined by the program and the type of information captured.
   - Sessions are automatically overwritten as the number of checkpoints increases using a first-in, first-out method.

3. **Active**—The active session (referenced as session number 1) is the last information captured. This session is overwritten each time a sample is taken.

For Linux systems, the session information for each session is stored in an individual text file called surveyCCYY-MM-DD-HH-mm-ss.txt. (The double letters represent the date and time when the Survey Utility was run.) These files are located in the /var/compaq/survey/ directory.

Note

When using the Survey Utility from a browser, sessions will be listed by the date and time of the session rather than by the number of the session.

## 16.8.5   Collecting Information

The three methods for initiating data collection with the Survey Utility are as follows:

- Periodic capture
- User-initiated collection
- Scheduled intervals

### 16.8.5.1   PERIODIC CAPTURE

After it is installed on the server, the Survey Utility automatically captures a session each time the server is restarted.

Because most significant configuration changes require a server restart to be recognized, these capture points help provide maximum coverage for detecting changes. If a significant change is recognized, it is tagged as a checkpoint and stored. Any configuration differences are also recorded.

Minor changes are also logged, such as the amount of used disk drive space, but they do not become checkpoints. Only major changes, such as a drive being removed or added, cause the snapshot to become a checkpoint.

### 16.8.5.2   USER-INITIATED COLLECTION

The Survey Utility enables you to initiate a new session on demand. Although this feature can also be used when the Survey Utility is configured for periodic capture, it proves particularly useful for one-time immediate collection.

To create a session on demand on a Linux server using the Survey Utility, enter **survey** at the command prompt.

To create a session on demand on a Windows server using the Survey Utility, follow these steps:

1. Select Start, Run.
2. Enter **C:\compaq\survey\survey.**

To create a session on demand on a NetWare server using the Survey Utility, enter the following commands at the NetWare system prompt:

1. **Unload survey**
2. **Load survey**

### 16.8.5.3   SCHEDULED INTERVALS

You can configure the Survey Utility to create a session at a regularly scheduled interval. Although the default setting for this feature is once per week, the interval is configurable using command-line parameters. You can adjust the interval to occur as often as once a day.

This scheduled interval feature enables the configuration audit trail to capture views of the systems on restart. It also captures and identifies differences and significant configuration changes during regular server operation. For example, this feature identifies software changes made without a required reboot (such as when loading and unloading NetWare modules).

### 16.8.6   Web Browser View

The Survey Utility Web browser interface, shown in Figure 16–6, enables remote control and facilitates transfer of Survey information from remote systems to a service provider.

The requirements for browsing to a device using the Survey Utility are (1) the TCP/IP protocol is installed on the server, and (2) a Web browser installed with the following features is supported and enabled:

- HTML tables
- HTML frames
- Java
- JavaScript
- Accept all cookies

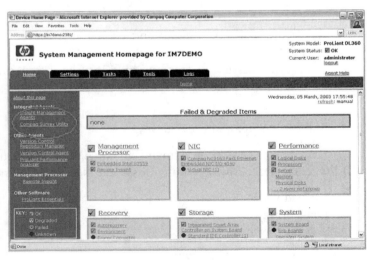

**Figure 16–6**   *HP Survey Utility Web browser interface.*

HP recommends either Microsoft Internet Explorer or Netscape Navigator. For the minimum supported version of Internet Explorer or Netscape Navigator, refer to http://h18007.www1.hp.com/support/files/server/us/ WebDoc/630/Surveyug.pdf.

## ▲ Summary

This chapter discussed the foundation of the HP Management solution: the HP management agents.

This chapter then provided an overview of four key technologies enabled by the management agents:

- The HP Prefailure Warranty
- Automatic Server Recovery
- The HP Systems Management home page
- Point management

This chapter concluded with a high-level overview of the following HP management products:

- HP Insight Manager 7
- HP Systems Insight Manager
- HP OpenView
- HP Survey Utility

## ▲ LEARNING CHECK

1. *List four key HP technologies supported by the HP Insight Management agents.*

2. *In the event of subsystem failures, HP Insight Management agents initiate* _____ *to the management console.*
    - A. Traps
    - B. Alerts
    - C. Pages
    - D. MIBs

3. *Name the program that helps system administrators prevent unnecessary downtime by providing advance notification of potential server failures and facilitating proactive part replacement.*

4. *Name the driver that sets the ASR timer and also monitors system temperature and system fans.*

5. *You attempt to connect to a managed HP server by entering http://192.168.1.1. However, an unexpected Web page loads instead of the management home page. Why did this occur?*

6. *In which of the following environments would point management provide a viable management solution?*

    A. A large network with about 1,000 devices

    B. A medium-size network with about 500 devices

    C. A small network with fewer than 100 devices

7. *Which of the following is* not *a capability or feature of HP Insight Manager?*

    A. Integrates with Microsoft SQL Server

    B. Sends e-mails or pager notifications when specific events occur

    C. Provides management of groups of devices

    D. Provides automatic identification and comparison of configuration changes

8. *Which component is* not *a part of the new HP Systems Insight Manager?*

    A. HP Servicecontrol

    B. HP Insight Manager 7

    C. HP TopTools

    D. HP Survey Utility

9. *Which of the following are components of HP OpenView service management integration?*

    A. OpenView Operations

    B. Service Navigator

    C. Service Desk

    D. Network Node Manager

10. *You need to recommend a management tool that allows for the proactive configuration monitoring of file systems, system BIOS, and the Windows Registry. What HP management tool is designed for this purpose?*

    A. Service Controller

    B. Configuration Manager

    C. Insight Manager

    D. Survey Utility

11. *Which of the following is not a valid session type for Survey Utility running under Windows?*

    A. Original

    B. Checkpoint

    C. Snapshot

    D. Active

12. *Which command creates a session on demand on a Windows server?*

    A. **C:\compaq\survey\survey**

    B. **C:\hp\survey\survey**

    C. **Load Survey**

    D. **survey**

# HP Lights-Out Management Technologies

This chapter provides you with the knowledge and skills to do the following:

- Explain HP Lights-Out technologies.
- Describe iLO standard and iLO Advanced Pack.
- Describe RILOE II.
- Compare the differences between RILOE II and iLO.
- Explain how Lights-Out devices are managed.
- Explain the network options for connecting Lights-Out devices.

HP recognizes the need for remote systems management and offers the HP Lights-Out technology to manage ProLiant servers from a remote system.

**17.1** **HP Lights-Out Technologies**

Lights-Out management provides virtual on-site management capabilities. Instead of calling the remote site to have another person issue keyboard commands and listening to the other person describe the response from the server, you can view server operations and manage the server directly, as illustrated in Figure 17–1.

HP Lights-Out technology includes two main solutions: RILOE II and iLO.

RILOE II is a PCI card that provides full control of hardware and operating systems for a server through a client browser. RILOE II has a dedicated processor, memory, *network interface card* (NIC), and an AC adapter that makes it completely independent of the host server operating system and hardware. It is the successor of the RILOE card. The major difference is the faster processor on the RILOE II card (200MHz PPC against 66MHz i960).

iLO is an intelligent processor and firmware integrated on selected ProLiant servers. This technology also supports collection of ProLiant BL p-Class rack information.

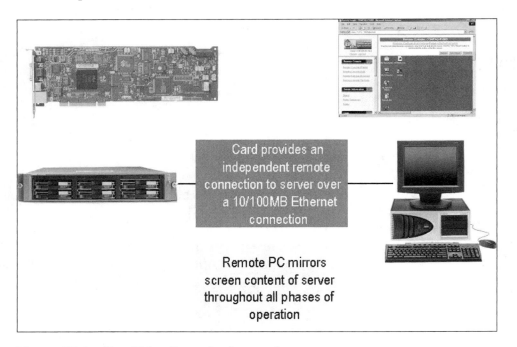

**Figure 17–1** *How Lights-Out technology works.*

Both products offer many of the same features with a few exceptions, which are noted in this chapter. Both types are configured through the *ROM-Based Setup Utility* (RBSU), which is accessed by pressing F8 at server startup.

### 17.1.1 Key Features of HP Lights-Out Technologies

The key features of HP Lights-Out management options include the following:

- **Autoconfiguration of IP address**—Provides automatic network configuration, which includes a default name and *Dynamic Host Configuration Protocol* (DHCP) client.

- **Browser accessibility**—Allows access to the remote host server regardless of the state of the host server or operating system.

- **Dedicated LAN network connectivity**—Provides a dedicated network connection that is capable of selecting speeds between 10 and 100Mb/s.

- **Microsoft Emergency Management Service (EMS) console**—Provides a text-based screen to access the host server. A feature of Microsoft Windows Server 2003, EMS enables you to display running processes, change process priority, and halt processes. Without a Lights-Out device, you need a physical connection to the server using a serial cable. However, with Lights-Out devices, you can use EMS through a Web browser.

- **Integrated Management Log (IML)**—Allows access to the IML of a host server even when the server is not operational.

- **Integration with HP Insight Manager**—Provides support for *Simple Network Management Protocol* (SNMP) trap delivery, SNMP management, a management processor, and grouping of Lights-Out devices. In addition, an application launch task can be configured to start the Group Administration Utility on RILOE II devices. Insight Manager also provides a hyperlink on the server device page to launch and connect to iLO and RILOE II devices.

- **Power cycle (reset)**—Enables you to initiate a cold reset from the remote console to bring the host server back online when it is not responding. This type of restart does not shut down the server operating system gracefully, but proves useful in situations when the operating system is unresponsive.

- **Remote firmware update**—Enables you to update the firmware of the Lights-Out device.

- **SNMP alerts**—Allows access to server alerts such as SNMP alerts and unauthorized access alerts.

- **Single-mouse cursor mode**—Enables single-mouse cursor mode in the remote console. To enable the single-mouse cursor, the administrator must install the Sun Java plug-in version 1.3.1 or greater. You must download the Java Virtual Machine applet and install it on the client machine. (The Java Virtual Machine applet is available at http://www.hp.com/servers/manage/jvm.)

- **User administration and security**—Enables additional users with custom access rights, provides secure password encryption, and uses Secure Sockets Layer (SSL) encryption of HTTP data transmitted across the network.

- **Virtual power button**—Enables remote operation of a power button on a host server.

## 17.2 Integrated Lights-Out

The iLO is an *application-specific integrated circuit* (ASIC) embedded on the system board on select ProLiant servers, as shown in Figure 17–2. iLO consists of an intelligent processor and firmware that provide standard and advanced levels of Lights-Out functionality.

iLO comes in two flavors: Standard and Advanced. iLO Standard provides basic system board management functions, diagnostics, and essential Lights-Out functionality. iLO Advanced provides advanced functionality and can be licensed with the optional iLO Advanced Pack.

**Figure 17–2**

*iLO chip.*

### *17.2.1   iLO Standard*

iLO Standard features include the following:

- **Virtual text remote console**—Embedded hardware remote console capabilities are provided for text mode screens. The operating system–independent console supports text modes that display remote host server activities, such as startup and shutdown operations.

- **Virtual power button**—You can access iLO through a supported browser interface to operate the power button of a remote server to power-up, power-down, or restart the server. A press-and-hold option is available if a momentary press is insufficient to power-off a server with a failed operating system.

- **Control of the unit ID LED**—A unit ID LED located in the front and rear of the server is monitored and controlled by iLO. iLO can display the status of the unit ID LED, can enable and disable the unit ID LED, and can blink the unit LED to indicate that iLO is engaged in an activity that should not be interrupted (for example, flashing the firmware).

- **Easy to set up and use**—iLO provides autoconfiguration using *Domain Name Service / Dynamic Host Configuration Protocol* (DNS/DHCP). It includes a *ROM-Based Setup Utility* (RBSU), and is accessible using Microsoft Internet Explorer 5.0 or later.

- **Always on and running**—The iLO processor is powered through the auxiliary power plane of the server, so the processor is always powered-on regardless of the state of the server. If the server is powered-off, the processor is still accessible. If the server fails because of an operating system error, monitoring of the server can continue.

**The server must be plugged into an AC power source for this feature to function.**

- **System board management**—With iLO, you can monitor the system for *Power-On Self-Test* (POST) error messages. In addition, you can diagnose the system using the events recorded by the IML and iLO event log.

- **Headless server deployment**—iLO features allow servers to be controlled seamlessly without local keyboards, pointing devices, monitors, or KVM switches.

- **Integration with Insight Manager**—Efficient, centralized administration is provided through integration with Insight Manager.

### 17.2.2   iLO Advanced Pack

The following additional features are licensed with the iLO Advanced Pack:

- **USB-based virtual media**—Enables a remote host server to be powered-on and use standard media from any network location, which saves time and increases efficiency by eliminating the need to visit a host server to insert and use a disk or CD.

- **Virtual graphical remote console**—Operates independently of the operating system and supports graphic modes, which display remote host server activities such as shutdown and startup operations.

- **Directory integration (firmware version 1.40 or greater)**—The Integrated Lights-Out integrates with enterprise-class directory services to provide secure, scalable, and cost-effective user management. Directory services, such as Microsoft Active Directory and Novell eDirectory, can be used to authorize directory users with assigned user roles to Integrated Lights-Out processors.

- **Terminal Services integration (firmware version 1.5 or greater)**—Integrated Lights-Out integrates with Microsoft Terminal Services to provide a high-performance graphical remote console by automatically switching to Microsoft Terminal Services when the operating system is fully loaded and available on the host system. When the operating system is not operational, iLO continues to provide its secure, hardware-based Lights-Out console for end-to-end remote access to the host server.

#### 17.2.2.1   OBTAINING ILO ADVANCED FUNCTIONALITY

The iLO advanced functionality can be licensed by ordering the Integrated Lights-Out Advanced Pack. The iLO Advanced Pack provides a license key that is entered into iLO via the Web browser, to enable the advanced functionality.

For a list of supported operating systems, go to http://www.hp.com/servers/manage.

### 17.2.3    *iLO Device Drivers*

The following device drivers that support iLO are included on the HP SmartStart CD and are available on the HP Web site:

- **Advanced Server Management Controller driver**—Provides system management support and support for management agents.
- **iLO Management Interface driver**—Allows the system software and SNMP Insight agents to communicate with iLO.

## 17.3    RILOE II

RILOE II is a Lights-Out PCI card that provides remote server manageability for ProLiant servers.

The following items are included in the RILOE II kit. The numbers correspond to the items shown in Figure 17–3.

1. External power adapter
2. PCI extender bracket
3. RILOE II card
4. Remote Insight cable (30-pin)
5. Virtual Power Button cable (4-pin)
6. Remote Insight cable (16-pin)

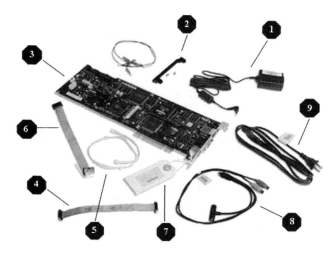

**Figure 17–3**  *RILOE II kit.*

7. Network settings tag
8. Keyboard/mouse adapter cable
9. Power cord
10. System documentation and support software CDs (not shown)

### 17.3.1  Hardware Overview

RILOE II can be configured using either the keyboard/mouse cable or the Remote Insight cable. With the former configuration, shown in Figure 17–4, the keyboard, mouse, and monitor cables are rerouted to the RILOE II connectors. The latter configuration connects the mouse and keyboard to the server connectors.

During normal operation, RILOE II passes the keyboard and mouse signals to the server and functions as its primary video controller. This enables several features. First, it provides transparent substitution of a remote keyboard and mouse for the server keyboard and mouse. Second, it saves video captures in memory for later replay. And finally, it provides simultaneous sending of video to the server monitor and a remote management PC monitor.

The RILOE II board contains its own VGA controller to ensure that a compatible controller is available for remote console operation. However, the BIOS on most systems can only detect a video card on a primary PCI bus. This means that the RILOE II board video can only be detected in certain PCI bus slots.

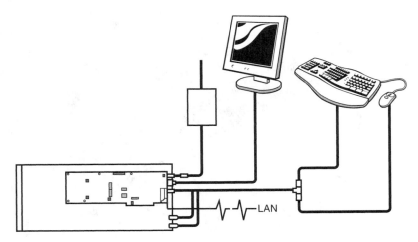

**Figure 17–4**  *RILOE II direct connect configuration.*

The server PCI slot and cable matrix identifies the appropriate cabling and video switch settings for the server.

**All recent ProLiant servers with 16- or 30-pin cables do not require a Y-connection or a power supply.**

The most current RILOE II server PCI slot and cable matrix is available at http://www.hp.com/servers/manage.

For a list of supported operating systems, go to http://www.hp.com/servers/manage.

### 17.3.1.2   RILOE II DEVICE DRIVERS

The following device drivers that support RILOE II are included on the SmartStart CD and are available on the HP Web site:

- **Advanced Server Management Controller driver**—Provides system management support and support for management agents.
- **RILOE II Management Interface driver**—Allows the system software and SNMP Insight agents to communicate with RILOE II.

## 17.3.2   *Comparing RILOE and iLO*

Use the following table to compare RILOE II and iLO.

| Feature | RILOE II | iLO |
| --- | --- | --- |
| Autoconfiguration of IP address | X | X |
| Browser accessibility | X | X |
| Dedicated LAN network connectivity | X | X |
| Directory integration | X | Advanced Pack only |
| Terminal Services integration | | Advanced Pack only |
| EMS console | X | X |
| Independent event log | X | X |
| IML | X | X |
| Integration with HP Insight Manager | X | X |
| Power cycle (reset) | X | X |
| Remote firmware update | X | X |
| SNMP alerts to a management console | X | X |

*(continues)*

| Feature | RILOE II | iLO |
|---|---|---|
| Scripted configuration | X | X |
| Single-mouse cursor mode | X | X |
| User administration and security | X | X |
| Virtual power button | X | X |
| Virtual text remote console | X | X |
| Group administration | X | X |
| Auxiliary power | X | X |
| External power backup | X | |
| Pocket PC access | X | |
| Reset and failure sequence replay | X | |
| Survey Utility | X | |
| Remote console (dual cursor) | | X |
| Virtual media | X | Advanced Pack only |
| Virtual graphical remote console | X | Advanced Pack only |
| Virtual indicators | X | X |

## 17.4 Managing Lights-out Devices

Lights-Out devices typically are connected to the corporate network, which facilitates *virtual private networking* (VPN) remote access. However, certain considerations may dictate other networking configurations.

Lights-Out devices are accessed through a client browser using the IP address or DNS name of the device, as shown in Figure 17–5. When you access the device for the first time, a security certificate dialog box displays. You must agree to proceed or install the certificate to log on to the device.

When you log on to a Lights-Out device, a navigation frame and the Status Summary home page displays.

The navigation frame on the left side of the screen displays at all times during a session, except when the remote console is displayed in full-screen view. This frame contains functional categories and hyperlinks to functions within each category.

### 17.4.1 Configuring the Management Client

Performance improves on the management client if the Lights-Out device is accessed using a supported browser.

For the most recent list of supported browsers, go to http://www.hp.com/servers/manage.

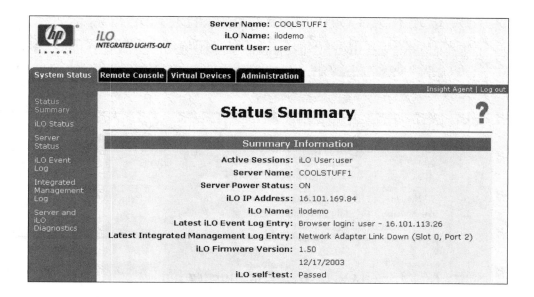

Server Name: COOLSTUFF1
iLO Name: ilodemo
Current User: user

System Status | Remote Console | Virtual Devices | Administration

Insight Agent | Log out

## Status Summary

Status Summary
iLO Status
Server Status
iLO Event Log
Integrated Management Log
Server and iLO Diagnostics

### Summary Information

| | |
|---|---|
| Active Sessions: | iLO User:user |
| Server Name: | COOLSTUFF1 |
| Server Power Status: | ON |
| iLO IP Address: | 16.101.169.84 |
| iLO Name: | ilodemo |
| Latest iLO Event Log Entry: | Browser login: user - 16.101.113.26 |
| Latest Integrated Management Log Entry: | Network Adapter Link Down (Slot 0, Port 2) |
| iLO Firmware Version: | 1.50 |
| | 12/17/2003 |
| iLO self-test: | Passed |

**Figure 17–5** *Lights-Out Status Summary home page.*

The settings on the remote server determine the performance of the graphical remote console for iLO and RILOE II. The remote server operating system resolution should be the same resolution or smaller than the management client. The higher the resolution on the remote server, the slower the overall performance becomes. For best results, use the following settings on the management client:

- Set the colors option to at least 256 colors.
- Select a screen area higher than the resolution of the host server operating system.
- Set the mouse motion speed to the middle setting.
- Set the mouse motion acceleration setting to Low or None.

## 17.4.2    User Settings and Administration

Each user can be assigned a different access level. A user can have supervisor status with the ability to create, modify, or delete other users. Users without supervisor status can be denied access to the remote console and remote reset features of the board.

### 17.4.2.1 ILO AND RILOE II USER SETTINGS DIFFERENCES

iLO supports up to 12 users, whereas RILOE II can support up to 25 users. The following table lists the user settings associated with each Lights-Out device.

| iLO | RILOE II |
|---|---|
| Allows user to access Windows Server 2003 EMS<br>Allows user to view or clear logs | Access restricted to a predefined IP address |
| Allows user to modify settings<br>Allows user to update firmware<br>Allows user to diagnose system | Deny login access to user |

## 17.4.3 RILOE II Group Administration

You can manage multiple RILOE II devices through Insight Manager. Four components are required for group administration:

- Remote Insight Board Command Language (RIBCL)
- HP Lights-Out Configuration Utility (cpqlocfg.exe)
- Query definition in Insight Manager
- Application launch

Insight Manager uses the Lights-Out Configuration Utility to send a RIBCL file to a group of RILOE II devices. The devices perform the action designated by the RIBCL file and send a response to a log file.

The Lights-Out Configuration Utility must reside on the same server as Insight Manager; however, it can be used through either Insight Manager or the batching process.

Download the Lights-Out Configuration Utility from http://www.hp.com/servers/manage.

The following statement illustrates the cpqlocfg.exe command line and switches:

```
cpqlocfg.exe  -s  server_name  -f  c:/ribclfile.txt  -l
c:/logfile.txt -v
```

Where

- -s denotes the RILOE II board to be updated.
- -f provides the location and name of the RIBCL file.
- -l defines the path and filename of the log file to be generated. When this switch is omitted, the file is stored in the directory where cpqlocfg.exe is launched and the log filename is the DNS name or IP address.
- -v enables the verbose messaging system.
- -c checks the XML syntax, but does not open a connection to the board.

The Lights-Out Configuration Utility generates two types of error messages: runtime and syntax. Runtime errors occur when an invalid action is requested. Syntax errors occur when an invalid XML tag is encountered. This interrupts the utility, and the runtime script error is logged in the output log file.

An example of a syntax error is as follows:

```
expected USER_LOGIN=userlogin but found USER_NAME=username
```

Supported Lights-Out Configuration Utility functions include the following:

- Add, modify, or delete a user
- View user configuration information
- Modify network settings
- Modify global settings
- Clear the RILOE II event log
- View firmware version
- Update firmware
- Obtain and set virtual floppy status
- Insert, copy, and eject a virtual floppy image
- Configure remote console hot-key settings
- Obtain and set virtual power status
- Obtain the server power status
- Reset the server

### 17.4.4 Global Settings

Global settings on Lights-Out devices enable you to do the following:

- Set the amount of time a session can remain idle before being terminated.
- Control access to the RBUS. If access is enabled, any user with physical access to the host server can run the utility and modify settings.
- Modify the port setting that provides access to the Web-based interface of the Lights-Out device.
- Modify the port setting that provides secure access to the Web-based interface of the Lights-Out device.
- Modify the port setting for remote console communications with the host server through the Lights-Out device.

#### 17.4.4.1 ILO GLOBAL SETTINGS

The iLO global settings page also includes the following security settings:

- **Enable Lights-Out Functionality**—The option to enable and disable iLO functionality.

> If you disable iLO functionality, you must set the iLO Security Override switch on the host server to re-enable functionality.

- **Virtual Media Port**—The ability to modify the port setting for iLO virtual media. This modification may be necessary if another application uses the same port or to minimize the number of open ports on a firewall.
- **Minimum Password Length**—Allows you to change the minimum number of characters allowed for a user password. The character length can range from 0 to 39.

> If zero is the set minimum length, a blank password will be acceptable. Note that this will subject the host server to many security vulnerabilities.

### 17.4.4.2 RILOE II GLOBAL SETTINGS

The RILOE II global settings page also includes the following security settings:

- **Emergency Management Services**—Disables EMS console functionality.

- **Bypass Reporting of External Power Cable**—Prevents a degraded status from being reported in Insight Manager when the external power cable is not attached.

- **Remote Console Port Configuration**—Modifies the default port setting, 23, generally used for Telnet. However, popular port numbers are vulnerable to port scans, which can be used for nefarious purposes.

- **Remote Access with Pocket PC**—Enables wireless or dial-up access from a handheld device.

- **Remote Console Data Encryption**—Disables data encryption for Telnet access. Telnet does not support encryption.

- **SSL Encryption Strength**—Designates the encryption level required to access the Lights-Out device through a browser interface. Some client browsers do not support 128-bit encryption.

- **Current Cipher**—Displays the encryption algorithm currently being used to protect data during transmission between your browser and RILOE II.

- **Host Keyboard**—Enables or disables the keyboard on the host server.

- **Level of Data Returned**—Associates management processors with servers and controls the amount of information returned to Insight Manager:

  - **High**—All data related to the host server displays on the summary page for the Lights-Out device in Insight Manager.
  - **Medium**—Summary page includes less detail.
  - **Low**—Server and management processor are listed as separate entities in the device list if SNMP pass-through is not supported.
  - **None**—No data is sent to Insight Manager.

The following table lists the information associated with each data level.

| Display Information | High | Medium | Low |
|---|---|---|---|
| Product name | Y | Y | Y |
| Server serial number | Y | Y | |
| Server state | Y | | |
| Management processor status | Y | Y | Y |
| Management processor serial number | Y | Y | |
| Rack topology | Y | Y | |
| Hardware revision number | Y | | |
| Firmware revision number | Y | | |
| Device home page URL | Y | | |

## 17.5    Network Configuration Options

Lights-Out devices can be connected directly to a corporate network, which allows the device to be accessed from any location on the network. In addition, this configuration reduces the amount of networking hardware and infrastructure required to support Lights-Out devices. Figure 17–6 shows a configuration typical of a nondedicated management network.

Some corporate networks operate at 1000Mb/s. Lights-Out devices only support 10/100 speeds. Performance problems can result if you attach a Lights-Out device to a gigabit-only switch port.

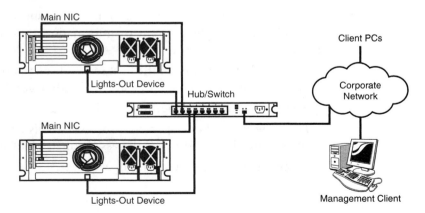

**Figure 17–6** *Nondedicated management network configuration.*

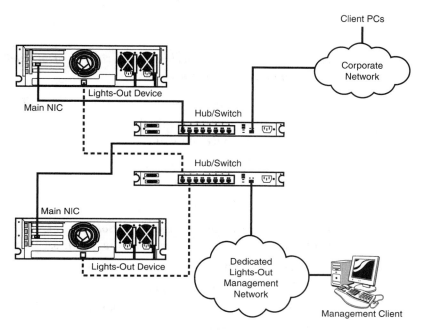

**Figure 17–7**    *Dedicated management network configuration.*

A separate, dedicated, network for Lights-Out devices, as shown in Figure 17–7, not only addresses potential performance problems, but also improves security. This configuration enables you to physically control which clients are connected to the management network.

## ▲ Summary

This chapter explained HP Lights-Out management technologies, iLO and RILOE II, including the following:

- iLO Standard and iLO Advanced Pack
- RILOE II
- Network configuration options for managing Lights-Out devices

## ▲ LEARNING CHECK

1. *Which HP management technology is comprised of intelligent firmware integrated in select ProLiant servers?*

2. *Which of the following are technologies provided in iLO Advanced Pack in addition to features in iLO Standard?*

   A. USB-based virtual media

   B. Directory integration

   C. Virtual power button

   D. Virtual text remote control

3. *When using the graphical remote console for iLO and RILOE II, how should the display resolution be set on the remote server operating system?*

   A. Higher than the management client

   B. The same as the management client

   C. The same as or less than the management client

   D. It has no effect

4. *What are two advantages of a separate, dedicated network for Lights-Out devices?*

# Performance

**A**n Accredited Integration Specialist will be able to set up and configure a server to meet a customer's need for optimal performance. Strategies for optimizing performance are explained in Part 6.

Here is an overview of the chapters in Part 6.

## Chapter 18   Installing Hardware Options and Upgrades

Chapter 18 explains the basic procedures for installing hardware upgrades and options, including processors, memory, drives, and PCI cards.

Chapter 18 also explains the process for removing hardware options and upgrades and how to troubleshoot a failed component installation.

## Chapter 19   Availability

Chapter 19 focuses on availability. Availability is a measure of the time that a server system or component is functioning normally and of its ability to maintain services despite hardware or software failures, planned or unplanned.

An Accredited Integration Specialist should be able to determine a customer's need for availability and recommend the right server components to ensure the required level of availability is obtained.

## Chapter 20   Optimizing Storage

Chapter 20 explains key concepts for optimizing storage. Storage can be optimized by choosing a stripe size most suitable for the type of data transfer common to your system and by changing the read/write cache ratio in the Smart Array controller.

# Installing Hardware Options and Upgrades

After reading this chapter, you should be able to explain the basic procedures for the following:

- Installing processors
- Installing memory
- Installing drives
- Installing PCI cards
- Removing hardware options
- Troubleshooting failed upgrades and installations

This chapter explains the basic procedures for installing hardware upgrades and options, including the following:

- Processors
- Memory
- Drives
- PCI cards

This chapter also explains the process for removing hardware options and upgrades and how to troubleshoot a failed component installation.

A couple of notes are very important up front:

- First, when installing hardware options and upgrades, always refer to the documentation that ships with the component. Save this documentation for future reference.
- Second, heat-dissipation accessories included with the upgrade kits must be installed according to the instructions. Otherwise, component overheating could result in erratic system behavior or even system shutdown.

## 18.1 Installing Processors

ProLiant servers ship from the factory with one or more processors installed. You can replace one processor with another or you can add additional processors.

Before installing a processor, you should be aware of these precautions:

- Processor socket 1 must be populated with a processor at all times. The system fails to boot if the socket is not populated.
- You should not mix processors of different types or speeds.
- You must correctly align the processor pins to seat the processor into the socket.

To install a processor, follow these steps:

1. Power down the server and remove the access panel.
2. Align the notched corner of the processor with the notched corner of the socket.
3. Insert the processor and close the locking lever on the processor socket.
4. Remove the plastic cover on a new, unused heat sink to expose the thermal interface material.

Always use a new heat sink with thermal interface material when replacing processors. Failure to use new components may result in damage to the processor.

5. Install the heat sink.
6. Carefully install the heat sink–retaining clip and close the locking lever on the heat sink–retaining clip.
7. Install a *power-processing module* (PPM) in the corresponding slot, if the slot is empty.

PPM slots must be populated when processors are installed. If PPM slots are not populated, the system does not boot.

8. Replace the access panel.

If installing an additional processor module, you also must install an additional *voltage-regulator module* (VRM). Processor modules acquired from HP will include the additional VRM.

To install a PPM or a VRM in a ProLiant server, refer to the Maintenance and Service Guide for that server.

You can access technical documentation and service advisories for ProLiant servers from the HP Reference Library site at http://h71025.www7. hp.com/support/home/selectproduct.asp?destination=reflib.

## 18.1.1 Mixing Processors

The desire for investment protection and a growing need to scale processing power make the ability to mix processors in dual-processor and multiprocessor systems a significant customer benefit.

To ensure full protection and support under manufacturer warranties, always configure processors according to manufacturer guidelines. In addition, you must reconcile the guidelines of the processor manufacturer, the server manufacturer, and the operating system vendor.

> **! IMPORTANT**
>
> Four-way platforms, starting with the Intel Xeon processors, no longer support processor mixing.

### 18.1.1.1 PROCESSOR STEPPINGS

Processor steppings are versions of the same processor model with slight variation, usually to improve performance or manufacturing yield. Each stepping requires changes to the system ROM.

Each Intel processor stepping has a microcode patch for inclusion in the system ROM. The microcode patches are stored in a table within the system ROM. HP and other server vendors must continually add newly released Intel patches to keep their ROMs current.

If a processor is installed in a ProLiant server that does not contain the correct microcode in the current system ROM, the ROM generates the following error message to prevent the user from operating the processor with the wrong microcode:

UNSUPPORTED PROCESSOR DETECTED. SYSTEM HALTED.

> **EXAMPLE**
>
> If a customer has a four-way ProLiant server containing two processors and decides to upgrade by adding two more processors, the new processors could be of a different stepping. To ensure that the system ROM contains the latest microcodes, you must flash the ROM on that server using an updated System ROMPaq before installing the new processors.

 After a processor has been installed, stepping identification can be problematic because a heat sink typically covers the top of the processor chip. Utilities provided with operating systems might help. You also can use the Survey Utility to view the steppings of installed processors.

### 18.1.1.2 INTEL SUPPORT FOR PROCESSOR MIXING

Based on the information available on the Intel Web site at the time of this writing, Intel supports mixed steppings of processors only under these conditions:

- All processors in a system must have identical family and model numbers as indicated by the CPU ID instruction.
- All processors in a system must operate at the same frequency—that is, at the highest frequency rating commonly supported by all the processors.
- All processors in a system must have the same cache size.
- The processor with the lowest feature set must be the bootstrap processor.

### 18.1.1.3 OPERATING SYSTEM SUPPORT FOR PROCESSOR MIXING

Like Intel, operating system vendors support the mixing of processors only if all processors in a system

- Have identical family and model numbers.
- Operate at the same frequency.
- Have the same cache size.

The processor with the lowest feature set must be the bootstrap processor. The most common operating systems typically do not inhibit the operation of servers containing multiple processors with different steppings.

**Note**

Processor steppings were introduced in Chapter 2. Refer to that chapter for a discussion of industry processor stepping guidelines.

### 18.1.1.4 HP SUPPORT FOR PROCESSOR MIXING

HP supports the mixing of processors in ProLiant servers under the following conditions:

- All processors in the server must be of the same processor family and model. For example, Intel Pentium II Xeon processors cannot be mixed with Pentium III Xeon processors.
- The 500/550MHz Pentium III Xeon processors cannot be mixed with 700MHz or higher-frequency Pentium III Xeon processors.
- The core frequency for the 900MHz Pentium III Xeon processors must be locked. The 900MHz Pentium III processors cannot be mixed with any other Pentium III Xeon processors.

- The core frequency of each processor in the server must be set to the frequency of the slowest processor. Switches on the system board (or the ROM) can be used to reset the frequency of Pentium Xeon processors. However, Pentium III and Pentium II processors are locked to the frequency ratio at which Intel intends them to run. HP does not support mixing Pentium II or Pentium III processors with different frequencies.

- No processor core should be set to a frequency higher than the processor is rated for.

- When using Pentium II Xeon or Pentium III Xeon processors with different cache sizes, the processors must be installed in pairs with the same cache size: the first pair in Slot 1 and Slot 2; the second pair in Slot 3 and Slot 4; the third pair in Slot 5 and Slot 6; and the fourth pair in Slot 7 and Slot 8.

- The processor with the lowest stepping must be installed as the bootstrap processor.

> **! IMPORTANT**
>
> Four-way Gallatin-based ProLiant server platforms, starting with the Intel Xeon processors, no longer support processor mixing.

To ensure that a ProLiant server containing mixed processors operates correctly, flash the system ROM before installing the processors.

To obtain the latest HP ROM available on the HP Web site, visit http://h18007.www1.hp.com/support/files/server/us/index.html.

You can find more information about processor mixing at http://h18000.www1.hp.com/products/servers/processor-mixing/.

## 18.2 Installing Memory

The electrical traces from the memory chips are routed from the memory chips to gold pins located at the bottom of the memory module. The pins snap into slots on the motherboard or a memory board.

When *single inline memory modules* (SIMMs) are used, they must be installed in pairs. *Dual inline memory modules* (DIMMs) have memory chips on both sides, and each side has separate pins, for a total of 144 pins. Some DIMMs have 168 pins. The extra pins handle *error checking and correcting* (ECC) capabilities.

> **! IMPORTANT**
>
> DIMMs with tin/lead pins must be used on system boards with tin/lead-plated contacts for the memory sockets. DIMMs with gold pins must be used on system boards with gold-plated contacts for the memory sockets. Mixing dissimilar-metal-contact DIMMs and their related sockets causes memory problems because of electrolysis-induced corrosion and damages the memory socket on the system board.

Memory must be added in banks of four DIMMs. Mixing of 50ns and 60ns memory is permitted; however, each bank of four DIMMs must contain the same size and speed DIMMs. Performance will default to the slower of the two speeds (that is, 60ns).

Installing memory modules with mismatching capacity (256MB, 512MB, and so forth) or configuration (single or double banked; buffered, registered, or unregistered) within the same multi-DIMM bank can result in errors. Problems such as boot failures, lockups, uncorrectable parity errors, or numerous correctable memory errors also can occur if the memory technology (EDO, PC100, PC133, and so forth) is not supported by the system in which the DIMMs are installed.

If memory errors occur, verify that the memory modules within each bank are matched in capacity, configuration, and technology. You can best accomplish this by matching the first eight digits of the nine-digit HP/Compaq part number. If they do not match, replace the memory modules with the correct spares kit.

At the next system *Power-On Self-Test* (POST), the server should report the new memory. The server will automatically incorporate the upgrade and start the operating system without any intervention. You might notice that the system executes more quickly.

## 18.3  Installing Drives

The process of installing a CD-ROM, tape backup, or hard drive is very straightforward:

1. Shut down the server.
2. Open the chassis cover.
3. Find the appropriate position for the part.
4. Remove any placeholders.
5. Install the component.

Installing a hot-plug drive is even simpler because no shutdown is needed. Use these steps:

1. Pick a bay.
2. Insert the drive.
3. Secure the latch.

You must mount non-hot-plug devices using the included hardware (rails, screws, and so on.). If required, you must set the jumpers before mounting. Finally, for a non-hot-plug upgrade, you must connect power, drive, and other applicable cables. This kind of upgrade usually requires a Torx or Phillips-head screwdriver. After installing the part, save any included documentation and items removed from the server in case of future need.

At the next system POST, the server should report the new component, unless it is an IDE device. The server will automatically incorporate the upgrade and start the operating system without any intervention.

Hot-plug parts do not require jumper setting or system restarts and are incorporated automatically, with the exception of hot-plug hard drives. Hot-plug hard drives must be configured using the *Option ROM Configuration for Arrays* (ORCA) or the *Array Configuration Utility* (ACU) if an HP Smart Array controller is present. You might need to apply a software driver to the operating system, requiring a server restart.

| 18.4 | |
|---|---|

## Installing PCI Cards

PCI Hot Plug technology simplifies card installation because you do not need to shut down the server. At the next system POST after installation, the server reports the new component and starts the operating system without intervention. You might need to apply a software driver to the operating system, requiring a restart.

The addition of an HP Smart Array controller to a system will generate POST errors regarding an unconfigured drive controller or array. To clear these errors, you must execute the *ROM-Based Setup Utility* (RBSU), ORCA, or the ACU to configure the controller or array.

ProLiant servers that support dual-peer PCI buses provide aggregate I/O throughput capability as high as 267MB/s. The dual-peer PCI buses increase configuration flexibility and allow higher levels of overall performance. However, attaining peak performance requires carefully balanced I/O loading across both PCI buses. This means careful planning of which expansion slot to use for each device in the initial configuration, as well as planning for future expansion.

Networks continue to require increasingly higher throughput to support the bandwidth requirements brought on by the demands of the Internet, multimedia applications, large files, increased use of e-mail, and faster processors. In addition to upgrading the *network interface cards* (NICs) to satisfy these requirements, you can configure redundant NICs for fault tolerance and failover support. Support for a redundant NIC configuration eliminates the network connection as a single point of system failure. One NIC is operational while another is ready as a hot standby

## **18.5** Removing Hardware Options and Upgrades

A situation might arise when you need to remove a hardware component from a server. At its simplest, removing a hardware component is as easy as uninstalling the software driver from the operating system, shutting down the server, opening the chassis cover, removing the component, and replacing any items removed during the installation.

Removing a hot-plug device other than a hard drive is even easier: Use the operating system procedure to stop the device, and then remove it when prompted; no shutdown is needed. To uninstall a hot-plug hard drive, you must use ORCA or the ACU to remove the drive from the array before removing it from the system.

**Warning**

Failure to properly remove a drive from an array could result in data loss.

## **18.6** Troubleshooting a Failed Installation

Not all upgrades go as planned. Unforeseen incompatibilities, defective hardware, and user error are some ways an installation can be unsuccessful. It is important to gather all relevant system information and follow all instructions when planning and installing additional hardware.

Some reasons why upgrades fail include the following:

- Unsupported hardware
- Defective hardware
- Defective hardware slot or bay
- Other hardware problems, such as power or cabling
- Unsupported software
- Software incompatibility
- User errors

The first step to recovering from the failure is to review the information and the instructions. Questions to ask include the following:

- Was the right part ordered for the computer?
- Were the hardware installation instructions followed correctly?
- Were all cables or accessories connected properly?
- Did the hardware activate at system power-on?
- Did the computer display an error during the POST process?
- Were the software installation instructions followed correctly?
- Were any known incompatibilities addressed?
- Did the operating system or software display an error?

You can use logic and reason to eliminate possibilities. For example, if all procedures were followed properly, and the device is unresponsive or unacknowledged, it is likely that the part is defective. The operating system or software may or may not display an error if a part is faulty. Always check the included documentation for help or any known issues or last-minute errata.

Replacing the newly installed but suspect part with another one is the easiest way to determine or verify where the fault lies. This is also true in most cases of an installed part that fails, such as a fan in a power supply. However, this is not always practical because of inventory costs or time constraints. In such cases, eliminating as many failure points as possible can expose the true cause of the problem.

A repeated failure in one part can be the symptom of a problem in another part. For instance, if PPMs repeatedly fail, it could be that there is nothing wrong with the PPM, but actually a problem with the processor board, power supply, or even line voltage.

HP PPMs monitor power currents to proactively detect and prevent potential problems.

## ▲ Summary

This chapter explained concepts critical for Accredited Integration Specialists, including how to do the following:

- Install processors
- Install memory
- Install drives
- Install PCI cards
- Remove hardware options
- Troubleshoot failed upgrades and installations

Especially critical are the warnings provided in this chapter.

Accredited Integration Specialists should completely understand the rules for processor mixing.

## ▲ LEARNING CHECK

1. *What happens if processor Socket 1 is not populated with a processor?*

2. *You have just installed a processor in a ProLiant server and you see the following error message:*

   UNSUPPORTED PROCESSOR DETECTED. SYSTEM HALTED

   *What is the most likely cause of this error?*

3. *Which type of memory must be installed in pairs?*
   A. SIMMs
   B. DIMMs

4. *To remove a hot-plug device other than a hard drive, you must shut down the server before removing the device.*

   ❏ True

   ❏ False

5. *You can install DIMMs with tin/lead pins on a system board with gold-plated contacts, and vice versa.*

   ❏ True

   ❏ False

# Availability

After reading this chapter, you will be able to do the following:

■ Define *availability* and describe the critical application classes, percentages of availability, and server availability level classifications.

■ Explain how to increase server availability by implementing power protection.

■ Explain how to increase server availability by implementing memory technologies, such as the following:

• Online spare memory

• Single-board mirrored memory

• Hot-plug mirrored memory

• Hot Plug RAID Memory

*Availability* is a measure of the time that a server system or component is functioning normally and of its ability to maintain services despite hardware or software failures, planned or unplanned. Availability is expressed as a percentage and is measured against a period of one year. The best possible rating, 100%, indicates that the system is available all the time.

Availability can be defined in terms of

- Critical application classes.
- Percentages of availability.
- Availability server level classifications.

This chapter first explains availability in terms of the various levels of application classes and their availability requirements, the methods for measuring availability, and the availability-level server classifications.

The chapter then explains how to increase overall server availability by (1) implementing power protection, and (2) increasing memory availability.

## 19.1     Critical Application Classes

Critical applications are software essential to business continuity, and can be classified as either *mission-critical* or *business-critical*.

Mission-critical applications require 100% uptime. The unavailability of one of these systems can have tragic or extreme consequences. Examples of mission-critical applications include such functions as air traffic control, 911 emergency call centers, stock exchange trading floors, and aerospace mission control.

As compared to mission-critical applications, business-critical applications can tolerate minimal interruptions. A business-critical application is extremely important to a company, but small amounts of downtime are allowed. These applications include the following:

- Electronic transfers in banking
- Company payroll systems
- Human resources systems
- Workgroup applications
- Reservation systems
- Cash machine systems
- Transportation logistics systems
- Messaging (e-mail) systems
- E-commerce sites

## 19.2 Percentages of Availability

A useful matrix for evaluating system availability refers to uptime as a number of nines. One nine is 90%, two are 99%, three are 99.9%, and so on. Most system vendors quote system availability as the percentage of time the system is up and running using nines. Some vendors guarantee uptime ranging from 99.9% all the way to 99.9999%.

Availability of 99% in a 24×7 operation translates to more than 87 hours of downtime a year. In a system that is 99% available, there can be 1 failure during the year that lasts 3.5 days, or there can be 10 failures, each lasting more than 8 hours, or there can be 87 outages of about 1 hour each. Although 87 different 1-hour outages over 1 year might be tolerable, an outage that shuts down a business for 3 consecutive days could be extremely costly.

| Uptime % | Downtime % | Downtime per Year | Downtime per Week |
|----------|-----------|-------------------|-------------------|
| 98% | 2% | 7.3 days | 3 hours, 22 minutes |
| 99% | 1% | 3.65 days | 1 hour, 41 minutes |
| 99.8% | 0.2% | 17 hours, 30 minutes | 20 minutes, 10 seconds |
| 99.9% | 0.1% | 8 hours, 45 minutes | 10 minutes, 5 seconds |
| 99.99% | 0.01% | 52.5 minutes | 1 minute |
| 99.999% | 0.001% | 5.25 minutes | 6 seconds |
| 99.9999% | 0.0001% | 31.5 seconds | 0.6 seconds |

**Note**

Availability of a standalone server includes only the availability of the server itself, not the operating system, application, or network connections.

## 19.3 Availability-Level Server Classifications

The computing industry has defined four *availability-level* (AL) classifications for servers. These classifications define the consequences of a system failure, and are described in the following table.

| Level | Characteristics |
|-------|-----------------|
| AL1— Data availability | Work stops. An uncontrolled shutdown results. Data integrity is ensured. System is available 95% of the time. |
| AL2— Standard availability | User is interrupted, but can log on again. User might have to rerun some transactions from a journal file. Possible performance degradation can result. System is available 95% to 99% of the time. |
| AL3— High availability | User stays online. Current transaction might need to be restarted. Performance degradation can possibly result. System is available approximately 99.9% to 99.99% of the time. |
| AL4— Continuous availability | Process is transparent to user. No work is interrupted. No transactions are lost. No performance degradation results. System is available 99.999% to 100% of the time. |

Standalone ProLiant servers are rated AL1. If the server is down, all work being performed by that server stops. ProLiant clusters can achieve AL2 or AL3. The user might notice a small interruption or degraded performance. HP also provides systems ranked AL4, including the NonStop Himalaya systems. Guaranteed uptime requires HP Global Services.

Although every business would like its servers to be always available, many businesses do not operate 24 hours a day, so availability greater than AL1 is not driven by the operating requirements. However, to maximize server availability within that classification, a company can employ technologies and create configurations that minimize time lost as a result of problems, including the following:

- Increasing availability through power protection (discussed in this chapter).

- Increasing memory availability to reduce memory errors and faults (discussed in this chapter).

- Optimizing storage for fault tolerance and recovery (discussed in the next chapter).

## 19.4    Increasing Availability Through Power Protection

Data centers cannot rely on utility power grids as a source of continuous power for critical equipment. HP has developed a full line of power-management products that protect and manage computer systems ranging from individual workstations to distributed enterprises including *uninterruptible power systems* (UPSs) and *power-distribution units* (PDUs).

For applications that require a high level of fault tolerance, the power source for the equipment should be protected by a UPS. The UPS is connected between the equipment and the electrical outlet or PDU.

## 19.5    Improving Server Availability with Memory Technologies

Chapter 3 explained key memory concepts along with technologies used to detect and correct memory errors. This subsection explains methods and technologies relating to memory that can be used to improve server availability, including the following:

- Online spare memory
- Single-board mirrored memory
- Hot-plug mirrored memory
- Hot Plug RAID Memory

### 19.5.1    Online Spare Memory

Online spare memory technology enables a ProLiant server to remain available even if a DIMM records an excessive number of single-bit errors. Online spare memory increases availability by enabling an administrator to wait until a scheduled downtime to replace a faulty DIMM.

Online spare memory provides a spare memory bank for systems that detect excessive single-bit errors. When a memory bank with a faulty DIMM is detected, it automatically fails over to (is replaced by) a spare bank of DIMMs, as shown in Figure 19–1.

In earlier-generation servers and in servers without online spare memory, when a memory module experiences an excessive number of correctable single-bit errors, the system issues a prefailure warning and the DIMM continues to function in its degraded state. If this occurs, the recommended procedure is to power-off the server as soon as possible, replace the faulty DIMM, and restart the system.

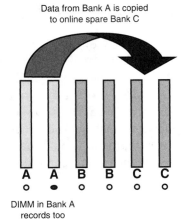

Data from Bank A is copied
to online spare Bank C

A  A  B  B  C  C

Bank A — In use          DIMM in Bank A
Bank B — In use            records too
Bank C — Online spare    many errors

**Figure 19–1** *Online spare memory.*

With online spare memory, a memory bank with a faulty DIMM automatically fails over to a spare bank of DIMMs. One pair of DIMMs functions as the spare bank. Up to two other memory banks can be installed in the other slots.

When the faulty DIMM reaches a predefined single-bit error threshold, the ROM starts copying the contents of the failing bank to the spare bank in 128KB increments. During this time, the failing bank provides all read accesses. Data is written to both banks during the copy process.

**Because the spare bank must be able to hold all the information from a failing bank, the DIMMs in the spare bank must be the same size as, or larger than, the other banks.**

After memory copying is complete, the system ROM makes the switch to the spare bank. At that point, no more reads or writes are made to the failing bank. All reads and writes are made to the spare bank.

During a scheduled shutdown, the faulty DIMM is replaced with a functioning DIMM. When the server restarts, the memory banks resume their normal functions.

The advantage of online spare memory is that the shutdown to replace the failing DIMM can be scheduled for a time when there is little activity on the server. When the server restarts, the memory banks resume their normal functions.

### 19.5.1.1 SPECIAL REQUIREMENTS

Online spare memory has the following requirements:

- Online spare memory must be configured in the *ROM-Based Setup Utility* (RBSU). If you do not configure the server for online spare memory, all memory slots can be used for main memory up to the system maximum.
- ProLiant G2 servers allow any bank to be defined as a spare bank.
- If you are using online spare memory, the spare memory bank is not counted during the *Power-On System Test* (POST) and is not added to the system memory count reported to the operating system.
- The DIMMs in the spare bank must be the same size as or larger than the other banks.

You can find the complete special memory requirements in the user guide that shipped with the server.

### 19.5.1.2 CONFIGURING ONLINE SPARES

Before you configure an online spare, HP recommends that you perform the following steps to test the new memory:

1. From the Advanced Options screen in the ROM-Based Setup Utility (RBSU), disable POST speedup.
2. From the Advanced Memory Protection screen, disable Online Spare with ECC support.
3. Restart the system to begin testing the memory. This may take a few minutes, depending on how much memory is installed in the system. After the memory has been tested, you can enable POST speedup again for faster system starts.

After the memory has been tested, power-down the system and verify that bank C is populated with memory no smaller than either bank A or B. To configure the online spare, follow these steps:

1. Power-on the server. Online spare memory is disabled by default; therefore, all the memory is initially counted and configured as available primary memory.
2. At the prompt, press F9 to enter RBSU.
3. From the Advanced Memory Protection screen, enable Online Spare with ECC support. Press Esc twice to return to the main RBSU menu.
4. Press F10 to exit RBSU and restart your server. When your server restarts it will enable online spare memory and display the following message: xxxxMB System Memory and xxxxMB memory reserved for Online Spare.

If the memory size requirements for proper operation are not met, RBSU will not allow you to enable online spare memory and will display this message: Caution: Current memory configuration does not support Online Spare.

### 19.5.2 Single-Board Mirrored Memory

Single-board mirrored memory provides a higher level of availability than online spare memory by adding protection against multibit errors using a mirrored memory bank. When a failure occurs, the system rereads the correct data from the mirrored bank. The system performs all future reads from the mirrored memory bank until the server can be shut down and the memory replaced.

Single-board mirrored memory in ProLiant servers protects against multiple noncorrectable multibit errors without degrading the performance of the memory system.

A single memory board contains two memory banks. One of the banks is designated as the primary bank and the other as the mirror. Data sent to memory is written by the memory controller to both banks simultaneously, but the system reads from the primary bank only, as illustrated in Figure 19–2.

During a read operation, if a multibit error is detected on one or more DIMMs in the primary bank, the system reads from the mirrored bank instead. This process occurs without service intervention or server interruption. Service personnel can replace the failed DIMM during a regularly scheduled shutdown.

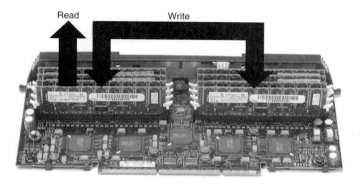

**Figure 19–2**  *How single-board mirrored memory works.*

Mirroring protects against multibit errors so long as system and mirrored DIMMs do not fail in the same cache line at the same time (a highly unlikely event). All read and write operations in a mirrored memory configuration are handled by the memory controller.

Although data is always written to both banks in the mirrored pair, data is read only from the primary bank. To ensure that all DIMMs are functioning properly, every 24 hours the system switches the primary and mirror designations and begins reading from the other bank.

### 19.5.2.1  SPECIAL REQUIREMENTS

The requirements for mirrored memory are as follows:

- Mirrored memory must be configured in the RBSU. If you do not configure the server for memory mirroring, all memory slots on a single board can be used for main memory.

- If you are using mirrored memory, only half of the physical memory is counted during POST and subsequently reported to the operating system.

- Each DIMM in a bank must be the same size as its mirror in the other bank.

When implementing mirrored memory, follow these steps:

1. Start the server with POST speedup disabled and memory mirroring disabled. This enables the system to check the status of all the memory.
2. After the POST process verifies the memory, restart the server and configure memory mirroring and POST speedup.

### 19.5.3 Hot-Plug Mirrored Memory

Hot-plug mirrored memory provides a higher level of availability than online spare memory by adding protection against multibit errors. When a failure occurs, the system rereads the correct data from the mirrored bank on the other memory board. The system performs all future reads from the other memory board until the failed bank can be hot-plug replaced without shutting down the server, as shown in Figure 19–3.

Hot-plug mirrored memory is targeted to customers who cannot afford to take a server offline to replace a failing DIMM.

Hot-plug mirrored memory works like single-board mirrored memory. The difference is that the primary banks and mirrored banks are located on different memory boards.

To use hot-plug mirrored memory, a server must have two identical memory boards, each containing several banks of DIMMs. The memory controller writes the same data to identically configured banks of DIMMs on both memory boards. The memory controller reads data from only one group.

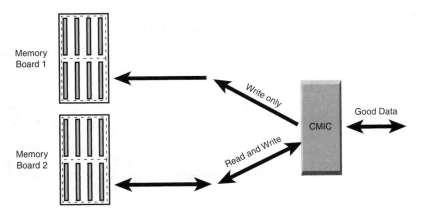

**Figure 19–3** *How hot-plug mirrored memory works.*

If any bank of DIMMs has a multibit error, the system performs the following actions:

1. Rereads the correct data from the mirrored bank on the other memory board
2. Performs all future reads from the other memory board
3. Provides notification of the DIMM failure through the QuickFind diagnostic display, the memory board LEDs, the front-panel internal-health LED, and Insight Manager 7

If no errors occur, the system periodically switches which set of banks it reads from to ensure that both sets are monitored for memory errors.

> **! IMPORTANT**
>
> If a DIMM exceeds the limit defined by HP for single-bit correctable errors, the system will not fail over to the redundant banks, but will notify you of the condition through Insight Manager 7.

Hot-plug mirrored memory also provides hot-plug replacement capability. You do not have to wait for a scheduled shutdown to replace the failed DIMM. You can remove a memory board that has a failed or degraded bank on it without shutting down the server.

After replacing the bank of DIMMs, you can reinstall the memory board when the server is still running. After the board is reinstalled, the system automatically returns to mirrored status. You can also perform a non-hot-plug replacement of failed or degraded DIMMs during a scheduled shutdown.

The special requirements described in the "Single-Board Mirrored Memory" section also apply to hot-plug mirrored memory.

Hot-plug mirrored memory offers two main advantages over single-board mirrored memory. First, you can mirror more than one bank of DIMMs. Second, no server downtime is necessary to replace a defective DIMM or bank.

### 19.5.4    Hot Plug RAID Memory

Hot Plug RAID Memory enables a memory subsystem to withstand a complete DIMM failure and continue to operate normally in a manner similar to hot-pluggable hard drives in a RAID 4 configuration. The system corrects future reads from parity information until the failed DIMM can be hot-plug replaced without shutting down or restarting the server.

Originally, the term *RAID* was used to describe a fault-tolerant hard disk drive technology. The same RAID theory can be applied to DIMMs. HP calls this *Hot Plug RAID Memory.*

Hot Plug RAID Memory allows memory to be added, replaced, and upgraded without shutting down or even restarting the server.

Servers with Hot Plug RAID Memory use five memory controllers to control five SDRAM DIMMs. The memory controllers are part of a next-generation chipset designed by HP. Each one is an *application-specific integrated circuit* (ASIC).

To write data to memory, a cache line of data is split into four blocks and distributed among the controllers. Four of the memory controllers write one block of data on their associated DIMMs. A RAID engine calculates parity information, and the fifth memory controller stores the parity information on the fifth DIMM.

RAID memory takes memory protection and correction beyond the capabilities of ECC. With RAID memory, multibit errors and full DRAM failure can be corrected. Errors in the ECC detection system can also be detected, but not corrected.

Although a failure of the ECC detection system can allow memory corruption and ultimately a system failure, it might not cause problems in the system if there are no memory errors to detect or correct. The RAID memory system in the ProLiant 700 series servers allows for the detection of a failure of the ECC system, which can be corrected by replacing a memory cartridge.

#### 19.5.4.1   HOW RAID MEMORY WORKS

In a method similar to the way data bits are re-created in a RAID 4 drive storage system, an entire data word can be re-created from parity in a RAID 4 memory system.

When a 64-bit cache line is read out of storage into memory, the F8 chipset breaks the cache line into four 16-bit data words, which are distributed to the four memory controllers on memory cartridges 1 through 4. Before being sent to the memory controllers, however, the data words go

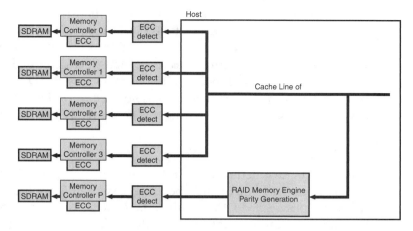

**Figure 19–4** *How RAID mirrored memory works.*

through the chipset hardware XOR engine for a parity calculation. Parity data is sent to the memory controller in the fifth cartridge for storage, as illustrated in Figure 19–4.

During data transactions, whether to or from memory, the chipset performs a check and ensures that each data word is valid. If there is a problem, the chipset can re-create the cache line based on any four of the five data words and the parity from the fifth cartridge.

If data from more than one of the five sources is corrupt, the read process will fail in a fashion similar to any normal **RAID 4** system.

### 19.5.4.2 COMPARING RAID MEMORY AND DRIVE ARRAYS

Although RAID memory is similar in concept to hard disk drive arrays, there are some differences.

RAID memory does not have the mechanical delays of seek time and rotational latency associated with hard disk drive arrays. Storage subsystem arrays use a single bus to write the stripes sequentially across multiple drives. In contrast, RAID memory uses five parallel connections so that data is written simultaneously across multiple DIMMs.

In addition, RAID memory eliminates the write bottleneck associated with typical storage subsystem RAID implementations. In a storage array, the RAID controller generally performs a read operation of existing parity before a write operation can be completed. If a dedicated parity drive is being used, a bottleneck occurs. However, because RAID memory operates on an entire cache line of data, there is no need to read existing parity before a write operation, thus eliminating this performance bottleneck.

### 19.5.4.3  HOT-REPLACE SUPPORT

The hot-replace functionality of RAID memory in the ProLiant DL700 series servers is transparent to the operating system and application. It enables users to replace failed DIMMs when the server is running. All operating systems and applications support this feature without any changes or updates.

### 19.5.4.4  HOT-ADD/UPGRADE SUPPORT

The hot-add or hot-upgrade procedures require *operating system vendor* (OSV) and *independent software vendor* (ISV) support. This feature enables users to add banks of new DIMMs when the server is running.

Operating systems that support the hot-add/upgrade feature include the following:

- Microsoft Windows Server 2003
- Caldera OpenUNIX 8 (ProLiant DL760 G2 only)
- SuSE and Red Hat Linux

The Oracle 9i/9i *Real Application Clusters* (RACs) database supports the hot-add/upgrade feature.

Applications that support the hot-add/upgrade feature include the following:

- SAP
- PeopleSoft
- JD Edwards
- Siebel
- Lotus Domino

#### 19.5.4.5 MEMORY CAPACITY

Only 80% of the server memory is available for the operating system to use in a system that supports Hot Plug RAID memory. If a server supports a total of 80GB of physical memory, for example, only 64GB of that memory is addressable by the operating system. The other 16GB (20% of the memory) is used for RAID overhead (or parity).

> There are no configuration parameters for the RAID memory array. The parity memory cartridge can be left unpopulated. However, this configuration provides no redundancy and no fault tolerance, and is not a recommended configuration. The parity memory cartridge cannot be added to the array as addressable memory.

## ▲ Summary

An Accredited Integration Specialist should be able to determine a customer's need for availability and recommend the right server components to ensure the required level of availability is obtained. Standalone HP ProLiant servers are rated at *availability level 1* (AL1).

Availability can be increased through additional power protection and server memory technologies, such as online spare memory, single-board mirrored memory, hot-plug mirrored memory, and Hot Plug RAID Memory.

## ▲ LEARNING CHECK

1. *A mission-critical application requires what percentage of uptime?*
   A. 100
   B. 99
   C. 95
   D. 90

2. *Which of the following would be considered business-critical applications?*
   A. Air traffic control
   B. 911 call center
   C. ATM machine systems
   D. E-commerce sites

3. *If a server is available 95% of the time, and if downtime causes a work stoppage but data integrity is ensured, what is the server availability level?*

   A. AL1

   B. AL2

   C. AL3

   D. AL4

4. *Which statement(s) is/are true regarding online spare memory?*

   A. It must be configured with RSBU, otherwise it will be used as main memory (up to the server maximum).

   B. The spare memory bank is counted during POST.

   C. The DIMMs in the spare bank can be equal to, or greater than, the DIMMs in the other banks.

   D. ProLiant G2 servers allow any bank to be defined as a spare bank.

5. *How does hot-plug mirrored memory provide a higher level of availability than online spare memory?*

# Optimizing Storage

In this chapter, you will learn to optimize storage by choosing a stripe size suitable for the type of data transfer common to your system and changing the read/write cache ratio for a Smart Array controller.

Proper array configuration is critical to maintaining availability, performance, and capacity. HP provides reliable array controllers for storage needs that include RAID *advanced data guard* (ADG), 5, and 1+0. For customers, recognizing the advantages and risks of specific RAID configurations on HP Smart Arrays can minimize unplanned and costly downtime.

## 20.1 Array Performance Tuning

Two main ways to optimize the performance of your array are as follows:

- Choose a stripe size more suitable for the type of data transfer common to your system.
- Change the read/write cache ratio in the Smart Array controller.

### 20.1.1 Disk Striping

To speed operations that retrieve data from disk storage, you can use disk striping to distribute volume segments across multiple disks. The most effective way to distribute volume segments is to do so equally across the disks. Striping improves disk response time by uniting multiple physical drives into a single logical drive. The logical drive is arranged so that blocks of data are written alternately across all physical drives in the logical array. The number of sectors per block is referred to as the *striping factor*.

Depending on the array controller in use, the striping factor can be modified, usually with the manufacturer's system configuration utility. Many of the HP Smart Array controllers can be modified online with online utilities that indicate the status of the logical drives and arrays and display the completion percentage of the rebuild process. For NetWare, this utility is CPQONLIN.NLM and for Windows, it is the *Array Configuration Utility* (ACU). For Linux, you must run the ACU from the SmartStart CD.

**On HP controllers released before the Smart Array 3100ES, changes to stripe size are data-destructive. In addition, any change to the logical volume geometry (such as striping factor, volume size, or RAID level) can be data-destructive.**

If you stripe disks on two or more SCSI controllers (called *controller multiplexing*), the operating system must calculate where to place the data in relation to the striping, in addition to other calculations that contribute to processor overhead. For best performance, stripe disks only on the same controller or use an HP Smart Array controller with multiple channels (a multichannel card uses only one interrupt) and specific circuitry for handling these calculations. The HP Smart Array 5300 and 6400 series controllers feature two or more channels for enhanced performance and capacity.

If a disk containing a spanned volume fails, the entire volume must be restored from a backup across all segments before you can use it again.

In Windows, the recovery process is automatic (as it is on hardware controllers). Windows also automatically rebuilds the volume when you replace the faulty drive. It begins the background process of reconstructing the data on the new drive the same way it handles I/O requests automatically. The process slows performance (more with software RAID than on an accelerated controller), but when reconstruction is finished, system operations return to normal.

RAID 0 striping improves volume I/O because you can read data and write data concurrently to each disk. If one of the disks fails, the entire volume becomes unavailable. To provide fault tolerance, you should mirror the segments of volumes that span devices.

When configuring RAID 5 on a Linux server, you must have at least one native partition that contains the /boot directory. The kernel must load the drivers that support RAID from a native disk before it can mount the RAID array. This requirement affects the way the drives in the array are partitioned and how you recover from a failure of the particular drive that contains the native partition.

### 20.1.1.1 OPTIMIZING THE STRIPE SIZE

Selecting the appropriate stripe (chunk) size is crucial to achieving optimum performance within an array. The stripe size is the amount of data that is read or written to each disk in the array when data requests are processed by the array controller.

The terms *chunk, block,* and *segment* are used interchangeably. Chunk is used most often when discussing storage.

The following table lists the available stripe sizes and their characteristics.

| Fault-Tolerance Method | Available Stripe Sizes (KB) | Default Size (KB) |
| --- | --- | --- |
| RAID 0 | 128, 256 | 128 |
| RAID 1 or 1+0 | 8, 16, 32, 64, 128, 256 | 128 |
| RAID 5 or RAID ADG | 8, 16, 32, 64 | 16 |

The default stripe size delivers good performance in most circumstances. When high performance is important, you might need to modify the stripe size.

If the stripe size is too large, there will be poor load balancing across the drives.

If the stripe size is too small, there will be many cross-stripe transfers (split I/Os), and performance will be reduced.

Split I/Os involve two disks, and both disks seek, rotate, and transfer data. The response time depends on the slowest disk. Split I/Os reduce the request rate because there are fewer drives to service incoming requests.

| Type of Server Application | Suggested Stripe Size Change |
|---|---|
| Mixed read/write | Accept the default value |
| Mainly read (such as database or Internet applications) | Larger stripe sizes work best |
| Mainly write (such as image manipulation applications) | Smaller stripes for RAID 5, RAID ADG |
| | Larger stripes for RAID 0, RAID 1, RAID 1+0 |

### 20.1.2  Changing the Read/Write Cache Ratio

The array accelerator on the Smart Array controllers dramatically improves I/O performance. Depending on the controller, it can have a size of 4, 16, 32, 64, 128, or 256MB.

The array accelerator uses an intelligent read-ahead algorithm that anticipates data needs and reduces wait time. It detects sequential read activity on single or multiple I/O threads and predicts what requests will follow. The data is gathered and stored in the high-speed cache. As soon as the data is requested by the operating system, the data is delivered 100 times faster than a disk can deliver data.

By default, the array accelerator cache capacity is equally divided between reads and writes. If your server application has significantly more reads than writes (or vice versa), you might need to change this setting to improve performance. This change can be accomplished online without restarting the system. The optimal ratio setting is application-dependent.

Whenever random-access patterns are detected, read-ahead is disabled because reading ahead data under random I/O slows down the system instead of making it faster.

If the disks are busy, new writes can be stored in the cache and written to the disk later when there is less activity (write-back). Some smaller blocks can usually be combined into larger blocks, resulting in fewer but larger blocks written to the disk, thus improving performance.

The Smart Array 5300 and 6400 controllers are the only array controller families with upgradeable cache modules.

## ▲ Summary

An Accredited Integration Specialist should be able to recognize the advantages and risks of specific RAID configurations on HP Smart Array controllers.

Two ways to optimize array performance are optimizing the stripe size and changing the read/write cache ratio.

Selecting the appropriate stripe size is crucial to achieve optimal array performance. In most situations, the default stripe size delivers good performance.

By default, the array accelerator cache capacity is equally divided between reads and writes. If a server application has significantly more reads than writes (or vice versa), you might need to change the read/write cache ratio to improve performance.

## ▲ LEARNING CHECK

1. *If the stripe size is too large, what might the consequence be?*

   A. Too many cross-stripe transfers will cause reduced performance.

   B. Poor load balancing across the drives will occur.

2. *If the stripe size is too small, what might the consequence be?*

   A. Too many cross-stripe transfers will cause reduced performance.

   B. Poor load balancing across the drives will occur.

3. *What utility is used to modify the striping factor if the server is running NetWare?*

   A. ACU

   B. CPQONLIN

   C. SmartStart

# Problem Resolution

**A**n Accredited Integration Specialist will be able to effectively deal with system problems in both proactive and reactive ways.

Here is an overview of the chapters in Part 7.

### Chapter 21   Backup Strategies

One of the cardinal sins in information technology is loss of data. The only way you can truly ensure that data is never lost is to have an effective backup strategy.

Chapter 21 provides an overview of backup strategies and technologies that HP recommends to ensure that vital data is never lost.

### Chapter 22   Problem Resolution, Performance Issues, and System Maintenance

Notwithstanding all that can be proactively done to prevent problems, problems will inevitably occur anyway. An Accredited Integration Specialist will know how to resolve these problems in an effective and efficient manner.

Chapter 22 provides a high-level troubleshooting methodology, recommended by HP, for identifying and resolving problems that occur with an HP ProLiant server, as well as problems that occur in a networked server environment.

# Backup Strategies

This chapter explains how to do the following:

- Choose a backup method.
- Select and install backup hardware.
- Select and install backup software.
- Determine a backup tape rotation scheme.
- Plan for offsite storage.
- Plan for disaster recovery.
- Use the HP StorageWorks Backup Sizing tool.

**421**

RAID and other fault-tolerant systems protect data against drive failures, but only a backup system can protect against deleted files, natural disasters, or theft. Backup processes copy important information to magnetic tape or other permanent storage media. This enables you to restore one file or an entire system, depending on the circumstance.

The media and devices for performing backups are often referred to as *secondary storage* to distinguish them from primary storage, which refers to the disks where data is stored for immediate access and use.

To develop a successful company-wide backup strategy, you must understand the network architecture and the demands placed on the system by its users.

Equipped with that information, you can then conduct a network or enterprise backup needs analysis. This needs analysis will help you (1) determine which data must be backed up, (2) understand when and how often data is modified, and (3) establish the best time to perform the backups.

To create and implement an effective backup solution, you need to do the following:

- Choose a backup method.
- Select and install hardware.
- Select and install software.
- Determine a backup tape rotation scheme.
- Plan for offsite storage of backup media.

## 21.1　Choosing a Backup Method

Your main options for a backup method are as follows:

- **Back up to a single tape device**—Tape libraries with removable cartridges provide the most complete, comprehensive, and effective means to protect enterprise-wide data.

- **Use stripe tape devices (redundant array of independent tape [RAIT])**—RAIT-5 provides the optimum balance between speed and safety because it writes to a set of tapes as an array and uses a parity stripe to provide checksum information. This technique permits file restoration even when there has been some data loss on a single tape in the array.

- **Back up to local disk devices**—Backing up locally keeps backup traffic off the LAN and the server, reducing network bottlenecks.
- **Back up across the network**—Centralized backup management enables users to share tape devices and libraries.

## 21.2    Selecting and Installing Hardware

The main factor driving backup hardware selection is the relationship of performance to cost. Speed is an essential component of performance, because the faster the drive system, the faster the backup. Backup performance can be almost tripled (from 30 to 84.5GB/hr) with hardware that provides data to the tape drives quickly. Performance also can be increased with multiple jobs, but only with adequate feed speed.

Unattended backups can significantly reduce administrative costs. Deploying sufficient backup capacity and automation, if needed, to make unattended backups possible is often a significant cost saver for the long term.

For unattended backups, the tape drive and media must meet backup requirements in terms of overall storage capacity and backup performance. Both performance and capacity vary with the type of drive technology selected.

When deciding the hardware most suited to your backup solution, consider also whether backups will be made of individual user data. Because large hard drives can hold gigabytes of software, backing up a user's hard drive could be a time-consuming task, even if it is automated. Related to this is the extra network bandwidth consumed by pulling such large amounts of data over the company network. If project files are being centrally stored on a server, the ideal solution is to back up that data and leave client backups up to the individual user.

Although an autoloader option will increase the cost of the *digital audiotape* (DAT) backup, it will make unattended backups much easier. Depending on the size of the magazine, tapes could be loaded in the order desired to make a week's worth of backups completely automated.

### 21.2.1   Calculating Required Performance

Performance requirements determine the type of tape drive you should use. You can calculate your performance needs by dividing the amount of information (in gigabytes) that must be backed up by the size of the backup window (in hours), as shown in Figure 21–1. This simple calculation yields the required performance as an overall transfer rate expressed in GB/hr.

**Figure 21-1**
*Required transfer rate formula.*

$$\frac{\text{DATA (Gigabytes)}}{\text{Backup Window (Hours)}} = \begin{array}{c} \text{Required} \\ \text{Transfer Rate} \\ \text{(GB/hr)} \end{array}$$

Consider these factors when choosing the type of tape drive you will use:

- The maximum capacity of uncompressed data that each drive can store on a cassette
- The transfer rates for reading and writing uncompressed data with each drive
- Typical system transfer rates when performing a local backup using each drive in a system
- The typical time for that system to perform a 10GB backup using each of the drives
- The number of tape cartridges that must be loaded and unloaded during the backup operation

By comparing the results of the required transfer rate with typical backup performance rates of the drive, you can determine whether the backup performance you need is achievable.

## 21.3   Selecting and Installing Software

After you have installed the backup hardware, you must apply any drivers and then install any third-party backup software. After this is complete, you can configure jobs using the built-in wizards. Using the Backup Wizard, you can easily select files, directories, entire hard drives, and even the system state. The complement to the Backup Wizard is the Restore Wizard.

A feature introduced with Windows Server 2003 is *Automated System Recovery* (ASR). Using the ASR Wizard, you can create a backup of the system files and an ASR disk that you can use to restore the system in the event of a major system failure.

You must have a separate backup of the data to restore the system completely.

## Determining a Backup Tape Rotation Scheme

Backups must be performed on a disciplined, scheduled regimen, carefully designed to address certain issues, including the following:

- The schedule for backups
- Whether to use partial or full backups
- Whether partial backups should be incremental or differential

The terms *full, partial, incremental,* and *differential* describe the amount of information that is copied and backed up. All backups, whether full or partial, can be performed online or offline.

The archive bit is a file attribute that identifies whether the file has been backed up. If a file is changed after the last backup, the archive bit is cleared until the file is backed up again.

Full backups back up all the selected data on the hard drive and reset the archive bit.

Differential backups back up all the data since the last full backup but do not reset the archive bit.

Incremental backups back up only the changed data from the last full backup and reset the archive bit.

### 21.4.1  Full Backup

A full backup is a complete backup of the entire server or client. A server backup includes all volumes, directories, and files. A client backup includes all drives, directories, and files.

The two types of full backups are normal backup and copy backup.

#### 21.4.1.1  NORMAL BACKUP

A normal backup backs up database files and then the transaction log files. It then deletes the transaction log files from the directory. You can have circular logging disabled because your backup software deletes the log files.

Therefore, if you are performing regular backups, you will not have a problem with log files filling your drive. To restore a normal backup, you only need to restore your last normal backup set and then start the service.

#### 21.4.1.2 COPY BACKUP

A copy backup is similar to a normal backup, but it does not purge the log files on your drive and does not update the backup context in the database files. A copy backup is practical when you want to back up your data without disrupting your normal backup schedule.

### 21.4.2 Partial Backup

A partial backup can be either incremental or differential.

#### 21.4.2.1 INCREMENTAL

An incremental backup copies all files that were changed after the last backup, regardless of what kind of backup it was.

Use an incremental backup when you must maintain every revision of a file. If you use the same tapes for consecutive incremental backups, do not allow the newer versions of backed-up files to overwrite earlier versions. Instead, append the newer files to the backup medium.

An incremental backup works only on the log files. Like a normal backup, an incremental backup purges log files after backing them up, providing another way to rid log files from your drive without compromising recoverability.

To restore an incremental backup, you must return to your last normal backup set that contains your database files. Restore those database files, restore every incremental backup set made after the normal backup, and then start the service. Do not start the service until you have restored all the backup sets; otherwise any logs restored after the backup set will not be played forward.

#### 21.4.2.2 DIFFERENTIAL

A differential backup copies all files that were changed after the last complete backup.

Use differential backups when you only need to save the latest version of each file. If you use the same tapes for consecutive differential backups, the newer versions of backed-up files often overwrite older versions of the same file on the tape. Backup programs typically do not reset the archive bit after a differential backup. Rather, the archive bit remains enabled until the next complete backup.

To restore a differential backup, return to the last normal backup and restore the differential backup that contains log files generated after the last normal backup. Do not start the service until you have restored all the backup sets.

### 21.4.3   Grandfather-Father-Son Tape Rotation

The *grandfather-father-son* (GFS) tape rotation scheme is the most commonly used scheme, requiring a weekly backup capacity of at least double the server storage capacity. Providing different levels of data retention, this scheme uses three levels of backup to supply redundancy and security.

The system administrator can select which generation of tapes to store temporarily and which to archive.

GFS backup requires the following:

1. Monthly grandfathers
2. Weekly fathers
3. Daily sons

> **EXAMPLE**
>
> The system administrator typically performs a full backup every Monday (father) and incremental backups on Tuesdays, Wednesdays, and Thursdays (sons). The administrator performs another full backup at the end of the week (father) and another at the end of the month (grandfather).

The GFS tape rotation scheme is intended to ensure that a company can always restore lost data to within a day of a disaster. Businesses dedicated to helping get a company back online after a disaster can make computer equipment, tape drives, phone equipment, and so forth available to a company quickly.

The tapes containing the weekly and monthly backups are usually stored in a location away from the site of the server. To help reduce media costs, many companies reuse older weekly backup tapes.

Never overwrite a recently used backup tape. If a hard disk crash should occur during the backup, not only would all the data on the disk be lost, but also the tape will no longer be useful for a complete restoration.

In some cases, customer requirements might be better met by performing differential backups for the daily sons rather than incremental backups. In a few cases, daily full backups might be required. The trade-offs between the various types of partial and complete backups relate to the following:

- Amount of data that will be backed up each day
- Time required to complete the backup session
- Number of tapes required to recover data to the server after a disaster

## 21.5    Planning for Offsite Storage

It is imperative for backed-up data to be moved regularly to an offsite storage facility. If something were to happen to the facility, backup media could be retrieved from safe, offsite storage.

Depending on the importance of the data, there can be several offsite storage facilities. Companies that provide offsite storage service will pick up and deliver media when they need to be rotated.

Be careful about choosing a location for backup media. Magnetic fields can destroy data on media. Keep media away from electronic devices such as video monitors, analog telephones, and so on.

## 21.6    Planning for Disaster Recovery

Just having a backup set of data tapes is no guarantee of recovery. Backup sets should be tested for their ability to restore as well. Many times a critical restore has failed because of a physical problem with the tape or corruption in the backup data. A regular backup strategy helps to mitigate the potential negative impact of a bad backup. An even more robust backup strategy, however, incorporates a disaster recovery plan.

A disaster recovery plan is an integrated strategy of backup, restore, and recovery in the event of a disaster. It involves a regular backup rotation, a proven restore process, offsite storage of media, and procedures for re-creating the affected environment.

Another aspect often overlooked is access to operating system media and license materials. Although new backup software technologies allow "bare-metal restores," it is good practice to keep a copy of the operating system media and license keys at an offsite facility so that the affected system can be restored to a minimal state before the restore is applied.

> **EXAMPLE**
>
> If fire were to damage a server room, a replacement server could be ordered, a SmartStart installation of the operating system could be performed, and then the restore could be applied to return the system to its predisaster state. Assuming that replacement equipment was readily available and backup media could be quickly retrieved, the organization could be up and running again in a matter of hours.

## 21.7 Using the StorageWorks Backup Sizing Tool

The StorageWorks Backup Sizing tool enables you to size and configure your ideal backup solution using information you provide. This tool

- Displays a complete backup schedule for your environment.
- Recommends solutions for tape drives and libraries that support your performance and business requirements.
- Simplifies the configuration process through a Windows-based graphic user interface (GUI)
- Lists updates to product compatibility in the EBS compatibility matrix.
- Supports Windows Server 2003.
- Offers a good /better /best recommended backup solution based on price, capacity, and performance.
- Provides information about HP tape backup products and solutions.

For operating systems certifications, compatibility matrices, and access to tape tools, visit http://h18006.www1.hp.com/products/storageworks/tapecompatibility.html.

The Backup Sizing tool is available in an online version or can be downloaded. HP strongly recommends the use of the online version, which you can run from any system that has Web access. The online version always has the latest version of software as well as compatibility information.

You also can download the HP StorageWorks Backup Sizing tool to run offline. Although limited in functionality, the offline version enables you to

- Generate and save solutions.

- Upload saved solutions to the online version of the tool, so you can then view and update your solutions online.

> **! IMPORTANT**
>
> HP strongly recommends that you print a copy of the installation instructions and read the steps carefully before installing the offline tool. The steps for installation have changed significantly, including installation of Microsoft Internet Information Services (IIS) as a prerequisite.

## ▲ Summary

Only a backup system can protect against deleted files, natural disasters, or theft. Backup processes copy important information to magnetic tape or other permanent storage media.

The main factor driving backup hardware selection is the relationship of performance to cost.

Unattended backups can significantly reduce administrative costs.

Backups must be performed using a very disciplined, scheduled regimen.

A full backup is a complete backup of the entire server or client.

A partial backup can be either incremental or differential. An incremental backup copies all files that were changed after the last backup. A differential backup copies all files that were changed after the last complete backup.

The *grandfather-father-son* (GFS) scheme is the most commonly used tape rotation scheme.

Backed up data needs to be moved regularly to an offsite facility in case something happens to the main facility.

A disaster recovery plan involves a regular backup rotation, a proven restore process, offsite storage of media, and procedures for re-creating the affected environment.

## ▲ LEARNING CHECK

1. *When selecting a backup method, which option provides the optimum balance between speed and safety?*
   A. Backing up to a single tape device
   B. Using a stripe tape device
   C. Backing up to local devices
   D. Backing up across the network

2. *What happens to the archive bit if a file is changed after the last backup?*
   A. It is marked as "changed."
   B. It is cleared, indicating that the file needs to be backed up.
   C. It is left in its current state.

3. *What are the two types of partial backups? (Select two.)*
   A. Incremental
   B. Archive
   C. Differential
   D. GFS
   E. Copy backup

4. *The GFS tape rotation scheme requires how much backup capacity?*
   A. Equal to the server storage capacity
   B. 1.5 times the server storage capacity
   C. 2 times the server storage capacity
   D. 3 times as much as server storage capacity

# Problem Resolution, Performance Issues, and System Maintenance

As an Accredited Integration Specialist, you will be expected to be able to do the following:

- Identify when an HP ProLiant server is not performing as it should and establish a performance baseline.
- Use the HP troubleshooting methodology to troubleshoot problems with ProLiant servers.
- Use HP system information resources to gather vital data about the system you are working with.
- Use tools to collect and analyze information relating to server performance.
- Use HP utilities to perform troubleshooting tasks.
- Troubleshoot problems relating to networking.
- Troubleshoot problems relating to processors.
- Troubleshoot problems relating to storage.
- Troubleshoot problems relating to memory.
- Resolve issues relating to software and drivers.

**433**

This chapter provides a comprehensive troubleshooting methodology, and introduces you to the tools that enable you to effectively use the troubleshooting methodology. By following this methodology and using the tools provided by HP, you will be able to accomplish each of the objectives listed at the beginning of the chapter.

## 22.1   Assessing Normal Operation

Before you can begin to identify a system failure, you must understand how the system should operate under normal circumstances. Recognizing when a system is performing normally as well as understanding what a system requires to operate properly will help you identify a malfunctioning system.

You also should be able to recognize the warning signs of a failed or failing component. These signs or symptoms may include consistent or intermittent error codes, loss of functionality, or a change in the time the system takes to perform a task.

Among other things, you should understand the following:

- Which LEDs illuminate when and why
- The order in which system components power-up
- The importance of SCSI termination
- The order in which files load during the boot sequence

Not understanding how a system or subsystem operates can lead to unnecessary part replacement, unneeded software upgrades, as well as wasted time and effort. These actions lead to unnecessary downtime and negatively impact customer satisfaction.

When you understand how a system operates under normal circumstances, you are ready to begin implementing the HP troubleshooting methodology on a malfunctioning system.

## 22.2   HP Troubleshooting Methodology

The high degree of interaction between the server system, options hardware, operating system, and application software can make it difficult to isolate the root cause of a problem. Intermittent problems and problems generated by multiple subsystem malfunctions can be especially difficult to troubleshoot.

HP has developed a six-step troubleshooting methodology, shown in Figure 22–1, to systematically get to the core of a problem, resolve it, and take steps to limit the possibility of it happening again. These six steps are as follows:

1. Collect data.
2. Evaluate the data to determine potential subsystems causing the issue.
3. Develop an optimized action plan.
4. Execute the action plan.
5. Determine whether the problem is solved.
6. Implement preventive measures.

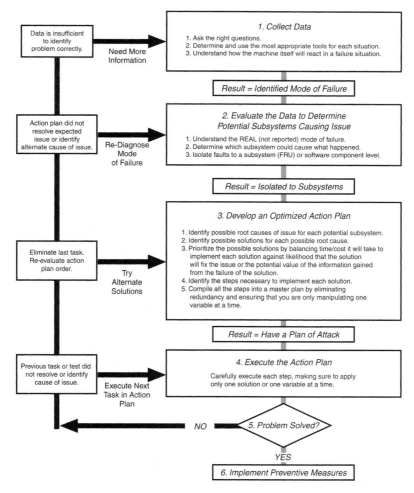

**Figure 22–1** *HP troubleshooting methodology flowchart.*

As part of any change management process, altering only one variable at a time can show the impact of that change. If manipulating one variable does not result in any performance increase, revisiting the data to determine the next variable to manipulate is the next step. By following the HP troubleshooting methodology, you can use a standard approach to reduce possibilities until a solution set is found.

This methodology provides a logical framework to troubleshoot system problems and reach problem resolution. A logical framework also provides a consistent and solid foundation for other technicians and system engineers to work from when escalation is necessary.

## 22.2.1 Troubleshooting Step 1—Collect Data

The first step in troubleshooting a problem involves spending the time and effort to gather helpful information. There are actually two skills involved in this step: (1) asking the right questions, and (2) using the appropriate tools and methods to gather and analyze system data.

### 22.2.1.1 ASKING THE RIGHT QUESTIONS

As you begin the troubleshooting process, start by asking a series of questions that will help you thoroughly understand the nature of the problem. Here are some of the questions you could ask:

1. What happens when the system fails?
2. What specific component is failing and when?
3. What errors display?
4. Can you duplicate the failure at will or is it random?
5. Do you notice anything unusual that you think would be helpful?
6. What has recently changed?

Through experience and logic, the answers to these kinds of questions will help you narrow down the possible causes and will help you focus your efforts as you begin collecting additional data on your own.

### 22.2.1.2 COLLECTING SYSTEM DATA

After you have determined the answers to the general questions, you now begin the process of collecting very specific information about the system.

The specific data information you collect should include each of the following items:

- The hardware components physically installed in the system
- The software installed in the system (including patches, service packs, and other incremental updates)
- Specific information about the failure, such as the following:
  - Stop/abend/trap messages
  - HP Insight Manager error conditions
  - Critical error log messages
  - *Power-On Self-Test* (POST) messages

HP provides several tools for viewing system data. Some of these utilities are integrated into the server itself, but all complement each other. These utilities include the following:

- Integrated Management Log
- Integrated Management Log Viewer
- Integrated Management Display
- Integrated Management Display Utility
- Enhanced Integrated Management Display Service

Each of these utilities is described briefly later in this chapter.

### 22.2.1.3   SETTING A PERFORMANCE BASELINE FOR WINDOWS SYSTEMS

As part of the information gathering process, you establish a performance baseline.

> **! IMPORTANT**
>
> This should be done before any changes are made to a system.

Windows Server 2003 (and earlier versions) includes a useful utility called Performance. This utility is located under the Administrative Tools icon in the Control Panel. It is used to monitor either local or remote system performance. After the needed counters are chosen, Performance can track and record them. This is useful for real-time monitoring and logging for a baseline. Over time, this data can help identify system bottlenecks.

After the tool is started, you can add various counters to the System Monitor feature to track performance of a local or remote computer. You can choose related counters and specific instances from several performance object categories. Specific instances refer to the ability to choose all or specific processors or page files. (Not all counters have instances to choose from.)

Although some of the counters represent averages for read/write requests, separate counters for read and write operations can be used to gain a more specific view of activity instead.

**To get an explanation of each counter, click Explain from the Add Counters window after clicking the plus sign (+) icon in System Monitor.**

Some counters have different scales, so it is important that the scale of one counter does not affect the readability of the other counters. Counter scales can be adjusted by right-clicking the counter in the legend area at the bottom of the Performance windows and selecting Properties, and then Data. On this tab in the System Monitor Properties window, you can adjust the color, scale, width, and style of each counter. Other tabs enable you to adjust the properties of source, graphs, colors, and fonts.

A Web browser provides a convenient way to monitor these counters. After the counters are selected and optimized for readability, they can be saved as an HTML-format file by right-clicking the graph. The file can then be opened in a browser on any computer.

## 22.2.2   Troubleshooting Step 2—Evaluating and Interpreting the Data

After you have gathered the data, the next step is to evaluate and interpret the data to determine which subsystem or subsystems could be causing the problem.

The evaluation and interpretation of the data enables you to do the following:

1. Determine which components could cause what happened.
2. Isolate faults to a hardware or software subsystem.
3. Understand the mode of failure.

After you have determined what is most likely causing the problem to occur, you are ready to move to Step 3.

### 22.2.3  Troubleshooting Step 3—Develop an Optimized Action Plan

After collecting the facts and isolating the specific mode of failure, your next step in the troubleshooting process is to develop an optimized action plan. The action plan is developed through the following steps:

1. Identify specific root causes for the specified mode of failure.
2. Identify possible solutions for each possible root cause.
3. Rank the possible solutions in a priority order by balancing the time and cost that it will take to implement each solution against the likelihood that the solution will resolve the problem. (It is possible that the initial possible solution will not solve the problem, but it might yield additional helpful information that will help solve the problem.)
4. Identify the steps necessary to implement each solution.
5. Compile all the steps into an optimized action plan by eliminating redundancy and ensuring that only one variable is being manipulated at a time.
6. Incorporate an escalation plan into the master action plan. You should be prepared to escalate the situation for additional technical assistance. The escalation plan should contain a list of whom to contact and the information the escalation recipient would need.

### 22.2.4  Troubleshooting Step 4—Execute the Action Plan

In Step 4, you implement the optimized action plan you created in Step 3. It is critical that you carefully observe and record the results of each step. Even if the action plan does not solve the problem, it might provide more clues to solving it.

To execute the action plan, you carefully execute each step, implementing only one solution (that is, modifying only one variable) at a time.

As you implement each step, observe and record the results of each step, including any error messages or changes in functionality.

### 22.2.5  Troubleshooting Step 5—Determine Whether the Problem Is Solved

Step 5 is to evaluate the results of each step until the problem has been isolated and resolved. If the problem is not resolved, you cycle back through the troubleshooting methodology by doing the following:

- Collecting more data
- Utilizing the information gathered from implementation of the action plan
- Evaluating the information
- Developing another optimized action plan
- Implementing the optimized action plan
- Repeating as necessary, escalating when appropriate

### 22.2.6 Troubleshooting Step 6—Implement Preventive Measures

As soon as the problem is resolved, you implement the necessary preventive measures that will ensure that the problem is not repeated (if possible). You should also look at opportunities to improve or increase system availability.

To implement preventive measures, follow these steps:

1. Determine the root cause of the problem.
2. Determine proactive steps that can prevent the problem from recurring.
3. Devise a system test to verify changes and procedures before implementing them into production.
4. Implement a new set of procedures, software, and administrative maintenance to attain a higher level of availability.
5. Perform preventive maintenance, including checking for loose cables, reseating boards, and checking for proper airflow.
6. Add fault-tolerant elements to critical subsystems, where applicable.

The HP troubleshooting methodology provides you with a structured approach to solving problems in an efficient manner.

## 22.3  Using HP System Information References

The manuals and CDs that ship with HP systems and options can help identify normal activity and proper system setup. HP also provides two other very useful resources for troubleshooting:

- Maintenance and Service Guides
- PartSurfer Service Parts Information

Depending on your situation, you might find the online or printed reference more useful for finding a part number, upgrade information, jumper setting, or other detail.

### 22.3.1 Maintenance and Service Guides

*Maintenance and Service Guides* (MSGs) provide system specifications as well as symptoms of failures and troubleshooting hints.

An individual MSG is published for each HP computer product line. The MSG is designed to be used as a troubleshooting guide and reference tool when servicing HP computers.

MSGs are available by product category from the HP Reference Library at http://www3.compaq.com/support/home/selectproduct.asp?destination= reflib.

### 22.3.2 PartSurfer Service Parts Information

The PartSurfer Service Parts Information tool, shown in Figure 22–2, provides access to parts information for a wide range of HP products.

HP PartSurfer provides fast, easy, online access to parts information for a wide range of HP products.

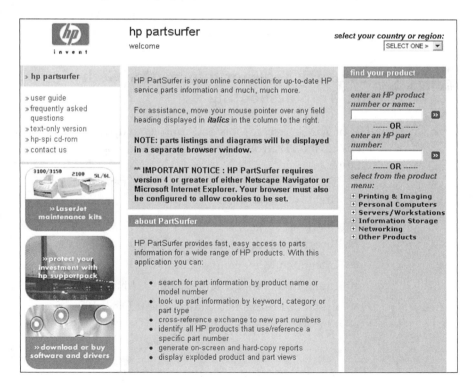

**Figure 22–2** *PartSurfer Web site.*

With this PartSurfer, you can

- Look up failure codes.
- Search for part information by product name or model number.
- Look up part information by keyword, category or part type.
- Cross-reference exchange to new part numbers.
- Identify all HP products that use or reference a specific part number.
- Generate onscreen and hard-copy reports.
- Display exploded product and part views.

Because of occasional performance issues on the Internet, many customers prefer to use the HP Service Parts Information CD-ROM as a complement to HP PartSurfer. The Service Parts Information CD accesses the same data as HP PartSurfer, but with a slightly different interface.

You can access the HP PartSurfer and also Server Parts Information at http://partsurfer.hp.com/cgi-bin/spi/main.

For information on how to order the Service Parts Information CD, go to http://partsurfer.hp.com/hp-spi/.

## 22.4  Using HP Tools for Information Gathering and Troubleshooting

HP provides several tools and utilities that will help you with several of the steps in the HP troubleshooting methodology described previously in this chapter.

You should be familiar with the capabilities and functions of the following products:

- Integrated Management Log
- Integrated Management Log Viewer
- Integrated Management Display
- Integrated Management Display Utility
- Enhanced Integrated Management Display Service
- HP Server Diagnostics

### 22.4.1  *Integrated Management Log*

The HP *Integrated Management Log* (IML) is a utility integrated into the server to record all server-specific events. Events are abnormal system occurrences. The log tracks events recorded by the health drivers, such as operating system information and ROM POST codes.

This nonvolatile (that is, information is recorded to a file rather than being stored in volatile memory) log records events and errors for a post-diagnosis review, thus helping system administrators to identify server failures promptly. The information displayed for each log entry includes a description of the event, the number of times this specific event has occurred, the initial time and date the event occurred, and the time and date the event was last updated.

## 22.4.2   *Integrated Management Log Viewer*

The HP Integrated Management Log Viewer is a utility that enables you to view and manage the IML system event entries on a local or remote system.

This utility is based on client/server architecture. It can run on any machine and connect to any machine on the network that is running the HP ProLiant Remote Monitor Service.

By using the viewer, you can accomplish the following tasks in relation to the IML entries:

- Sort by description, class, severity, count, update time, and initial time
- Filter by class, severity, update time, and initial time
- Print the entries
- Export the information to a comma-separated file (for import into third-party applications such as spreadsheets) or save the information in a binary format for viewing at a later date or different location

In addition to manipulating the displayed entries, you can also effect changes to the IML on a system. With appropriate administrator privileges, you can accomplish the following tasks:

- Enter maintenance notes
- Mark selected entries as repaired
- Clear the IML of all entries (effectively deleting the log from non-volatile memory)
- Acknowledge pending alerts on the *Integrated Management Display* (IMD)

The Integrated Management Log Viewer is available for the following platforms:

- Microsoft Windows Server 2003
- Windows 2000
- Windows NT 4.0
- Novell NetWare
- Linux

> **! IMPORTANT**
>
> Invoking the IML Viewer on a Windows 2000 server to remotely view the IML on a Windows NT 4.0 server (and vice versa) is not supported. However, the IML logs can be viewed locally at the server or remotely using HP Insight Manager 7.

### 22.4.3 Integrated Management Display

The HP *Integrated Management Display* (IMD) is an optional peripheral on the front of legacy servers. The IMD provides the following useful benefits:

- Displays server processes such as power-up, POST, and errors
- Simplifies management with the capability to report or alert from an endless list of critical events
- Improves server manageability and uptime by providing easy-to-read information without the use of a monitor
- Simplifies menu navigation
- Enables users to display customized information
- Integrates easily in rack-mounted servers

### 22.4.4 Integrated Management Display Utility

The HP Integrated Management Display Utility enables you to set the text displayed on the IMD. This utility is based on client/server architecture. It can run on any machine and connect to any machine on the network that is running the HP Remote Monitor Service.

The Integrated Management Display Utility is available for the following platforms:

- Windows Server 2003
- Windows 2000
- Windows NT 4.0
- Novell NetWare

## 22.4.5   *Enhanced Integrated Management Display Service*

The HP Enhanced Integrated Management Display Service is different from the Integrated Management Display Utility in that it enables you to view multiple items in the IMD Idle screen of the IMD.

The Enhanced Integrated Management Display Service is available for the following platforms:

- Windows Server 2003
- Windows 2000
- Windows NT 4.0

## 22.4.6   *HP Server Diagnostics*

HP Server Diagnostics is a resource for server testing and problem resolution. The Test Computer feature of it provides diagnostic tests for system components. Use this feature to

- Perform burn-in testing.
- Diagnose intermittent problems with components such as memory and drives.
- Verify the condition of individual components.

Server Diagnostics can test more components than the Embedded Diagnostic Utility available from the System Maintenance menu.

You can access the System Maintenance menu by pressing F10 when prompted during POST.

### 22.4.6.1   TEST COMPUTER

Test Computer provides three types of diagnostics routines, described in the following table.

| Routine | Description |
|---|---|
| Quick Check Diagnostics | This option will run high-level diagnostics on all detected hardware in the system. However, any errors found with this test would most likely be hard failures and would have already been reported during POST. In such a case, running diagnostics would not be necessary because the POST code will detail the failure. |
| Automatic Diagnostics | This option is most useful for burn-in testing of all devices. The "continuous looping" feature continues testing all devices until it is stopped by pressing Ctrl+Break; or, if the Stop on Errors option is checked, until it finds an error with a device. Unattended testing without continuous looping will run all tests once and then stop. |
| Prompted Diagnostics | Use this option to test individual devices. This proves most useful in troubleshooting intermittent errors, such as a high number of *error checking and correcting* (ECC) memory errors or problems with a drive. It can also be used to verify that a particular component has failed and that its replacement is fully operational. |

**These diagnostic tests were written specifically for HP-supplied equipment. For accurate results, remove any third-party equipment in the unit before testing.**

### 22.4.6.2   DIAGNOSTIC TESTS

Any of the three routines of Test Computer can perform the tests listed in the following table.

| Test | Function |
|---|---|
| Primary Processor Test | 100 Series error codes. Identifies failures with processor and system board functions. To ensure they are working properly, corrective action may require replacement of the following:<br>• System boards or processor assemblies<br>• Numeric coprocessor<br>• DMA controller<br>• Interrupt controller<br>• Port 61 |

| Test | Function |
|------|----------|
| | • CMOS RAM<br>• CMOS interrupt<br>• CMOS clock<br>• Refresh detect signal<br>• System speaker, and speaker, to ensure that they are working properly |
| Memory Test | 200 Series error codes. The System Memory Test will run the following address tests (tests only the first 16MB in the system) to check the functionality of the address lines:<br>• **Write, Read, Compare Test**—Uses static patterns to exercise memory.<br>• **Noise Test**—Checks the integrity of data transfer through data lines.<br>• **Random Data Pattern Test**—Uses random data patterns to exercise memory.<br>• **Random Address Test**—Uses random data patterns written to random addresses to exercise memory.<br>• **Random Long Test**—Uses four patterns to exercise long memory. It scans 1MB of memory after testing each test block, looking for errors induced in other locations. This test takes up to 10 minutes per megabyte. Corrective action may require replacement of the memory expansion board, the memory modules, or the processor assembly. |
| Keyboard Test | 300 Series error codes. |
| Parallel Printer Test | 400 Series error codes. |
| Diskette Drive Test | 600 Series error codes. |
| HP Smart Array Controller Test | The following options are under the HP Smart Array Controller Test:<br>• **Drive Monitoring Diagnostic Test**—Performs a check on the drive monitoring functionality.<br>• **Controller Diagnostic Test**—Verifies that the hard drive controller can be accessed and is functional.<br>• **Seek Test**—Performs sequential seeks over the hard drive, and then performs random seeks.<br>• **Read Test**—Performs a random head seek test followed by a test of the hard drive and reports the number of unusable tracks, if any.<br>• **Select All the Above Tests**—Runs the Drive Monitoring Diagnostic Test, the Controller Diagnostic Test, the Seek Test, and the Read Test.<br>• **Surface Analysis**—Performs multiple write/read/compares on each track of the drive in search of more unusable tracks. It de-allocates sectors or formats tracks to be unusable when errors are found. |

*continues*

| Test | Function |
|---|---|
| Serial Test | 1100 Series error codes. |
| Modem Communications Test | 1200 Series error codes. |
| Fixed Disk Drive Test | 1700 Series error codes. |
| Tape Drive Test | 1900 Series error codes. |
| Advanced VGA Board Test | 2400 Series error codes. |
| 32-Bit DualSpeed NetFlex-2 Controller and 32-Bit DualSpeed Token Ring Controller Test | 6000 Series error codes. |
| SCSI Fixed Disk Drive Test | 6500 Series error codes. |
| CD-ROM Drive Test | 6600 Series error codes. |
| SCSI Tape Drive Test | 6700 Series error codes. |
| Server Manager/R Board Test | 7000 Series error codes. |
| Pointing Device Interface Test | 8600 Series error codes. |

## 22.5 Troubleshooting Networking Problems

Poor network server or workstation performance is often associated with physical network problems. In an overly congested or poorly designed network, the performance level of a server or workstation can do little to improve overall network performance. In a resource-sharing environment, the network communications subsystem, because of its heavy use in this environment, is one of the most likely places for network performance problems. The resolution can involve adding more *network interface cards* (NICs) and rebalancing the network load or adding more network bandwidth.

> **! IMPORTANT**
>
> When making modifications to any network, document all modifications to ensure that accurate records are available if a similar network problem occurs at a later date.

The network subsystem is the entry point for all server data. NIC performance problems limit the amount of data that can be handled by the server. Monitoring this subsystem involves the following:

- Eliminating NIC queuing
- Identifying bandwidth deficiencies
- Controlling processor and I/O bus overhead attributed to the NIC
- Optimizing NIC-related configuration parameters
- Properly configuring the network infrastructure

In Microsoft Windows 2003, the following features affect network performance:

- Domain Name System (DNS)
- Domain controllers
- Environment
- Global catalog servers
- Operation masters
- Kerberos authentication and public key infrastructure

Often performance problems can be traced to the networking components in the server, or to the network infrastructure that is external to the server.

When evaluating the network subsystem, start by making an inventory of the existing network and identifying any existing bottlenecks. Performance Monitor can help you isolate performance bottlenecks. Using the Performance Monitor and its logging facility will help you identify problem areas.

The main concern when searching for bottlenecks is how the network subsystem interacts with the memory, processor, and disk subsystems. Performance data for the network subsystem is collected from the Network Interface Performance object.

## 22.5.1  Network Interface Counters

The Network Interface Performance object allows independent observation of each NIC. You must install the *Simple Network Management Protocol* (SNMP) service and TCP/IP to monitor the network interface object.

The following table describes the most useful network interface counters.

| Counter | Description |
| --- | --- |
| Output Queue Length | The length of the output packet queue (in packets). If this is longer than two, delays are being experienced and the bottleneck should be found and eliminated if possible. Because the requests are queued by the network driver interface specification (NDIS) in this implementation, this will always be zero. |
| Current Bandwidth | An estimate of the current bandwidth of the interface in bits per second. For interfaces that do not vary in bandwidth or for those where no accurate estimation can be made, this value is the nominal bandwidth. |
| Bytes Total/s | The rate at which bytes are sent and received on the interface, including framing characters. |

## 22.5.2   Network Segment Counters

The Microsoft Network Monitor agent is required to monitor the Network Segment object. With the Network Monitor agent installed from the *ProLiant Support Paq* (PSP), you can gather performance data using Performance Monitor on the Network Segment object. Data is sourced through the agent and passed to the System Monitor.

The following table describes the Network Segment counters.

| Counter | Description |
| --- | --- |
| Network Segment: % Network Utilization | Displays a percentage of the network bandwidth being used. It confirms data provided by the queuing counter and measures the degree of the bottleneck. Segmenting and upgrading the network infrastructure yields measurable improvements in latency and bandwidth when sustained usage is greater than 60%. |
| Network Segment: Frames/s | Counts the number of frames transmitted on the network per second. |
| Network Segment: Bytes/s | Displays the number of bytes transmitted on the network per second. This counter indicates segment saturation. <br> *Note*: To convert bytes/s to Mb/s, use the following formula: <br> Mb/s = [(bytes/s * 8) / 1024] / 1024 <br> If the Mb/s calculation approaches 60% of the network capacity, the segment has surpassed maximum efficiency and might need to be segmented. |
| Network Segment: Broadcasts/s | Displays the number of broadcast frames on the network. |
| Network Segment: Multicasts/s | Displays the number of multicast frames on the network. |

The Network Segment object can negatively impact system performance. The data collection for this performance object places the NIC in a promiscuous mode. When a network card is in a promiscuous mode, it reads all the network packets.

**! IMPORTANT**

Additional NICs do not improve performance if the current NIC is not close to saturation.

## 22.5.3 Running the HP ProLiant Network Configuration Utility 7

The HP ProLiant Network Configuration Utility 7 enables you to configure and monitor HP NICs running under Windows 2003.

There are two ways to access the ProLiant Network Configuration Utility 7:

1. From the Windows Control Panel, double-click the HP Network icon.
2. Double-click the HP icon in the system tray.

The ProLiant Network Configuration Utility 7 displays NICs recognized by Windows Server 2003 in its list. The icons used by the ProLiant Network Configuration Utility 7 are described in the following table.

| 10Mb/s and 100Mb/s Icons | Gigabit Icons | Description |
| --- | --- | --- |
| | | **Active OK**—NIC is operating properly. The driver is installed in the Registry and the driver is loaded. If the NIC is a member of a team, this is the active NIC. |
| | | **Installed inactive**—NIC is installed but not active. |
| | | **Cable fault**—NIC is installed in the Registry and the driver is loaded. The broken cable indicator means the cable might be unplugged, loose, or broken; or the switch/hub might be defective. |

*continues*

| 10Mb/s and 100Mb/s Icons | Gigabit Icons | Description |
|---|---|---|
| | | **Inactive cable fault**—A cable fault occurred when the NIC was inactive. |
| | | **Hardware failure on the NIC**—NIC is installed in the Registry and the driver is loaded. The driver is reporting a hardware problem with the NIC. This indicates a serious problem. Contact your service provider. |
| | | **Unknown (teamed NICs only)**—NIC is unable to communicate with the driver. The NIC is installed in the Registry, but the driver is not loaded. If you just installed the NIC, it will be in this state until the machine is restarted. If the NIC is in this state after the system is restarted, the driver might have not loaded or the Advanced Network Control Utility is unable to communicate with the driver.<br>**Unknown (in systems that support PCI Hot Plug)**—A teamed NIC is displayed as *unknown* if you have a system that supports PCI Hot Plug. Remove the teamed NIC.<br>**Unknown NICs**—On Windows 2000 systems, when you physically remove a NIC from the system, the NIC Registry entries are not removed until you uninstall the NIC using the Device Manager. Therefore, some removed NICs might display as unknown until they are removed through the Device Manager. |
| | | **Disabled**—NIC has been disabled through Device Manager or the network control panel tool. |

If you see the cable fault icon next to the NIC, recheck the network connections and ensure that the switch or hub is working properly. After the connection is restored, you should no longer see this icon.

Only teamed NICs display as unknown. If you power-off a teamed NIC, it becomes unknown. When you restart the NIC, its appropriate state is restored (active or nonactive).

## 22.5.4  *Tuning the Network Subsystem*

Numerous options are available when optimizing a network subsystem and network segments. These techniques are listed in the suggested order of priority.

### 22.5.4.1  ELIMINATING UNNECESSARY PROTOCOLS

Never use more protocols than needed. Unnecessary protocols place an additional load on the processor and memory subsystems. Using unnecessary protocols also puts an extra load on the network because browsing is performed separately for each protocol. Most networks require only the TCP/IP protocol.

### 22.5.4.2  USING PCI BUS MASTERING DEVICES

PCI devices provide the highest possible bandwidth, using *direct memory access* (DMA) burst modes. The PCI interface provides the highest possible throughput efficiency compared to processor utilization. This reduces processor involvement, saving processor bandwidth for applications.

### 22.5.4.3  SEGMENTING THE LAN USING SWITCHED NETWORK TECHNOLOGY

Network switches reduce the collision rate and increase bandwidth by allowing several nodes to communicate simultaneously through the switch. The traffic is directed to the ports only where the addressed servers are connected.

- **Switched LAN**—Uses a switch between the server and workstations. This is the simplest, quickest, and most cost-effective method of network segmentation. It requires no server reconfiguration because the topology remains intact. However, broadcast traffic could be transferred to all ports.

- **Router-segmented LAN**—Gives somewhat better bandwidth usage and reduces the impact of broadcast storms, which are error conditions resulting in a high broadcast rate that consumes a major part of the bandwidth. Router-segmented LANs can be reconfigured from an SNMP console using switches with *virtual local area network* (VLAN) capabilities.

- **Emerging LAN technologies**—New features such as channel aggregation, fiber technology, wireless LAN, switching routers, and more.

### 22.5.4.4 ADJUSTING NIC SETTINGS

NIC drivers can yield slow or unreliable performance in a Windows environment if they are not adjusted properly. You can use the ProLiant Network Configuration Utility 7 to optimize these parameters for your server.

### 22.5.4.5 MULTIPLE NICS

Multiple NICs enable you to share the network load between separate networks. This can increase performance by splitting the network traffic between different segments. However, adding NICs does not improve performance if the current NIC is not close to saturation.

**Note**

If NetBIOS name support is enabled, the NICs must be connected to separate LANs to avoid name conflict.

### 22.5.4.6 DISABLING AUTODETECT FEATURES

Parameters that are set by the autodetect feature of the NIC card can be unreliable in a Windows 2000 environment. These issues are seen especially in a Windows 2000 Terminal Services environment. HP recommends that you use the ProLiant Network Configuration Utility 7 to hard code the settings for the following:

- **Media type**—*Unshielded twisted-pair* (UTP) and *shielded twisted-pair* (STP) are twin copper wires twisted together and typically used for telephone or Ethernet networks. The difference between the types is the shielding used in the STP cable functions as a ground to limit electromagnetic interference. UTP cable is cheaper, but the shielding makes STP cable better suited for the demands of faster networks.

- **Duplex setting**—Full-duplex Ethernet data is transferred in both directions simultaneously, doubling the available bandwidth over half-duplex Ethernet. If your network equipment supports full-duplex Ethernet, migrating your servers to full-duplex Ethernet can dramatically increase performance and reduce user response time.

- **Speed**—Ethernet, Fast Ethernet, and Gigabit Ethernet move data at 10, 100, and 1000Mb/s respectively. Faster is better, but only if your network infrastructure can support it.

### 22.5.4.7  USING ADAPTIVE PERFORMANCE TUNING

The NIC sends interrupt signals to notify the server processor that a packet or group of packets is ready to be processed and to request processor cycles for that process. A low number of interrupts per second is not necessarily a good performance indicator nor does it automatically equate to higher processor utilization.

Too few interrupts leads to latencies that reduce throughput, and too many interrupts leads to high processor utilization. If the NIC sends too few interrupts, packets will form bottlenecks in the receive buffer and the system idles. The result is that latencies are introduced into the operation of the NIC, which in turn negatively affects server performance.

Tuning the hardware and software for optimal throughput is the key. Logically, the rate of interrupt signals should strike a balance where it does not hinder the processor or cause too many packets to overload the NIC.

Use the ProLiant Network Configuration Utility 7 to fine-tune the number of packets received before an interrupt is triggered. The Adaptive Performance Tuning option sets the number of frames the adapter receives before triggering an interrupt. Under normal operation, the adapter generates an interrupt each time a frame is received.

RECEIVE INTERRUPTS • Setting a low value for the receive interrupts parameter causes a high rate of receive interrupts. (That is, a setting of the lowest value will result in an interrupt for every frame received.) This increases NIC bandwidth, but might reduce processor efficiency, slowing your computer.

Setting a high value for this parameter reduces the interrupt rate (that is, increases the number of frames the adapter receives before generating an interrupt). This improves processor efficiency, but might reduce NIC bandwidth.

The default setting is 1536. The range is 0 to 4096 (in increments of 32).

After monitoring processor utilization, this parameter can be adjusted to decrease processor activity. The system should be thoroughly baselined before and after adjusting this setting to determine the effectiveness.

RECEIVE BUFFERS • This parameter in the ProLiant Network Configuration Utility 7 specifies the number of buffers used by the driver when copying data to the protocol memory. In high network load situations, increasing receive buffers can increase performance. Increasing buffers, however, also increases the amount of system memory used by the driver. If too few receive buffers are used, performance suffers. If too many receive buffers are used, the driver unnecessarily consumes memory resources.

The default is 750. The range is 4 to 4000.

The receive buffers parameter is available on Netelligent NICs only.

RECEIVE DESCRIPTORS • The number of descriptors used by the driver when copying data to the protocol memory can be adjusted. In high network load situations, increasing receive descriptors can increase performance. The trade-off is that this also increases the amount of system memory used by the driver. If too few receive descriptors are used, performance suffers. If too many receive descriptors are used, the driver unnecessarily consumes memory resources.

The default is 48. The range is 8 to 1024 (in increments of 8).

### 22.5.4.8 TEAMING NICS

The design goal of HP NIC teaming is to provide fault tolerance and load balancing across a group of two or more NICs. The term *team* refers to the concept of multiple NICs working together as a single NIC, commonly referred to as a *virtual network adapter*. Multiple NICs are required to make a team, but like a single NIC, a team connects only to one network.

Before you configure teaming NICs, consider the following:

- In a load-balancing configuration, the NICs must run at the same speed.
- The NICs must use proper protocol configuration.
- Do not depend on a *Dynamic Host Configuration Protocol* (DHCP) server to assign an IP address.
- Do not depend on a static NIC configuration to ensure proper network function.
- Ensure that protocols for the Virtual Miniport, which represents the team, have been configured.

To configure protocols for the Virtual Miniport, highlight the Virtual Miniport, select Properties, and edit the properties as needed.

Install the NIC teaming driver from the HP PSP for Windows 2003 by following the instructions provided with the PSP.

The most common reasons that NICs failover are physical link failures and heartbeat failures.

A physical link failure is anything that causes the link light on the back of the network adapter to go out, such as a pulled cable, switch power loss, or other such condition.

> **Note**
> A failed link LED could indicate a physical link failure when none actually exists.

ProLiant NICs also failover when they detect heartbeat failures, such as when heartbeat packets are not successfully transmitted and received from one network adapter to another via the network infrastructure. They are only transmitted to increment the receive counter on a NIC that has been idle to verify that the NIC still has network connectivity.

All ProLiant Ethernet NICs support the following three types of teaming:

- Network fault tolerance
- Transmit load balancing
- Switch-assisted load balancing

| Teaming Capability | Network Fault Tolerance | Transmit Load Balancing | Switch-Assisted Load Balancing |
|---|---|---|---|
| Number of adapters supported per team | 2–8 | 2–8 | 2–8 |
| Fault tolerance | Yes | Yes | Yes |
| Transmit load balancing | No | Yes | Yes |
| Receive load balancing | No | No | Yes |
| Requires 802.3ad-compliant switch | No | No | Yes |
| Can connect a single team to more than one switch for switch redundancy (must be same broadcast domain) | Yes | Yes | Switch dependent |
| Uses heartbeat for network integrity checks | Yes | Yes | No |
| Can team NICs that do not support a common speed | Yes | No | No |

*continues*

| Teaming Capability | Network Fault Tolerance | Transmit Load Balancing | Switch-Assisted Load Balancing |
|---|---|---|---|
| Can team NICs operating at different speeds as long as the NICs support a common speed | Yes | Yes | Yes |
| Maximum theoretical transmit/receive throughput in Mb/s with maximum number of 100Mb/s NICs | 100/100 | 800/100 | 800/800 |
| Maximum theoretical transmit/receive throughput in Mb/s with maximum number of 1000Mb/s NICs | 1000/1000 | 8000/1000 | 8000/8000 |
| Load balances TCP/IP | No | Yes | Yes |
| Load balances protocols other than TCP/IP | No | No | Yes |

Switch-assisted load balancing was formerly referred to as *Fast EtherChannel / Gigabit EtherChannel* (FEC/GEC) teaming.

The following table lists teaming options that are supported by Windows 2000.

| Teaming Options | Windows 2000 Protocols |
|---|---|
| Network fault tolerance | IP, NetBEUI, IPX (NCP), IPX (NetBIOS) |
| Transmit load balance | IP |
| Switch-assisted load balancing | IP, NetBEUI, IPX (NCP), IPX (NetBIOS) |

### 22.5.4.9 NETWORK FAULT TOLERANCE

Network fault tolerance provides simple redundancy with two to eight NICs in a fault-tolerant team. Each server can support up to eight teams where one NIC per team is defined as the primary NIC. All other NICs are secondary. Network fault-tolerance teaming functions at any speed, on any media. It is switch-independent and can be split across OSI Layer 2 switches, but must be in the same Layer 2 domain.

Network fault tolerance is a simple, effective, and fail-safe approach to increase the reliability of server connections. It enables you to set up link recovery to the server NIC in case of a cable, port, or NIC failure. By creating a team, the network fault-tolerance approach enables you to maintain uninterrupted network connectivity.

During normal operation, the backup NIC has transmit disabled. If the link to the primary NIC fails, the link to the secondary (backup) NIC automatically takes over.

### 22.5.4.10   TRANSMIT LOAD BALANCING

Transmit load balancing, formerly known as *adaptive load balancing*, incorporates all the features of network fault tolerance and takes teaming one step further by adding load balancing of all outgoing server traffic. It is also switch-independent and can be split across Layer 2 switches; however, all transmit load balancing members must be in the same Layer 2 domain. Transmit load balancing increases a server's transmission throughput.

---

**EXAMPLE**

A transmit load-balancing team containing four HP Fast Ethernet NICs, configured for full-duplex operation, can provide an aggregate maximum transmit rate of 400Mb/s and a 100Mb/s receive rate. In this example, total bandwidth is 500Mb/s.

---

With transmit load balancing, traffic received by the server is not load balanced. One NIC is primary, and as many as seven other NICs are secondary. The primary NIC transmits but is also responsible for receiving all traffic destined for the server. The secondary NICs only transmit data. The transmit load-balancing agent adjusts the data flow evenly between the multiple NICs. An algorithm that uses the last 1 or 2 bits of the source and destination MAC or IP addresses determines which port is used for a particular server-to-client communication flow.

Under transmit load balancing, all NICs in the team operate under the same IP address, but different *Memory Access Controller* (MAC) addresses. If one of the secondary connections fails, the server driver redirects the information flow from the failed connection to the remaining NIC team members. If the primary NIC in the team fails, one of the secondary NICs assumes the MAC address and the duties of the primary NIC.

### 22.5.4.11   SWITCH-ASSISTED LOAD BALANCING

Cisco Systems developed FEC technology based on the *Institute of Electrical and Electronics Engineers* (IEEE) 802.3 full-duplex East Ethernet specification. Switch-assisted load balancing incorporates all the features of network fault tolerance and transmit load balancing. If any of the NICs fail, the remaining NICs share the data load.

The operating system sees the multiple NICs as the same IP and MAC address and therefore as one NIC. The HP Intel-based Fast Ethernet NICs that support switch-assisted load balancing also support PCI Hot Plug technology, so that NIC servicing is possible during normal work hours without interrupting network services.

The differences between transmit load balancing and switch-assisted load balancing center around three design issues:

- All network connections transmit and receive data simultaneously, enabling a maximum transfer rate of up to 1600Mb/s.
- Switch-assisted load balancing is supported on IEEE 802.3ad-capable intelligent switches only.
- All ports must be connected to the same switch.

For more information on the IEEE 802.x standards, refer to http://www.ieee.org.

## 22.5.5   *Gigabit Ethernet*

Networks continue to require increasingly higher throughput to support the bandwidth requirements brought on by the demands of the following:

- The Internet
- Multimedia applications
- Large files
- Increased use of e-mail
- Faster server processors

Customers are also expecting increased reliability, availability, and scalability from their servers without comprising on manageability or flexibility.

Gigabit Ethernet is an evolving technology that supports ultra-high-speed connections along the backbone of Internet and intranet networks. It provides a raw data bandwidth of 1000Mb/s and includes both full- and half-duplexing modes. It can also play an important role in connecting certain types of high-demand servers to the network as a whole.

### 22.5.5.1  ADVANTAGES AND DISADVANTAGES OF GIGABIT ETHERNET

The biggest advantage of Gigabit Ethernet is the boost it gives to data transmission over existing Category 5 cabling. Performance increases up to ten times compared to Fast Ethernet (100Mb/s) solutions, which is especially critical for servers, workstations, and Pentium 4 desktop computers that are bottlenecked by aging 10/100 Ethernet networks. This congestion is the result of an increased use of network-oriented applications such as automatic file backup, e-mail, messaging, streaming business video, and *network attached storage* (NAS) applications.

In addition, Gigabit Ethernet is a natural outgrowth of the existing Ethernet base and can be considered an incremental technology rather than a complete replacement for the existing infrastructure.

Gigabit Ethernet can greatly improve the network subsystems, but it will also bottleneck other network and server devices if they are not upgraded as well. Gigabit Ethernet can deliver one and a half million small packets per second with an interpacket latency in nanoseconds. This stream of information will overwhelm slow routers that are connected to the network. Before deploying Gigabit Ethernet, you should understand and upgrade the Layer 3 packet forwarding devices on the network.

In the same manner that it has the potential to flood routers on the downstream side, Gigabit Ethernet can saturate the server on the upstream side. The data transfer from a Gigabit Ethernet NIC will generate so many interrupts that most servers will be crippled.

HP offers several Gigabit Ethernet products, including switches and NICs. All Gigabit Ethernet NICs offered by HP support a technology called *interrupt coalescence* that is designed to take the gigabit load off the server. NICs that support interrupt coalescence have the intelligence on-board to hold back interrupts during periods of high packet offloading. Essentially, the NIC generates one interrupt for a group of packets rather than creating an interrupt for each. When the network is not heavily loaded, the NIC resumes one-for-one, packet-to-interrupt processing.

| 22.6 |
|---|

# Troubleshooting Processor Problems

Processor performance is probably the most debated factor in system performance. Although it is true that a faster processor executes instructions faster, it can only execute about one instruction per clock cycle. When processor speed increases, other system component factors must be considered, in addition to their overall integration. For these reasons, a 3GHz processor is not exactly ten times faster than a 300MHz processor.

Further complicating the issue are multiprocessor systems. Two processors do not double the speed of the system, because both the operating system and application must be able to scale to the extra processor to leverage maximum performance from the system. As with processor speed, multiprocessor configurations do not increase speed geometrically.

Considering that processors sit idle most of the time, replacing a slower processor or adding a second one might not lead to the expected performance increase.

### 22.6.1 Evaluating the Processor Subsystem

Two useful counters in the Processor category of performance objects are % Interrupt Time and % Processor Time.

The % Interrupt Time counter indicates the percentage of time the processor spent receiving and servicing hardware interrupts during the sample interval. This value is an indirect indicator of the activity of devices that generate interrupts, such as the system clock, the mouse, disk drivers, data communication lines, NICs, and other peripheral devices. These devices normally interrupt the processor when they have completed a task or require attention. Normal thread execution is suspended during interrupts. Most system clocks interrupt the processor every 10 milliseconds, creating a background of interrupt activity. This counter displays the average busy time as a percentage of the sample time.

The % Processor Time counter indicates the percentage of time that the processor is executing a non-idle thread. This counter was designed as a primary indicator of processor activity. It is calculated by measuring the time that the processor spends executing the thread of the idle process in each sample interval, and subtracting that value from 100%. (Each processor has an idle thread that consumes cycles when no other threads are ready to run.) It can be viewed as the percentage of the sample interval spent doing useful work. This counter displays the average percentage of busy time observed during the sample interval. It is calculated by monitoring the time the service was inactive, and then subtracting that value from 100%.

## 22.7    Troubleshooting Storage Problems

Many factors affect storage subsystem performance. If bus or controller bandwidth is too narrow, read/write requests will be delayed and the disk drives might be underutilized as a result. If the drives themselves are too slow, read/write responses will be delayed. If both bandwidth and the drives are experiencing excessive utilization, the overall system is approaching saturation. Excessive page file hits can reduce the I/O bandwidth needed for other transactions. If an array controller is present, its read/write priority and stripe-size setting can also have an effect. The type and speed of the drive are also factors.

### 22.7.1   Evaluating the Storage Subsystem

Two useful counters in the PhysicalDisk category of performance objects are % Disk Time and Average Disk Queue Length.

The % Disk Time counter indicates the percentage of elapsed time that the selected disk drive is busy servicing read or write requests.

The Average Disk Queue Length indicates the average number of both read and write requests that were queued for the selected disk during the sample interval.

## 22.8   Troubleshooting Memory Issues

As the operating system loads, it allocates available memory to itself and other components. When applications load, they get clearance to occupy desired memory from the operating system. Operating systems and applications also set aside memory for temporary usage, which can grow considerably under heavy load. At some point, lower-priority transactions are cached in a temporary file on the hard disk to optimize remaining memory. Not enough system memory can result in excessive temporary file access, which slows the system down because accessing the hard disk is slower than accessing RAM.

### 22.8.1   Evaluating the Memory Subsystem

Two useful counters in the Memory category of performance objects in the System Monitor are Available Bytes (or Kilobytes or Megabytes) and Pages/Sec.

The Available Bytes (or Kilobytes or Megabytes) counter indicates the amount of physical memory available to processes running on the computer, in bytes. It is calculated by summing the space on the Zeroed, Free, and Standby memory lists. Free memory is ready for use; Zeroed memory is pages of memory filled with 0s to prevent later processes from seeing data used by a previous process. Standby memory is memory removed from the working set of a process (its physical memory) on route to disk, but is still available to be recalled. This counter displays the last observed value only; it is not an average.

The Pages/Sec counter indicates the number of pages read from or written to disk to resolve hard page faults. (Hard page faults occur when a process requires code or data that is not in its working set or elsewhere in physical memory, and must be retrieved from disk.) This counter was designed as a primary indicator of the kinds of faults that cause system-wide delays. It is the sum of Memory: Pages Input/sec and Memory: Pages Output/sec. It is counted in numbers of pages, so it can be compared to other counts of pages, such as Memory: Page Faults/sec, without conversion. It includes pages retrieved to satisfy faults in the file system cache (usually requested by applications) and noncached mapped memory files. This counter displays the difference between the values observed in the last two samples, divided by the duration of the sample interval.

## 22.9    Evaluating Other Subsystems

Other useful troubleshooting counters include Paging File: % Usage and System: Processor Queue Length.

The Paging File: % Usage counter provides the amount of the page file instance in use in percent.

The System: Processor Queue Length counter indicates the number of threads in the processor queue. There is a single queue for processor time even on computers with multiple processors. Unlike the disk counters, this counter counts ready threads only, not threads that are running. A sustained processor queue of greater than two threads generally indicates processor congestion. This counter displays the last observed value only; it is not an average.

These counters are useful for their ability to monitor typical aspects of a system. Deeper inquiry requires more specific counters within a performance object category.

## 22.10    Resolving and Preventing Software Issues

Another bottleneck could result from outdated drivers or control software. The performance of hardware drivers and control software typically increases over time as their development is optimized. In a computing environment, it is possible that performance issues could be a combination of older components and heavy usage reaching a point where degradation is beginning to occur. You might need to assess the organization's IT infrastructure to establish a software version control baseline.

Updating drivers or software is not a difficult task, but it can become a daunting one in a large or complex environment. HP has developed several methods to manage the download and application of new drivers and control software.

At its simplest, updating the driver or software on a system is as easy as locating the update, retrieving it, and applying it. For simple environments, going to the HP Web site and downloading an individual update for a single computer is the most efficient. In a large or complex environment, use a combination of HP Insight Manager 7, Version Control Repository Manager, and Version Control agents to manage a centralized repository that distributes HP system software.

### 22.10.1   Obtaining Software and Drivers

The HP Web site is the first place to look for updated drivers and software. Software packages called *SoftPacks* are posted on the Web site upon release and are available for download. This method of distribution is faster than waiting for a software distribution on CD to ship.

At the Software and Drivers home page, select the product platform, and then search by computer family, model, language, and operating system to locate the correct SoftPack. Instructions for each SoftPack are contained in a Read-me file, which is downloaded automatically with the SoftPack.

All the drivers, utilities, support software, and ROMs you need to keep HP products running at peak performance are available from http://h18007.www1.hp.com/support/files/index.html.

### 22.10.2   System Software Maintenance Strategy

A carefully planned system software maintenance strategy maximizes server stability and availability. By developing well-regulated system software baselines for business servers, you can reduce the time required to update or troubleshoot existing servers and ensure that new servers are set up with tested and stable software configurations.

HP provides two agent-layer applications, *Version Control Repository Manager* (VCRM) and *Version Control agents*, which are used for HP software deployment. These applications facilitate both version management and updates of HP system software running on HP ProLiant servers.

The VCRM catalogs HP system software either proactively downloaded into the customer's environment through ActiveUpdate or manually downloaded from the HP Web site. You can create custom groupings of HP system software.

The Version Control agents maintain system software status for a single HP ProLiant server by comparing the software contents of the target server with the most recent contents of the VCRM, or through a PSP or customer-defined Support Paq within the VCRM. The Version Control agents also enable you to upgrade individual components or Support Paqs on a single-server basis.

When the Version Control agents are used in conjunction with Insight Manager 7, you can view software status and update system software across multiple servers.

### 22.10.3 Software Maintenance Architecture

To ensure that HP servers provide maximum uptime with minimal maintenance, HP has developed ProLiant advanced server management technologies to integrate the following:

- ActiveUpdate
- Version Control Repository Manager
- Version Control agents
- Insight Manager 7

The tight integration of these advanced technologies reduces server management efforts, enabling administrators to work issues, resolve problems, and deploy server software from remote locations by means of a standard Web browser.

Insight Manager 7, together with Version Control agents and VCRM, introduces an architecture for version managing and updating HP system software. The software maintenance architecture enables you to select a baseline set of software (BIOS, drivers, and agents) as the point of reference for version control across a portion of or the entire managed environment.

VCRM and Version Control agents are Web-enabled management agents. Insight Manager 7 uses these management agents and others to facilitate the following management tasks:

- System identification
- Communication with systems
- Presentation of common data
- Software and firmware deployment

### 22.10.3.1  ACTIVEUPDATE

ActiveUpdate is a Web-based client application that keeps IT administrators directly connected to HP for proactive notification and delivery of the latest software updates.

Content delivered through ActiveUpdate includes the following:

- Product change notification (PCN)
- Customer advisories
- Management application updates
- PSPs
- Device drivers
- System ROMs
- BIOS images
- Software utilities

**Note**

Refer to the ActiveUpdate user guide for a complete description of all ActiveUpdate functions. The user guide is included in the ActiveUpdate download.

For online help, click the question mark icon in the upper-right corner of the ActiveUpdate window.

ActiveUpdate uses software filters and a customizable profile to ensure that users receive only those software updates relevant to their environment. The subscription pages topic tree structure enables users to drill down and select not only their hardware platforms but also the operating system they are running.

From the Web site, you can select the models, operating systems, and languages for the SoftPack files you want to download. You must submit your subscription to receive downloads.

ActiveUpdate benefits include the following:

- Saves time by downloading and storing new updates automatically
- Delivers customized information
- Provides easy-to-understand descriptions about the software updates
- Simplifies access to the latest software updates for HP servers, desktops, portables, and workstations by providing a single point of access

You can install the ActiveUpdate client software from the Management CD or by accessing http://h18000.www1.hp.com/products/servers/management/ activeupdate/index.html.

### 22.10.3.2 VERSION CONTROL REPOSITORY MANAGER

VCRM is a Web-enabled agent designed to manage a repository containing PSPs and individual server software Smart Components.

The repository is maintained by using ActiveUpdate or by copying software directly to the repository from the SmartStart CD, another repository, or the HP Web site.

Users with administrative privileges can access the repository to perform repository maintenance tasks manually. The agent automatically updates a database whenever a PSP or Smart Component is added to the repository. All activities that affect the repository are logged to a log file on the server where the VCRM agent is installed.

The VCRM enables administrators and operators to perform the following tasks to maintain the repository:

- Display a list of PSPs and Smart Components stored in the repository
- Delete multiple PSPs and Smart Components from the repository
- Copy multiple PSPs and Smart Components to another repository
- Create customer-defined Support Paqs based on multiple Smart Components

In addition to managing repositories, VCRM integrates with Insight Manager 7 to provide a catalog of software that is available in the repository.

The VCRM is available through the Change Management software option.

### 22.10.3.3 VERSION CONTROL AGENTS

Version Control agents are Web-enabled agents designed to display the software inventory of the server on which the agents are installed. Version Control agents also allow the installation, comparison, and update of server software from a repository that is managed by VCRM.

Users with administrator and operator privileges can access the Version Control agents to maintain the software inventory of the server manually. The agents query the SNMP *Management Information Base* (MIB) each time the user views the inventory page. All activities that affect the software inventory are logged to a log file. Component installations are logged to a log file at the server, such as software installations; however, installations performed outside the Version Control agent do not display in the log.

The Version Control agents enable administrators and operators to perform the following tasks to maintain the software inventory of the server:

- Viewing PSPs and Smart Components that are installed on the server or available for installation

- Obtaining software status and comparing file versions of installed PSPs and Smart Components with software available for deployment

- Updating the software inventory of the server from a repository

Version Control agents integrate with Insight Manager 7 to enable administrators and operators to use the one-to-one deployment capabilities of the agent and to deploy PSPs and Smart Components on multiple target servers that need server software updates.

Deploying PSPs and Smart Components from a single repository or multiple repositories saves time and is important in standardizing software maintenance and deployment procedures on distributed systems. For maximum manageability and flexibility across operating system platforms, each repository that is created should be located on shared network drives managed by a Windows domain or Active Directory security. It should be updated automatically by ActiveUpdate, and it should be managed by VCRM.

## 22.10.4   *Creating a Software Repository*

You can create a software repository on any system by using standard operating system commands to create a folder or directory. You can create a default repository folder when you install Insight Manager 7. Create the repository folder, browse to the Version Control repository, and point to that folder from the Options panel.

Insight Manager 7 is not limited to using the repository on the Insight Manager 7 server. Insight Manager 7 can use and deploy software from any repository, provided that the following two conditions are met:

1. The repositories are available to Insight Manager 7 on the network.
2. VCRM manages and is trusted to Insight Manager 7.

For optimal integration with the software deployment features of Insight Manager 7, ensure that VCRM manages each repository.

## 22.10.5   Maintaining a Repository with ActiveUpdate

After you create a repository, it must be populated with PSPs and Smart Components before deployment on the target servers. You can maintain the repository by using ActiveUpdate, the HP Web site, or the HP SmartStart CD.

ActiveUpdate is the preferred solution for maintaining repositories automatically. ActiveUpdate delivers the latest PSPs and Smart Components directly to a specified repository. Each installation of ActiveUpdate maintains one repository. The repository can be located either on the server where ActiveUpdate was installed or on a remote network drive. In both cases, the system user ID that updates the repository must have write access to the repository.

By using the network-based repository feature of ActiveUpdate, you can ensure that all updates are always readily available for deployment from standardized locations.

## 22.10.6   Software Management and Deployment Solutions

Insight Manager 7 simplifies software maintenance and resolves some of the problems users experience. To deploy software, know the following properties about the devices that are managed:

- Status of each device to be updated
- Software or firmware that needs to be upgraded on each device
- Successful or failed results of the installation
- Changes that have been made to the repository where the software is stored
- Tasks created based on certain deployment specifications
- Tasks executed based on software or firmware criteria

### 22.10.6.1   SOFTWARE MANAGEMENT CONSIDERATIONS

Administrators and operators should (1) have access to a repository, and (2) understand the options for selecting a PSP. "Equal to" is the only comparison you can use with a PSP.

Insight Manager 7 cannot determine whether a PSP was actually installed on a system, only whether all the components in a PSP are installed on a system. A device will be returned by this query if, and only if, every component in the PSP is on the device.

> **! IMPORTANT**
>
> Create a copy of the PSP used on your system before you deploy to other systems to ensure that the same configurations are used.

Ensure that the query results are correct. Information is accessed from the SQL database table that was populated by a Software Version Status Polling task. This table is updated when software is installed with the Deploy Software or Firmware Insight Manager 7 task. If software was installed or uninstalled on systems without using Insight Manager 7 and after a Software Version Status Polling Task last ran, this query might not return the correct results.

For detailed information, refer to the Software Deployment user guide at http://ww.hp.com/support.

### 22.10.6.2  SOFTWARE MANAGEMENT AND DEPLOYMENT OPERATING SYSTEMS REQUIREMENTS

Insight Manager 7 is the primary engine used to perform one-to-many version controls. The Version Control agents identify what software needs to be installed and then pull the software from the Version Control repository.

To ease the deployment, the software already installed on managed servers displays. Software from multiple operating systems can be deployed, including Windows Server 2003.

### 22.10.6.3  DEPLOYMENT OPTIONS

The two deployment methods are one-to-one (1:1) and one-to-many (1:$n$).

With 1:1, only one device is updated. This deployment option enables you to browse to the Version Control agent and see a simple software inventory page for a list of installed components.

With 1:$n$, several devices are updated at the same time. This method

- Queries machines that have or do not have one or more selected software components.
- Queries machines that match or do not match one or more selected PSPs.
- Deploys selected components and bundles to a list of machines.
- Views installation status.

To create a 1:*n* deployment task, you must create a query defining the devices and then attach a control task to the query.

### 22.10.7  Product Change Notification

The PCN service provides the latest information on hardware and preinstalled software changes for HP products. Through ActiveUpdate 2.0 or the PCN Web site, HP communicates changes as soon as they are identified, which gives customers adequate time to plan. The PCN program provides up to 60 days advance notice of upcoming hardware and software changes to HP products.

HP Change Control is another facet of PCN. HP Change Control and PCN programs have two goals. First, to minimize potentially disruptive changes to Intel-based HP desktops, workstations, and servers. And second, to provide advance notification of changes to these product lines.

Features of HP Change Control and PCN include the following:

- **Roadmap sharing**—Provides a six-month roadmap snapshot of upcoming technologies
- **PCN Web site**—Communicates changes up to 60 days in advance as soon as they are identified, thus ensuring ample time to plan ahead
- **Proactive e-mail notification**—Sends e-mail notification of upcoming changes that affect platforms specified in user-configured custom profiles

The secure PCN Website can be accessed at http://www.hp.com/united-states/subscribe/.

## ▲ Summary

The six-step HP troubleshooting methodology enables you to pinpoint problems and design a solution. HP software utilities enable your customers to manually and automatically maintain their system software.

System information tools such as QuickFind 2000, Maintenance and Service Guides, and the Service Quick Reference Guide, enable a technician to prepare to address potential issues with customer servers. The IML and IMD enable the technician to gather system data to help identify and narrow the problem. HP diagnostic tests are run to further isolate potentially faulty subsystems before setting a performance baseline. The technician needs to evaluate the network, memory, storage, processor, and other subsystems before developing an optimized action plan.

## ▲ LEARNING CHECK

1. *What are the six steps of the HP troubleshooting methodology?*

2. *Which is more important, understanding the customer's reported problem or understanding the true failure?*

3. *What criteria should you consider when optimizing your action plans?*

4. *If executing the entire action plan did not solve the problem, what is the next step to try?*

5. *List at least three things you should do after solving the problem.*

6. *List three typical system bottlenecks.*

7. *What are four ways to manage software version control?*

# AIS Competencies

The *Accredited Integration Specialist* (AIS) competencies were defined by a group of subject-matter experts who specialize in HP ProLiant servers and associated technologies.

This appendix provides a high-level overview of the competencies identified by this group of experts for an individual seeking to achieve the HP ProLiant AIS-level credential. Each of the competencies identified below has been defined in greater detail by the HP technical training and certification teams and has been used as the foundation for building the technical training and certification materials that support the AIS credential.

Important: This book does *not* cover all the competencies listed here. To prepare for the AIS exam, use this book as a resource in your preparation, but also attend the HP hands-on trainings, complete the labs, and ensure you meet the recommendations for industry experience.

**475**

| Competency 1 | Explain and Recognize Fundamental Server Technologies |

1.1 Explain and recognize processor technologies.

1.2 Explain and recognize memory technologies.

1.3 Explain and recognize I/O bus technologies.

1.4 Explain and recognize storage technologies.

1.5 Explain network technologies.

1.6 Explain and recognize system architectures.

1.7 Explain and recognize power/thermal and hardware management technologies.

1.8 Explain availability and cluster technologies.

1.9 Describe partner products (operating systems and server applications) and how to categorize them.

1.10 Explain operating system architectures.

1.11 Classify and describe server applications and their profiles.

1.12 Explain mission critical concepts and environmental requirements.

1.13 Understand systems management fundamentals and associated technologies

| Competency 2 | Perform the Planning and Design Necessary to Achieve a Deployable Solution |

2.1 Gather data.

2.2 Use HP configuration tools to validate design.

2.3 Design the correct customer server solution.

2.4 Write scope of work.

2.5 Obtain customer buy-off.

2.6 Gather necessary tools and resources.

2.7 Perform proof of concept.

| Competency 3 | **Install, Configure, Set Up, and Upgrade Systems and Options** |

| 3.1 | Install and configure storage. |
| 3.2 | Identify StorageWorks key differentiators. |
| 3.3 | Summarize the ENSA features and components to support the StorageWorks concept of storage as a utility. |
| 3.4 | Install and configure hardware. |
| 3.5 | Install operating systems with SmartStart. |
| 3.6 | Install and configure management agents. |
| 3.7 | Configure operating system networking services. |
| 3.8 | Configure fault tolerant options. |
| 3.9 | Install OS with Multi-server deployment tool. |
| 3.10 | Explain, install, and configure clustering. |
| 3.11 | Describe rack and power/infrastructure options. |
| 3.12 | Validate and test system and storage installation. |
| 3.13 | Use Survey/Insight Diagnostics to document the solution. |

| Competency 4 | **Solution Performance Tuning and Optimization** |

| 4.1 | Identify server performance problems. |
| 4.2 | Use HP system information resources to collect and analyze information related to server performance. |
| 4.3 | Use operating system tools to collect and analyze information relating to server performance. |
| 4.4 | Apply server performance-tuning methodologies. |

| Competency 5 | **Perform Troubleshooting of Server and Storage Problems** |

| 5.1 | Describe and apply HP troubleshooting methodology. |
| 5.2 | Collect server performance data using system and storage tools. |
| 5.3 | Evaluate data to determine problem. |
| 5.4 | Develop an optimized action plan. |
| 5.5 | Execute the plan. |

5.6    Implement preventive measures taking necessary steps to ensure the problem is not recurring.

5.7    Use fault management techniques.

**Competency 6**   ## Use HP Management and Serviceability Tools and Resources

6.1    Identify performance management process.

6.2    Use performance management tools.

6.3    Record baseline measurements.

6.4    Resolve performance bottlenecks.

6.5    Document changes, results, and recommendations.

6.6    Perform volume management.

6.7    Identify common performance issues.

6.8    Set performance thresholds.

**Competency 7**   ## Perform Administrative and Operational Tasks

7.1    Install and configure *Version Control Repository Manager* (VCRM) and *Version Control Agent* (VCA).

7.2    Use change/configuration management tools.

7.3    Perform system upgrades.

7.4.   Identify and describe certificate technologies.

7.5    Perform security admin.

7.6    Resolve a virus problem.

7.7    Perform backups.

**Competency 8**   ## Explain the Industry-Standard Systems Marketplace and Competitive Positioning

8.1    Identify and describe HP service capabilities.

8.2    Install service-delivery tools.

8.3    Use service-delivery tools, including support CDs and Quickfind.

# Answers to Learning Checks

# Chapter 1 Learning Check

1. *Which type of system board is most commonly found in HP ProLiant servers and has active embedded chipsets?*

   A. Active

   B. Passive

   C. Modular

   *Answer:* A

2. *Which type of memory is most commonly found in server memory subsystems?*

   *Answer:* DRAM

3. *What is the function of the address or control bus?*

   *Answer:* The address or control bus identifies the desired location within a target device where data might reside. It also carries control signals that indicate the purpose of the data transfer, such as whether a device is supposed to read or write the data.

4. *What is a dedicated, centrally managed, secure information infrastructure that enables direct and physical access to common storage devices or a storage pool known as?*

   A. Drive array

   B. Direct-attached storage

   C. Storage area network

   D. Network attached storage

   *Answer:* C

5. *Which server component coordinates the activity of the server components and regulates server data flow?*

   A. Memory

   B. Processor

   C. System clock

   D. System bus

   *Answer:* C

# *Chapter 2 Learning Check*

1. *Define the term chipset.*

   ***Answer:*** A chipset is a collection of the microchips on a server mother-board that control the features and the functions of the motherboard. The chipset determines how much memory can be installed, which processors can be used, and which types of interfaces the computer can support.

2. *What are the two main performance bottlenecks in the original PC chipset?*

   ***Answer:***
   (1) Only one device could use the system bus at a time.
   (2) All bus transfers, both system and I/O, were restricted to the same bus speed.

3. *What was the main benefit of the dual independent bus architecture? Where was the bottleneck with this architecture?*

   ***Answer:*** This design allowed the memory bus between the processor and memory to operate at a higher speed than that of the I/O expansion bus. The bottleneck was the I/O bridge.

4. *What server subsystem was the point of contention with bus mastering technology?*

   ***Answer:*** Memory

5. *What were the three main functions of the memory and I/O (MIOC) technology?*

   ***Answer:***
   (1) Bus arbitration
   (2) Timing
   (3) Buffering between the processor, memory, and I/O

6. *Which system architecture first provided peripherals with independent access to processors and memory?*

   ***Answer:*** Parallel I/O bus architecture

7. *Which architecture provided dual-peer PCI buses and employed dual memory controllers that processed memory requests in parallel?*

   ***Answer:*** Highly Parallel System Architecture

8. *What innovation enabled each of the five main ports to transfer data at high speed to each of the other ports, allowing concurrent read/writes between processors, memory, and I/O?*

   ***Answer:*** Crossbar switch

9. *What chipset uses a two-port (bus) memory design with 1.6GB/s memory bandwidth (2 × 800MB/s), allowing simultaneous access to memory on both ports?*

   ***Answer:*** ProFusion

10. *What three advantages does the F8 chipset have over the NUMA architecture?*

    ***Answer:***

    (1) Eliminates potential bottlenecks by using very high bandwidths to match the processing power of the Xeon MP processor

    (2) Eliminates potential bottlenecks using optimized crossbar switch capabilities

    (3) Expands online replacement capabilities to include Hot Plug RAID Memory

# *Chapter 3 Learning Check*

1. *What is an instruction?*

   ***Answer:*** An instruction is an order (such as add, subtract, or compare) that a computer program gives to a processor. Instructions are written in binary code, which means they are represented by 1s and 0s.

2. *Match the processor component with its function.*

   ***Answer:***

   Prefetch unit:  A holding place for instructions and operands that a processor will need

Decode unit: A component that breaks an instruction into its constituent parts

Execution unit: A component that performs the actual data processing, such as adding and subtracting

Control unit: A component that acts as a scheduler for the execution units

Registers: A small number of memory locations used by the control and execution units to store data temporarily

L1 cache: A small, fast memory area that holds recently used instructions and data

Branch target buffer: A register that stores recently taken branches to aid in branch prediction

Bus interface unit: A component that controls access to the address and data buses

3. *Put the following steps in order to describe how a processor handles input:*
    A. Executes instruction
    B. Writes data
    C. Fetches instruction
    D. Transfers data
    E. Decodes instruction

    *Answer:* C, E, A, D, B

4. *Match the technology with its description.*

    *Answer:*

    Pipelined: A processor that does not wait for one instruction to be completed before it begins another

    Superscalar: A processor that can execute more than one instruction per clock cycle

    Hyper-pipelined: A processor with an expanded number of steps that it uses to complete an instruction

    Branch prediction: A technology in which the first time a branch instruction is executed, its address and that of the correct branch are stored in the branch target buffer

    Out-of-order execution: A processor technology that can process instructions first that do not depend on another instruction

EPIC: A processor in which the compiler tells the execution units which instructions can be processed in parallel

5. *Match the technology with its description.*

   *Answer:*

   Asymmetric multiprocessing: Tasks are assigned to specific processors.

   Symmetric multiprocessing: The next task is executed on the next available processor.

   Loosely coupled: Each processor has memory assigned to it and, in a sense, acts as an independent computer.

   Tightly coupled: All processors share all memory.

6. *When mixing processors, to which processor core frequency should the core frequency of each processor be set?*

   *Answer:* The highest frequency rating commonly supported by all the processors.

7. *Which processor should be installed as the bootstrap processor?*

   *Answer:* The processor with the lowest feature set must be the bootstrap processor.

# *Chapter 4 Learning Check*

Answer the first four questions with DRAM, SRAM, or both.

1. *Which technology uses capacitors to store data?*

   *Answer:* DRAM

2. *Which technology is faster?*

   *Answer:* SRAM

3. *Which technology is used in cache?*

   *Answer:* SRAM

**4.** *Which technology stores data in a grid?*

*Answer:* Both

**5.** *What innovation did DDR RAM introduce?*

    A. Transfers data on both the rising and falling edge of each clock cycle

    B. Distributes data across DIMMs in two banks

    C. Adds a parity bit to each byte when it writes it to memory

    D. Corrects single-bit errors

*Answer:* A

**6.** *Which memory technology doubles the amount of data obtained in a single memory access from 64 bits to 128 bits?*

    A. DDR RAM

    B. Online spare memory

    C. Hot Plug RAID Memory

    D. Interleaved memory

*Answer:* A

**7.** *Match the fault-tolerant technology with its description.*

*Answer:*

Parity: The memory controller adds a bit to each byte when it writes the byte to memory based on the number of 1s in the byte.

ECC: This technology uses a checksum to analyze an error, determine which byte is corrupt, and correct it.

Advanced ECC: This technology corrects multibit errors that occur on a single DRAM chip.

Online spare memory: A memory bank with a faulty DIMM automatically fails over to a spare bank of DIMMs.

Hot-plug mirrored memory: The memory controller writes the same data to identically configured banks of DIMMs on two memory boards.

Hot Plug RAID Memory: Four memory controllers each write one block of data to one of four DIMMs. A fifth memory controller stores parity information on a fifth DIMM.

8. *What is the benefit of cache in a server?*
   A. Fills data requests from the processor more quickly than memory
   B. Doubles the amount of data that can be stored on the hard drive
   C. Decodes instructions to make the processor work faster
   D. Increases the clock speed of the memory bus

*Answer:* A

9. *Which cache stores the first data checked by the processor?*

*Answer:* Level 1

10. *Which bus connects the L2 cache to the processor?*
    A. Frontside bus
    B. Backside bus
    C. System bus
    D. PCI bus

*Answer:* B

11. *What is the function of the Tag RAM?*

*Answer:* Tag RAM stores the memory address for the data in each cache line. When the processor requests a piece of data, the cache controller compares the address in the request with the addresses in the Tag RAM. If the cache controller finds the address, it returns the associated data to the processor.

12. *Match the cache implementation to its definition.*

*Answer:*

Look-aside:  Both cache and memory receive memory requests. If there is a cache hit, the cache controller terminates the request to the other devices.

Look-through:  If there is a cache hit, no request makes it to the system bus.

Fully associated:  Data from main memory can be stored in any cache line.

Direct mapped:  A group of memory addresses is assigned to each cache line.

Set-associative: A group of memory addresses is assigned to a specific group of cache lines.

Write-through: The system must write the data through all the memory levels before it can be used again.

Write-back: A bit attached to the cache line is flagged to indicate that the data has not yet been written to memory.

Bus snooping: A cache controller listens in to system bus traffic for any memory requests made by bus masters.

Bus snarfing: When a bus master is trying to write to memory, the cache controller captures the data being written and writes it to cache.

# *Chapter 5 Learning Check*

1. *What is bus width?*
   A. The number of bus cycles that occur per second
   B. The number of electrical lines in a bus
   C. The process used to transfer data
   D. The amount of data that can flow across a bus during a period of time

   *Answer:* B

2. *Over what system bus are control signals usually sent?*

   *Answer:* Control bus

3. *What is the formula for maximum transfer rate of a bus?*
   A. (Speed × Width)/Clock cycles per transfer
   B. (Speed × Clock cycles per bus cycle)/Width
   C. (Width × Clock cycles per bus cycle)/Speed
   D. Speed/(Clock cycles per bus cycle × Width)

   *Answer:* A

4. *What are four fundamental adjustments that can improve system performance?*

   ***Answer:*** Any four of the following are acceptable answers:

   (1) Increase the speed at which bus cycles take place. This usually means increasing the clock speed of the processor.

   (2) Increase the speed at which devices, especially system memory, can communicate with the processor. This involves implementing high-speed memory or adding a cache.

   (3) Increase the width of the data bus to increase the amount of information passed in a single bus cycle.

   (4) Implement modified bus cycles, such as a burst cycle.

   (5) Add concurrent processes, such as dual independent buses or multiprocessing.

5. *What is a bus master device?*

   ***Answer:*** A device connected to the bus that communicates directly with other devices on the bus without going through the processor.

6. *How many expansion slots operating at 66MHz can a PCI-X bus segment support?*

   ***Answer:*** Four or more.

7. *How long does PCI-X allow for the decode logic to occur?*

   ***Answer:*** 7ns

8. *Match the following terms and descriptions.*

   ***Answer:***

   PCI Express: Defines a packetized protocol and a load/store architecture

   PCI-X 2.0: Incorporates error checking and correcting

   USB: Enables you to hot plug peripheral devices without restarting or reconfiguring the system

## *Chapter 6 Learning Check*

1. *Define ATA and IDE, and explain the differences.*

   *Answer:* The ATA interface is the drive controller interface and the standard that defines the drive and how it operates. IDE is the actual drive and the 40-pin interface and drive controller architecture designed to implement the ATA standard.

2. *What are the three major SCSI standards?*

   *Answer:*

   SCSI-1—The original SCSI standard, approved by ANSI in 1986, defined the first SCSI bus.

   SCSI-2—SCSI-2 was approved in 1994 as an extensive enhancement to the original standard that defined support for many advanced features.

   SCSI-3—SCSI-3 was approved in 1996. SCSI-3 is a group of specifications that define the implementation of SCSI protocols on different physical layers.

3. *What is the main difference between a single-ended and differential SCSI interface?*

   *Answer:* On a single-ended interface, data travels over a single wire known as the signal line. There is a corresponding ground wire for the signal line. However, voltage is carried only on the signal line. A positive voltage is a 1, and ground voltage is a 0.

   Differential SCSI uses a paired plus and minus signal level to reduce the effects of noise on the SCSI bus. Each signal is carried on a twisted pair of wires. A 1 is represented by a positive voltage on one wire and an equal but opposite negative voltage on another wire. A 0 is electrical ground, or zero voltage, on both wires.

4. *Which one of the following terms identifies the process in which the controller agrees on a transfer rate with each connected device during the initialization phase?*

   A. Disconnect/reconnect

   B. Tagged command queuing

   C. Negotiation

   D. None of the above

   *Answer:* C

5. *What is the purpose of tagged command queuing?*

   ***Answer:*** Tagged command queuing (TCQ) enables a drive to receive many commands and perform those commands without involving the SCSI bus. This allows other devices to use the bus.

6. *How many terminators should be on a SCSI bus and where should it/they be placed?*

   ***Answer:*** You must terminate each end of the SCSI bus.

7. *What are the three new features included with Wide-Ultra3 SCSI-3?*

   ***Answer:***
   - Doubles the data burst of Wide-Ultra SCSI to 80MB/s, providing greater system throughput.
   - Quadruples the maximum cable length of a Wide-Ultra SCSI-3 bus to 12m, allowing increased flexibility when adding external storage or configuring clustered servers.
   - Maintains backward compatibility, allowing all previous SCSI implementations to be used on the same bus.

# *Chapter 7 Learning Check*

1. *What are four major benefits of RAID storage that are offered over nonarrayed storage systems?*

   ***Answer:*** Any four of the following:
   - Effective high-speed data transfer rates
   - Ability to handle simultaneous multiple requests
   - Increased storage capacity
   - Flexibility in configuring data
   - High reliability

2. *What are the two major types of RAID implementations?*

   ***Answer:*** Software-based and hardware-based

3. *Which RAID level obtains the highest read and write operations?*

   ***Answer:*** RAID 0

4. *Which features are supported by hot-pluggable hard drives? (Select three.)*

    A. Replacement of a failed drive in a fault-tolerant array

    B. Addition of drives and arrays

    C. Expansion of arrays

    D. Replacement of an array controller when the machine is online

*Answer:* A, B, C

5. *RAID 1 is considered to be an inexpensive solution providing complete fault tolerance.*

    ❏ True

    ❏ False

*Answer:* False

6. *RAID ADG will support how many simultaneous drive failures without loss of data?*

*Answer:* Two

## *Chapter 8 Learning Check*

1. *Which of the following is not a part of a complete Fibre Channel solution?*

    A. Hardware platforms

    B. Storage systems

    C. Operating systems

    D. Applications

    E. Bus termination

*Answer:* E

2. *Match the Fibre Channel term with its definition.*

*Answer:*

Node: A Fibre Channel device.

Node ID: Unique identifier.

Port: A connection point between each node that provides access to other devices.

Link:  A pair of optical fibers. One of the fibers carries information into the receiver port; the other fiber carries information out of the transmitter port.

Topology:  An interconnection scheme that connects two or more Fibre Channel N_ports.

3. *Fibre Channel is an industry-standard interconnect and high-performance serial I/O protocol that can deliver a new level of reliability, throughput, and distance flexibility for the server industry.*

   ❏ True
   ❏ False

   *Answer:* True

4. *Which one of the following are the three Fibre Channel topologies?*
   A.  Parallel to serial, SCSI IDs, and switched fabric
   B.  Point to point, arbitrated loop, and switched fabric
   C.  Point to point, arbitrated loop, and RAID 0
   D.  Point to point, fabric arbitrated loop, and storage fabric

   *Answer:* B

5. *What is a gigabit interface converter (GBIC)?*

   *Answer:* The GBIC translates the electrical impulse into the optical signal used with the fiber-optic medium. It contains a device that emits an optical signal used for transmission along the fiber-optic cable.

6. *Which Fibre Channel topology uses Fibre Channel hubs?*

   *Answer:* FC-AL

7. *What is the function of an E_port on a Fibre Channel switch?*

   *Answer:* This interswitch expansion port is used to connect to an E_port of another switch to build a larger fabric

8. *What are the two types of Fibre Channel cabling?*

   *Answer:* Copper fiber and optical fiber

9. *Which one of the following best describes attenuation?*
   A.  The bending of a cable past a specific radius
   B.  The loss of power over a distance

C. The ratio of velocity in a vacuum

*Answer:* B

10. *What is the name for a network of switches in a Fibre Channel environment?*

*Answer:* Fabric

11. *What is the only standards-based technology designed from the beginning for simultaneous data, voice, and video transmission?*
    A. ATM
    B. Fibre Channel
    C. IP over Fibre Channel
    D. Multimode Fiber
    E. Point-to-Point topology

*Answer:* A

12. *What technology enables Fibre Channel information to be transmitted over the network between SAN facilities?*

*Answer:* IP over Fibre Channel

# *Chapter 9 Learning Check*

1. *What are the two criteria by which HP servers are positioned?*

*Answer:* Line and series

2. *Which server is best suited to act as a file and print server that can grow as the number of saved documents grows?*
    A. ML370
    B. DL320
    C. DL560
    D. DL760
    E. BL10e

*Answer:* A

3. *Which server is best suited to handle a large database and allow for future internal system expansion?*
    A. ML370
    B. DL320
    C. ML570
    D. DL760
    E. BL10e

*Answer:* C

# Chapter 10 Learning Check

1. *What hardware component managed through HP Power Management software is required to manage multiple platforms with one UPS?*

    *Answer:* The HP Multi-Server UPS Card provides system administrators with the flexibility to manage multiple platforms with one HP UPS. If the network is down, the HP Multi-Server UPS Card can still conduct prioritized shutdowns.

2. *If a UPS is beeping every five seconds, what problem could be indicated?*

    *Answer:* Power outage

3. *What should you do with an HP UPS that is clicking repeatedly?*

    *Answer:* All HP UPSs make a clicking sound when the internal relay makes a switch from a buck-to-boost status or from a boost-to-buck status. This is a normal occurrence. If the UPS is clicking repetitively, run a self-test by following the steps outlined in the UPS user guide. If a problem is detected, an audio alarm sounds and an LED illuminates. If the self-test passes, have a qualified electrician test the A/C utility power for input voltage variations.

4. *Match each of the following to the correct description.*

    *Answer:*
    Leveling feet:  Take the full weight of the rack
    Coupling kit:  Required for multiple rack configurations

Console switch: Provides a direct connection to multiple servers

Stabilizing feet: Required for standalone racks

Rack Builder Online: Rack-configuration tool

## Chapter 11 Learning Check

1. *What technology is implemented in HP SCSI adapters to accept commands simultaneously, sort them efficiently, and minimize response time?*

   **Answer:** Tagged command queuing

2. *List the ways that HP drives differ from original manufacturer drives.*

   **Answer:**
   - Reorganization of the drive geometry
   - Self-monitoring of performance characteristics
   - Support for HP Prefailure Warranty
   - Added functions
   - Enhanced diagnostics
   - Enhanced error detection and correction

3. *What determines the SCSI ID of a hot-pluggable SCSI drive?*

   **Answer:** The bay position of the drive automatically determines the SCSI ID.

4. *What does a flashing amber light mean on a hot-plug SCSI drive?*

   **Answer:** An attached hot-pluggable hard drive has entered a degraded status.

## Chapter 12 Learning Check

1. *Where should first-generation 10,000rpm drives be installed?*

   **Answer:** Direct-connect drive carrier

2. *List three advantages of DAS.*

   ***Answer:***
   - High performance
   - Easy deployment
   - Relatively inexpensive to acquire, maintain, and expand
   - Fast server-to-storage data transfer
   - Easy migration to SAN solutions

# *Chapter 13 Learning Check*

1. *RAID ADG offers higher fault tolerance than RAID 5.*
   - ❏ True
   - ❏ False

   ***Answer:*** True

2. *What is the maximum number of drives recommended by HP for a RAID 5 implementation?*
   A. 6
   B. 12
   C. 14
   D. 56

   ***Answer:*** C

3. *What is the recommended maximum number of drives per array for a RAID ADG implementation?*
   A. 6
   B. 12
   C. 14
   D. 56

   ***Answer:*** D

4. *Which array utility executes out of the option ROM that is located on an array controller, and is designed for situations that have minimal configuration requirements?*

    A. Array Diagnostic Utility (ADU)

    B. Array Configuration Utility (ACU)

    C. Array Configuration Utility XE (ACU XE)

    D. Option ROM Configuration for Arrays (ORCA)

*Answer:* D

5. *What is a potential disadvantage of setting a high rebuild priority when an online spare drive is implemented?*

*Answer:* Selecting a high rebuild priority results in reduced server performance while the rebuild is in progress.

6. *Which of the following LED statuses indicate that a drive has failed?*

    A. On

    B. Blinking

    C. Off

    D. Blinking amber

*Answer:* D

# *Chapter 14 Learning Check*

1. *What information are you trying to gather during the needs analysis? (Select three.)*

    A. The types of problems the customer is experiencing

    B. How reliable a customer expects a server to be

    C. The customer's thoughts on solving his current IT problems

    D. The customer's existing physical environment

    E. The customer's physical security

*Answer:* A, B, C

2. *What information are you trying to gather during the site survey?*

   A. The types of problems the customer is experiencing

   B. How reliable a customer expects a server to be

   C. The customer's thoughts on solving his current IT problems

   D. The customer's existing physical environment

   E. The customer's physical security

   *Answer:* D, E

3. *A customer was referred to you and tells you that his recently installed server is no longer working. After inspecting the server, you discover that the customer has placed the server under a desk and too near a wall, blocking the airflow through the server. Which of the following steps was likely omitted when you first talked to the customer about purchasing a new server?*

   A. Conducting a needs analysis

   B. Conducting a site survey

   C. Determining business value

   D. Choosing the right server

   *Answer:* B

4. *Which of these might help you determine the business value of a server to a customer? (Select three.)*

   A. Reliability

   B. Performance

   C. Site survey

   D. Security

   E. RAID level

   F. Operating system

   *Answer:* A, B, D

# Chapter 15 Learning Check

1. *Name the utility that RBSU replaces.*

   *Answer:* The legacy System Configuration Utility (SCU)

2. *During the system startup process, what should you press to access RBSU?*

    A. F8

    B. F9

    C. F10

    D. F12

*Answer:* B

3. *List three differences between RBSU and the SCU.*

*Answer:* Any three of the following:

- With SCU, you must save changes before exiting.
- SCU displays warnings when conflicts are resolved.
- SCU is disk-based; can be installed on system partition.
- SCU has only one version that supports all servers.
- SCU is device-oriented and file-driven.
- SCU has no direct replication utility support except through configuration backup.

4. *Which utility delivers enhanced functionality for the 4MB ROM?*

    A. Embedded Inspect Utility

    B. RBSU

    C. ORCA

    D. ROM-Based Diagnostics Utility

*Answer:* A

5. *What is ORCA?*

*Answer:* Option ROM Configuration for Arrays

6. *What are three differences between ORCA and the ACU?*

*Answer:*

ORCA does not require the use of disks or CDs.

ORCA executes out of the Option ROM.

ORCA is designed for users who have minimal configuration requirements.

7. *Which of the following is not a function of ORCA?*

    A. Testing logical drives

    B. Creating logical drives

    C. Setting interrupts

    D. Setting boot controller order

    *Answer:* C

8. *List three server deployment solutions from HP.*

    *Answer:*

    SmartStart

    SmartStart Scripting Toolkit

    Rapid Deployment Pack

9. *What does PSP stand for?*

    *Answer:* ProLiant Support Paq

10. *What is a difference between the Remote Deployment Utility (RDU) and Remote Deployment Console Utility?*

    *Answer:* The functionality of the command-line-based Remote Deployment Console Utility is identical to the graphical RDU but enables unattended scripted deployment.

## *Chapter 16 Learning Check*

1. *List four key HP technologies supported by the HP Insight Management agents.*

    *Answer:*

    • HP Prefailure Warranty

    • Automatic Server Recover

    • HP Systems Management home page

    • Point management

2. *In the event of subsystem failures, HP Insight Management agents initiate _____ to the management console.*

A. Traps

B. Alerts

C. Pages

D. MIBs

*Answer:* B

3. *Name the program that helps system administrators prevent unnecessary downtime by providing advance notification of potential server failures and facilitating proactive part replacement.*

*Answer:* HP Prefailure Warranty

4. *Name the driver that sets the ASR timer and also monitors system temperature and system fans.*

*Answer:* HP Server Health Driver

5. *You attempt to connect to a managed HP server by entering http://192.168.1.1. However, an unexpected Web page loads instead of the management home page. Why did this occur?*

*Answer:* You did not specify a port number and the server was running as a Web server.

6. *In which of the following environments would point management provide a viable management solution?*

A. A large network with about 1,000 devices

B. A medium-size network with about 500 devices

C. A small network with fewer than 100 devices

*Answer:* C

7. *Which of the following is not a capability or feature of HP Insight Manager?*

A. Integrates with Microsoft SQL Server

B. Sends e-mails or pager notifications when specific events occur

C. Provides management of groups of devices

D. Provides automatic identification and comparison of configuration changes

*Answer:* D

8. *Which component is not a part of the new HP Systems Insight Manager?*

 A. HP Servicecontrol

 B. HP Insight Manager 7

 C. HP TopTools

 D. HP Survey Utility

 *Answer:* D

9. *Which of the following are components of HP OpenView service management integration?*

 A. OpenView Operations

 B. Service Navigator

 C. Service Desk

 D. Network Node Manager

 *Answer:* A, B, C

10. *You need to recommend a management tool that allows for the proactive configuration monitoring of file systems, system BIOS, and the Windows Registry. What HP management tool is designed for this purpose?*

 A. Service Controller

 B. Configuration Manager

 C. Insight Manager

 D. Survey Utility

 *Answer:* D

11. *Which of the following is not a valid session type for Survey Utility running under Windows?*

 A. Original

 B. Checkpoint

 C. Snapshot

 D. Active

 *Answer:* C

12. *Which command creates a session on demand on a Windows server?*

    A. C:\compaq\survey\survey

    B. C:\hp\survey\survey

    C. Load Survey

    D. survey

*Answer:* A

# Chapter 17 Learning Check

1. *Which HP management technology is comprised of intelligent firmware integrated in select ProLiant servers?*

*Answer:* iLO

2. *Which of the following are technologies provided in iLO Advanced Pack in addition to features in iLO Standard?*

    A. USB-based virtual media

    B. Directory integration

    C. Virtual power button

    D. Virtual text remote control

*Answer:* A, B

3. *When using the graphical remote console for iLO and RILOE II, how should the display resolution be set on the remote server operating system?*

    A. Higher than the management client

    B. The same as management client

    C. The same as or less than the management client

    D. It has no effect

*Answer:* C

4. *What are two advantages of a separate, dedicated network for Lights-Out devices?*

*Answer:*

    (1) Enhanced performance

    (2) Improved security

## Chapter 18 Learning Check

1. *What happens if processor Socket 1 is not populated with a processor?*

   ***Answer:*** The system will fail to boot.

2. *You have just installed a processor in a ProLiant server and you see the following error message:*

   UNSUPPORTED PROCESSOR DETECTED. SYSTEM HALTED.

   *What is the most likely cause of this error?*

   ***Answer:*** The processor installed in the server does not contain the correct microcode in the current system ROM.

3. *Which type of memory must be installed in pairs?*
   - A. SIMMs
   - B. DIMMs

   ***Answer:*** A

4. *To remove a hot-plug device other than a hard drive, you must shut down the server before removing the device.*
   - ❑ True
   - ❑ False

   ***Answer:*** False

5. *You can install DIMMs with tin/lead pins on a system board with gold-plated contacts, and vice versa.*
   - ❑ True
   - ❑ False

   ***Answer:*** False

# *Chapter 19 Learning Check*

1. *A mission-critical application requires what percentage of uptime?*
   A. 100
   B. 99
   C. 95
   D. 90

   *Answer:* A

2. *Which of the following would be considered business-critical applications?*
   A. Air traffic control
   B. 911 call center
   C. ATM machine systems
   D. E-commerce sites

   *Answer:* C, D

3. *If a server is available 95% of the time, and if downtime causes a work stoppage but data integrity is ensured, what is the server availability level?*
   A. AL1
   B. AL2
   C. AL3
   D. AL4

   *Answer:* A

4. *Which statement(s) is/are true regarding online spare memory?*
   A. It must be configured with RSBU, otherwise it will be used as main memory (up to the server maximum).
   B. The spare memory bank is counted during POST.
   C. The DIMMs in the spare bank can be equal to, or greater than, the DIMMs in the other banks.
   D. ProLiant G2 servers allow any bank to be defined as a spare bank.

   *Answer:* A, D

5. *How does hot-plug mirrored memory provide a higher level of availability than online spare memory?*

   ***Answer:*** Hot-plug mirrored memory adds protection against multibit errors.

# Chapter 20 Learning Check

1. *If the stripe size is too large, what might the consequence be?*

   A. Too many cross-stripe transfers will cause reduced performance.

   B. Poor load balancing across the drives will occur.

   ***Answer:*** B

2. *If the stripe size is too small, what might the consequence be?*

   A. Too many cross-stripe transfers will cause reduced performance.

   B. Poor load balancing across the drives will occur.

   ***Answer:*** A

3. *What utility is used to modify the striping factor if the server is running NetWare?*

   A. ACU

   B. CPQONLIN

   C. SmartStart

   ***Answer:*** B

# Chapter 21 Learning Check

1. *When selecting a backup method, which option provides the optimum balance between speed and safety?*

   A. Backing up to a single tape device

   B. Using a stripe tape device

   C. Backing up to local devices

   D. Backing up across the network

   ***Answer:*** B

2. *What happens to the archive bit if a file is changed after the last backup?*
    A. It is marked as "changed."
    B. It is cleared, indicating that the file needs to be backed up.
    C. It is left in its current state.

*Answer:* B

3. *What are the two types of partial backups? (Select two.)*
    A. Incremental
    B. Archive
    C. Differential
    D. GFS
    E. Copy backup

*Answer:* A, C

4. *The GFS tape rotation scheme requires how much backup capacity?*
    A. Equal to the server storage capacity
    B. 1.5 times the server storage capacity
    C. 2 times the server storage capacity
    D. 3 times as much as server storage capacity

*Answer:* C

# Chapter 22 Learning Check

1. *What are the six steps of the HP troubleshooting methodology?*

*Answer:*
    (1) Collect data.
    (2) Evaluate the data to determine potential subsystems causing the issue.
    (3) Develop an optimized action plan.
    (4) Execute the action plan.
    (5) Determine whether the problem is solved.
    (6) Implement preventive measures.

2. *Which is more important, understanding the customer's reported problem or understanding the true failure?*

   ***Answer:*** Understanding the true failure

3. *What criteria should you consider when optimizing your action plans?*

   ***Answer:*** Ensure that only one variable is manipulated at a time.

4. *If executing the entire action plan did not solve the problem, what is the next step to try?*

   ***Answer:*** Escalation

5. *List at least three things you should do after solving the problem.*

   ***Answer:*** Any three of the following:
   - Determine the root cause of the problem.
   - Determine proactive steps that can prevent the problem from recurring.
   - Devise a system test to verify changes and procedures before implementing them into production.
   - Implement a new set of procedures, software, and administrative maintenance to attain a higher level of availability.
   - Perform preventive maintenance, including checking for loose cables, reseating boards, and checking for proper airflow.
   - Add fault-tolerant elements to critical subsystems, where applicable.

6. *List three typical system bottlenecks.*

   ***Answer:*** Network, processor, memory

7. *What are four ways to manage software version control?*

   ***Answer:***
   Manual
   HP Insight Manager
   Version Control Repository Manager
   Version Control Agents

# Sample AIS Exam

1. What is the function of the ALU in a microprocessor?

   **A.** It decodes instructions.
   **B.** It is used to address local units.
   **C.** It assists in the fetching of instructions.
   **D.** It performs basic mathematical operations.

2. Which processors support the EPIC architecture? Select two.

   **A.** Alpha
   **B.** Itanium
   **C.** ItaniumII
   **D.** Pentium III
   **E.** PowerPC

3. You are upgrading an HP ProLiant server with hot-plug mirrored memory. How should you configure the memory?

   **A.** Using RBSU
   **B.** Using ORCA
   **C.** Using switch settings on the memory boards
   **D.** Using switch settings on the system board

4. Which storage device category must be terminated manually during installation of a ProLiant server?

   **A.** USB
   **B.** SCSI
   **C.** ATAP
   **D.** ATA/IDE
   **E.** IEEE 1394

5. A customer using SmartStart 5.xx wants to install Red Hat Linux 8.0 on an HP ProLiant ML330 G1 server. Which installation path must the customer choose?

   **A.** Remote installation
   **B.** Manual installation
   **C.** Replicated installation
   **D.** Assisted installation

6. You want to optimize the consolidation of multiple applications onto one SMP server. Which ProLiant Essentials Foundation Pack should you use?

    **A.** Performance Management Pack
    **B.** Workload Management Pack
    **C.** Recovery Server Option Pack
    **D.** Rapid Deployment Pack
    **E.** Integrated Lights-Out Advanced Pack

7. You recommend that your customer use the Survey Utility to initiate the collection of data following each restart. Which options should the customer use to initiate the data collection? Select two.

    **A.** User initiated
    **B.** Periodic capture
    **C.** Scheduled intervals
    **D.** Object intervals
    **E.** Data capture

8. A disk array consists of 4 identical drives in a RAID 0 configuration. What is the recommended average disk queue length for this disk array?

    **A.** 1
    **B.** 2
    **C.** 4
    **D.** 8
    **E.** 16

9. Which Windows monitoring tool enables you to view hardware resources consumed by installed hardware components?

    **A.** Device Manager
    **B.** Event Viewer
    **C.** System Monitor
    **D.** Task Manager

10. When installing your Windows server, you installed the Insight Management agents with SmartStart. You decide that you do not need to monitor the NIC subsystem. What method can you use to disable the NIC agents?

    **A.** Edit the Insight.reg file.
    **B.** Edit the Agentset.txt file.
    **C.** Run the Insight agents setup file.
    **D.** Use the HP Management agents applet.

11. You selected the Trust by Name option during the Version Control Repository Manager (VCRM) installation. However, you inadvertently clicked the Finish button before adding names. How will this affect the security level of the VCRM?

   A. You will not be able to access the VCRM because the trust mode is in an unstable state.
   B. The device will not trust any other Insight Manager 7 server.
   C. The device will trust all other Insight Manager 7 servers.
   D. You will be able to access the VCRM, but you will not be able to configure the repository.

12. You need to upgrade the operating system on an HP ProLiant server. What should you update on the server before installing the new operating system?

   A. Diagnostics utilities
   B. System firmware
   C. HP Management agents
   D. Smart components

13. You are asked to explain the benefits of PCI-X enhancements over conventional PCI technology. Which are benefits of PCI-X enhancements? Select two.

   A. Increased bus frequency
   B. Support for more devices per bus
   C. Split transactions
   D. Capability of additional buses to move 64 bits at 33MHz

14. You want the best data protection and performance for your drives. Cost is not a factor. Which RAID level would you use?

   A. RAID level 0
   B. RAID level 1+0
   C. RAID level 5
   D. RAID level 1

15. Which technology provides the highest data transfer speed?

   A. Ultra ATA/133
   B. Ultra SCSI-3
   C. Wide-Ultra3 SCSI-3
   D. 100MB Fibre Channel

16. What is an advantage of a differential SCSI interface over the standard SCSI controller?

    **A.** Termination is not required.
    **B.** It has greater noise immunity.
    **C.** Signal voltage is carried on a single line.
    **D.** Both single-ended and differential devices can share the bus.

17. You are installing two SCSI controllers on a single bus. How should each SCSI controller ID be set?

    **A.** One SCSI controller ID is 7, and the other ID is 6.
    **B.** The SCSI controller ID in both systems is set to 7.
    **C.** One SCSI controller ID is 0, and the other ID is 15.
    **D.** The SCSI controller ID in both systems is set to ID 15.

18. Theoretically, which system architecture should have the greatest performance?

    **A.** Multi-peer PCI buses
    **B.** Bridged PCI buses
    **C.** Multi-peer PCI-X buses
    **D.** Bridged PCI-X buses

19. What is a function of the Secure Sockets Layer (SSL)?

    **A.** Provides an encrypted channel of communications between the server and the browser
    **B.** Provides a secure management communication between SNMP and TCP
    **C.** Provides a protocol layer that lies between SMTP and TCP that allows secure e-mail to be sent from a management agent to a centralized management console
    **D.** Provides a protocol layer that lies between DLL and TCP

20. What is a major limitation of parallel ATA?

    **A.** Bulky ribbon cables
    **B.** Only two devices supported per channel
    **C.** Slower speed
    **D.** Smaller drive capacity

21. Where can you find the HP Solution Sizer tools?

    **A.** Support Software CDs
    **B.** SmartStart CD
    **C.** Gartner TCO/ROI Web site
    **D.** HP Enterprise Configurator Web site

22. How can you access the Integrated Management Log Viewer on a Linux server running X Windows?

    **A.** Open the cpqimlview Web page.
    **B.** Go to a shell prompt and type cpqmgmt.
    **C.** Go to a shell prompt and type cpqimlview.
    **D.** Look for the Integrated Management Log Viewer under System > Tools > cpqimlview.

23. During configuration of the ProLiant Support Paq deployed by the Remote Deployment Utility to a server, you are asked to set the device authentication relationship. Which relationship is the most secure?

    **A.** Trust All
    **B.** Trust by Name
    **C.** Trust by Certificate
    **D.** Trust Administrator

24. You are using NetIQ to resolve alerts in your enterprise. Where can you find the Management Information Base (MIB) for ProLiant servers?

    **A.** OnSite Agents Reference Set
    **B.** MIB directory on the SmartStart CD
    **C.** ProLiant Essentials – NetIQ Integration Pack
    **D.** Compaq directory of the NetIQ distribution CD
    **E.** Management Toolkit Directory on the Management CD

25. Which feature of HP Remote Insight Lights-Out Edition (RILOE) enables you to initiate a cold reset and bring the host server back online after the operating system has become unresponsive?

    **A.** Remote reset
    **B.** Graphical remote console
    **C.** Server failure alerting
    **D.** Reset and failure sequence replay

26. When memory is the only component to be tested, which diagnostic option should you select?

    **A.** QuickCheck
    **B.** Automatic
    **C.** Prompted
    **D.** CPQSET+

27. What is the problem when you receive only audible codes (beeps) during POST?

    **A.** The monitor signal cable is not connected.
    **B.** The system sees intermittent memory parity errors.
    **C.** No memory modules are present.
    **D.** The monitor is in power-saver mode.

28. You have installed additional memory in an HP ProLiant server. The server fails to recognize the new memory. What should you try first?

    **A.** Replace the new memory modules.
    **B.** Replace the system board.
    **C.** Reseat the memory modules.
    **D.** Run the Server Setup Utility.

29. Which Windows 2000 System Monitor counter reports the percentage of processing time the system spends executing the kernel and I/O?

    **A.** % Kernel Time
    **B.** % Privileged Time
    **C.** % Processor Time
    **D.** % User Time

30. You have 10GB of data on your system on a single disk. Approximately less than 100MB of data is modified daily. Backup routines are run each day, using different tapes. You are using a 12/24GB internal DAT drive.

    Which backup method will use the least number of tapes and provide the fastest restore if the disk fails?

    **A.** Full
    **B.** Full + Incremental
    **C.** Full + Differential
    **D.** GFS

# INDEX

# informIT